WITHDRAWN

Jl

Golden River to Golden Road

SOCIETY, CULTURE, AND CHANGE IN THE MIDDLE EAST

SOCIETY, CULTURE, AND

IN THE MIDDLE EAST

PHILADELPHIA

Golden River to Golden Road

CHANGE

BY RAPHAEL PATAI

UNIVERSITY OF PENNSYLVANIA PRESS

Printed in Great Britain
by Adlard and Son, Ltd., Dorking, Surrey.

Preface

FROM THE Golden River, the Spanish colony of Río de Oro in West Africa, to the Golden Road leading from Khurasan to Samarkand in Turkestan, immortalized in English literature by Flecker, stretches the huge land mass of the Middle East. The distance from the Golden River to the Golden Road is roughly five thousand miles in a west-easterly direction, while from the Black Sea coast of Turkey in the north to Aden and Sudan in the south is about two thousand miles. The land area of the Middle East is about 7,156,000 square miles, or almost two and a half times that of the continental United States. Its population, however, is only 156 million, as against the 180 million of the United States.

This huge territory, though inhabited by peoples speaking many different tongues and exhibiting many different physical features, is nevertheless the domain of one basically identical culture. The core area of the Middle East, stretching from the Nile to the Tigris, is the locale of the oldest recorded history of mankind. From here, in successive waves, cultural influences spread in all directions, reaching their climax thirteen centuries ago when the new Islamic variety of Arabian culture became superimposed on pre-existent cultural layers all over the Middle East, resulting in the characteristic pattern still predominant to the present day.

To the southwest, Muslim conquests have brought the entire northern third of Africa under the rule not only of Arab dynasties, but also of Arab culture, which rapidly spread from Arabia across North Africa to the territory of Río de Oro on the Atlantic coast. To the northeast, the Golden Road has for centuries been traversed by men who were carriers of Middle Eastern culture, which has become dominant in areas today held by the Soviet Union, notably the former Khanat of Bokhara and the Turkoman Republic.

Basic cultural identity, of course, does not mean surface homogeneity or monotony. On the contrary, upon closer inspection significant local differences can be discerned in each part of the

5

Middle East that give its culture areas a coloration and character of their own. But beneath localized developments and variants, the observer familiar with the whole of the Middle East recognizes the same basic pattern, the same fundamental features whose presence sets Middle Eastern culture apart from the cultures of contiguous world areas.

Cultural characteristics do not always coincide with international boundaries. It happens, therefore, that part of a country belongs culturally to the Middle East while another part of it extends beyond the limits of this world area. Such countries are the Mali Federation and the Republic of Sudan; the northern parts of both of them belong culturally to the Middle East, while their southern parts show very close affinities with the great Negro cultures of Africa. To the east, one finds that beyond the borders of Iran and Afghanistan peoples very similar culturally and in mode of life inhabit the western part of West Pakistan, which traditionally goes by the name of Balujistan, while the eastern part of West Pakistan belongs culturally to the Indian subcontinent.

The present volume deals with three interconnected topics. The first of these is Middle Eastern culture in general, including a discussion of the problems presented by the delimitation and subdivision of the Middle Eastern "culture continent." The second treats of a number of significant aspects of Middle Eastern social organization. The third is devoted to an analysis of the vital sociocultural changes taking place at present in the Middle East.

Most of the material contained in this book is printed here for the first time. Several chapters, however, are based on my previously published studies or on papers presented to scholarly conferences and utilized here in a rewritten and expanded form. Thus a shorter version of Chapter 1 was first published in the Winter 1952 issue of the *Middle East Journal* under the title "The Middle East as a Culture Area." The substance of the first part of Chapter 2, never published, was presented at a supper-conference of the Wenner-Gren Foundation for Anthropological Research on May 2, 1952. Some of the material included in Chapters 4, "The Family," 5, "The Position of Women and Sex Mores," and 9, "The Middle Eastern Town," was previously published in my book *The Kingdom of Jordan* (Princeton University Press, 1958).

A brief summary of the results of Chapter 7, "Dual Organization," was presented on December 29, 1952, at the Annual Meeting of the American Anthropological Association in Philadelphia. Chapter 9 also incorporates part of a paper presented at the Colloquium on Islamic Culture at Princeton University in September, 1953, and subsequently published in the Bombay magazine *United Asia* (Vol. 6, No. 4, 1954) under the title "Culture Change in the Muslim Town: A Challenge for Research," and in the Arabic volume *Al-Thaqāfa al-Islāmiyya wal-Hayāt al-Muʿāṣira,* edited by Muḥammad Khalafallah, Cairo, 1956; as well as parts of the chapters entitled "The Town," written by me jointly with Fahim I. Qubain, and published in the three handbooks, *The Kingdom of Jordan, The Republic of Lebanon,* and *The Republic of Syria* (Human Relations Area Files Subcontractor's Monographs, New Haven, 1956) edited by me. Chapter 6, "Cousin Marriage," includes a portion dealing with a man's right to marry his cousin, a shorter version of which was published in the Winter 1955 issue of the *Southwestern Journal of Anthropology* under the title "Cousin-Right in Middle Eastern Marriage." Most of Chapter 12, "The Dynamics of Westernization," was printed in the Winter 1955 issue of *The Middle East Journal.* Only one single chapter, Chapter 10, "Religion in Middle Eastern, Far Eastern, and Western Culture," is the unaltered reprint of an article originally published in the Autumn 1954 issue of the *Southwestern Journal of Anthropology.* Chapter 11, "Social and Cultural Determinants of Middle Eastern Nationalism," was presented to the Institute on Nationalism in the Middle East held at the University of Chicago in November, 1959. I gratefully acknowledge the permission given to me by the Princeton University Press, *The Southwestern Journal of Anthropology, The Middle East Journal,* and the magazine *United Asia* to reprint or to utilize in an altered form these chapters and articles.

New York, September, 1961   RAPHAEL PATAI

Contents

Maps and Tables

Maps

Tables

I. The Middle East as a Culture Continent

ACROSS THE middle of the three continents of the Old World stretches a vast desert-and-steppe zone, reaching from the West African littoral to Mongolia and separating the great northern zone of agriculture extending from Spain to Siberia from the southern zone of agriculture comprising Central Africa and Southern and Southeastern Asia.[1] This central zone can be divided roughly into two distinct halves: a southwestern half, reaching across North Africa and Arabia and lying largely to the south of latitude 38° N.; and a northeastern half, extending across Central Asia, to the north of the same parallel. The two halves are joined in the middle by a relatively narrow isthmus, bounded by the Persian Gulf to the south and the Caspian Sea to the north.

Students of culture have repeatedly dealt with the problem of the cultural identification of the peoples inhabiting these areas, within the context of classifying the cultures of the two continents, Asia and Africa.[2] The present discussion is confined to the cultural characteristics of the western half of the desert-and-steppe zone of the Old World, together with the more fertile regions immediately contiguous with it or contained islandlike within it.

To delimit it geographically, the entire northern part of Africa from the Mediterranean down approximately to latitude 15° N. as well as the whole of west Asia is considered. On the northwest and southeast, this area is bounded by the natural limits of great bodies of water: the Atlantic, the Mediterranean, the Black Sea, the Caspian Sea, and the Arabian Sea, with the Persian Gulf and the Red Sea as great inland divides. To the south lies the humid tropical zone of Central Africa with the intervening steppe and savanna belt clearly marking the transition not only between two distinct geographical regions, but also between two different types of cultures. To the north, between the Black and the Caspian seas, the Caucasus forms a limit almost as definite as that of the seas

13

themselves. To the northeast, the transition is more gradual, though here the northern and eastern limits of the Iranian Plateau and the sudden drop toward the Turkestan and Indian lowlands (separated by the narrow range of the Hindu-Kush mountains) can be taken as the marginal area. It is suggested that the entire area as here described be designated by the name *Middle East.*[3] In the following pages the cultures of the peoples inhabiting this area will be investigated, as far as this is possible within the confines of a short chapter in order to determine the justification of regarding it as a cultural entity distinct from contiguous cultural entities and at the same time sufficiently homogeneous within itself.

It has to be stated preliminarily that in such an enormous land mass, many times larger than any of the culture areas determined in the Americas by Wissler[4] or in Africa by Herskovits or Murdock, one will necessarily find a considerable range of internal variation

AREAS AND POPULATIONS OF THE POLITICAL UNITS IN THE MIDDLE EAST*

Political Unit	Area Sq. Miles	Population Midyear, 1960
1. *North Africa* (from west to east)		
Mauritania, Islamic Republic of	418,120	725,000
Spanish Sahara (Rio de Oro and Saguia el-Hamra)	102,700	19,000
Morocco	172,100	10,550,000
Ifni (Spanish possession)	571	53,000
Ceuta and Melilla (Spanish)	82	146,000
Mali Federation (northern part only)†	200,000	1,500,000
Algeria	851,000	10,930,000
Niger, Republic of	458,976	2,555,000
Tunisia	48,300	3,954,000
Libya	679,350	1,172,000
Chad, Republic of	501,000	2,600,000
Egypt	386,280	25,770,000
Sudan (Northern and Central only)‡	716,205	6,000,000
II. *Asia Minor and the Fertile Crescent*		
Turkey	300,000	26,881,000
Syria	72,230	4,267,000
Lebanon	4,000	1,550,000
Israel	8,000	2,105,000
Jordan	37,500	1,658,000
Iraq	175,000	6,590,000

III. *The Arabian Peninsula*

Saudi Arabia	617,750	6,025,000
Yemen	74,000	4,500,000
Aden Colony (British)	78	151,000
Aden Protectorate (British)	111,922	650,000
Muscat and Oman	82,000	550,000
Trucial Oman (Seven shaikhdoms)	83,600	87,000
Qatar	8,000	40,000
Bahrein	213	143,000
Kuwait	15,540	219,000

IV. *The Eastern Wing*

Iran	628,000	20,805,000
Afghanistan	270,000	13,150,000
Balujistan (part of Pakistan)§	134,000	1,000,000
Total	7,156,514	156,345,000

* Sources are United Nations publications and other official sources. The populations are midyear 1960 estimates. Areas in sq. miles.

† Total area, square miles: 463,500; total population: 3,700,000
‡ „ „ „ „ 967,500; „ „ 11,390,000
§ „ „ „ „ 370,311; „ „ 80,000,000

as one proceeds from one area to another. If, nevertheless, in the following pages *the culture* of the Middle East is discussed, this does not mean that the significance of these variations is overlooked, or that an attempt is made at unwarranted generalization and artificial schematization. The culture of the Middle East is in fact in the sense employed here not of the same order as that of any single culture area of America or Africa. The geographic locus of this culture, as delimited above, is of such magnitude and it contains so many internal variations that the term "culture area," coined for the native cultures of America, is too narrow to be meaningfully applied to it. It is therefore suggested that the world area inhabited by the carriers of Middle Eastern culture be termed a "culture continent," a designation that both indicates the huge size of the geographical area concerned and allows for the internal variation among its constituent regions.

The concept "Middle Eastern culture continent" can be compared to the long familiar concept of modern Western culture whose geographical locus could be termed "Western culture continent." Both culture continents are characterized by a certain cultural homogeneity that demarcates them against contiguous culture continents, and, at the same time, by considerable internal variations as between one and another of their constituent cultures.

It will be shown later that one of the basic features of Middle Eastern culture is the interaction between the population groups inhabiting the desert and people living in the cultivated regions. Utilizing this point of view, the Middle East can be subdivided into four major geographical regions, each with a desert-and-steppe area in its center and with a more fertile, cultivated perimeter encircling it. These four regions are: North Africa, the Arabian Peninsula, the Iranian Plateau, and Asia Minor. By far the largest, and characterized by the least favorable desert-sown ratio, is North Africa; second in both respects is the Arabian Peninsula; third is the Iranian Plateau; and fourth, Asia Minor. Somewhere in the general area of the grazing steppe between the desert and the sown[5] are located, as a rule, the typical old Middle Eastern towns which (in addition to the coastal towns) are the cultural centers of their respective areas.

If, in a general overview of the Middle East, the relative extent of the desert and the sown is taken as a basic consideration, the impression gained is one of an arid land mass more than overwhelmingly desert, only a very small percentage of which is utilized for agricultural pursuits. Exact data are lacking, but it is estimated that not more than 5 to 10 per cent of the total area of the Middle East is utilized for cultivation with either hoe or plough, and that the lands actually under cultivation at any given time are considerably less even than this small figure. With regard to surface area, therefore, the Middle East as a whole is an overwhelmingly desert-and-steppe area, and the ways of human adaptation to life in the desert and the steppe through pastoral economies seem to be its most significant characteristics.

A very different picture is, however, obtained if the percentage of the population supporting itself by animal husbandry and agricultural pursuits respectively is taken as the basis of estimate. In this case, it is found that the Middle East as a whole is a predominantly agricultural area. Between 65 and 75 per cent of the total working population is engaged directly in agriculture. An additional percentage either lives in villages rendering services to agriculturists, as artisans, teachers, religious personnel, barbers, watchmen, etc., or engages in supplementary or irregular agriculture. Some 12 to 14 per cent of the total population of the Middle East lives in towns and cities. This leaves roughly 10 to 15 per cent only for the nomadic and seminomadic peoples who eke out a living on the noncultivable steppes and deserts of the area.

Just as each area of the Middle East comprises both desert and sown and transitional zones between these two extremes, so also the demographic picture of each country is composed of at least three types of population elements that constitute a recurrent configuration in every part of the area. The desert is the habitat of the camel nomad, the steppe belt the domain of the sheep and goat nomad, and the sown the home of the agriculturist. Transitional stages and localized variations of these population types make for additional diversification.

The camel nomads rely on their camels for sustenance to a degree unparalleled by the exploitation of any other animal species in any other culture.[6] The camel nomads spend their life in seasonal wandering over fairly extensive tribal territories in constant search of pasture for their camels.

The nomads of the steppes breed sheep and goats or occasionally cattle in place of the camels of the true nomads. This difference in itself determines the total gamut of divergences in the ways of life of these two groups. Sheep and goats are less hardy than the camels, they cannot stay away from water for days, they need better and softer pasture, and thus their mobility is much more limited. Consequently, the sheep and goat nomads stay within the grazing steppe belt or, more precisely, in that part of the steppe belt which represents the transition between it and the sown. The annual cycle of seasonal wandering is the rule also for them, but their wandering territory is much smaller and their movements are much slower than those of the camel nomads. In the Sudan, south of latitude 13° N., cattle-grazing seminomads (the so called Baqqāra) take the place of the sheep and goat nomads of the northern outskirts of the desert. Cattle gain in importance also in Southern Arabia.

A special kind of nomadism is practiced by the peoples of the

mountainous regions of the Middle East, especially around the
Iranian Plateau, but also in Morocco. In this type of wandering,
called "transhumance," the characteristic annual cycle of movement takes the tribal groups high up into the mountains in the
summer, and again down to the warmer and milder valleys or the
lower levels of the plateau in the winter. Transhumance is therefore the vertical variant of the horizontal nomadism discussed
hitherto.

Characteristic of all the true and seminomads, whether of the
horizontal or of the vertical variety, is the black hair tent, the only
shelter used by them. The basic identity of the black hair tent all
over the Middle East is one of the indications that the entire
territory is truly one single culture area. The only place outside
the Middle East where the black hair tent is used is Tibet, and its
presence there must be accounted for by diffusion.[7]

Another characteristic shared by all the wandering peoples of
the Middle East, as well as by some of the settled population of
the area, is the tribal structure. Each tribe is a homogeneous social
unit whose native members are social equals. This definition excludes people who joined the tribe from the outside, and slaves.
The tribe as such has little actual significance since tribal affinity
constitutes a rather vague tie. The actual functioning unit is the
wandering group, which varies greatly in size as well as in standing
within the tribal structure. The number of unit-levels or of successively larger groupings of which the tribe consists also varies, so
that in one place one may find a small wandering unit that is an
independent and unaffiliated tribe in itself, while elsewhere a much
bigger wandering unit may be merely a subdivision of a subgroup
of a subtribe.

In contrast to the classless structure of each tribe in itself, the
totality of wandering tribes shows a considerable range of variation with regard to degree of social standing, or "nobility."
Distinction is being made between noble and client tribes such as,
for example, the Saʻadī and Marabṭīn tribes of Cyrenaica of
whom more will be said in Chapter 8. In general it can be stated
that the camel nomads are in most cases regarded as noble tribes,
while the artisan groups (the so-called ṣunnāʻ), attached to them
temporarily, count as low-status people or even as vassals. Between

the two rank the sheep and goat nomads and the semistationary inhabitants of the Iraqi marshes. Despised by all as standing beneath the tribal hierarchy are the settled cultivators, the slaves of the soil.

Tribal structure is such an unmistakable hallmark of nomadism that wherever it exists among settled villagers it can be taken as definitely indicating that they are the descendants of nomads who, in the not very remote past, settled down to sedentary agricultural life. Examples can be found all across the Middle East, but the most typical are the Kurds who, though settled in village strongholds, have retained not only the tribal structure but also several other characteristics that distinguish the roaming nomads from the settled cultivators.

The interrelationship between one wandering unit and another is governed by certain principles validated by tradition, enjoying unquestioned authority, and constituting everywhere the basis of tribal ethos. Among these can be mentioned the principle of collective responsibility expressed in such institutions as the blood feud, raiding, and the inviolate laws of hospitality and sanctuary, as well as in such concepts as honor, *wajh* ("face"), and nobility. All these ideas and ideals appear in their most intensive form among the camel nomads, and they successively lose their power and significance as one proceeds across the range from them to the sheep and goat nomads, to the almost sedentary groups, and finally to the completely sedentary cultivators.

The main areas of cultivation in the Middle East are those that either receive sufficient rain to make cultivation of field crops possible or can be irrigated from rivers or wells for a more intensive utilization of the land. One or both of these types of cultivated lands are present in every part of the Middle East, the typical example of the former being found in the more northerly or mountainous countries (Turkey, Iran, Syria, Morocco), while the latter is best exemplified by the riverine agricultures of the Nile and the Tigris-Euphrates valleys or the oases of the Sahara and the Arabian Desert.

Material equipment, which has to be closely adapted to the nomadic and sedentary modes of life respectively, shows considerable differences between the two sectors of the Middle Eastern peoples. Moreover, since material equipment under the technologically backward conditions still prevailing in many parts of the Middle East has to depend on the locally available raw materials, this aspect of culture reveals marked differences not only between nomads and cultivators, but also among the settled villagers themselves from one area to another. The nomadic camp is largely the same all over the Middle East: black hair tents pitched at a comfortable distance from one another, and in a definite orderly pattern. The village, on the other hand, shows a highly nucleated, closely packed structure, in which house leans against house, with narrow winding paths leading between them, without any plan or design, and in which the limiting influence of the available raw materials is strongly felt. The building material of the Middle Eastern village is stone in the mountains, mud or adobe on the plains, reed in the marshes, and palm leaves and fronds in the far south. Despite this diversity of building material, the floor plan of the houses shows an almost identical range in most parts of the Middle East. The simplest structure everywhere is the square one-room building (an exception being the so-called beehive houses in some villages in the Alawite region of Syria), which can be increased by a simple budding process into two, three, four, five, or even more stories and a correspondingly larger number of rooms. The common feature of all these houses is that they are inhabited by only one single extended family. In fact, family and house are so closely associated that in ancient as well as in modern Semitic languages the same word is used to denote both.

Comparable variations could be shown to exist with regard to clothing, furnishings, utensils, household articles, and the like; again, however, with the reservation that these differences seem significant only when material objects from different areas of the Middle East are compared with one another; when, on the other hand, they are compared with articles hailing from adjacent culture continents (Negro Africa, Europe, India, or Central Asia), the local differences all but disappear and melt into an over-all Middle Eastern type.

Notwithstanding the more obvious variations between the cultures of the Middle Eastern nomads and of the settled agriculturists, conditioned by the difference between a nomadic pastoral mode of life and a settled agricultural existence, a considerable number of basically similar or almost identical cultural features can be shown to exist between these two archetypes of Middle Eastern life. The most important of these is undoubtedly *the family,* which occupies a focal position in Middle Eastern culture and whose structure and functioning are practically identical not only among nomadic breeders and settled cultivators, but also among them as compared with urban populations.

The family in traditional Middle Eastern society—that is, in every place where Westernization has not yet made appreciable inroads—is patrilocal, patrilineal, patriarchal, endogamous, and occasionally polygynous. It is usually headed by an elderly male, and its membership comprises all his sons with their wives and children, and the unmarried daughters and granddaughters (sons' daughters). The entire family, which may consist of several dozen members, resides together, in a cluster of neighboring tents in the nomadic camp, in a single house, or in several buildings clustered around a common courtyard in the villages and towns. When the grandfather dies, the extended family breaks up into as many new units as there are sons, each of whom will then become the head of a new and separate extended family.

Marriage customs, sex mores, the position of women and the division of labor between men and women are completely analogous and in many cases identical in the nomadic camp, the agricultural village, and the town (with the exception of the upper class and the still relatively thin but growing middle class in the town). Marriage is highly endogamous, the preferred mating being between children of two brothers. Polygyny is permissive and sporadic and certainly less than 5 to 10 per cent of the married men have more than one wife simultaneously. The relationship between the sexes is governed by rigid sex mores that place special emphasis on female purity and chastity, both premarital and marital, though veiling and total seclusion of women is practiced mainly in the tradition-directed middle and upper class society of the towns. Men still claim the ancient right to kill their daughters and sisters (but not their wives) if caught in illicit sex relations. A man can easily divorce his wife at will or whim; a woman has no legal way of obtaining a divorce; she can only run away and take refuge with her own consanguineous family.

Economically, too, the extended family is the basic unit. In the nomadic tribe, the extended family holds all property—that is, camels and other livestock—in common; in the village, the extended family owns jointly the lands from whose cultivation it derives its livelihood; while in the towns it owns and manages jointly the enterprise from which its members make a living. Earnings are pooled as a rule and the expenses of the household are defrayed from the common purse controlled by the *pater familias*. The women may help in the field, if their husbands work land that they own or rent; otherwise, their place is at home and their main task is to make the meager earnings of the men go as far as possible by working hard and economizing tightly, sharing the household chores or taking turns in performing them.

The Middle Eastern birthrate is among the highest in the world; but it is counterbalanced by a very high rate of infant and child mortality as a consequence of which general life expectancy is cut down to appallingly low averages. Institutionalized schooling in its traditional form means religious education; it is, however, the privilege of the few only, and is rudimentary. Social conditioning is usually achieved informally, and takes place within the family circle. The children begin at a tender age to participate in the work of their parents, whereby an early differentiation between the sexes appears, the boys being introduced into male occupations by their father or elder brothers, and the girls into those of women by their mother or elder sisters. Girls, when they marry at or frequently before puberty, are whisked away from the parental home, and their relationship with their parents then becomes loose and remote, except in the case of cousin marriage. Otherwise, the Middle Eastern bride becomes absorbed into the household of her husband's family. The tutelage of her own mother is supplanted by the more rigid one of her mother-in-law, and only many years later, after she has given birth to children, and especially to sons, and these are on their way to manhood, can she begin to assert herself as a *mater familias* in her own right.

The achievement of independent status comes as tardily to the son as to the daughter. He takes a wife when his father can spare the bride-price. After marriage he continues to live within the extended family of which his father is either the head or a member. Age is an asset in Middle Eastern outlook, so that the older a man becomes, the smaller the number of the males in the extended family older than himself and the greater the number of those younger than he, the more he grows in esteem, the greater the weight of his opinion, and the more easily he can live according to his own inclinations.

The family is beyond doubt one of the most important institutions in Middle Eastern culture. It may therefore serve as an example to illustrate, briefly at least, the marked differences between the Middle East and each one of the contiguous culture continents.[8]

To the northwest of the Middle East, in Europe, the typical family is the small biological family in which descent is reckoned bilaterally; as a rule it is neither patrilocal nor matrilocal, but neolocal; in it the role and the status of husband and wife are balanced to a much greater extent than in the Middle East. There is a great variety in the way of choosing spouses; endogamy, in the sense of marriage between close relatives, is comparatively rare, while the marriage of relations as close as first cousins is not countenanced by the Christian religion. Only monogamy is lawful. However, the relationship between the sexes is much freer than in the Middle East; premarital and to a lesser extent also extramarital sexual relationships are tolerated. Divorce proceedings can be instituted by either husband or wife.

To the south of the Middle East, in Negro Africa, the typical family is the extended one: either patrilineal, headed by the oldest surviving brother in a given generation or matrilineal, headed by the mother's oldest brother. After the death of the original head of the family it does not break up, as it does in the Middle East, but continues to function as a unit under the new headship of the next oldest brother. Marriage is exogamous, the totemic or rarely nontotemic clan being the exogamous unit. Sexual mores show a wide range of variety. Divorce can be initiated by either the husband or the wife.

To the southeast of the Middle East in the subcontinent of India, the rule is the patrilineal, patrilocal, and patriarchal extended family, though matrilineal descent also occurs. Upon the father's death the oldest son becomes the head of the family; in this respect the Indian family stands nearer to the African than to the Middle Eastern counterpart. The extended family or larger kinship group (*gotra*) is exogamous; the endogamous unit is the subcaste. Monogamy is the rule among the Hindus, though polygyny occurs, as well as some localized polyandry. Sex mores show a wide range of variation, with the prevalence of purdah or seclusion of women, and sati, the burning alive of widows (now prohibited by law) in direct ratio to caste status. Divorce is not allowed by Hindu tradition.

To the northeast of the Middle East, in the Central Asian culture area, the family is patrilineal, patrilocal, extended, and exogamous. Upon the death of the family head, his eldest surviving brother takes his place. Polygyny is permitted, as in the Middle East. Sex mores are lax; there is no emphasis on female purity, no veiling, and no seclusion of women. Women can have no legal recourse to divorce.

With respect to marriage and the family the Middle East is thus clearly set off against the four adjoining world areas; while the similarity of traits within it serves as an additional indication of its character as a distinct culture continent.

Also with regard to social units larger than the extended family, the three main sectors of Middle Eastern society show a number of basic correspondences. The Middle Eastern towns, however, have been for several decades centers of foreign (Western) cultural influences, as a consequence of which much of the original Middle Eastern tradition in social organization has been obliterated in them (especially in the middle and upper classes) and can be found only in the villages and the nomadic tribes.

Nomadic camp and agricultural village, however, must not be conceived as two opposite forms of local aggregates. The existence of a continuous range of transitional forms between the two clearly shows that camp and village are merely the two extreme forms of a variety of possible mixtures of elements taken from both. The presence of these "mixed" forms of local aggregates is due not only to the continued processes of sedentarization; the reverse process is also known to have taken place repeatedly: settled villagers have taken up nomadism, either completely or partially.

The cultivation of the soil and animal husbandry can, moreover, mutually complement each other. When the observer is confronted with the habitat of a human group making a living in both ways, he may not be able to decide whether it should be counted as a village or as a nomadic encampment.

The nomadic wandering unit often consists of not just one, but two or even more groups of extended families, each one of which is sometimes called *ḥamūla*; similarly, also, the settled village may contain two or more groups, each with a great inner cohesion, and varying degrees of mutual tension. The nomadic *ḥamūla*, as a rule, pitches its tents together in one part of the camp; the village group (also called *ḥamūla* in some parts of the Middle East) inhabits one quarter of the village. The *ḥamūla*, whether in village or camp, is definitely a kinship group, and as such commands the loyalty of its member families.

The place of the individual within his society is determined, first, by his membership in an extended family, and secondly, by the membership of his extended family in a *ḥamūla*. This means that in traditional Middle Eastern society participation in social groups larger than the family is a family affair and not an individual concern. Adherence to larger groups can never cut across family ties. On the contrary, the fact that the family belongs to a larger social group only strengthens the family unity, for the stronger the family as a whole the greater its weight within the larger unit.

The largest traditional social grouping to be found all over the Middle East is a loose, informal twofold faction which, at the same time, is powerful in its hold over the population, whether nomadic or sedentary. This social grouping resembles in several respects the kind usually referred to by the term "moiety" or "dual organization." In some parts of the Middle East (e.g., in Arabia and the Levant coast) entire tribes and villages belong to one or the other of such dual factions known by name pairs such as Qaḥṭān and ʿAdnān, Yafaʿ and Ḥamdān, Hināwī and Ghāfirī, Qays and Yaman. In other places, the individual villages are split into two sections or moieties. One of the two moieties in a village may be bound by ties of friendship or allegiance to corresponding moieties in other villages, while the other moieties of the same villages form another confederation. Whether the villages as a whole or only one half of each of them belong to a moiety, there is usually much competition and rivalry, and frequently even bloody fights between the two sides. In many cases political initiative has made use of the existing dual organization with the result that the moieties today often have political significance, though differences in descent and custom are by no means forgotten. A detailed examination of Middle Eastern dual organization will be found in Chapter 7.

With regard to social control, distinction must be made between the local and the higher level. On the local level, the social control of the typical and traditional Middle Eastern village resembled until recently (roughly up to the end of World War I) that of the nomadic tribe to a considerable degree. It was the same kind of semiautocratic and semidemocratic, highly variable and informal social control characteristic of the nomadic tribe, which makes difficult a description in concrete terms. The village headman (called *mukhtār* in the Fertile Crescent countries, *muhtar* in Turkey, *'omda* in Egypt, *aga* in Kurdistan, *amīn* in North Africa) corresponds to the tribal *shaykh*; he is usually the head of the most influential family or group of families in the village. The office of headmanship is inherited from a man by a son or another near relative, but succession also requires the approval of the elders of the village. These elders make up the informally (and recently more frequently formally) constituted village council, the *majlis* (*jema'a* in North Africa).

The balance of power between the headman and the council depends upon the personality of the headman. The authority of the tribal *shaykh* rests not on force, which as a rule does not stand at his disposal, but on the esteem, renown, and prestige he enjoys. The same is true to a more limited extent of the village headman, though the latter usually wields more influence over his council, and his power over the simple villagers is also correspondingly greater. One of the reasons for this difference may be seen in the lack of mobility of the cultivators inhabiting the villages as compared to the much greater freedom of movement of the nomadic tribesmen. A dissatisfied tribesman can, if worst comes to worst, leave his tribe and join with his family and flocks another tribe, even though such a move may mean loss of status; an agriculturist villager who has been antagonized or even oppressed by his headman has no such way out. Another reason is the frequent indebtedness of the villagers to the headman or to a wealthy absentee landowner whose representative he is; such a situation can easily be exploited by the headman to make the debtor subservient to him.

In the heyday of Turkish rule over the Middle East the village could and would rely as little on any central governmental authority as the nomadic tribe. The only difference between the two was that the volatile nomadic tribe was never successfully bent under the yoke of taxation, while the lot of the villagers was to bear a heavy yoke of oppressive taxes. The official political or administrative contact between the village and the higher (district or central) authorities was largely confined to conscription and tax collection. The taxes were (and are) a heavy burden on the villagers, in return for which they received nothing: no services, no help, no protection. As long as the village headman delivered the taxes, he and his village were left alone and could continue undisturbed in their traditional ways of life.

In recent decades, this pattern has been undergoing considerable change. The nomadic tribe occupies today more or less the position held by the village half a century ago; it has to pay taxes to the central government as the village does, although there is a marked difference even here: many nomadic tribes receive, in the person of their *shaykhs*, considerable governmental subventions that sometimes equal the sums collected in taxes. One of the results of this development is that the position of the *shaykh* has become stronger vis-à-vis his council and tribesmen, and that he can assume a more autocratic attitude.

The village, on the other hand, has become a more and more integral part of the state, politically, economically, educationally, and in several other respects. The old, traditional village institutions such as the mosque, the *kuttāb* (Koran school), the guest house, the communal threshing floor, and the like survive; but recent decades have witnessed the great innovation that, for the first time in thousands of years, the villagers receive something from the state in return for their taxes: schools, sanitation, economic aid, police and military protection. These services, however, are still in their infancy.

In general, the socioeconomic conditions characteristic of the Middle Eastern cultivators today can be summed up in a few somber lines. Most of the cultivators are subsistence farmers living on their produce, with a predominantly cereal diet which, though perhaps barely adequate in caloric value, is lacking in protein and protective foods. As a consequence of this and the generally low standards of hygiene, the incidence of disease is high, in some areas appallingly so. Adequate water supplies are rare; because of the perennial irrigation method practiced in some riverain tracts and the presence of stagnant waters elsewhere, malaria is the most prevalent single disease in many regions. The vast majority of the cultivators in the Middle East are either dwarfholders, share-cropper tenants, or landless laborers. A small number of wealthy, often extremely rich landowning families concentrate in their hands a substantial proportion of the cultivated land, a situation in which land reforms have only recently begun to make a dent. Lands owned by smallholders in villages were until recently often held under the ancient system of communal ownership.[9]

It is very difficult to reach valid generalizations with regard to governmental and political forms in the Middle East. At present, the tendency prevails in most Middle Eastern states to follow Western patterns of government—which is consistent with the readiness of urban upper-class Middle Easterners to adopt Western techniques. Thus we find republics and kingdoms with houses of representatives, ministers of state, and the like. However, these are rarely more than new façades behind which still stand the old structures of autocratic rule exercised by small, wealthy, and powerful feudal groups. Several Middle Eastern countries passed from traditional despotism, through a brief period of experimentation with parliamentary democracy, to modern dictatorship. In some Middle Eastern states, even of the external forms of Western governmental techniques only a few have been adopted: no distinction, for instance, is being made to this day between state income and expenditure on the one hand and the ruler's privy purse on the other. This is part of the age-old Middle Eastern governmental tradition, which also includes the feudal rule of the few based on the power of a mercenary army, often of foreign extraction. Under such circumstances, dynastic constancy is rare; the throne or the power is more often usurped than inherited. While on the local level (in tribes and villages) the rule of persons other than of the blood would be unimaginable, on the highest level foreigners can succeed in attaining positions of sovereignty.

The relationship of the cities to the countryside in the Middle East today is reminiscent of that between town and country in medieval Europe. The Middle Eastern towns, of which more will be said in Chapter 9, are the undisputed industrial, commercial, financial, political, judicial, educational, literary, recreational, artistic, intellectual, medical, and religious centers of their respective hinterlands. Externally the *sūq*, or bazaar, is undoubtedly the most characteristic as well as the most fascinating part of the towns, with its narrow alleys, covered with vaulted stone arches or with matting or awning, and with each trade occupying a separate street. Organizationally, the *sūq* is the most tangible expression of the existence and activities of the craft guilds (now largely defunct) such as those of tailors, outfitters, slipper and sandal makers, saddlers, embroiderers, goldsmiths, etc. Each of these guilds has its head, its provost, its council, its grades of apprentices, journeymen, and masters, its constitution, rules, and other organizational trappings.[10] In most cases artisanship, and with it membership in a guild, are hereditary; sometimes, as in Tunis, guild membership as well as the position of guild chief has to be passed on from father to son.

The presence of social classes is characteristic of the Middle Eastern towns, in contrast to villages and nomadic tribes. The urban class structure shows great vertical mobility. The great majority of the townspeople belong to the lower class, and make their living as craftsmen, shopkeepers, itinerant vendors, unskilled laborers, porters, workers employed in services, fishermen (in coastal towns), beggars, etc. The thin but growing middle class is made up of master craftsmen, merchants, teachers, other professional people who do not belong to the "great" families, minor officials, small house-owners, and others of moderate means. The very small but extremely powerful upper class consists in each country of a few "great" families whose members, sometimes referred to as "notables," occupy key positions in many fields and are the mainstay of the feudal oligarchy. They are, as a rule, the leaders of society, of political life (the political parties often utilizing family affiliations, moieties, or religious orders), of economic, financial, and industrial enterprises. In most cases, the initial wealth of such families is due to the concentration in their hands of landed property. Westernization, which is centered in the towns, is most advanced among the upper class, less so among the middle class, and has only begun on the lower levels.[11]

Nationalism, a modern urban phenomenon in the Middle East, is the result of two trends. One of these, xenophobia, has been a traditional attitude in the Middle East for several centuries. It means hatred of non-Muslims, or even of Muslims not belonging to the locally prevalent sect. This indigenous substratum of sentiment has been overlaid in the course of the last few decades by a Western type of nationalism that is probably the only Western *idea* deeply to impress itself on the Middle Eastern mind. While in general Westernization means almost exclusively the adoption of nothing but Western material equipment and techniques, an exception was made in the case of nationalism, which happened to fit in well with the pre-existing scheme of ideas. Westernization thus, somewhat paradoxically, means the adoption of Western techniques on the one hand and the upsurge of nationalism and intensification of the traditional hatred of foreigners on the other.

Towns are the centers of Westernization, and not only because they are the homes of the few wealthy families who are economically in a position to emulate the manners and customs of the West. Western influences are diffused from the town over the surrounding area as a consequence of the not infrequent visits paid to its bazaars, cafés, banks, stores, motion-picture theaters, law courts, and other offices by both villagers and tribesmen. Interaction, manifested mainly in commercial contacts between nomads and agriculturists, is an important characteristic of Middle Eastern social life everywhere, and a major part of this interaction occurs in the towns. Even when direct trading between a village and a nomadic tribe is precluded by hostile relations, merchants and customers can meet in the town where, as individuals, they feel safe and free to deal with one another. The commercial contact taking place in the towns actually is a three-way process: the town sells the products of its crafts and industry; the village its agricultural products; and the nomadic tribe its animals, hides, wool, rugs, clarified butter (*semn*), etc.; and each buys its necessities from the other two. The town, of course, profits in addition in its role of the middleman, buying from the villager and selling to the tribesman and vice versa. Exporting and importing, often on a large scale, are also concentrated in the towns.

To pass from the socioeconomic aspects of culture to mental equipment, we must first consider the question of literacy. Located between Europe with its high rates of literacy and Negro Africa with its nonliterate cultures, the Middle East is the home of the oldest literate cultures and has produced some of the greatest masterpieces of world literature. Nevertheless it is characterized today, as it was throughout its six-thousand-year history, by extremely high rates of illiteracy. Even in the towns the illiteracy rates reaches 80 per cent; in the villages it climbs up to over 90 per cent; among the nomadic tribes it is practically 100 per cent. In recent years, slow changes have begun in certain areas with the opening of elementary schools and the introduction of compulsory education. However, the over-all picture is still that of very high rates of illiteracy, higher among women than among men; among Muslims than among non-Muslims (Christians and Jews); among nomads than among settled people; among villagers than in the urban population.

Illiteracy, however, means neither a lack of familiarity with the intellectual and spiritual products of preceding generations nor an ignorance of the events of the contemporary world. Middle Eastern illiterate culture shares with the nonliterate cultures of the Old World the possession of a rich storehouse of oral literature, consisting of folk stories and legends, poetry and songs, riddles, sayings, and proverbs; it is, moreover, residual heir to the age-old and famed "Wisdom of the East," lending a flavor of mellow maturity to all aspects of everyday life, to activities, judgments, and values. As to the events of the contemporary world, the grapevine of the bazaars, cafés, markets, village wells and threshing floors, council chambers or tents, and caravan serais always surprises the Western observer with its rapidity, efficiency, and penetration.

Poetry is so much part of everyday living that the ambulant vendors in the streets of Oriental towns praise their wares in rhymed ditties recited to special tunes. Schoolchildren in the old-fashioned Koran schools compete with one another in composing poems by way of a pastime, and in many lands versification is indulged in by people in all walks of life, rich and poor, literate and illiterate.

Inseparable from poetry is music, which is perhaps the most individualistic of arts in the Middle East. Not only will two performers never give the same interpretation of a traditional musical piece, but the same musician will only rarely play or sing the same song twice in exactly the same manner. The performer is usually also his own composer, and even when playing a well-known tune he will inevitably introduce variations and additions of his own, under the spur of the moment's mood. Moreover, the Middle Eastern musician, as a rule, also builds his own musical instrument; his musical training as an apprentice to a master begins by learning how to make for himself an instrument of his own.[12] In the shadow theater, a favorite though at present rapidly declining pastime, the master of the theater makes his own figures, writes his own plays, directs the performance, and plays the main roles.[13] Similarly, the storytellers who can be heard in cafés during the festive nights of the fast month Ramadan, although bound by certain general traditional lines, nevertheless combine the arts of the novelist, the poet, and the actor, and often those of the composer and instrumental performer as well. The distinction sharply drawn in the West between creative artist and performer simply does not exist in the Middle East, where every performance involves the creation of at least a new, individual variation on the original theme.

Tradition also determines the framework of the visual arts; but here too the frame can be filled in in varying ways, according to the talents and inclinations of the individual artist or artisan. What is, however, even more significant for the cultural picture as a whole is the fact that in traditional Middle Eastern culture almost all branches of everyday work are permeated with aesthetic qualities; the beauty of objects everywhere complements their utility. Art is called upon to embellish everything. The richer a man the more time he spends in practicing and enjoying the arts, but the poor as well, the great masses of the simple people, live a life enriched by aesthetic values.

No definite line can be drawn between the arts and crafts in Middle Eastern culture. Articles of clothing such as headgear, mantles, belts, and sandals are in style, color, and decoration closely dependent upon custom fixed by age-old tradition which allows individual talent and taste to express themselves only in relatively minor variations. At the same time, the absence of mass production and the factory system and the corresponding prevalence of handcrafts, mean a greater reliance on trained skill and dexterity, on the ability of the individual artisan to design and execute an article according to the discriminating taste of individual customers. The execution of a piece of work, whether it be a shoe, chair, water pipe, brass tray, rug, lamp, camel litter, basket, or earthenware jug, from its inception to its completion, gives the artisan a deep sense of satisfaction and a keen interest in his work. Most artisans are actually artists whose aesthetic judgment plays an important role in their work. Thus aesthetics is an integral part of artisanship.

Aesthetic tradition is closely linked to religious tradition in the Middle East. Although religious rituals may in principle be performed everywhere, they have always been preferably localized at temples and shrines that are highly aesthetic foci of visual and vocal arts all over the Middle East. Annual religious festivals, which are great events in the life of Middle Eastern peoples, are aesthetic-religious-emotional affairs rich in artistic pageantry.

Although officially the vast majority (about 95 per cent) of the Middle Eastern peoples belong to one of several sects of Islam, actually their religious life contains many elements going back to pre-Islamic and even to pre-Christian and pre-Hebrew times. The belief in and propitiation of various spirits, ghosts, and demons (*ghūls, jinns, 'afrīts, zārs* etc.), many of them connected with natural objects; divination and interpretation of dreams and omens; belief in the evil eye; the use of charms and amulets; the practice of making vows and sacrifices; these are in the main the

2

more ancient elements of belief and ritual that are often overlaid
with only a thin veneer of Islamic doctrine and practice. This is
true of both nomads and sedentary peoples, though the latter are
generally more inclined to venerate saints at annual pilgrimages
to their tombs and to observe the Five Pillars of the Faith,[14]
which are almost entirely ignored by the nomads. The absence of
ancestor worship from this quasi-animistic religious complex is
remarkable.

It is a sign of the complexity of Middle Eastern religious culture
that, side by side with the persistence of such early manifestations
of religion, one finds such developments as theological schools and
colleges, and religious doctrines spiritually and ethically equal to
those of Judaism and Western Christianity. Significant in this
connection are the religious orders and brotherhoods whose
members dedicate their lives to the service of God by voluntarily
denying themselves worldly goods to varying degrees, and by
following special "paths" and rituals of their own, often for the
purpose of inducing ecstasy. These confraternities, one of the most
important of which is that of the Senussi in Cyrenaica, sprang
primarily from Sufism (Islamic mysticism), but they often became,
very soon after their initial success, strongly political and practical
in character.

More significant, however, than the varieties of religious doctrine and practice, is the basically religious orientation of the
Middle Eastern peoples. The totality of life is permeated with
religion, which holds supreme sway over the great majority of the
population, and especially in the nomadic camp and the agricultural village that have been the strongholds of religious traditionalism. Religion is thus the fundamental motivating force
behind most aspects of culture, and has its say in practically every
act and moment in life. Observance of traditional forms and rites,
whether of the official or the popular kind, is an integral part of
everyday life. Religion not expressed in formal observance is
inconceivable. Morality, too, always appears in the guise of
religion and is merely one of its manifestations; moral law disso-
ciated from religion does not exist for people steeped in Middle
Eastern culture.

The connection between religion and art has been touched

upon already, but it goes further than the stimulus given by religion to the arts or the service rendered by them to religion. The scope of Middle Eastern art is itself closely circumscribed by religion, to the extent that certain fields are excluded and others concentrated upon intensively. The decorative arts and architecture in which the Middle Eastern artistic genius most fully expresses itself are the fields most closely associated with religion. But religion claims its due even in the secular uses of art, as exemplified by the ever recurring use of the name of Allah and of Koranic passages as decorative devices on a multitude of objects including tiles and trays, lamps and daggers, vases and plates, etc., made of such divers materials as glass, clay, china, wood, and various precious or common metals.

All custom and tradition are basically religious; for whatever is old and customary and traditional is hallowed by religion that itself is mainly tradition and custom, and only to a small extent doctrine and law. Thus the entire field of custom, wide and infinitely ramified in its permeation of everyday life, is incapable of being divorced from religion either in theory or in practice. Whatever man does in his waking or sleeping hours during his entire lifespan on this earth, and also what is done to him in his prenatal and post-mortem existence, always conform to custom, tradition, and religion. These three, then, religion, tradition, and custom, form an inseparable three-in-one constellation that rule the skies of Middle Eastern life.

Another characteristic trait of religion in the Middle East is its distinctly dual aspect of materialism on the one hand and spiritualism on the other. The two neatly balanced main concerns of Middle Eastern religion are physical well-being in this world and spiritual welfare after death. God is expected to dispnese material blessings to his people in this life, and to compensate the unfortunate but deserving with his blessings in the after life. Hence the accent of righteousness, on the purity of the soul, as the only real achievement of man, in contradistinction to worldly goods that are viewed as worthless encumbrances. The supreme good man can acquire is of a moral quality, but moralism always involves ritualism. For the great masses of the poor, many of whom live in poverty unknown in our Western world, religion with its moralistic and spiritualist tenets and with its great promise of future reward is an asset of inestimable psychological value. Owing to the sway religion holds over performance, and the grooves it cuts into thinking and feeling, life with its vicissitudes and disappointments is appraised from a wider angle, from a long-range perspective, in which sojourn on this earth with all its possible gains and losses appears as a mere lower and lesser half of a great totality of existence whose essentials and ultimates lie in the Beyond. Spiritual outlook thus moves on a higher plane, beyond the reaches of discomfort, pain, anguish, and privation. Hence that composure, that peace of mind, preserved even in the face of great adversity, which ever and again astonish Western observers. The other side of the picture is that religious systems able to give *this* to their followers almost inevitably exercise a powerful hold on them and create a state of mind conducive to intolerance, fanaticism, and cleavage to narrow sectarian lines.

To sum up, the following features characterize traditional Middle Eastern culture: (1) A basic ecologic dichotomy: on the one hand, camel-breeding nomadic tribes living on animal husbandry and, on the other, settled villagers living on agricultural cultivation, corresponding to the desert and the sown regions. (2) The presence of transitional or intermediary types of human societies ranging from sheep and goat or cattle herders practicing a limited nomadism, through seminomadic tribes in various stages of sedentarization, to almost completely settled tribes. (3) The nomadic and seminomadic groups exhibit a tribal structure that is practically identical everywhere. (4) The village is usually divided along kinship lines, but is fairly homogeneous as far as occupational structure is concerned, practically all its inhabitants engaging in agricultural pursuits. (5) Constant commercial exchange takes place between the settled and the nomadic population in each area, with the local town as its focus. (6) Until a few decades ago, however, the nomadic tribes often raided the weaker villagers, regarding them as their legitimate prey. (7) The urban population, and more precisely its middle and upper class, though numerically insignificant, takes in every respect the leadership (in religion, education, art, politics, business, etc.).

(8) The triple class structure is pronounced in the towns, rudimentary in the villages, and almost nonexistent in the nomadic camp. (9) Westernization is centered in the towns and, within the towns, is strongest among the upper class, less advanced in the middle class, and incipient in the lower class. (10) The extended, patrilineal, patrilocal, patriarchal, endogamous, and polygynous family is the basic social and economic unit in camp, village, and town, the individual being subordinated to the family. (11) Strongly marked double standards of sexual morality prevail, with great emphasis on premarital virginity and female purity. (12) Veiling of women is practiced sporadically, being most prevelant in the conservative middle and upper classes of urban society. (13) In the nomadic camps and the villages, the social units larger than the family are based on kinship lines. (14) In the towns such associations as the guilds are based on occupation but membership is often inherited. (15) The individual participates in social groupings larger than the family not on an individual basis but through his family membership. (16) Indications of a dual organization can be found everywhere. (17) On the local level (in camps and villages) social control and political leadership are based on family ties and influences, with the powers divided between headman and council. (18) On the higher level, in the capitals and other centrally located towns, the feudalistic, oligarchic, and at times despotic rule is slowly being mitigated by newly introduced Western forms of government, respectively transformed into dictatorship with capitalistic control and a disproportionate accumulation of wealth in the hands of a few "great" families. (19) Poverty, subsistence-level life, with extremely high incidence of disease, high birth rate, high death rate, and low life expectancy are general, with the situation somewhat better in the towns than in the villages and camps. (20) Very high rates of illiteracy all over the Middle East stamp it with the character of an illiterate culture. (21) There is a great preoccupation with folklore: folk poetry, folk song, folk tales, folk music, riddles, proverbs. (22) There is also an intensive permeation of everyday life by the aesthetic element, with the fields and the overall forms of aesthetic expression being determined by traditione (23) One of the most outstanding characteristics is an all-pervasive

religiosity, consisting of elements of belief, ritual, custom, and morality, and embracing a wide range of variation regarding concrete content. (24) The belief in God and His will is intense and general, but is accompanied by the belief in spirits, demons, and ghosts and by saint worship in the villages ; ancestor worship, on the other hand, is absent. (25) Finally, a broad outlook on human existence can be found everywhere, including the firm belief in a reward and punishment in an after life and accompanied by detachment from material values and indifference to adversity.

II. Some Problems of the Middle Eastern Culture Continent

CHARACTERISTICS OF THE CULTURE AREA

OBSERVATIONS ON the culture of the Middle East may be made in the light of four characteristics that are generally taken to indicate a culture area type of spatial distribution.

The first of these four characteristics is the existence of a certain correlation between a culture area and the geographical area that is its locus. Culture areas roughly correspond to ecologic areas. Certain elements in the culture evince a dependence on geographic and ecologic factors. There is thus a definite relationship between the culture and its geographic environment.

The second characteristic derives from the observation that there are cultures in which traits group themselves geographically, and others in which they do not.[1] This observation was made by Ruth Benedict and, in accordance with it, Herskovits has stated some fifteen years later than "Experience has shown ... that it [the idea of culture areas] is not adapted to use where the distribution of geographical differences between peoples is overridden by class stratification resulting from a high degree of specialization that ... characterizes larger population aggregates" such as the literate societies of Europe and America. "The typical behavior of social class or occupational group is important here. Categories derived from distinctions drawn empirically on the basis of local differences are obviously inapplicable to such cases, and should be replaced by those that are functionally relevant."[2] Translated into quantitative terms, the second characteristic of the culture area could, therefore, be expressed as follows: the less the social and occupational stratification in a geographical area, the greater the theoretical applicability of the culture area concept.

The third characteristic of the culture area is that its center is well defined but its margins are rarely, if ever, clearcut. Boas has pointed out that the areal distribution of different aspects of culture, such as technology, beliefs, social forms, religion, art, and music, may be nonconcordant.[3]

This means that the usefulness of the culture area concept as a classificatory tool is limited, since it frequently leaves doubt as to the borderline that divides two contiguous culture areas from each other. This criticism has been met only partially by stressing the fact that, as Kroeber put it, "the culmination of these [different] aspects [of culture] tend actually to coincide in the same centers" which therefore "are to be construed as foci of radiation."[4] Wissler has accordingly mapped his areas in America only schematically, emphasizing their centers in which the culture is most typical and intensive.[5] Implicit in this discussion about the clear-cut center and dubious borders is the quantitative assumption that the greater the cultural homogeneity within an area and the clearer its limits, the less doubtful its culture area character.

The fourth characteristic of the culture area refers to the time aspect. Wissler stated that "a distribution of narrow range may be suspected of being an innovation, whereas one of wide range would be of respectable age."[6] Kroeber, further generalizing, emphasized that the culture area "is primarily classificatory and descriptive, therefore static; but like every sound 'natural' classification it implies a genetic one."[7] A culture area is thus assumed to be the result of historical processes. One could tentatively formulate a quantitative relationship between age and area: the larger the spatial extent of the culture area, the longer the historical processes that went into its making.

The "Culture Continent" Character of the Middle East

Let us now examine the Middle East in the light of these four characteristics. With regard to the first characteristic, the dependence of culture on habitat, it can be stated categorically that there are few world areas in which there is such a close correlation as in the Middle East between the geographic pattern of the natural environment and the cultural pattern of the peoples. Between 90 and 95 per cent of the entire area is desert or desert-like steppe, interspersed everywhere, however, as well as surrounded by fertile regions of cultivated or cultivable land. This alternation of desert and sown with a transition either sudden or gradual from the one into the other is the basic ecologic pattern of the Middle East. To the south this area is bounded by the humid forest region of central Africa; to the north by the Mediterranean and the Black Seas; and to the southeast by the Arabian Sea and the humid forest region of the Indian subcontinent. To the northeast, in Central Asia, is found the only contiguous area that to some extent is comparable geographically to the Middle East. However, the Middle East with its true deserts lies south of latitude 38° N., whereas the Central Asian steppes lie to the north of the same latitude. Differences in elevation, water resources, and climatic conditions further set off the two regions, and make different cultural adaptations necessary. The limits of the natural area of the Middle East are thus drawn clearly enough and, as we shall see instantly, are closely concordant with the limits of the Middle Eastern culture continent.

When we examine the cultural correspondences to this geographic area and pattern, we are actually shifting our attention from the first to the second characteristic of the culture area, according to which a geographic patterning of cultures within a larger region is a criterium of the applicability of the culture area concept.

The Middle East lies in this respect, just as it does geographically, in the middle between Negro Africa and Europe. Negro Africa is characterized by chiefly geographic groupings of cultures almost as suitable for classification on an areal basis as are the native cultures of America. In the Middle East no area shows a cultural homogeneity comparable to that of a typical culture area in Negro Africa. On the other hand, neither does the Middle East partake of the European pattern with its accent on social classes and occupational groupings.

The specifically Middle Eastern sociocultural pattern is characterized by the presence in every part of the area of two main population categories, each with a typical ecologic adjustment of its own: nomadic tribes inhabiting the deserts and steppes on the

2§

one hand, and settled groups concentrated in those regions capable of agricultural cultivation on the other. This schematic dichotomy into nomadic and settled aggregates reveals, of course, under closer inspection a much more complicated picture of social structure. With the exception of the townspeople, these further subdivisions show a close correspondence to finer distinctions within subtypes of geographic environment, and thus further corroborate the first characteristic of the culture area, according to which a definite correlation exists between a culture area and the geographic area it occupies.

Between the true desert and the sown there is in most parts of the Middle East a transitional semidesert belt, barely suited for agricultural purposes but offering much better pastures than the true desert. This semidesert belt is the home of the sheep- and goat-breeding nomads whose wandering territory is much more restricted than that of the true or camel nomads. Again, in the mountainous sections of the Middle East, is found yet another type of seminomads: the mountain nomads who practice transhumance. In the cultivable areas, for example, along the Mediterranean littoral and the great riverbeds of the Nile, the Tigris, and the Euphrates, in the oases and the mountain tracts, are found agricultural villages with a population in many respects different from any of the nomadic varieties. These sedentary peoples who form more than 85 per cent of the total population of the Middle East are mostly villagers but, in addition, they range from small-townpeople to big-city folk with a display of occupational specialization increasing in proportion to the size of the urban aggregates they inhabit.

Starting out from a big city such as Damascus in Syria, Cairo in Egypt, Tripoli in Libya, or Casablanca in Morocco, one can find first a number of agricultural villages situated in the midst of cultivated territory, then a steppe region utilized by goat and sheep herders practicing a limited nomadism, and finally the desert where are encamped the camel-breeding Bedouin tribes, all within a radius of fifty miles or less. Were one to apply the culture area concept to such a narrowly delimited tract alone, one would find that four separate culture areas can be distinguished in it: urban, agricultural, seminomadic, and true nomadic. However, as one proceeds from one country to another, from one region to another, one finds this same spatial sequence repeated again and again, so that the fourfold division appears as a single unit showing a definite configurational patterning. The entire Middle Eastern culture continent thus appears as a tissue consisting of a number of cells, each one of which has an identical or very similar inner structure.

Such a cell pattern in itself is not a uniquely Middle Eastern phenomenon. It is known to exist to a smaller or larger extent in most human societies. In the modern Western world one finds it represented by the ubiquitous range from city to village or farm. But unique for the Middle East is the specific structure of the cell with its four components, the urban, agricultural, seminomadic, and nomadic population elements. In fact, this pattern of social structure with its local heterogeneity that recurs consistently all over the area is so typical for the Middle East that it must be regarded as one of the most important criteria when an attempt is being made to determine its limits.

In turning now to the third characteristic, the one that can be reformulated as stating that a culture area is only as good as its boundaries, let us attempt to draw the borderline of the Middle East with both the geographic and the cultural angles in mind. This task is made relatively easy because in no geographic area contiguous to the Middle East is either the typical Middle Eastern desert-sown pattern or the equally typical Middle Eastern sociocultural configuration duplicated.

Even if we disregard for a moment the nomadic-and-settled pattern and concentrate on the nomadic element alone, no contiguous geographic area is found to contain a nomadic population sufficiently similar to the Middle Eastern nomads to raise serious doubts as to the delimitation of the Middle Eastern culture continent.

The only comparable nomadic culture in any world area contiguous to the Middle East is found in Central Asia. However, in addition to the environmental factors referred to above, cultural factors that can be isolated by a careful perusal of documentation available from both areas show that Central Asial nomadism and Middle Eastern nomadism constitute two very distinct cultures,

different enough to preclude their inclusion under one cultural
entity.[8] It is sufficient to refer to one complex only that can serve
both as a characteristic of the nomadic element in all parts of the
Middle East and as a clearly marked distinguishing feature
between it and the Central Asian nomads. This is the type of
shelter used all over the Middle East by the nomads and seminomads: the black hair tent, which essentially consists of a single
large rectangular piece of tent cloth made of camel's and goat's
hair, spread upon a number of poles and held in place by long
outstretched ropes pegged to the ground. This black hair tent is
practically the only type of shelter used by the nomads and seminomads of the Middle East, its form and construction showing
only minor and insignificant variations from Morocco and Río de
Oro in the west to Afghanistan and Balujistan in the east. In the
Indus Valley the nomadic camp is replaced by settled agricultural
villages that are the westernmost outposts of the cultures of the
Indian subcontinent.

In the Plain of Turkestan the place of the Middle Eastern black
tent is taken by the *yurt*, the round dome-capped tent built around
a complex and solid frame of latticelike rods of willow or beech-
wood, tied together with rawhide, and covered with white or gray
sheep's felt. The boundary line between the black hair tent and
the *yurt* is sharply drawn. To its northeastern edge the Iranian
Plateau is the domain of the Iranian tribes with their black hair
tents; down in the plains, beginning with the Gorgan Valley
within the political boundaries of Iran and Afghanistan, and to the
northeast for thousands of miles is the territory of the Turkoman,
Kirgiz, Kazak, and Mongol *yurt*-dwelling tribes. Wherever *yurts*
appear further to the west, that is, within the Middle East, they
belong to isolated Turkoman tribes who in the course of their
wanderings reached these western lands. On the other hand, a
variety of the black hair tent reappears to the east in Tibet, after
a break of several hundreds of miles. What is, however, more
significant for a delimitation of the Middle East is the fact that no
intermediary or transitional forms exist between the black hair
tent and the *yurt*, and that consequently the spatial distribution of
each is even more clearly marked off against the other.

The black hair tent is, of course, much more than a single item in the material equipment of nomadic tribes. It is the symbol and the tangible expression of a highly coordinated, complex, and specific way of life: Middle Eastern pastoral nomadism. The hair tent means a special set of material equipment; it indicates animal husbandry concentrating on camels and/or sheep and goats; it is an evidence of seasonal wandering, tribal organization, and of a definite system of values and social attitudes. Wherever it is found it thus testifies to the presence of the nomadic or seminomadic component of the Middle Eastern sociocultural configuration.

The nomads and seminomads, however, are only part of the Middle Eastern sociocultural pattern. They have, in every section of the Middle East, clearly patterned contacts with the settled population. That is, the interaction among the different parts of the local cells is largely the same all over the area. In fact, this specific dynamism and functional interdependence among the different population elements is everywhere the inevitable concomitant of the structural patterning referred to earlier.

Equally significant for a study of the Middle East from the culture area point of view is the fact that in all those aspects of culture not contingent upon ecologic adjustment a surprising homogeneity can be observed among the population elements inhabiting the area, however different the economic bases of their existence.

More about the definiteness of the boundaries of the Middle Eastern culture area can be said within the context of its time aspect. The correlation between time and space was stated to be the fourth characteristic of the culture area. The problem of Americanists such as Wissler was to reconstruct probable historical processes from a study of geographic distribution. Their age-area concept began with observed data in a geographic area and aimed at reaching an understanding of otherwise unknown occurrences in past ages.

In the Middle East, we are faced with a reversed situation. Owing to the specific trends of interests, first religious and later scientific, an enormous amount of attention has been focused on the history and archaeology of the Middle East, to the relative neglect of its present-day cultures. The result is that we know more about several phases of life in ancient Egypt or in ancient

Mesopotamia than in modern Egypt or Iraq. Compared to what
we know about cultural interchange and influences among the
great cultures of ancient Near Eastern civilization, our knowledge
of the distribution and formation of modern cultures in the area
is meager. In such a situation, the quest from the known to the
unknown must, obviously, proceed in the opposite direction from
the one familiar to Americanists and to anthropologists in general.
Our rich historical knowledge of the area must be brought to bear
upon the problems of the spatial distribution and interrelation of
the present-day cultures in the area.

If Wissler's dictum that a wide distributional range indicates
respectable age is true also in the reverse, the unparalleled age of
documented cultures in the core area of the Middle East will lead
us to expect an extremely wide spatial distribution of the modern
culture that is the end result of this long cultural history. In other
words, we will expect to find widely diffused over an uncommonly
extensive geographic region cultures or cultural complexes going
back ultimately to ancient Near Eastern origins.

Yet another consideration will strengthen us in this expectation·
The culture areas in America were found roughly to correspond to
ecologic or natural areas. As against the relatively small size of
these areas in America, and especially in North America, one
encounters in the Middle East a huge area characterized by a more
or less uniform overriding geographic pattern, to which a similarly
large area of cultural diffusion can be expected to correspond.
The two factors, historical and geographic, represent an exceptional set of circumstances that facilitated the spread of Middle
Eastern culture from the old core area until it reached the
present-day dimensions of the Middle Eastern culture continent.

In a rough diachronic scheme, three major elements can be
distinguished in the cultural configuration of each part of the
Middle East: two making for homogeneity and a third for
diversity. The two homogenizing influences are those of Islam and
of the ancient Near Eastern civilizations, while the diversifying
factor is the local tradition of greatly varying age.

Islamic culture started out from Arabia in the seventh century
and spread over the entire Middle East within a century after the
death of Mohammed (632). Islam, it may be reiterated here, is

more than a religion in the sense in which this concept is known
to us from the Western world. It is rather comparable to Hinduism, notwithstanding the basic differences between the two with
regard to concrete content, insofar as both Hinduism and Islam
are *total ways of life*. Islam as a total way of life is founded on a
tradition that goes back to Mohammed, either actually or
fictitiously, or to his companions and first disciples. It incorporates
religious, cultic, and doctrinal elements, and was in its very
beginnings a mixture of Mohammedan innovation and local
Ḥijāzī tradition and folk custom, which it disseminated in the
course of its conquests from Sind to Spain, from the Golden
River to the Golden Road.

However, the distribution of Islam is considerably wider than
that of Middle Eastern culture. There is, moreover, a marked
difference between the cultures of the Middle Eastern Muslim
peoples and those of the large Muslim ethnic aggregates residing
beyond the boundaries of the Middle East. This brings us to the
older, pre-Islamic processes of cultural diffusion that took place
in the area. For some four thousand years preceding Alexander
the Great, the ancient Near East was the primary center of cultural development and dissemination over a major part of the three
continents of the Old World. Influences from this core area
emanated in a sequence of waves. It would be extremely fascinating and instructive to collate the available information as to the
differences in the spatial spread of ancient Near Eastern cultural
influences on the one hand and of Islamic cultural influences on
the other, all around the margins of the Middle East. This,
however, cannot be done at the present time. Only from one contiguous area, that of African cultures, can a few data be adduced
illustrating the problem and at the same time helping to reach
a clearer understanding of the relationship between age and area
in the Middle East.

THE BOUNDARIES

Historical data as to the spread of ancient Near Eastern culture
into Negro Africa are meager, but a study of the spatial distribution of certain cultural elements points the way. There are
several cultural traits or complexes that originated in antiquity

somewhere in the general area of the ancient Near East, and which today are no longer found in the Middle East but have survived in Negro Africa.

One of these is the extremely significant complex of *sacred kingship*, which occupied a focal position in ancient Near Eastern

━━━━━━ The sacred kingship

━ ━ ━ ━ The myth of the message that failed

━·━·━· Multiple-headed spears and staves

Map 1. The northern boundary lines of the present-day distribution of three ancient Near Eastern cultural features in Africa cultures, and spread far beyond the present boundaries of Islam in Africa. Within the Middle East itself, sacred kingship has been obliterated by Islam with the result that sacred kingship and Islam form two mutually exclusive complexes sharply delimited against each other.[9]

Although the socioreligious complexes of Islam and sacred kingship respectively are of outstanding importance in the life of the peoples concerned, they in themselves would not be sufficient to delimit the southern boundary line of the Middle Eastern culture area. However, we find that this boundary line is roughly the same as that of several material traits that too originated in the ancient Near East and were subsequently superseded in the Middle East by more recent developments, to survive in the ancient form only in Negro Africa. *Multiple-headed spears* are a case in point. Bidents or two-headed spears were ritual objects in ancient Egypt and adjoining Libya in prehistoric as well as historic times. In ancient South Arabian (Sabaean and Minaean) inscriptions bidents, together with tridents, appear as symbols of lightning. The trident as a symbol of lightning and as a royal or divine attribute is known from the Hittites, the Assyrians, the Babylonians, and later the Greeks. Actual tridents survive from ancient Persia and countries to the southeast.

In the modern Middle East multiple-headed spears do not exist. In one place, Morocco, their ceremonial use disappeared about a hundred years ago. In Negro Africa, however, the multiple-pointed spear is very much in evidence to this day, as a badge of office, a ceremonial weapon, a royal emblem, or a cult object. The northern boundary line of its present-day distribution is practically identical with that of sacred kingship.

The distribution of the multiple-headed spears to the east of the Middle Eastern area is not as clear as one would like to have it. But it seems that the further away one moves from the Middle East, the more recent are the specimens found, until one reaches the East Indies, South East Asia, and China, where bidents and tridents have been in use as ceremonial or actual weapons down to the present time.[10]

The disappearance of multiple-headed spears from secular use can be explained by its suppression by Islam as an emblem of

sacred kings, and a subsequent extension of this suppression also
to its secular use. That sacred kingship itself could not be tolerated
by a strictly monotheistic and in its origins highly puritanistic
faith such as Islam is easily understandable.

The monotheistic-puritanistic origins of Islam are responsible
for the suppression and complete elimination of yet another
important ancient Near Eastern culture complex from most of the
Middle Eastern area. The *plastic representation* and portraiture of
living beings, animal, human, and divine, was of such significance
in the ancient Near East that without them ancient Near Eastern
religions (with the exception of the religion of the Hebrews from
the sixth century B.C. onward) would have been inconceivable.
And since religion was in its earliest Near Eastern manifestations
as much a total way of life as it is today in the Middle East,
everyday life in the ancient Near East would also have been
unthinkable without the esthetoreligious satisfactions offered by
plastic arts, and secondarily also by graphic arts. Masterpieces of
ancient Egyptian, Syrian, Mesopotamian, Anatolian, and Iranian
plastic art survive to this day as splendid witnesses to highly
developed cultures with definite artistic orientations. Islam,
continuing the late-Hebrew tradition of aversion against plastic
(as well as graphic) representations, put an end to this great
artistic efflorescence, and forced the artistic genius of the peoples
converted to its creed into such limited expressions as afforded by
decorative arts. The Middle East has thus become artistically an
essentially sculptureless area, to such an extent that even the
Coptic church, the largest, oldest, and most Middle Eastern of
all the Eastern Christian churches, foregoes any plastic representation of Jesus, Mary, and the saints.

Only to the northeast of the Middle Eastern culture area do we
encounter another culture that is likewise devoid of representative
art. In Central Asia, Islam has had the same effect in this respect
as in the Middle East: it eliminated any plastic art that may have
existed previously. To the north, in the Mediterranean area of
Christian Europe, sculpture is a significant element in religious
life in the Catholic as well as the Orthodox churches. To the south,
the borderline that marks the limits of the distribution of the
sacred kingship and the multiple-headed spear also marks the

borders of the vigorous Negro sculpture zone. To the southeast, in India, sculpture occupies in Hindu as well as in Buddhist cults a position similar to the one it has in Southern Europe.

With regard to *music*, it is the contention of musicologists who studied the Middle East that it is an area with definite musical characteristics of its own. It is pointed out that the same musical instruments are used and the same types of music are produced all over the area. Some of these musical instruments are old in the area, and certainly antedate Islam. Other ancient Near Eastern instruments disappeared from the area itself and survive in Negro Africa. A concrete example of the latter is the peculiar ancient Egyptian harp, known from its pictorial representation on ancient monuments, which does not exist any longer in any part of the Middle East but survives in unchanged form among the Azande and the Baganda in East Africa, and among the Jukun, Busawa, Igbira, Chamba, Verre, and others in West Africa.[11] All these tribes are grouped along the southern borders of the Middle Eastern culture continent, and just outside its limits.

Our last example to illustrate the same type of spatial distribution and the same position of the borderline is taken from the world of *myth*. In the literatures of the ancient Near East there is a type of story or myth known as "The Perverted Message" or "The Message That Failed." Frazer has shown that the Biblical story of the fall of man and the loss of his immortality is one version of this story.[12] In the modern Middle East no traces of this story are known to have survived. But the story of the message that failed reappears in a well-documented distribution in Negro Africa, again just south of the limits of the Middle Eastern culture area.[13]

If these examples could be sufficiently multiplied, they would show the Middle Eastern culture as occupying that centrally located geographic area in which the Islamic culture has superseded ancient Near Eastern culture complexes. Just outside its limits, however, many ancient Near Eastern culture complexes survive. This marginal survival is best documented in Negro Africa. In other contiguous areas more research is needed to demonstrate the same phenomenon, although hypothetically its presence seems most probable. The Middle Eastern culture continent would thus be found to comprise those regions which are Islamic at present and which in the past were under the cultural sway of the great ancient Near Eastern cultures. Regions that were reached by only one of these two great cultural waves are marginal to the Middle Eastern culture continent, and lie outside its boundaries proper. The area thus defined historically is coextensive with the geographically determined desert and sown area, as well as with the ethnographically delimited distribution of the nomadic and settled configuration.

The proposed southern delimitation of the Middle East in Africa has recently received important corroboration by the work of George Peter Murdock. After a careful examination of the culture groups of Africa, Murdock compiled three distribution maps of its culture provinces (all the three south of what is suggested above as the southern boundary of the Middle East) as well as a distribution map of East African pastoralists.[14] The northern boundary line, resulting from a superimposition of these four maps on one another, coincides generally with the southern boundary line proposed above. This line can thus be considered fairly well established.

To the northeast, the limits of the Middle East run roughly along the Caucasus and the northern borders of Iran and Afghanistan. Elsewhere the writer has adduced evidence to show that Middle Eastern nomadism can be clearly distinguished from Central Asian nomadism and that, strictly speaking, the limits of the Middle East should be drawn where the typical Middle Eastern black hair tent is replaced by the yurt, the round, dome-shaped felt tent, equally typical of Central Asian nomadism.[15] This delimitation excludes a corner of Iran (the Gorgan valley to the southeast of the Caspian Sea) and part of northern Afghanistan from the Middle Eastern culture continent. We shall, nevertheless, discuss briefly this marginal area at the end of our listing of the culture areas of the Middle East.

To the east, the boundary line of the Middle East runs roughly north to south across the middle of Western Pakistan. To the west of this line live the nomadic Balujis who are a definitely Middle Eastern people by all criteria. To the east of it live the Sinds, in every respect a South Asian (Indian) population.

THE PROBLEM OF SUBDIVISION

The problem of how to subdivide the vast land area of the Middle East into cultural subareas has received only scant attention. Especially its Asian part has remained neglected in this respect. Those who put forward suggestions as to the mapping of culture areas in the African part of the Middle East were without exception Africanists, interested more in the "black" two thirds than in the "white" northern one third of Africa.

The first attempt to map the major regions of Africa was made by an ingenious Frenchman, A. de Préville, in 1894.[16] Taking the main animal species bred by the pastoral peoples as the basis of classification, he generalized broadly and divided North Africa into four roughly horizontal strips, which he then extended over into the Asian part of the Middle East, giving them an upward slant. As the map opposite page 14 in his book shows at a glance, he regarded the entire north coast of Africa as far south as approximately the 30th parallel as the region of horsemen (*cavaliers*). In southwest Asia he assigned to this region a broad belt north of a line drawn from the southern tip of the Sinai Peninsula to the northern end of the Persian Gulf and thence continuing in a northeasterly direction. South of this lay his second zone, the region of camelmen (*chameliers*), which comprised most of the Sahara, Central Arabia, and southern Iran. The third one was the much thinner region of goatmen (*chevriers*), stretching from the Atlantic coast of Africa south of Río de Oro, across the Red Sea and the southern part of the Persian Gulf, to southern Iran. His southernmost zone within our area was the region of cattlemen (*vachers*), corresponding roughly to the area between the 12th and the 16th parallels all through the width of Africa, turning south to include most of Ethiopia and Somalia, then across the Bab el-Mandeb along the South Arabian coast, and finally across the Gulf of Oman into the southeastern corner of Iran.

Although there is little in this attempt that can stand the test of time, credit must be given to Préville for the idea of the geographic plotting of regions in the Middle East on the basis of types of animal husbandry.

The next attempt, made by Jerome Dowd in 1907, constitutes

what was in fact a step backward as compared to the work of
Préville. Quite apart from the numerous untenable hypotheses
contained in Dowd's book, he divided the entire northern third
of Africa into two zones only: a northern "camel zone" and a
southern "cattle zone." His dividing line between the two regions
was drawn from west to east somewhere in the middle of Préville's
region of goatmen.[17]

Completely different from these early amateurish attempts was
the one made in 1924 by an outstanding Africanist, Melville J.
Herskovits. Although Herskovits titled his first published paper on
the subject "A Preliminary Consideration of the Culture Areas of
Africa,"[18] he retained the general outline in two subsequent
revisions with a few changes confined to Negro Africa. In this
revised form he reprinted his map of the "Culture Areas of Africa"
in his *Man and His Works*.[19]

As an Africanist, Herskovits' main interest as well as field
experience lay in Negro Africa. In the discussion accompanying
his map he described at some detail the culture area he named
"Western Sudan," which comprises the southwestern corner of the
African part of the Middle East (as delimited above, p. 13), as
well as the northwestern areas of Negro African cultures; but he
dismissed in a few lines the areas he termed "Eastern Sudan,"
"Desert Area," and "Egypt."[20] As to the north coast of Africa,
down to a distance of over three hundred miles from the Mediterranean coastline of Tunisia, Algeria, and Morocco, he excluded it
entirely from his scheme on the ground of "its close affinity to
Europe."[21]

To any student of the Middle East it is beyond doubt that the
North African coastal area constitutes one of the most characteristic varieties of typical Middle Eastern culture, and that its
affinity to Europe, although closer than that of most of the rest
of Africa, about equals in degree that of Lower Egypt and the
Levant coastal area.

The east-west dividing line Herskovits draws between the
"Desert Area" and the "Western Sudan" runs directly through
the very middle of the Tuareg area and cannot, therefore, be
regarded as meaningful. Similarly, his north-to-south dividing
line between "Western Sudan" and "Eastern Sudan" runs through

the Kanuric-speaking East-Saharan area, and should therefore be moved some three hundred miles to the west.

In 1929, the German Africanist, Richard Thurnwald, published a study on the "Social Systems of Africa."[22] Thurnwald did not attempt to map culture areas, but he classified African social systems into nine types, of which, however, only two have representatives in the Middle Eastern part of Africa as well. Conversely, the great majority of the social systems found in this part do not fit into any of Thurnwald's nine categories. Evidently, this prominent Africanist has also paid but scant attention to the northern one third of the continent of his specialization.

In 1937, Wilfrid D. Hambly in his *Source Book for African Anthropology*[23] mapped the culture areas of Africa. The Middle Eastern part of Africa was divided by him as follows: (1) The Nile Valley; (2) "A region of migration of northern Hamites," occupying the entire north coast of Africa, from Mauretania in the west to close to the Nile delta in the east, and extending approximately 440 miles southward from the Tunisian-Algerian-Moroccan coast line; (3) "The Saharan region of camel-keeping cultures," subdivided into (3*A*) Tuareg (west-central Sahara), (3*B*) Tebu, Tibbu and Teda of Tibesti, and (3*C*) Arabs of the Libyan oases. This No. 3 covers the entire Sahara, and borders in the south on the narrow east-west beltlike area (4), termed "A region of pastoral nomads possessing cattle, sheep, goats, horses, and perhaps camels also." Hambly included in this area most of the region between the Nile and the Red Sea. To the south of (4), again beltlike in its east-west stretch, lies (5), the dividing line between the two running in a roughly straight line touching the Senegal River, the northern bend of the Niger, and Lake Chad. This is stated to be a "parkland area" and a pastoral region with seasonal migrations.

The main advance of this scheme as against the earlier one of Herskovits is in the adumbration of a threefold subdivision of the Sahara area (No. 3). Apart from this, the criticism leveled against Herskovits applies also to Hambly.

The most recent mapping of the culture provinces in Middle Eastern Africa has been made by George Peter Murdock in his volume *Africa: Its Peoples and Their Culture History.*[24] While the

writer found himself in agreement with Murdock with regard to
the delimitation of the southern boundary of Middle Eastern
cultures in Africa, he must disagree with him as to his classifications.

Murdock treats the entire Middle Eastern Africa in three of the
eleven parts of this book. In Part 4, entitled "North African Agricultural Civilizations," he discusses the Berbers (Chap. 15) and
the Saharan Negroes (Chap. 16); in Part 9, "East African
Pastoralism," one chapter deals with the "Beja" (Chap. 40);
while Part 11, "North and West African Pastoralism," comprises
four chapters, "Bedouin Arabs" (Chap. 52); "Tuareg" (Chap.
53); "Baggara" (Chap. 54), and "Fulani" (Chap. 55).

The over-all classificatory point of view, therefore, is ecologic:
the population is grouped into an agricultural and a pastoral
category. This in itself is perfectly sound, and in agreement with
the present writer's own elaboration of the basic dichotomy of all
the Middle Eastern peoples into nomads and cultivators.[25]
However, this ecologic classification is of little use when the
purpose is to isolate criteria with whose help the Middle East can
be divided into culture areas, since, as is pointed out repeatedly
in the present volume, both nomads and cultivators are found in
every part of the Middle East. Moreover, for the same reason, the
breakdown into agricultural and pastoral peoples is not coterminous with linguistic, religious, racial, or ethnic classification, nor
with over-all geographic subdivisions. Under the general ecologic
classification indicated in his titles of parts 4, 9, and 11, Murdock
nevertheless treats ethnic or linguistic groups inhabiting certain
geographic areas. He therefore involves himself in numerous
difficulties and contradictions.

The first chapter in the book that deals with a Middle Eastern
group is Chapter 15, entitled "Berbers." This is one of the chapters contained in Part 4, "North African Agricultural Civilizations" (pp. 111 ff.). Murdock adopts "a strictly linguistic classification in segregating the Berbers from the Arabs in North
Africa" (p. 111); in other words, he regards as Berbers only those
groups who still speak Berber. These, he finds, fall into 29 groups
(totaling four and a half million people), practically all of whom
are located in northwestern Africa, i.e. north of latitude 15° N.

and west of longitude 15° E. Of them, 17 groups (or 3,271,000) are stated to be sedentary cultivators; four groups, numbering 733,000, are semisedentary or practice transhumance; three, numbering 450,000, are nomads. As to the remaining three groups, no data are supplied. Geographically, however, the largest part of the Berber language area is inhabited by nomadic groups, the Tuareg. In fact, the Tuareg are treated again, and in greater detail, in Part 11 under "North and West African Pastoralism." A classification which thus places the same population group into two different categories cannot be regarded as satisfactory. Murdock's explanation, that the Tuareg have adapted to a desert environment involving "so many innovations as well as borrowings from the indigenous Negroes and the Bedouin Arabs, that we shall treat them separately in Chapter 53" (p.115), does not eliminate the inconsistency. If his Chapter 15, "Berbers," treats of a population group belonging to "North African Agricultural Civilizations," it is impermissible to include in it Berber-speaking groups which for nearly a thousand years have not been agricultural but nomadic pastoral, and which in addition not only differ from but in fact contrast with the agricultural Berbers in descent rules, social organization, sex mores, material culture, etc. It is obvious that in this case the inconsistency was caused by the attempt to utilize simultaneously an ecologic and a linguistic classification. This cannot work, simply because not all Berbers are agriculturalists.

The inconsistency resulting from the application of these two conflicting classificatory criteria is even more pronounced in Part 11. Here, as the first group of "North and West African Pastoralists," the "Bedouin Arabs" (Chap. 52, pp. 392 ff.) are discussed. "Bedouin Arabs" are, of course, the prototype of desert-dwelling, animal-herding nomads. But the criterion applied by Murdock in listing groups under this heading was, as in the case of his "Berbers," the linguistic one. He lists here *all* the Arabic-speaking groups of North and West Africa, 42 in number, with a total of 32 to 33 million people. Of these, however, only 12 groups numbering close to two million are nomadic pastoralists; three more, numbering a few hundred thousand, are seminomadic or consist of mixed nomadic and sedentary subgroups; and 21 groups, numbering about 30 million, are sedentary cultivators. The ecologic character of the five remaining groups is not stated. Again Murdock tries to smooth over the inconsistency by stating that among the 42 groups listed by him as "Bedouin Arabs" "a number of Arabic-speaking peoples who are descended from the coastal populations that participated fully in the earlier Greco-Roman civilization" should "be segregated." These he terms "Littoral peoples" (Algerians, Cyrenaicans, Egyptians, Jebala, Moroccans, Sahel, Tripolitanians, and Tunisians), and describes as "sedentary and partially urbanized," who, although Islamized and Arabized in the first period of Arab political conquest, "remained to a considerable extent aloof from the Hilalian Bedouins" who invaded North Africa in the eleventh century and established in it the prototype of Bedouin culture (pp. 396 f.). Their economy is based primarily on cereal agriculture with auxiliary arboriculture, animal husbandry, urban handicraft, and trade. They thus contrast with the Bedouin Arabs who "retained, wherever possible, the nomadic pastoral economy they brought with them from Arabia" (p. 397). It is puzzling, to say the least, why a language group of 33 million should be named after its smallest component element, which constitutes about 6 per cent of the total, when over 90 per cent is not Bedouin but sedentary, not pastoral but agricultural, and not even Arab, as far as descent is concerned, but merely "Arabized." If the Berber nomadic Tuareg are classed among "North African agricultural civilizations" because prior to the Hilalian invasion their ancestors were cultivators, then certainly the 30 million "littoral peoples," who were cultivators for centuries prior to the Hilalian invasion and remained agriculturalists to this day, should also be classified under the same "North African agricultural civilizations."

The first conclusion from the foregoing critical consideration of previous attempts at classifying the cultures in North Africa is that in trying to solve the problem of the subdivision of the Middle East into culture areas one must, first of all, liberate the culture area concept from its close association with the geographic area that characterized it in its original application to native American cultures and still haunts those who are engaged in studies of spatial distribution of non-Western cultures. Culture is, of course,

carried by human groups, and these, in turn, must have geographic loci as their habitat. In this sense, clusterings of cultures
are correlated to geographic areas in the Middle East as well as
in any other part of the globe. But, a mapping of cultural similarities and differences in the Middle East does not result in contiguous
and clear-cut geographic areas. Instead of regarding the Middle
East with its constituent cultures as a patchwork quilt, one has to
regard it as a "Kelim" rug, that famous woven variety of Persian
carpetry in which the patterning is achieved by the skillful way
in which once the warp and once the woof is allowed to emerge to
the surface. The basic material consists, throughout the entire area
of the carpet, of the same two types of yarn; yet the patterns
can nevertheless show considerable variation when one corner of
the carpet is compared to another.

This is exactly the case with the specific configuration the
component cultures evince in all parts of the Middle East. Unless
one were to delimit a culture area extremely narrowly, such as a
single oasis cluster or a single nomadic tribal territory, one encounters everywhere both the warp and the woof of the cultural
texture, both the nomadic breeders and the settled cultivators.
Any attempt at a subdivision of the Middle East into culture areas
must find a place in its scheme for both. The proportion in which
the two are represented in an area or province and the question
of cultural predominance that undoubtedly is correlated with it—
these are criteria that can and must be used for purposes of subdivision and classification. The predominance of the Bedouin
element in Central Arabia, for instance, stamps that area with a
character greatly differing from that of the Nile Valley with its
exclusively sedentary population of fellahin.

A phenomenon similar to the one pointed out here has, in fact,
been recognized in connection with the mapping of the culture
areas of South America. Apart from the coastal area to the north
and the west, the entire land mass was divided in 1922 by Wissler
into a larger northern area called Amazon and a smaller southern
area called Guanaco. Kroeber, a year later, retained Wissler's
areas, but renamed them Tropical Forest and Patagonia, respectively.[26] In the great *Handbook of the South American Indians* of
the Smithsonian Institution these areas were drastically revised,

on the basis of a huge amount of additional information gathered
in the intervening years. The neat, straight lines and clearcut,
contiguous, almost geometric simplicity of the two areas completely disappeared. Instead, a considerable amount of mutual
interpenetration of two major culture types is shown. The area
still called the Tropical Forest is found to extend far down the
west coast, but contains several major and many minor pockets
inhabited by peoples who belong to what is called Marginal culture type, as well as a smaller number of pockets formed by the
Circum-Caribbean culture type. The Marginal cultures occupy
the entire southern tip of the continent, but their northernmost
pocket appears as far north as Venezuela.

This pattern, though complex when compared with the earlier
attempts, is simplicity itself in relation to the much more involved
interlacings found in the Middle East. Carriers of nomadic and
settled cultures are present everywhere, and in many places the
picture is further complicated by the presence of towns that dot
the area with partly Westernized population islands and thereby
obscure the differences between their hinterlands.

Next, the cultural variations evinced by one or both of the
constituent ecologic groups in each geographic area must be
considered. Both the bedouins of Arabia and the Tuareg of the
Sahara are, for example, camel-herding nomads with all the
cultural characteristics that this entails in material equipment, in
food habits, in the adaptation to desert conditions, and even in
social organization and values. Yet, at the same time, a number
of significant traits set the two groups sharply off against each
other. There are, for instance, marked differences in clothing,
language, descent rules, and sex mores.

Or, take the differences between two fellah groups: the Syrian
and the Egyptian. Here the clothing, language, descent rules, and
sex mores are, although by no means identical, at least very
similar. But there are clear differences in methods of work and
in the availability of leisure, as well as in temperament and character. Such are the criteria that can with advantage be utilized for
classificatory purposes.

The available data, meager as they are, indicate that we have
in the Middle East a continuum of nomadic culture and a parallel

continuum of settled culture. Starting out from the North Arabian desert as the presumable center of the Middle Eastern nomadic complex, one finds, upon moving up into Jordan and Syria, certain new traits giving nomadic culture there a somewhat different character. Progressing eastward into Iraq, again a new set of traits is added and upon crossing into Iran, yet another one. A similar progression of change can be observed when moving westward across the Red Sea and along the expanses of North Africa. As a concrete example the black hair tent can again be mentioned with its slight variations from tribe to tribe and more marked ones from area to area.

As to the settled cultures, they change in a like manner and even more pronouncedly. Sailing up the Nile from Cairo towards the Sudan frontier and across it, one has a fine opportunity for observing this gradual change. From one village to the next the difference is unnoticeable; having passed twenty or thirty villages and recalling the first one, it becomes discernible; at the hundredth, apparent; south of the Sudan borderline, striking. Thorough studies, including compilations of lists of such progressively increasing differences, will make it possible to plot the Middle Eastern culture areas with a solid factual basis to rely on, instead of conjecture and informed guesswork.

To them have to be added the observations made by old and new local authors and students of Middle Eastern history and society with regard to differences in value culture between one part of the area and another. To mention only one example of such general characterizations, Maqrizi, the fourteenth century Arab historian, quotes Ka'b al-Ahbār, one of the companions of the Prophet Mohammed, to the effect that when Allah created all things, He gave them each a companion. "I am going to Syria," said Reason; "I will go with you," said Rebellion. "I am going to the Desert," said Poverty; "I am going with you," said Health. "I am going to Egypt," said Abundance; "I shall accompany you," said Resignation.[27] Translated into our terminology, this means that the Syrians were regarded as clever but rebellious; the nomads of the Arabian Desert as poor but healthy; and the Egyptians as wealthy and submissive. Another version of this tradition substitutes for the Syrians bravery in the place of cleverness; and adds that the Iraqis are proud and hypocritical, and that the Yemenis are characterized by faith and modesty.

Nor must one overlook the interaction between the indigenous local cultures and the cultural influences that spread in successive waves from the core area toward the boundaries of the present-day Middle East. In spite of the power of these waves, and especially the last one, Islam, vestiges of the old local cultures have survived in many places, primarily among the settled rural populations of the regions remote from the core area. Even where no distinct "archaic" traits can be recognized, and where a thorough blending of the old and the new has taken place, the persistent effect of the old local cultures can be discerned in the resultant somewhat different local hue of the over-all color of Middle Eastern culture.

Yet another factor that has strengthened the differences among these local entities has been the absence of communications, especially on the folk level, between one localized society and the next. Isolation has not only enabled the old cultural differences to survive; it also favored the development of new differences in the shape of local variants of the superimposed imported cultures. These differences assume significance as soon as we shift our attention from the culture continent as a whole to its component parts. A study of local cultural histories is therefore indispensable for classificatory purposes.

These then are the main avenues of research that will have to be followed for a definitive classification of the Middle Eastern culture continent into culture areas: more descriptive ethnographic material is needed from practically every area; this has to be supplemented by anthropological analyses of the historical material, much of which is available to this day only in the Arabic or Persian or Turkish original. The task will be an arduous one, but the results will be richly rewarding: a fuller understanding of the present-day mosaic of the Middle East, and of the longest recorded cultural development that went into its making.

THE CULTURE AREAS OF THE MIDDLE EAST

For the time being, a preliminary and tentative mapping of the culture areas in the Middle East can be attempted on the basis of the presently available data. Let us begin with the North African part of the Middle East, and state at the very outset that the following outline could not have been arrived at without the huge amount of material assembled by Murdock in his *Africa: Its Peoples and their Culture History*, and the excellent detailed "Tribal Map of Africa" appended to that volume. While the author was constrained above to criticize the classifications adopted by Murdock, he wishes to acknowledge fully his indebtedness to Murdock's tribal map and his brief characterizations of the hundreds of tribes plotted on it. Only in a few instances did the author find it necessary to alter the boundary lines of groups drawn by Murdock, as for example in the case of some riverain and oasis groups to whom Murdock assigned unduly large territories.

No such careful listing or mapping of tribes was available for the Asian part of the Middle East. The lists and maps of the Arabian Bedouin tribes prepared by Baron Oppenheim[28] were of little help because all the tribes described by him had to be included in one single culture area (No. 10). Of greater usefulness was the ethnic and linguistic map of the Near East published in 1944 in *Petermans Geographische Mitteilungen*. In most cases, however, the writer had to draw upon his own familiarity with the area in deciding where to draw the boundary lines between what appeared to him as contiguous but different culture areas.

An added difficulty was presented by the ethnic complexities of major parts of the Asian Middle East. Especially rugged mountain areas, such as those inhabited by the Kurds and the Lur and Turkic-speaking tribes in western Iran, do not easily lend themselves to a mapping of culture areas. While the natural conditions tend to impose a definite way of life on all the inhabitants, the isolation resulting from lack of communications and from the frequent difficulty of establishing contact even across a single mountain range makes for the retention of cultural traits that may have been brought into the area many centuries ago by the remote ancestors of the present-day population. Thus, the typical picture in these regions is that of simultaneous existence side by side of representatives of two or more cultures, more often than not in overt or quiescent enmity. In western Iran, for example one finds side by side Sunni Muslim Kurdish tribes, Armenian-speaking Christians, Shī'ite Muslim Azerbaijani Turks, Aramaic-speaking Nestorian Christians, and Aramaic-speaking Kurdish Jews.

In such a case one has no choice but to regard this very mixture itself as a characteristic of the area and to delimit it against neighboring, more homogeneous areas as best possible. For these reasons, and several others too technical to enter into, the mapping of the culture areas in the Asian part of the Middle East must be regarded as even more tentative than the African.

1. *The Nile Area.* The material base is intensive irrigated cultivation extending from the delta into the Sudan. Religion is Muslim (with a small Christian minority); the language, Arabic; the physical type shows a mixture of ancient Egyptian stock with the Arabs who arrived in the seventh century from Arabia. Although it is the smallest area in the entire Middle East, it is by far the most populous; in fact, it is one of the most densely settled agricultural areas in the entire world. The nuclear political unit is the village; the family is of the typical Middle Eastern type. No nomads are to be found within this area; on the other hand, in Lower Egypt there are two cities of metropolitan dimensions and several towns. About 80 per cent of the people nevertheless live in villages, many of which are much larger than in any other part of the Middle East.

2. *The Coastal Agricultural Area.* Cultivation is less intensive, with irrigation applied only exceptionally. Terracing of mountain slopes is practiced. The area forms a contiguous strip along the Atlantic and Mediterranean coasts as far east as Tripolitania, and resumes, after a break in the Gulf of Sidra, on the northwestern coast of Cyrenaica. Sunni Islam predominates with a sprinkling of Senussi sectarianism in the east and strong saint cult in the west. The language is largely Arabic with considerable Berber elements in the western part of the area (especially in Morocco) and on its southern fringes. Nomads, in small numbers, practice transhumance and utilize the lands unsuited for agriculture. The biggest cities are located on the coast. Social and family organization is the typical Middle Eastern one. In the west (Morocco) the craft guilds show many archaic traits,[29] and the Arabic dialect has a markedly local character.

3. *Northwestern Oasis Area.* The geographic region of the north-western Sahara, characterized by a liberal sprinkling of oases, is inhabited largely by Berber-speaking peoples who practice irrigation agriculture and arboriculture. The surrounding steppe and desert is the grazing ground of the camels or sheep and goats tended by nomadic Arab tribes. The Berber-Arab ethnolinguistic division, however, is by no means coterminous with the ecologic one. There is a minority of settled Arab cultivators as well as of nomadic Berber pastoralists in the area, the latter especially in its western part. Both the Berbers and the Arabs are Muslims, several of the Berber groups belonging to the Ibādī sect. Most of the Berbers practice monogamy. Among the nomads, Islam is followed with varying degrees of laxity. Some of the oasis settlements reach impressive sizes, although large cities are absent. The interaction between nomads and cultivators, the family, and social organization are all of the typical Middle Eastern mold. The kelim-pattern referred to above (p. 59) is clearly apparent.

4. *The Northeastern Oasis Area.* This area is in many respects similar to the northwestern oasis area, but the Berber element is small. Practically all the nomads as well as the great majority of the cultivators are Arabs. The nomads' domain extends both in the west (the Sirtican coast of Libya) and in the east (the Libyan plateau of western Egypt) to the Mediterranean coast. Religion is Islam, with the Senussi sect predominating in the central part of the area. Family and social organization is of the general Middle Eastern pattern, with a certain relaxation, however, of the strict sex mores.

5. *The Southwestern Nomadic Area.* This area is separated from Area 3 by a huge uninhabited desert. Its population consists largely of Arab nomad tribes, with some small semi-Arabized Berber groups in the southwestern corner. In this area there are no sizable oases as in Areas 3 and 4, and, consequently, it is sparsely populated and the settled element is negligible. The southern border of this area coincides with the southern limits of the Middle East. The transition to its southern neighbors (Murdock's "Nuclear Mande" and "Fulani") is gradual, and southern influences can be felt well up to the north of the area. Neverthe-

less, in general, the family and social organization is of the over-all Middle Eastern pattern.

6. *The Tuareg Area.* Inhabited by Berber-speaking nomadic tribes, the Tuareg area has a scattering of oases in which cultivation is carried out by servile classes for their nomadic overlords. Family and social organization differ considerably from the general Middle Eastern pattern: Descent is matrilineal; the society is structured into distinct layers of status groups, which almost amount to castes; women have great freedom (it is the noble men and not the women who wear the veil); marriage is monogamous but sex mores are reported to be lax. Adherence to Islam is lukewarm. More women than men can read and write the old Tuareg script. In place of the usual Middle Eastern black hair tent, the Tuareg use hide tents dyed red or yellow—another archaic trait.[30]

7. *The East Saharan Area.* Separated from Area 4 by a large expanse of uninhabited desert, this area is again richer in oases and, although still a predominantly pastoral area, its southern part receives from 4 to 20 inches of rain annually, and consequently is savanna rather than desert with the importance of cultivation increasing as one proceeds southward. The area is inhabited by Saharan Negroes, many of whom have become converted to Islam as late as the eighteenth century. They speak a number of related languages called "Kanuric" by Murdock and "Central Saharan" by Greenberg.[31]

Most of the area is inhabited by nomadic tribes whose herds consist not only of camels and sheep and goats as in Areas 3 to 6, but in the southeast of cattle in addition: an influence of the adjoining camel-cattle area (see Area 8). Oases are scattered all over the area, but only in its eastern and western extremes do people engage in agriculture in large numbers.

8. *The Camel-Cattle Area.* This area is inhabited by Nubian tribes of mixed Arab-Negro ancestry whose main intermingling occurred following the Arab conquest of the region in the beginning of the sixteenth century. Most of them are nomadic or seminomadic with the camel as the main animal in the north, cattle in the south. The southern cattle herding tribes are often referred to collectively as *Baqqāra*, Arabic for "cattle herders." Among the

latter, agriculture plays a considerable role. Family and social organization resemble the general Middle Eastern type; however, a higher incidence of polygyny and an initial matrilocal residence are noted. Also, the Middle Eastern black hair tent is in this area frequently replaced by other types of temporary shelter. This detail illustrates the marginal character of this area in relation to the Middle East. The Baqqāra are warlike and fanatical Muslims.

9. *The Beja Area.* This lies between the Upper Nile and the Red Sea. Most Beja tribes have retained their own Hamitic language, called *tu-Bedawiye*, although one of them has adopted Arabic, and sections of another speak Tigre. Racially they are Caucasoid, their economy is pastoral nomadic with camels, cattle, sheep, and goats as the main livestock. Owing to poor grazing conditions, they must move in very small groups. Family and social organization conform to the general Middle Eastern pattern. South Arabian influences can be seen in their grass- and leaf-covered huts.

10. *The North Arabian Desert Area.* Moving across into Asia, we designate as Area 10 the large land mass that is the original home base of the Arabs who, during and following the lifetime of Mohammed, conquered the entire Middle East. It is the birthplace of much of the Muslim way of life that is still followed by the conservative population sectors all over the Middle East. The area includes the entire northern part of the Arabian Peninsula, as well as the Syrian Desert, the Negev Desert of Israel, the Sinai Peninsula and the Eastern Desert of Egypt. Although the majority of the population is settled in villages and towns and the sedentarization of the remaining nomads progresses apace, this is still a Bedouin area in two senses: geographically, the vast majority of its surface is utilized only by the nomadic herders, and psychologically it is their ethos and ideals that are still upheld by the entire population. The dominant religion in central Arabia is the puritanistic Wahhābī sect of Islam. The core of this area, together with Area 11 is the least Westernized of all parts of the Middle East. In it are found the typical Middle Eastern forms of family life and social organization at their fullest, with the retention of such elements, outmoded elsewhere, as slavery, large harems, eunuchs, despotic monarchy, bodily mutilation as punishment, and the like.

11. *The Southwest Arabian Area.* This comprises the Kingdom of Yemen and some of the territory around it. It is a mixed sedentary-nomadic area, with summer monsoon rains over a certain elevation, differentiated from Area 10 also by the physical type, language (or rather idiom), and religion of the people. The dominant sect in the central mountainous region of the area is that of Zaydī Shī'ite Islam, headed by the king or Imam, a combination of secular ruler with charismatic sectarian head. Addiction to the chewing of *qāt*, a stimulant shrub *(catha edulis)*, is prevalent in the area and does not occur outside it. The towns of this area are differentiated from those of Area 10 by the prevalence of high houses—up to five or six floors. In the interior of this area, and especially among the nomads, as far north as 'Asīr, the knee-length loincloth replaces the robe or full shirt worn elsewhere by the males. And, what is equally in contrast with the general custom prevalent elsewhere, the men often wear no head covering at all.

12. *The Eastern Arabian Area.* A mixed agricultural-nomadic area, here there is greater prevalence of cattle than in Area 11. Boating and fishing too play a greater role in the economy than in Area 11. On the other hand, the high houses in the towns are less in evidence here. The dominant religion is the Ibāḍī sect of Islam. On the Oman coast Iranian influences are felt.

13. *The Levant Coast Area.** This area, in many respects similar to Area 2 in North Africa, is characterized by agriculture, mainly rain fed, although in places irrigated, as well as arboriculture on terraced mountains. Practically all the people are Arabic-speaking settled cultivators, living in tightly clustered villages, most of them Sunni Muslims. Family and social organization conforms to the typical Middle Eastern pattern.

14. *The Mesopotamian Area.* This is another fellah-area like Area 13, but with flatland riverine agriculture and with a greater prevalence of irrigation. Ecologically, therefore, this area occupies a middle place between Areas 1 and 2 in North Africa. A special subarea within it is that of the Marsh Arabs in southern Iraq near

---

*In the above characterization of Area 13, the changes introduced into it by the Jewish immigration and the establishment of the state of Israel are left out of consideration.

the Persian Gulf. Most of the population is Muslim, Arabic speaking, but toward the south the Shī'ite element predominates over the Sunnite.

15. *The Turkish Area.* This comprises almost the entire extent of the Republic of Turkey with the exception of its southeastern corner, which belongs to Area 16. It is a clearly delimited area with the sea surrounding it on three sides. Its ecology is predominantly agricultural, with only the faintest traces of nomadism still discernible in its dry and arid central plateau. Urban development and Westernization are pronounced, especially in the western part. This is the only area in the Middle East in which a complete constitutional separation of church and state has been carried out, although practically all the inhabitants are Sunni Muslims. It is separated from the other areas also by its language, Turkish, which is spoken nowhere else outside its boundaries, although related Turkic languages are spoken in Areas 18 and 23.

16. *The Kurdish Area.* Politically bisected between Iran and Iraq, with a little corner of it in Syria and an outlying district in Soviet Russia, this area is inhabited by Kurdish Sunni Muslim mountaineers who practice either transhumant nomadism or agriculture or both, and who have retained even in their settled groups strong tribal ties; and by Aramaic-speaking Christian and Jewish minorities. Physical prowess, fearlessness, and temper are characteristics for which the Kurds pride themselves and are known among their neighbors. Marked differences between the garb of the Kurds and their neighbors facilitate the distinction between them, although on the borders there are large areas inhabited by both Kurdish and Turkish groups on the northwest, Kurdish and Azerbaijani groups on the northeast, and Kurdish and Persian groups on the southeast.

17. *The Azerbaijani Area.* This is a border area between the Middle East (Iran) and Soviet Russia, largely settled, with the population living chiefly in villages, although it boasts of several sizable towns and has also a sprinkling of seminomadic tribes. The dominant language is the so called Azerbaijani Turkish also known as *Azeri*, which differs considerably from the Turkish spoken in Area 15, and reflects Persian influences. The religion is Sunni Muslim.

18. *The West Iranian Tribal Area.* This is one of the most mixed areas in the entire Middle East as far as ethnic composition is concerned. It is however, precisely this mosaiclike appearance that stamps it with the character of a separate culture area, in addition to the fact that the majority of the population groups, whatever their provenance, language, religious affiliation, and physical appearance, practice transhumant sheep and goat nomadism. The northern half of the area is dominated by the Lurs, a huge tribal confederation of the Shī'ite faith and speaking Lur, which is an Iranian dialect. The southern part is the home of two large tribal confederations, the Bakhtiyārīs, another powerful Shī'ite tribal confederation, who speak another Iranian dialect and whose unveiled women enjoy greater freedom than is usual among tribal populations; and the Qashqais, a Turkic-speaking Sunnite Muslim tribal confederation, living to the east of the former.

19. *The Persian Area.* This area comprises most of Iran, as well as a detached smaller area in the northeastern corner of Afghanistan where the Persian-speaking inhabitants are known as Tajiks. The great majority of the population of this area consists of Persian-speaking Shī'ite Muslim villagers, practicing, as a rule, extensive rain-fed agriculture. In contrast to the rest of the Muslim Middle East, in this area pictorial representation of human beings and wine drinking is practiced. Love of physical exercises, gymnastics, and hot baths seems to be a survival of old Hellenistic influence, while nineteenth-century Russian influences are also discernible, especially in the towns. One of the characteristic local features of religion is the performance of annual passion plays provoking great emotional response in the audience. The area has developed a high urban civilization with great local refinements in the visual and musical arts.

20. *The Mongol Area.* Located entirely in the central and western parts of Afghanistan, the Mongol Area is inhabited by several groups that exhibit either a clear-cut Mongoloid physical type or a mixture of Mongoloid and Iranian features. The Hazara Mongols in central Afghanistan are Shī'ite Muslims, live in villages, cultivate the land, and speak an Iranian dialect, described by some students as "archaic." Hazara splinter groups are found

also in western Afghanistan and across the Iranian border, where they are Sunni Muslims, and were until recently nomadic. Another group belonging to this area is that of the Chahar Aymak (literally: Four Tribes), tribes of a mixed physical type, who live in yurts that indicate their Central Asian origin.

21. *The Afghan Area.* Southeastern Afghanistan as well as the adjoining area of West Pakistan comprise this area. The language is Pushtu (or Pakhtun), related to Persian; religion Sunnī Islam. The Afghans are the dominant element in Afghanistan, and comprise both nomadic and settled components, as well as townspeople. In the southeast, near the former Indian (now Pakistani) border, where the inhospitable mountains offered no adequate living even when stock breeding and agriculture were combined, the tribes traditionally supplemented their income by raiding caravans or selling them their protection.

22. *The Baluji Area.* The southeastern corner of Iran and the southwestern corner of Pakistan make up this area. Its inhabitants are Balujis, with the Brahuis forming an island in the middle of the area. Both the Balujis and the Brahuis are pastoral nomads, dwelling in the well-known Middle Eastern type of black hair tent, and practice transhumance, but their main livestock is not sheep and goats, as in the case of most other transhumants, but camels. Along the borders, the Balujis used to raid the Persian villages, and to give "protection" to those who paid for it. The Balujis speak an Iranian language, while the Brahuis speak a Dravidic tongue.

23. *The Turkoman-Uzbek Area.* This is marginal to the Middle East and extends far into Central Asia. Some Turkoman tribes live in Iran, near the southwestern shores of the Caspian Sea, others in northwestern Afghanistan, while the Middle Eastern Uzbeks are found in northeastern Afghanistan. The Turkomans, relative newcomers in this area, live in the typical Central Asian yurt and practice stock breeding, but supplement it with agriculture. They are Sunni Muslims, speak a Turkic language, and are Mongoloid in physical type. The Uzbeks, also of Central Asian origin, are similar to the Turkomans in every respect, but have become more sedentarized and more assimilated linguistically to their Tajik neighbors, with whom they often intermarry.

The Turkoman culture is differentiated from the Persian (Area 19) by the persistence of certain old features of Islam, by the retention of elements of the old Shamanistic religion side by side with Islam, and other features of Central Asian origin.[32]

III. The Desert
and the Sown

A BASIC GEOGRAPHIC characteristic of the entire Middle East, as has been indicated in Chapter 1, is a subdivision into two distinct land types: a region stretching usually along the seashore or the banks of great rivers, Mediterranean in character, with long, hot, and rainless summers, rainy, temperate winters, and a natural vegetation ranging from grass to open deciduous forests; and a second desert region, as a rule at greater distance from bodies of water, with great extremes of temperature, almost no rain at any season, and a very scanty vegetation of low grass and drought-resistant bushes. The first or Mediterranean region is under agricultural cultivation or at least is capable of such cultivation; the second, the desert region, is unfit for cultivation, and serves at the utmost as a seasonal grazing ground for flocks and herds.

In each country of the Middle East, from Río de Oro and Morocco in the west to Afghanistan and Balujistan in the east, these two regions can be distinguished; through each there runs a dividing line splitting it into desert and sown. "Dividing line" is, of course, merely a figurative expression, for in reality no such "line" exists. Only rarely, as for instance in Egypt along the banks of the Nile, do the desert and the sown run sharply and clearly against each other so that the boundary line between them can be drawn with an accuracy of a few yards. It has repeatedly been stated of Egypt that it is a country in which one can stand with one foot in the desert and with the other in a garden. More often, the transition between the desert and the sown is gradual; when reaching the outskirts of the cultivated land one usually finds that

3§

the spontaneously thriving vegetation diminishes little by little or that the cultivated patches become rarer, while the alternating unutilized and fallow stretches become larger and more numerous, until the cultivated areas disappear altogether and the only remaining plant life is the typical desert vegetation of scanty shrubs and thorns. In mountainous territories, as in central Anatolia in the north or Yemen in the south, the hills are almost entirely bare, except where patient terracing has transformed the barren slopes into gardens. In such regions, neglect of cultivation for even a single season means immediate reversion of the land to a state of wilderness.

In these mountain zones, where ground water usually lies too deep so that the only source of utilizable water is the seasonal rainfall, ingenious devices have been developed to catch every drop of rain and prevent its running off into a deep-lying and stony *wādī*-bed. But since rainwater can be caught and preserved only where it falls, the crests of mountain ranges often mark the boundary line between an arid region one side that remains dry and desolate and a region on the other side that receives precipitation during the rainy season owing to the prevailing winds.

The ratio between the desert and the sown varies from place to place in the lands of the Middle East. In general, the entire area is overwhelmingly desert: approximately 90 per cent. The least desertlike countries, Turkey and Lebanon, are in the north and on the North African shore, with the exception of Libya. The greatest expanse of desert lies in the countries among which are divided politically the Sahara and the Great Arabian Desert. But even in the countries with the most favorable desert-sown balance the presence of the desert is felt everywhere: precipitation is generally poor; humidity low, except on the seashore; the wind, though it has a steady prevailing trend, turns occasionally to bring a fine, powderlike dust from the desert across the sown lands; from time to time locusts invade the sown from their desert breeding grounds; and from practically every high mountain one can discern during the summer season the low black tents of the nomadic desert people, pitched on the borderline between the desert and the sown.

Not only is the boundary between the desert and the sown not sharply delineated in most cases; it also shifts considerably. The borders of the two different land types are constantly advancing and receding. A few years with insufficient rain may force the villagers to give up previously cultivated plots of land, which are then swallowed up by the desert. Conversely, a succession of rainy seasons with abundant precipitation may enable the agriculturalists to bring under plough or hoe some acreage that was formerly barren desert. In the case of irrigated lands, best exemplified by Egypt and, to a lesser extent, by Iraq, careful regulation of the great life-sustaining rivers means the conquest of valuable *feddans* or *dunams* from the desert, while neglect of the waterworks, either because of local mismanagement or lack of a strong central government, results in floods and waste or a silting up of river beds, with a consequent catastrophic curtailment of arable land.

A third factor affecting the fluctuation between the desert and the sown, in addition to water supply and labor, is *war*. Throughout all history, desert people waged wars against the settled sons of the sown, and if they prevailed the settlers had to retreat and abandon the outskirts of the sown, which were rapidly incorporated into the desert.

People of the Western World have, as a rule, some familiarity with the more common varieties of cultivated land, such as fields and gardens. Firsthand knowledge of the desert is much rarer. To many, the very word "desert" means endless, softly rolling sand dunes absolutely devoid of animal or vegetable life, a concept popularized by many motion pictures. There are, to be sure, such deserts in the Middle East, in North Africa, in the Arabian Peninsula, as well as in Iran; but they have throughout history remained uninhabited. Traditionally, they have been crossed by camel caravans traveling along long-established routes and, in recent years, also by motor vehicles. But the barren, empty deserts cannot provide a home base for even the most rugged nomads.

The desert in which the nomads make their home, and which represents for them the "wide-open spaces" with freedom of life and movement, is of a different character. Admittedly, it is a very unfriendly place, forbidding and frightening in its desolation. But, barren though it may be, it does enjoy some scanty rain and can even boast of a little ground water in the form of widely spaced and often brackish wells or waterholes. In the fall, with the onset of the rainy season, whose length varies in different parts of the Middle East, the yellow or reddish stony deserts or the grey lava fields become covered with a scanty vegetation and actually turn green, a welcome sight to the nomad's eyes and a blessing for his hungry herds. The rain and the grass lure the nomad deep into the heart of the desert, and only the scorching, parching sun of springtime drives him back again toward the more fertile approaches of the sown. Only this type of desert with its seasonal vegetation is inhabited, and it is inhabited only during the rainy season and for a few weeks after it. Habitability is, of course, a relative matter, and areas regarded as habitable by the nomadic desert dweller who displays a remarkable adaptability to his environment would be a "courtyard of death," as the Biblical phrase has it, for other peoples.

Nomadic herdsmen reside in every country of the Middle East. During all historic periods they were a constant menace to the settled communities within their reach; but being a threat they were also a stimulant. In the civilizations of the cultivators several traits can be distinguished that have evolved in response to contact with unpredictable and uncontrollable desert people. On the other hand, many traits of desert civilizations originated from the proximity of settled communities which, although individually weaker than the nomadic tribes, often proved stronger and superior when organized into a united force.

The cultivators, or *fellahin*, as they are called in Arab lands, are the most numerous, permanent, and immutable population element in the Middle East. They work their lands today in much the same manner as they did several thousand years ago. Once empires were established in the ancient Near East, and the cultivators broken into the yoke of taxes, the least important events affecting the lives of their great masses were of a political nature, such as dynastic changes or the conquest of one country by another. Of more significance were the periodically recurring natural events, such as a period of prolonged drought or of abundant rain, a plague, or severe onslaught of locusts. But most decisive for the fate of the people as a whole were events of an intellectual-spiritual nature, such as the appearance of a new religion. This has remained largely true to this day. The severe governmental crises, for instance, that "shook" Syria in 1949, and again in 1961, were affairs of minor importance to the Syrian population as a whole, of which the overwhelming majority are *fellahin*. A succession of good rainy seasons, on the other hand, means the difference between privation and plenty, between misery and ease, and even between death and life to a considerable number of Syrian farmers. The rate of survival has always been affected by events such as these throughout the long history of the Middle East, but the mode of life of the population at large has remained practically unchanged since the introduction of Islam thirteen centuries ago. The really important changes were initiated by new religions that profoundly altered the entire tenor of existence. And today, again, it is new ideologies—first of all Communism—that threaten to throw out of gear the life of populations quiescent for centuries.

The fellah and the Bedouin, prototypes of Middle Eastern populations, exhibit pronounced differences with relation to every phase of life. They are highly dissimilar in physical type and character, in religious outlook and degree of sophistication, in mode of life and occupation, in likes and dislikes. Yet the inhabitants of no Middle Eastern country—even disregarding the townspeople—can be clearly divided into either nomads or cultivators. The nomad, as exemplified by the proud Bedouin of Arabia, and the cultivator, as typified by the humble fellahin of Egypt, are but the two polar types. Between them can be found in practically every Middle Eastern country, with the exception of such places as Egypt where the demarcation between the desert and the sown is most abrupt, transitional groups whose mode of existence combines in varying degrees elements of nomadic and agricultural life. Camel nomadism, entailing the dependence of man almost exclusively on the single species of the dromedary, developed only about the end of the second millennium B.C.[1] But already a thousand years earlier nomadic Amorites roamed the outskirts of the sedentary zones of Syria and Mesopotamia (modern Iraq). The Amorites were organized into tribes, headed by chieftains, much as the Bedouin tribes of today, but their means of livelihood was cattle, sheep, and goat husbandry and their beast of burden was the ass, whereas both these functions are fulfilled by the camel among the "grand" nomads, as the French call the camel herders. In the absence of the camel, the Amorites of four thousand years ago could not utilize the arid open spaces of the desert in which only the camel can survive; they had to remain closer to the cultivable land and their mobility was limited. For nomads, limited mobility means small tribal groups; any undue increase forces them to split up and seek separate pastures, as happened in the case of Abraham and Lot whose combined flocks were too "heavy" for the land to bear.[2] The Amorites also lacked horses, which made them a much less ormidable enemy than the Bedouins of later times. Some idea of the outward appearance of the Amorites can be gained from the murals of Benī Ḥasan, which show a nomadic chieftain, Absha, accompanied by his tribesmen and their families. In these murals, dating from about 1900 B.C., both men and women are dressed in elaborately woven, multicolored woolen tunics; the men wear sandals, the women shoes. The arms, carried by the men, are composite bows, heavy throwing sticks, and spears. An eight-stringed lyre held by one of the men shows that these people were familiar with instrumental music.[3]

Tribes of steppe Bedouins, that is, nomads without camels or with only a few, whose mode of life is similar to that of the Amorites, are found to this day all over the Middle East. They are shepherds and goatherds, with limited mobility and a much smaller wandering territory than that of the camel Bedouins. Their life is tied to the outskirts of the sown, which they never can leave far behind. They are the enemies of the cultivators for whose fields a grazing flock means ruin. They must keep to the steppebelt between the desert and the sown, and in many cases they buy protection from the more powerful camel-herding tribes to whom otherwise they would fall easy prey. Their limited mobility, their closer contact with agriculturalists, the very difference between tending camel herds and sheep or goat flocks, all these result in their occupying an intermediate position between the settled population and the camel nomads.

The more significant characteristics of the culture of the camel nomads all over the Middle East can be summarized as follows: animal husbandry with reliance mainly on the camel as a means of transportation, source of food (milk and milk products as well as meat occasionally), supply of raw materials for tent and clothing from its hair, for leather utensils, containers, and trappings from its skin, and for fuel from its dung; seasonal wandering with the herd within a certain tribal territory, reaching in the rainy season deep into the heart of the desert, and in the dry summers near the steppe and the richer settled land; tribal organization based on real or imagined common origin and family groupings, headed by chieftains; collective responsibility expressed in such institutions as the blood feud, raiding, and the inviolate laws of hospitality and sanctuary, as well as in such concepts as honor, "face," and nobility; great familiarity with the natural features of the desert, and a remarkable degree of physical and mental adaptation to the unparalleled harshness of desert life.

It is more difficult to find a common denominator underlying the more diversified life forms of the Middle Eastern cultivators. The common elements characteristic of this group are relatively fewer, with a greater preponderance of regional or local traits. Geographic and climatic conditions as well as religious and ethnic differentiation make for greater variety. A village in the mountains of Kurdistan is necessarily very different from one on the banks of the Nile which, in turn, cannot resemble too closely one along the Moroccan coast. Likewise, a Maronite Christian village in Lebanon, a Shīʻite Muslim village in Iran, and a Druze village in the Jebel Druze each has its own peculiar characteristics.

In a Bedouin tribe each and every family subsists on animal husbandry; but a village has, in addition to its bulk of agriculturalists, also a few artisans such as cobblers, blacksmiths, weavers, or masons, as well as such other specialists as teachers, imams, watchmen, barbers, and the like. Social stratification parallels occupational specialization, so that in most villages landowners, tenant farmers, and day laborers occupy a definite place in the social hierarchy.

In the nomadic tribe, whose families traditionally trace their descent either to a real or, more often, to an eponymous or

mythical common ancestor, all men are equal; the power vested
in the chieftain of the tribe is given him voluntarily as a practical
expedient, and he is expected to act always in the interests of the
tribe as a whole. Ownership of property does not play an important role in the determination of personal status, for wealth,
reckoned in terms of numbers of camels, can quickly dwindle
after a few seasons of drought, or even more suddenly disappear
in the wake of enemy raiders; and vice versa, poverty can within
a few days turn into wealth in consequence of a single daring raid.
The status of a man within the group to which he belongs by
descent is determined by personal courage and valor and, later
in life, wisdom in counsel; and, the greatest blessing of all, a large
number of male offspring.

Among the settled populations the situation is quite different.
The tradition that all the resident families are descendants from
one common ancestor is much less frequent. Many villages are
characterized by the presence of two rival groups.[4] The social
status of the individual is strongly influenced by his wealth,
reckoned in terms of land and money. The head of the wealthiest
and therefore the most influential family is often recognized by
the village *de facto*, and by the government *de jure*, as head of the
village. As such, his effort is expended in three directions: increasing his own wealth; furthering the welfare of the village;
and representing the interests of the government. In many cases,
especially in Iran, Syria, Lebanon, and Egypt, the land of entire
villages belongs to an absentee landlord to whom the cultivators
have to pay often exorbitant rents in crop or cash: a situation
that only recently has begun to change owing to governmental
land reform measures.

The relationship between the nomadic tribes and the sedentary
population must have been very much the same four thousand
years ago, in the days of the roving Amorites, as it is today. The
attitude of the cultivators in ancient Babylonia toward the
Amorites was similar to that of the fellah today toward his
nomadic neighbors: a feeling of awe, inspired by the nomads'
warlike qualities, mixed with a certain contempt stemming from
an appreciation of his own higher living standards. These ambivalent feelings are admirably summarized in a few lines of an old

Sumerian poem in which the Amorites of the west are characterized as follows:

> The weapon is [his] companion ...
> Who knows no submission,
> Who eats uncooked flesh,
> Who has no house in his lifetime,
> Who does not bury his dead companion.[5]

The attitude of the nomad toward the settled cultivator, on the
other hand, is that of contempt mixed with envy. He feels contemptuous of the fellah because the latter is bound to the soil and
subject to constant drudgery, which appears to the nomad's eyes
as worse than slavery. The nomad also scorns the fellah's submissive nature and subservience to his landlord, to the tax-collector,
and to any petty effendi. At the same time, he cannot help
envying the fellah his comforts, which he, the proud and free
bedouin, can never enjoy in his life. He envies him the protection
of his stone or mud house against cold and heat; his better and
richer diet; and his relatively greater economic and social security,
especially under the somewhat improved conditions prevailing in
several Middle Eastern countries today. It is these advantages,
whether real or imaginary, that the camel-nomad and even more
so the less mobile sheep and goat nomad sees in sedentary life
that give him the first impetus towards sedentarization. Sedentarization, if spontaneous as in Syria and Jordan, is a gradual and
difficult process that can take many years to complete, if not
decades, turning the original Bedouin or his son or grandson into
a typical fellah who can be distinguished from other fellahin only
by a proud tradition of free Bedouin descent.[6] Where the government takes up the cause of sedentarization, the process can be
greatly accelerated, and, as happened in Saudi Arabia, entire
new villages of "pure-blooded" tribesmen can spring up within
a few months or years.[7]

The reverse process, that of cultivators turning into nomads,
is much rarer, but instances of it can be found both in ancient
history and in modern times. In the last century of the kingdom
of Judah (sixth century B.C.), the Rechabites, sons of Jonadab ben
Rechab, gave up building houses and living in them, sowing seeds
and possessing land, planting vineyards and drinking wine, and

took to dwelling in tents, "so that they may live many days on the face of the land."[8] This "return to the desert," which was motivated by purely religious considerations, was an exceptional phenomenon in the history of ancient Israel, though the remembrance of the nomadic days of old, clad in legendary colors, was kept alive in the consciousness of the people as the days when Israel "went with God in the desert, in a land that is not sown."[9] Several centuries later, in a similar situation, when the downfall of the Second Commonwealth and the Second Temple of Jerusalem was felt to be impending, a group of religious extremists again took to the desert, though this time it was not a tribal group like the Rechabites, but a sect, the Essenes, and instead of pitching tents for dwellings they built themselves houses or sought shelter in caves. It is among these groups who returned to the desert that the famous Dead Sea Scrolls originated.

In modern times, both groups and individuals have taken to the desert in flight rather than as an act of religious devotion. Oppressive governmental measures, threats by too powerful adversaries, feuds in which the weaker party could not hope to hold its own—these are some of the circumstances that have caused people seek out the lesser dangers of the desert.

According to J. Braslawski, who made a special study of the composition of the Bedouin tribes of the Negev (today part of Israel), the names of several of these tribes or tribal groups bear witness to their descent from non-Bedouin or sedentary peoples. The Zaghārne families of the Tiyāha tribe came from the town of Zughr at the southeastern end of the Dead Sea; the Saʿidiyyīn in Jordan have a tradition that they came from the village of Jebal near Kerak.[10] Some Bedouin tribes trace their descent to the Crusaders;[11] while others, though claiming the noblest descent among the Arabs, that of the prophet Mohammed, are actually of Albanian ancestry.[12]

In spite of these movements from the sown into the desert and the much more significant countermovements from the desert to the sown, both the settled cultivator and the nomadic herdsman remain to this day the two basic polar types in the Middle East. Future developments are difficult to foresee. Certain signs indicate that the sown is about to make significant encroachments upon the desert. In Egypt and in Iraq plans are being made to increase the irrigated areas. In Israel, successful beginnings have been made to bring water and agriculture to the Negev desert. The most valuable pasture land of the fringes of the desert will thus gradually slip out of the hands of the nomads. Moreover, the processes of sedentarization, sporadic and haphazard in the past, seem to be gaining momentum at present, a trend that will probably continue and may even increase in the future.

Yet all this means neither the vanishing of the desert nor the disappearance of the nomad in the Middle East. The greatest engineering efforts will in the foreseeable future not achieve more than an increase of the cultivated area by 10, 20, or perhaps 30 per cent, which corresponds to a decrease of the desert area by a mere 1, 2, or perhaps 3 per cent. The desert people will likewise remain. Most desert tribes live at subsistence level; this means that the numbers of their ranks lost through sedentarization are immediately replenished by a greater natural increase that is also aided by the rudiments of sanitation and hygiene beginning to reach the more accessible tribes now for the first time.

Only the nomads with their unique adaptation to the rigors of the wasteland and wilderness can live in the desert. Because of their presence in the desert over many centuries, a fine ecologic balance has evolved between the flora, the fauna, and human-kind—a balance that would be gravely disturbed if the human inhabitants were to depart. A different and perhaps more cogent consideration is the right of every human group to the way of life it has developed for itself and the intrinsic value of each particular culture for its carriers. From the long-range point of view of cultural history, the passing of the desert people would be regret-table, for it would mean the preclusion of even that slight chance still existing today that these people might again in the future, as they did in the past, contribute something unique, original, and valuable to the totality of human cultures in the world.

IV. The Family

Basic Characteristics

O F ALL the component features of Middle Eastern social organization the family is undoubtedly the most fundamental and most important. Beginning with the most ancient times from which historical records are extant and down to the present day, the Middle Eastern family has remained basically the same, has been composed of largely the same personnel, structured along the same lines, fulfilled the same functions, and commanded the same loyalty of its members.

With a few exceptions, of which more anon, the traditional family exhibits identical basic characteristics all over the Middle East. Whatever the religious, ethnic, social, national, or linguistic affiliations of the family, it is unmistakably stamped as Middle Eastern by a series of traits easily recognizable from one end of the area to the other, and not to be found again in its totality in any of the adjacent world areas. In general, it can be stated that the traditional Middle Eastern family is characterized by the following six traits: it is (1) extended, (2) patrilineal, (3) patrilocal, (4) patriarchal, (5) endogamous, and (6) occasionally polygynous. An explanation of each of these six terms gives us a more or less adequate picture of the structure and functioning of the Middle Eastern family.

1. The traditional Middle Eastern family is *extended*, that is, it is headed by an elderly man and consists of his wife (or wives), his unmarried daughters, his unmarried as well as married sons, and the wives and children of the latter. Daughters, when they marry, depart from their own extended families and become incorporated into the extended families of their husbands, although

84

their own consanguineal families still remain responsible for their moral conduct. The family, although it may comprise a dozen or more members, usually lives either in one house or in a number of adjoining houses or, in the case of the nomadic tribes, in a number of tents pitched next to one another. All property is held in common by the extended family and is controlled by its head. The extended family functions as an economic unit: all the men of the family work together in joint ventures such as animal husbandry, agriculture, artisanship, or business, and from the common income all the expenditures of each member and each part of the family are defrayed.

Very few studies of the size of families or households in Middle Eastern countries are available. Such studies as do exist were made mostly in Lebanon, Jordan, Mandatory Palestine, and Egypt, and refer to the settled population of towns or villages.

As to the towns, it was found that in Beirut, in a sample of close to 2,000 households studied in 1952-53, the average was 5.76 persons per household.[1] In Jordan, in towns ranging in size from 12,000 to 108,000 inhabitants, the average number of persons per household ranged (in 1952) from 5.48 to 6.57. The small Jordanian towns (from 2,500 to 8,500 inhabitants) showed a range of 5.19 to 6.94 persons per household.[2] In eight Lebanese villages studied in 1953 in connection with the Kasmie Rural Improvement Project it was found that the average number of persons per household range from 5.5 to 8.3.[3] An almost identical range (from 5.2 to 7.4) was found in five Arab villages in southern Palestine, studied in 1944.[4]

It should be mentioned that the Lebanese villages referred to above were inhabited by Shī'ite Muslims and the Palestinian villages by Sunnite Muslims. These figures can therefore be taken as an indication of the average number of persons belonging to the Muslim family in the Mediterranean littoral. As to the average size of the Christian families, this can be taken to be somewhat smaller, owing to the absence of polygyny and the lower birthrate. On the other hand there is reason to assume that in the more remote parts of the Middle East as well as among the nomads the average size of the family is larger than the above averages. In Morocco, an observer noted in the small Berber village of

Idirh in the High Atlas that the entire population of the village, about 200 persons, lived in about twenty houses. In other words, the average number of persons per family was about ten.[5]

2. The Middle Eastern family is *patrilineal*, that is, a person is regarded as belonging to the family to which his father belongs, and not the family of his mother. An Arabic proverb current in many countries expresses this succinctly: "The people rely in descent on the father and not on the mother; the mother is like a vessel of oil that is emptied." Inasmuch as social groupings larger than the extended family are practically always composed of extended families and not of individuals, every person automatically becomes and remains a member of that larger social group (such as clan, tribe, and to some extent even political party) to which his father's extended family belongs.

This is the general rule everywhere in the Middle East irrespective of religious affiliation: in other words, this rule prevails not only among the various Muslim sects but also among the Christians and Jews. The only major exception to the rule of patrilineal descent is that of the Tuareg in the Sahara. Among them descent is matrilineal, and therefore a man's status is determined by the social group to which his mother belongs. If a woman marries outside her own tribe, the children belong to her tribe, and, although the parental couple resides with the husband's tribe, the children eventually return to live with their mother's tribe. A noblewoman's children are nobles, irrespective of the father's status; and vice versa: a nobleman's children are noble only if their mother too is noble. In recent decades, however, it has become more and more evident that this ancient matrilineal rule tends to break down. Noble fathers, powerful enough to assert themselves, have often succeeded in passing off as nobles their children born to them of servile wives.[6]

Since the preferred marriage in the Middle East in general is between children of two brothers (cf. below, Chapter 6) or failing this, between children of other near relatives, or of families belonging to the same local or tribal group, patrilineal descent often does not alienate the children from their mother. Difficulties in the patrilineal family arise when the mother comes from a different group, and especially when hostilities break out between the father's family and the family of the mother's father. In such cases the children are expected to side with their father and to show no hesitancy in actively aiding their father's family in its fight or feud against their mother's family. While such situations may occasionally result in tragedies, or at least in grave psychological conflicts, especially in the case of women who stand between their fathers and their husbands, as a rule the marriage between the son of one family (or tribe or local aggregate) and the daughter of another is regarded as a bond of alliance between the two groups. The children issuing from such unions, although by tradition and mores belonging only to the father's group, are regarded with affection by the mother's family as well, and are therefore to some extent a guarantee of mutual friendship and good will for both sides. It has been a policy of long standing in the Middle East, practiced to this day especially by the ruling houses of the Arabian Peninsula, for princes and rulers to marry women of different tribes and peoples and thus to cement their allegiance to them.

Another outcome of the patrilineal mode of reckoning descent, combined with the institution of concubinage and the legal recognition of the children of concubines, was the occasional replacement of "white" by "black" heirs and successors. In various parts of the Middle East, and especially along the West coast of the Arabian peninsula and in North Africa, Somali, Abyssinian, Sudanese, or Negro slave girls have been incorporated into "white" households, and the offspring of these mixed unions have counted as full and equal members of the father's family and social group. If, as it at times happened, the only son of a man in ruling position was by such a dark-skinned concubine, there was nothing in the social or cultural traditions to prevent his becoming the heir to his father's position. The recently deceased Sultan of Morocco, for example, was as fair-skinned as any northerner, but his children are rather dark complexioned.[7] Discrimination on the basis of skin color is largely absent in the Middle East, and from the earliest days of Islam to the present Negroes and half-Negroes have always been able to rise to the highest positions, such as generals of the army, governors of provinces, and independent rulers.[8]

3. The Middle Eastern family is *patrilocal*, which means that generally upon marriage the young couple takes up residence in (or near) the home of the bridegroom's father. As a result of this custom brothers usually live together and form part of the extended family of which their father is the head or a member, while sisters live separately, away from one another and from their parents, each with her husband's family.

Investigation carried out in a Palestinian Muslim village in 1944 showed that "only one-third of the [male] children leave their parents' home after they marry."[9] In other words, two thirds of the newly married couples took up patrilocal residence. In Egypt "a married son continues to live in his father's house, into which he brings his wife and where his mother welcomes the daughter-in-law as a help in her household tasks."[10]

4. The Middle Eastern family is *patriarchal*, that is, the father is the master of his family, while the elderly male who is head of the entire extended family is the undisputed ruler of the entire group. In olden times, the rule of the family head comprised jurisdiction over life and death as well as over all other matters within his family.

The father's authority remains strong, especially in the rural family. In the study carried out in five Palestinian Muslim Arab villages referred to above it was found that the prevalent mores demand that the younger members obey and respect the decisions of the senior, and even when the head of the household reaches the ripe old age of eighty, and his son has become practically the head of the family, he will still always consult with his old father.[11]

As to the role of the mother in patriarchal families, the general observation has been made that lack of self-esteem as *women*, overdeference to the *pater familias*, and overvaluation of the male are characteristic of these families. "The companionship and reality interests denied to women [the wife] must compensate for in her relations with her children. Women in patriarchal cultures are prouder and more passionate mothers, over-tender to their sons, who largely constitute their own claim to social esteem."[12] In Egypt, for instance, it was observed that "the undisputed head of the individual family is the father. He is treated with respect and deference, and even grown-up and married sons submit to his authority." Sons, daughters, and wives kiss the hand of their father and husband.[13]

5. The Middle Eastern family is *endogamous*, meaning that there is a preference for marriages contracted within a relatively narrow circle. In theory, Koranic law permits a Muslim man to marry any woman, and a Muslim woman to marry any man, provided they accept Islam: "Marry not women who are idolaters, until they believe . . . and give not women who believe in marriage to the idolaters until they believe . . . ." (Koran 2: 200). Another passage in the Koran specifies that Muslims may marry daughters of the "peoples of the book," that is Jews, Christians, and Zoroastrians: "And ye are also allowed to marry free women that are believers, and also free women of those who have received the scriptures before you, when ye shall have assigned them their dower; living chastely with them, neither committing fornication, nor taking them for concubines" (Koran 5: 7). In the interpretation of this Koranic law there is a difference of opinion between two of the four Sunnite legal schools: the Ḥanafī school holds that marriages between Muslims and non-Muslim women who are not idolaters are permissible. The Shāfi'ī school, however, invoking an additional passage of the Koran, regards such unions as unlawful.[14]

While the legal endogamous circle is thus very wide and embraces all Muslims, even according to the Shāfi'ī school, in practice traditional custom has narrowed it down considerably. In general it can be stated that each social group in the Middle East tends to behave as an endogamous unit. Marriage outside one's own group is frowned upon, discouraged, forbidden, and not infrequently severely punished, occasionally even with the death penalty. These endogamous restrictions prevail everywhere in one form or another, and they apply usually with much greater strictness to women than to men. Groups which countenance or accept with disapproval marriage of their own men to women from groups of inferior status powerfully discourage, and often make it completely impossible, for their women to marry men of inferior status groups. Fulanain tells the tragic story of a shaykh of the noble Banī Sabah tribe of the Quraysh who, after having sojourned for twenty years as a fugitive among the Marsh Arabs of Lower Iraq, noticed that his only daughter was harboring tender feelings towards one of the youths of a marsh tribe. And although the two young people never met face to face, and the youth asked for the girl's hand in marriage, the old shaykh preferred to kill his only daughter rather than let her marry into a low-status tribe.[15]

The so-called noble (*aṣīlīn*) Bedouin tribes of the Syrian and Arabian Desert (see Chapter 8) guard most jealously their purity of blood, and do not permit either their men or their women to marry members of an inferior tribe. In choosing a marriage partner for either a son or a daughter satisfactory descent is an indispensable prerequisite.[16] Members of the noble Rwala, one of the leading tribes of the Syrian desert, cannot marry persons belonging to the Ṣleyb, Hawāzim, Fheyjāt, Shararāt, or ʿĀzim tribes which, although camel-breeders like the Rwala themselves, are low-status groups since they are unable to defend themselves, and pay *khuwwa*, protection-money, to the more vigorous tribes. The Rwala hold themselves aloof even from other free Arab tribes and discourage, though do not absolutely forbid, intermarriage with them. As to marriages with male slaves or slave girls, such occurrences are a legitimate reason for putting the offender to death. A Rweylī marrying a slave girl would be killed by his own kin, *ahl*, whom he defiled by his act. Intermarriage is forbidden for the Rwala also with the *ṣāniʿ* (pl. *ṣunnāʿ*) groups, those blacksmiths and tinkers who from time to time attach themselves to Rwala (and other Bedouin) camps, and of whom it is known to the Rwala that they have no marriage restrictions.[17]

The same restrictions exist also among the powerful Shammar tribes of Iraq and the Syrian Desert. No son of a Shammar tribe can marry a slave girl or a girl from an inferior tribe such as those mentioned above. If he did, his own people would kill him. If a noble tribesman takes up such trades as blacksmithing, salt-making, or salt-carrying, lime-burning, charcoal-burning, skinning animals and curing the skins, he makes himself dishonorable and the Shammar and other noble tribes will refrain from intermarrying with him and his.[18]

Similar limitations prevail in Southern Arabia where, for

instance, the Qara mountain tribesmen do not intermarry with the Shahara whom they regard as no better than slaves. The Shahara, again, do not marry outside their own people.[19]

Where different ethnic groups meet, even though all of them are Muslims, marriage limitations often restrict the choice of a mate to one's own group. In Afghanistan, for example, it seems that it is unlawful for a down-country man, that is, one from India, even though he be a Muslim, to marry an Afghan. Jewett reports a case where such a marriage was concluded, and the Afghan authorities kept the offender, a Muslim Pathan from India, in jail for about a year.[20] At the other or western end of the Middle East, in the town of Timbuctoo, which is inhabited by three distinct ethnic elements of differing statuses, men of high status groups can acquire wives or concubines from any status group, but the men of low status are limited by the fact that the high status women do not marry inferiors.[21]

An additional limitation in the choice of marriage partners stems from the socioeconomic stratification present to some extent everywhere in the Middle East. The three main ecologic groups of the nomads, villagers and townspeople from three distinct social classes among whom intermarriage is discountenanced in theory and rare in practice. As a South-Arabian proverb expresses it: "*Qūl bū'i Nūḥ: al-hegrī luh hegrah, al-'askarī luh 'askarīyah, wal-'abd luh gāriyah.*" "Said Father Noah: the ploughman to the plough-woman, the retainer to the retainer-woman, and the slave to the slave-woman."[22]

Yet another endogamous limitation is imposed upon the people by their preference for finding marriage partners within their own local group. A study carried out in the 1920's in Arṭās, a South-Palestinian Muslim Arab village, showed that the great majority of marriages were contracted by young men and women both of whom resided in the village or in its immediate vicinity.[23] This is not an isolated instance but typical for conditions in the Middle East in general. Among the fellahin of Egypt, for example, ". . . a woman or girl in this country will seldom consent, or her parents allow her, to marry a man who will not promise to reside with her in her native town or village."[24] Since a village is often inhabited by members of one or two (rarely more than two) extended family groups (called *ḥamūla* in several Middle Eastern countries), in-village marriage frequently also means in-family marriage. In Egypt to this day marriage to a stranger or to a woman met by chance outside the family's range is rare.[25]

The narrowest endogamous circle is drawn by the preference for marrying close relatives, if possible a father's brother's daughter (*bint 'amm*). In tradition-bound social strata a father is not allowed to give his daughter in marriage to anyone else unless he has obtained the consent (often in exchange for a consideration) of the girl's cousin. The right can be renounced by the *ibn 'amm* for a compensation paid to him by the suitor of the girl, who thus is a source of revenue for him.[26] In the towns cousin-marriage seems to be most frequent among the lower classes consisting of workers, artisans, and small employees.[27]

6. The Middle Eastern family, finally, is occasionally *polygynous*, that is, a man may marry more than one wife simultaneously. The prevalence of polygyny in the Middle East has been greatly exaggerated in the past by Western authors, observers, and travelers. Although it is true that polygyny is lawful among all Muslim sects as well as among the Oriental Jews, in other words among at least 90 per cent of the area's population, it has always been and recently is increasingly the exception rather than the rule. According to Koranic law a man can lawfully be wedded simultaneously to up to four women (Koran 4 : 3). In addition to marriage there is also the institution of concubinage, which makes it legal for a man to avail himself of the sexual services of slave girls owned by him, without limitation as to their numbers. Since, however, wives are acquired by payment of a bride price, while concubine slave girls have to be purchased forthright, the economic law has always been less permissive with regard to plural marriages than the religious law. Large harems were exceptions in the past and are extremely rare at present. In Saudi Arabia the king, the princes, and the rich still have sizable harems; in Syria, Jordan, Iraq, Egypt, however, the example of the leading families is that of monogamy, which cannot fail to have its effect on the upper class of society and ultimately also on the other classes, in the sense of serving as an example to be emulated. Of every hundred married men in the Middle East as a whole there

are probably not more than four or five married to more than one wife at a time.

In Cairo it was estimated well over a hundred years ago that "of one hundred married men in this city there certainly is not more than one who has two wives; and not more than one in five hundred who has more than two."[28] In Arabia in general most Bedouins have only one wife. "As a rule they only take another when the first is barren and they do not want to divorce her. The shaikhs often have three or four wives sometimes for political reasons, in order to be related to an influential family, sometimes, but more rarely, to give a home to a woman."[29] In Southern Arabia, too, the rule is that a man has only one wife, rarely two. When a man marries a second wife, it is customary for him to pacify his first wife with a gift equivalent to the bride price he pays for the new wife.[30] In this manner the second wife costs him at least twice as much as the first one had, a powerful deterrent from plural marriages. Most of the Iranian tribes are mono-gamous,[31] and the same rule prevails among the Berber tribes of North Africa.[32] In a random sample of 247 married Teda men (in the southeastern central Sahara), it was found that 35 had two wives and seven had three, making a total of 17 per cent of poly-gynous marriages.[32a]

In five Muslim Arab villages in Palestine, a study conducted in 1944 found that 10.6 per cent of the married men had more than one wife each. Of these 9.9 per cent had two, 0.5 per cent three, and 0.2 per cent four wives. Polygynous marriages were more frequent among the older men, and practically absent in the younger-than-thirty age group.[33]

A relatively high percentage of polygynous marriages was found among a group of Arab refugees from Palestine who had originally inhabited Upper Galilee around Lake Tiberias and up into the hills towards Nazareth and Safed, and had been agri-cultural folk. Of 200 heads of families interviewed in the course of a social survey carried out in July 1949 in the Khiss-Finn refugee camp, 32, or 16 per cent, were found to be polygynous.[34]

In the Sharqiyya province of Egypt in the 1930's 7.17 to 9.2 per cent of the married Muslim males were polygynous, while in the town of Zagazig this percentage was only 4.5.[35]

In a social survey carried out recently in Beirut among a representative sample of almost two thousand families only two plural marriages were found. In the one case the man had two wives, in the other three. The author of the report comments: "The economics of subsistence militates against plural marriages."[36] Data from other places seem to indicate that cultural influences must also be taken into consideration.

As against the rights of a man to marry more than one wife, he has certain obligations toward his wives that occasionally may make life difficult for him. Among several tribes of the Syrian-Arabian Desert a man has to divide his marital attentions equally between his two wives. He must alternately spend one night with one and one with the other. Each of the wives cooks for him a day in turn, and on that day it is the woman's right to have the husband spend the night with her, whether he cohabits with her or not. If the husband spends the night with one wife out of turn, he must compensate the other with a sheep or a goat as the price for her night. Sometimes the two wives strike a bargain and one of them buys a night from the other whose turn it is.[37]

"Be Fruitful and Multiply"

One of the motivations for large numbers of children is the emphasis on family coherence and family strength. Only a family with many children, and preferably boys, can be a strong family. The greater the number of children the greater also the prestige of the father and, through him, of the family as a whole. It is therefore the duty of every man in the family to beget as many children as possible. Even among the Christians this is found to be true. In Lebanon, for instance, ". . . a large family is desired . . . and a childless home is regarded as under a heavenly curse. Since the husband cannot divorce [his wife] (being Catholic) he loses all the hope of propagating himself. Children are wanted as a source of riches, comfort in old age, power against enemies, and, after death, to help into heaven. Therefore a bride who is robust, healthy and from a big family herself, is wanted."[38] The same attitude prevails among the Copts of Egypt.

The average number of children born to a married couple in

the Middle East is very high, resulting in sizable families in spite
of the effects of the high infant and child mortality. Unfortunately,
no adequate statistical studies are available on the rate of repro-
duction of women in most Middle Eastern countries. Some indication as to the results one may expect should such studies be
made can be found in data from Palestine, where, according to
1945 figures, the average number of children born to Muslim
women during their lifetime was between 9 and 10, of whom about
6 reached adulthood. Both the general conditions and the specific
motives believed to foster attitudes that make for large families
are found in the Middle Eastern countries in a rarely complete
combination. The general conditions are: illiteracy, great dependence on agriculture, isolation, a generally low standard of life, and
a fatalistic outlook; the specific motives comprise religious injunctions to be fruitful and multiply, the specific form of family
organization (the extended family), the widespread desire for
heirs and especially for male heirs, the high infant mortality as a
result of which relatively few children survive even if many are
born; also the absence of any economic motivation to limit the
number of children since the cost of satisfying the needs of the
children is small, and they begin to contribute to the family
income at an early age.[39] All these factors together constitute an
interlocking system of social and family organization resulting in
a strong pressure to reproduce. Only in the urban sector, and
especially in its middle and upper classes, are the families smaller.

In view of the great emphasis placed on having many children,
and the growth of the prestige of both man and wife with the
increase of the number of their (male) children, it will be understandable that a correlate of these attitudes is a resultant dim view
of sterility. A childless woman is regarded with contempt mixed
with commiseration, and is often believed to be cursed by God who
is the closer and opener of wombs. Such a woman will search
desperately for a remedy and will fall victim to quacks and
medicine men or women who still abound among the nomadic
tribes, the remoter villages, and even in the slums of the towns.
Should this search bring no result, the woman must resign herself
to being divorced, or to sharing her husband with a second wife
who, if fertile, will hold dominance over her. Although this

traditional attitude toward childlessness is being gradually mitigated under the impact of Westernization, traces of it are still
present even in the urban middle and upper classes.

Since all the motivations of the traditional Middle Eastern
family are directed towards having many children, birth control
is something to which a woman would as a rule resort only in
great secrecy, and only after she has given birth to a great number
of children. If a woman has three or four sons and she feels that
the frequent and continuing childbearing is too great a burden,
she may try one or more of the traditionally available contra-
ceptive methods, such as prolonged lactation (in the belief that
this prevents new conception), or one of the magical means offered
by the same medicine men or women whose help is invoked also
in the case of childlessness. Needless to say, these means are
inadequate, and one cannot speak of any effective traditional
method of family planning. As to the introduction of modern
family planning, the general atmosphere of the Middle Eastern
family and society is, for the time being, highly unfavorable to it
in spite of official pronouncements made recently by leading
religious authorities of the *el-Azhar* (the highest Muslim institute
of religious learning in Cairo, Egypt) to the effect that there is no
religious injunction in Islam against birth control.

"FAMILISM" AND SOCIALIZATION

The influence of the family on the life of the individual in the
Middle East is very great, much greater than usual in the modern
urban society of the Western world. In fact, the entire culture of
the Middle East is so permeated with family loyalty and influence
that the terms "familism" and "kinship culture" have properly
been applied to it. The individual is much more the product of
his family and much less that of other socializing factors than is
true in the West. Well beyond the onset of adulthood and deep
into his middle age, his life is joined to his extended family. Subservience to family authority and reliance on the advice of elders
remain characteristic traits of men in their thirties and forties.[40]
Ingrained habits of family loyalty are so strong that even in public
and official positions it is extremely difficult for the individual to
divest himself of a protective attitude towards his kinsmen, who

as a matter of course expect him to render special services and favors to them.

A most fundamental difference between the Western family and the Middle Eastern family can be found in the educational field: In the Western family efforts are made to educate the child from a very early age for independence. The parents take pride in a child who can do things for himself, who can find his way alone, and who therefore in their opinion is well prepared to take his place independently in a competitive society.

In traditional Middle Eastern society, on the other hand, the basic educational aim pursued by the family, whether consciously or not, is to mold the child into an obedient member of the family group, able to integrate into the working of his immediate social environment. Only very slowly and gradually, in most cases at a relatively advanced age, is he expected to act independently. The growing child, the adolescent boy has to learn to subordinate his wishes to those of his father and possibly to those of his elder brothers. He has to learn that the interests of the family come first and has to govern his actions with the family point of view in mind. Great stress is laid on coherence in the family because a divided family cannot hold its own in collective competition with the interests of other possibly stronger and more powerful families.

There is a considerable difference between the early socialization of a boy and of a girl and in this difference can be found one of the basic factors that make for the specific Middle Eastern flavor of the relationship between man and woman in adulthood. In the villages, both boys and girls are still swaddled, although in the cities modern women fight against it.[41] The period of lactation lasts one to two years in the case of a girl and two to three years in the case of a boy, which means that a boy is breast fed for almost twice as long as a girl. During the period of lactation, the mother as a matter of course is constantly at the disposal of the child, picking him up and giving him her breast. During the midday hour, when she takes a hot lunch to her husband and menfolk working in the field, she carries the baby along with her on her hip, shoulder, head, or back. With weaning, there is a sudden break in this close intimate relationship between mother and

4

child; thereafter, the mother no longer picks him up when he cries, no longer stands at his beck and call. When the mother leaves the house for the field or brings water from the well, she now leaves the child at home either in the care of an older sibling or completely alone to play in the dust of the small courtyard of the house. The child now cries unheeded, his customarily solicitous mother nowhere in sight. It is no exaggeration to say that weaning in the life of the Middle Eastern child is something of a traumatic experience.

This experience comes in the life of a girl at a very early age, when she is between one and two years old, and the formation of mental habits has not yet reached as advanced a stage as in the case of the boy who is weaned at twice her age. The impressions of the relatively short period during which the girl child is the object of maternal solicitude are very early overlaid by the new and lasting experience of finding herself neglected, of crying without being listened to, of being paid no attention. In later life, this experience is intensified and before long the girl learns that she is a rather unimportant member of the family, that her function is to serve her brothers, her elder sisters, her mother and father. When she is four or five, she is given some simple duties in the household and begins to help her mother in tending her smaller siblings. At about this time the mother very consciously begins to prepare the girl for her marriage, explaining to her whenever occasion arises that soon she will move into the house of her husband's parents and there will serve not only her husband but, primarily, her husband's mother. In this way the girl is conditioned for the subordinate role she will play in the home of her husband where for all practical purposes she will become a servant of her mother-in-law.

As to formal schooling of girls, this is still objected to by many Muslim villagers. In the villages studied in connection with the Kasmie Rural Improvement Project in Lebanon in 1952 it was found that 234 boys but only 13 girls attended elementary school. With regard to the Shī'ites in particular it was observed that they "do not encourage their daughters to attend schools. They feel that it is a hindrance to a happy marriage and often encourages disobedience to one's elders."[42]

The subordinate position of a girl, first in the house of her own parents, then in the house of her husband and his parents, serves as an additional motive for making a woman want to have as many children as possible and as soon as possible. The servile situation of a young wife changes only when children are born to her. She will still have to serve her mother-in-law, but her prestige increases with the birth of each child and especially with the birth of male children. It is when her sons grow up and marry that the woman reaches a period of life when the burden of everyday work is lightened by her daughters-in-law who now take over her chores. Just as the young girl learns in her parents' home how to behave in the home of her future parents-in-law, so the young wife is taught by her mother-in-law how to behave when she herself becomes a mother-in-law. In this manner both the mother-daughter relationship and the mother-in-law–daughter-in-law relationship is perpetuated from generation to generation.

Among the Christians this emphasis upon the desirability of bearing a boy is also present. "When the midwife announces a boy, there is much joy, firing of rifles, dancing, arak drinking. But she does not move if it is a girl, and later receives a small remuneration; everyone goes quietly after his daily task."[43]

To return now to the first years of a boy child's life. The lactation period lasts, as stated, from two to three years. During this time, certain definite expectations begin to form in the boy's mind. A two- to three-year-old boy who already can speak, walk, run, play, is still the master of his mother in the sense that whenever he wishes he may ask for her breast. As a result of this long period of lactation the boy child becomes imbued with the idea that his mother is there to serve him, that she must heed all his whims and wishes, and as he grows older, that the other womenfolk in the home also are there for the same purpose. The experience of weaning is of course a shock to the boy child as well, but, coming so much later than it comes for the girl, it does not eradicate the first impression he gained concerning his own relationship with the female world, namely that females are meant to serve him. Although corporal punishment is frequent, the boy may roam at will with older children and without the supervision of his parents. When the boy grows older his socialization and education are shifted from the hands of his mother to those of his father. He is taken by his father to the fields and allowed to help with the agricultural work. At the same time the boy notices that his mother or sisters serve him in more or less the same manner in which they serve his father: they bring food for him as well, also make his clothes, and so on. In this manner the impression that females are subservient creatures is reinforced in the male child's mind during the first decade of his existence. When he reaches adolescence and consciously observes the relationship between men and women, this impression is of course reinforced further and with it comes the recognition of the male role of leadership in the family and society at large. Naturally, this is translated into the expectation that, when he marries, his wife will be not so much his equal companion as a subservient fulfiller of his needs. When marriage actually occurs and the young bride is installed in the home that the boy shares with his parents and siblings, this expectation is fulfilled inasmuch as his own mother makes it clear what role his young wife must play in the household.

At the same time the boy, now a young husband, remains in an inferior position vis-à-vis his own father. He may accompany his father to his work in the fields and also to the deliberations of the village council, but he will have to take a back seat and is expected to listen quietly to his elders, discouraged from uttering any premature ill-considered opinion. Only when he himself becomes a father does his prestige slowly increase, and with each addition to his family, he is regarded as more of an authority in his own house.

EARLY MARRIAGE

Under traditional circumstances, which prevail to this day among practically all the nomads and villagers of the Middle East and many of the townspeople, marriages are arranged by the parents of the young people. A son or daughter is expected to carry out the decision of his or her parents in this, just as in other matters of greater or lesser importance. In view of the very early average age of marriage for girls, there seems to be some justification for the traditionally held view that parents are better judges of the suitability of a match for their daughter than the girl herself. The average age of marriage for men is higher, but in this case the fact that the family property is controlled by his father, who alone can make all decisions in connection with the bride price, serves as a powerful factor in making a son submit to parental choice. Moreover, in the extended patrilocal family set-up, for a son to bring into the house of his parents a bride to whom his parents object would be all but impossible.

In conservative villages and in the tradition-bound sectors of the urban population, very early marriages are still the rule. This is indicated by demographic studies which, unfortunately, are still sporadic. A study carried out in 1944 in five Palestinian Arab villages showed that 12 per cent of the women aged thirteen to seventeen and 89 per cent of the women aged eighteen to twenty-two were married. Among all Palestinian Muslims the average age at marriage for women was 20.2 in 1931 and 19.1 in 1938–39; for men 25.8 in 1931 and 26.6 in 1938–39.[44]

Taking twenty as the age limit, we find that in the United States, of all the women who were married in 1956, about 37 per cent were under twenty years of age; in England and Wales, about 20 per cent; in Egypt (1955), almost 50 per cent; in Jordan (1957), over 60 per cent; in the provincial and district capitals of Turkey, (1955), undoubtedly under the influence of Westernization, only 33 per cent.

In the age of the bridegrooms at marriage, the differences between the Western rates and those of the Middle East are in the reverse. In the United States in 1956, about 10 per cent of the men who married were under twenty years of age; in England and Wales, about 4 per cent; in Egypt, about 4 per cent; in Jordan, a little over 10 per cent; in the provincial and district capitals of Turkey, between 5 and 6 per cent.

In other words, fewer young men can afford to marry in Egypt, for example, than in the United States; but many more girls are married very young in the Middle East than in the West.[45]

Such early marriages for girls represent an age-old Middle Eastern tradition. The stated reasons often voiced to this day by conservative parents are: fear of unchastity and of losing the money expected in the form of the bride price (which is paid by the bridegroom or his father to the father of the bride who can

use it as he deems fit, although as a rule all or part of it is invested
into the trousseau of the bride); preference for educating the girl
in the house of her mother-in-law; preference for a young wife,
motivated by the relatively early aging of women; the often
present opportunity to exchange women, that is to give in marriage
the daughter (or sister) of one to another in exchange for the
latter's daughter (or sister); the desire of the groom's mother to
have household help.

Another result of these factors is that the percentage of people
remaining unmarried is very small, though somewhat higher
among the males than among the females. In Egypt (in 1937),
for instance, 99 per cent of the women in the forty to forty-nine
age group were married or widowed or divorced, while the
corresponding figure for males was 97 per cent.[46] In Turkey
(1935), the corresponding percentages were 97.5 per cent and
96 per cent.[47]

In recent decades several Middle Eastern countries have
passed laws fixing the minimum age of marriage. Article 4 of the
Syrian law on the status of the family stipulates that the fiancé
must have completed his eighteenth and the fiancée her seventeenth year of age for the marriage to be valid; and Article 88 of
the Turkish civil code prescribes the same ages as a condition of
marriage. In Egypt, legislation in 1923 fixed the minimum age
of marriage for girls at sixteen and for boys at eighteen. However,
the translation of such laws into practice is a difficult matter in
view of the persistence of the traditional preferences among the
people and the difficulty in enforcement. Thus, as a rule, there is
only a negligible difference between the average age of marriage
before the enactment of such laws as compared with that several
years after it.[48]

Such increase as has occurred in the average age of marriage is
largely confined to the middle and upper classes of the urban
population. In a representative sample of 1,665 male heads of
household in Beirut studied in 1952–53 it was found that 0.30
per cent had married at the age of fifteen or under; 11.23 per
cent between the ages of sixteen and twenty; and 27.33 per cent
between the ages of twenty-one and twenty-five, or a total of
38.86 per cent had married up to the age of twenty-five. Among the

fathers of these heads of household, that is, men one generation older, the corresponding figures were as follows: married at the age of fifteen and under, 8 per cent; sixteen to twenty, 24.0 per cent; twenty-one to twenty-five, 20.0 per cent; or a total of 52 per cent married up to the age of twenty-five. In other words, within one generation the percentage of men married up to the age of twenty-five, decreased from 52 per cent to 38.86 per cent, and the percentage of men married up to the age of twenty decreased from 32 per cent to 11.52 per cent.

PERCENTAGES OF AGE AT MARRIAGE IN BEIRUT, 1952–53[49]

Males	Former generation	Present generation
15 and under	8.0	0.30
16–20	24.0	11.23
21–25	20.0	27.33
25 and under	52.0	38.86
Over 25	48.0	61.14
TOTAL	100.0	100.00
Females		
15 and under	28.88	18.22
16–20	43.97	44.81
20 and under	72.85	63.03
Over 20	27.15	36.97
TOTAL	100.00	100.00

Among the mothers of the heads of household, 28.88 per cent had married at the age of fifteen or under, and 43.97 per cent at the age of sixteen to twenty. Among the female heads of household and the wives of male heads of household, the corresponding percentages were 18.22 and 44.81. There was thus a very considerable decrease within one generation in marriages of women at the age of fifteen and under, but no decrease, in fact a slight increase, in marriages at the ages from sixteen to twenty.

The same trend of later marriages seems to continue among the next generation (that is, the children of the heads of household studied), but the presentation of the data is such that no definite conclusions can be drawn from them.

Among the factors making for a higher average age at marriage can be mentioned the spread of education, as a result of which more and more girls are at school at an age when their mothers were married, and the increasingly longer period required of young men for establishing themselves in positions. Of course, these factors are present to an appreciable degree only in the urban upper and middle classes. Among the working class and the rural population early marriages are still the rule. In fact, in these latter circles a girl over twenty-four or twenty-five who has not yet married is regarded as having something wrong with her.

Again, only in the middle and upper classes of the urban population has the traditional family and marriage pattern undergone significant modifications in recent years. Children, both sons and daughters, who have had high school or even college education have increasingly emancipated themselves from the traditional type of paternal control with the result that not only paternal authority but also the traditional extended family experiences a definite decline (or if one prefers: modification) in these circles.

Since marriage is the most important event in the life of the family, a brief description of the attendant rites seems in place. These rites exhibit a wide range of local variations. The following summary refers to the Eastern Mediterranean area, where in the villages and in conservative urban circles two ceremonies precede marriage. The first is called *khuṭbeh* or unofficial engagement; the second, *katb el-ketāb* or signing of the contract. In the *khuṭbeh* a few relatives and friends are invited to the bride's house, where the parents of the bridegroom and bride announce to the guests the intended marriage. Some time later, the ceremony of *katb el-ketāb* is held. This ceremony is attended by an official of the Sharī'a Muslim Court and a large gathering of villagers. The official registers in the contract the consent of the couple to marry and the amount of dowry paid by the bridegroom. The dowry consists of two parts: one paid on date of contract, and the second deferred and paid in case of divorce. The dowry paid on date of contract may be wholly in money or partly in money and partly in land. The money is paid for the purchase of clothing for the bride, since custom dictates that the bride should take with her a bridal trousseau when she marries. The remainder of the money is used for the purchase of jewelry for the bride. In general, whenever the father can afford it, he furnishes the expensive clothing and all the dowry is used for the purchase of jewelry or land for the bride.

The actual marriage may take place immediately after this ceremony or more frequently, several months later. In towns, this period is usually longer and may extend to a year or even two. During the three days or the week that precede the actual marriage ceremony, the women villagers gather and dance in the bride's home. On the evening of the wedding a lavish feast is served in the bridegroom's house, attended by most of the villagers and also by guests from outside. Guests usually bring with them presents in money and in food such as rice, sugar, or sheep.[50]

DIVORCE

Divorce in Muslim society is extremely simple. The husband can divorce his wife at will by pronouncing the traditional formula, "I divorce you," in the presence of two witnesses. The wife does not have the right either to oppose such a divorce or to initiate it on her own behalf. Once the fateful sentence has been uttered, she must go back to her father's (or brother's) family, and can claim that portion of the bride price which is retained by the husband and paid to her only upon divorce. If a wife leaves her husband (by returning to her own family) and her husband agrees to divorce her, she forfeits this part of the bride price. After a divorce a man may remarry at once, but a woman must wait for three months to make sure she is not pregnant. Should she find herself pregnant, she cannot remarry until she gives birth to the child and weans it. During this time her former husband (the father of the child), must support her and the baby. According to Muslim law all the children of divorced parents belong to the father, and the mother must deliver them up to him, usually at

4§

the age of seven. It is important to note that among Muslim peoples no stigma attaches to divorce, and divorced women remarry, as a rule, soon after they are premitted by law to do so. In fact, among the Bedouins it is not at all rare that a woman marries several men in succession. A girl of the 'Ajmān, one of the nobles tribes of Arabia, by the name of al-Jāzī bint Muḥammed al-Hazām al-Hithlayn, who in her youth was a famous beauty, was married to King Ibn Saʿūd; then to his brother, the Amir Muḥammad; then to the king's brother-in-law, the Amir Saʿūd al-ʿArafa; then to the paramount chief of the Muṭayr tribe, Shaykh Bandar al-Duwīsh; then to a relative of the latter, Shaykh Mutluq al-Jabaʿa of the Qaḥṭān tribe; then to the chief of the 'Ajmān, Shaykh Rakān ibn Dhaydān al-Hithlayn. In between the above marriages, she was married two more times to King Ibn Saʿūd who was able, on both occasions, to persuade her then husband to divorce her because "I have not got over my love for her." Al-Jāzī was thus married no less than eight times within the relatively short period during which Bedouin women enjoy the youthful attributes and attractions of beauty.[51]

No statistical data are available from most Middle Eastern countries as to the frequencies of divorce and subsequent re-marriage, but that these frequencies must be high can be gauged from the observation made in Mandatory Palestine where among the women of five Muslim Arab villages aged thirty-eight or more no less than 30.8 per cent have been married twice or more.[53]

A glance at the frequency of divorces is also instructive. This can be measured by the number of annual divorces per 1,000 married couples, which in the United States was 8.9 in 1939–41 and 10.4 in 1949–51, the highest rates in the Western world. In the Middle East, however, these rates are higher still. In Egypt, the only country from which relatively reliable data are available, they were 13.6 in 1936–38 and 16.9 in 1946–48.[52]

These figures show that in the Middle East relatively more married women get divorced than in America. Nevertheless, there is considerable dissatisfaction in feminist circles in the Middle East with the divorce laws. The Arab Women's Congress in Cairo in 1944 resolved to demand reforms of the divorce law in two directions:

"The right to divorce is to be granted to women as well as men, and no divorce is to come into effect without the decision of the court." No unqualified condemnation of polygyny was resolved, since allowance for it was made in cases of sterility and incurable sickness, a fact that demonstrates how far custom and tradition still influence the Muslim women even of the educated class.[54]

FAMILY AND SOCIETY

The family in the Middle East is the traditional economic unit. That is to say, in the nomadic tribes the family jointly owns the herds and flocks; in the villages, the family jointly owns and works the land; and in the towns, unless Westernization has changed the situation, the family jointly owns and works in a craft, or trade, or business. Hand in hand with this goes the tradition of passing on occupations in inheritance from father to son or, failing a son, to a nephew or other relative. Where modern influences are prevalent this system suffers a breakdown and, with the disintegration of the traditional extended family, its young male members strike out more and more frequently into new and individual directions.

Inheritance of property is regulated in the Middle Eastern countries, with the exception of Turkey, by the religious laws of the community to which the family belongs. As far as the Muslims are concerned, there is a Koranic prescription (Sura 4), according to which, if a man dies, first his debts are paid from his estate, then his wife and other members of his family besides his children get certain shares, then the residual estate is equally divided among his sons (each of whom gets a full share), and his daughters (each of whom gets half a share). This rule is observed primarily among traditional townspeople and villagers. Among the nomads, ancient pre-Islamic usages and customary laws (*'urf*) still persist, and the rules of inheritance contained in them are followed. Among the Bedouins of Jordan and Syria, for example, daughters do not inherit, and the Turkish government attempted in vain to enforce the *sharī'a* (canon) law.[55] In addition to the exclusion of

daughters from inheritance, traditional law as followed by the
nomads permits a man to dispose of his entire property before
death as he chooses, while according to Muslim canon law he
has the right to give away at will only one third of it.

Adoption is recognized and practiced by the nomads, whereas
canon law rejects it (based on Koran 33 : 4 f., 37).

The main differences between the attitudes of the rural and the
urban families can be subsumed under the point of view of conservatism *versus* modernism. The typical rural family is conservative, tradition-bound, and averse to change. It is suspicious of
innovations, and values the *status quo*. It emphasizes the importance
of the family and its collective interests as against those of its
individual members. It expects subordination of individuals, and
especially of the younger generation, to the interests and wishes of
the family as a whole as expressed by its head and its older
members. It has great cohesion, which continues even when the
family branches out into several subdivisions located in different
places of residence. It protects its individual members and helps
them economically, socially, and with "string pulling" whenever
necessary.

When a rural family moves into the city many of these traditional features are lost. The individual often becomes separated
from his family or the nuclear family deprived of the protective
framework of the extended family. As a result, the old values
represented and upheld by the family tend to disappear. Only
rarely can the family in the city retain its tradition-directed tenor.
Traditionalism and modernism compete with each other even
within the family, causing not infrequently deep rifts between the
conservative older and the modern younger generations. The
transition from traditional familism to modern urban living and
the preservation of family mores, with which the problem of the
attitude toward religion is intrinsically interwoven, are regarded
by thoughtful people as basic difficulties in the path of Westernization. As Hourani put it,

> . . . the patriarchal family system remains in existence, but its
> days are probably numbered. The claims of the family are still
> prior to those of the individual member of it; but its solidarity is
> gradually being undermined by the ways of modern urban life

and by the emergence for large sections of the population of alternatives to the cultivation of inherited land in the ancestral village.

The structure of the family is being radically transformed by the change in the status of women. The change is particularly great among the urban middle class. Girls' schools have been opened, and it is possible for women to enter an ever-increasing number of occupations, including the liberal professions. But so far only the edge has been touched of the great problem, which like all great problems in this country is closely bound up with religion: how far is it possible in a modern society to retain the traditional Islamic view of women's status—seclusion and the veil, the theory and in a minority of cases the practice of polygamy, the divorce laws and so on? Of all the difficult questions which the process of Westernization raises, this is perhaps the most difficult; and its difficulty and urgency are likely to increase. The process of change is being speeded by one manifestation of Western civilization above all: the film which expresses a way of feminine life, and a conception of the relations between men and women, which are far from those prevalent in the Islamic world.[56]

DEMOGRAPHIC DATA

To supplement the foregoing analysis of the Middle Eastern family some demographic data might be useful. Such data, however, are very scanty in most Middle Eastern countries, and it is consequently necessary to extrapolate when generalizations are called for.

Even the most basic of all demographic data, the birth and death rates, are lacking in most Middle Eastern countries.

Only from two Muslim Arab populations (Egyptians and Palestinian Muslims) do we possess series of data extending over a number of years. These figures show that the typical crude birth rate ranges between 40 and 50, placing these countries into the top brackets of the so-called "high fertility countries." No general trend of either decrease or increase is observable, although the war years were accompanied by a definite drop in crude birth rates, the low having been reached in both countries in 1942.

The birth rates of the Christian population groups in the Middle East (Palestinian Christian Arabs; Cyprus, with its 80 per cent of Greek Christians; and also Lebanon with its slight Christian Arab majority) are lower. They range from 25 to 35.

High birth rate is usually accompanied by high death rate, and this is what we find in the Middle East. The Egyptian crude death rate ranged, in the course of the two decades of 1930 to 1950 between 25 and 29, reaching the low of 19.2 in 1950–52. The death rate of the Palestinian Muslims decreased from over 26 in 1932 to less than 20 by 1942. The Christian populations, characterized by a lower birth rate, show a correspondingly lower death rate, as well as a hesitant but noticeable trend for the decrease of the latter (from 16 in 1932 to less than 10 in 1945 in Palestine, and to 6.7 in 1953–55 in Cyprus).

The differential between crude birth rate and crude death rate gives the crude rate of natural increase, which shows an increasing trend in those populations of the Middle East that evince a decreasing trend in death rate.

As to the probable future trends of population movement in the Middle East only a few very general observations can be made. The most immediate demographic effect of industrialization, Westernization, and urbanization is a gradual improvement in the rate of infant mortality that can be noticed in several Middle Eastern countries already today. This is followed by a slower but no less definite decrease in general mortality, as a consequence of which the number of births increases over the number of deaths, and the total population embarks upon a more and more pronounced natural increase.

After a while, industrialization is followed by a fall in birth rate, as was shown not only in Europe but also in Japan. However, the decrease in birth rate in the Middle East may not become significant enough to be felt in the national or regional population movements for many more years to come. This means that for the next few years—possibly up to two decades or more—the increase in the number of children who once born will survive will not be counterbalanced or offset by a decrease in the number of children born. After the lapse of this transitional period, however, the onset of a decreasing tendency in the natural increase can be expected. The outlook and values of an ever-growing proportion of the population will undergo a slow and gradual change. The present deeply embedded values, powerful in their hold, safeguarded by social sanctions, will slowly and gradually give way under the impact of Westernization, of changing and improving economic and social conditions. The end result can well be a changed set of demographic traits approximating those of the Western world.

A very important figure in vital statistics is the rate of infant mortality, calculated as either the number of children dying under one year of age per every thousand live births during the year or the number of children dying under one year of age per every thousand children under one year of age at the middle of the year. The difference between the two methods is considerable, the second yielding a higher figure than the first.

The importance of the rates of infant mortality for drawing a demographic picture of any community lies in the fact that the higher the infant mortality rate the greater the waste of human lives, energy, emotional stress, and economic effort expended by the population in relation to every child who is successfully brought up to the age of maturity. Moreover, high general mortality rates usually go hand in hand with high infant mortality rates as well as with high birth rates; so that the end result (that is, the natural increase) of these three high rates together can be the same or only slightly higher than the end result of low birth rates coupled with low infant and general mortality rates. High birth rate and high infant mortality rate (as well as high child mortality up to five years of age) are conducive to a low standard of living because the earning capacity of the adult members of the family is divided among a large number of small children, a considerable percentage of whom does not reach the age of economic productivity.

Only scattered returns are available from a few Middle Eastern countries as to infant mortality, and even those are not reliable because of the probability of incomplete registration. Nevertheless, the figures indicate that infant mortality is on the decrease, as shown by the accompanying data (rates based on live births during the year):[57]

People	Year	Mortality	Year	Mortality
Aden Colony	1948	171.3	1958	137.7
Egypt	1944	152.3	1954	140.4
Cyprus	1948	66.9	1958	30.0
Palestine Muslims	1935	148.1	1945	93.9
Palestine Christians	1935	125.8	1945	89.0
Palestine Jews	1935	64.2	1945	35.8

The main single cause for the decrease in infant mortality which can be assumed to be characteristic for the major parts of the Middle East area, is undoubtedly the greater care, both medical and social, enjoyed by the newborn. The beneficial results of infant care can be demonstrated by referring to the extremely great difference in infant mortality rates in Egypt between children under the care of health centers and those not under the care of such centers. In 1945, the infant mortality rate per thousand among children under the care of health centers was 181, among those not under the care of centers, 323; by 1948 the rate of the first group was reduced to 80, while those in the second group showed a decrease to 241 only.

It is a remarkable fact that the male infant mortality is in every case higher, in some cases considerably higher, than the female infant mortality, even in Muslim populations who traditionally value their male children more than their female children, and who, therefore, presumably pay more attention to the health and well-being of a male infant than of a female.

Child mortality rate is the number of children per thousand live births who die before they reach their fifth birthday. The data for child mortality are even scantier than those of infant mortality, but we know, for instance, that in Egypt the rate is 340,[58] and it can be assumed not to be much different in other Middle Eastern countries in which conditions are similar to those of Egypt.

To put the above figures in the proper perspective, they should be compared not only with corresponding figures from the Western world, but also with those of Negro Africa.

In the tribal population of southern Sudan, which culturally has close affinities to Negro Africa, infant mortality seems to be several times higher than in the Middle East. Limited studies carried out among the Nuba mountain tribes resulted in the following infant mortality rates per 1,000 live births:

Tribe	Mortality
Heiban	423
Otoro	361
Tira	323

In the same three tribes it was found that the number of children born per mother was low (when compared with the Middle Eastern average), and that the number of children remaining alive per mother was scarcely sufficient to replace the present generation.[59]

Tribe	Number of women	Children born per mother	Children alive per mother
Heiban	100	4.2	2.3
Otoro	77	5	2.7
Tira	112	2.8	1.7
Koalib	33	3.2	1.7

These figures, when taken in conjunction with the estimated infant mortality of 600 in Mukalla in the Aden Protectorate,[60] indicate that the infant mortality rates of the more advanced regions of the Middle East, high though they are, represent a definite advance over the largely uncontrolled situation prevailing in most of Negro Africa and Southern Arabia.

TERMINOLOGY

The importance of the family and of family life is expressed, among other manifestations, in the extremely rich terminology centering around the family and used in the everyday colloquial in Arab countries. There is, for instance, a considerable number of nouns denoting the *family*, and used sometimes interchangeably, sometimes with fine gradations of meaning. The family consisting of father, mother, and children is called *'ayle* (variant: *'ēle*, or *'īāl*; in plural *'iyāl*, *'ayāl*, or *'ailāt*). Another term for the same concept is *bēt*, which, however, may also mean the extended family living in one house. The extended family is called *āl*, or *ahl*, or *finde* (variants: *fendi*, *fende*), or *feriq* (also pronounced *ferich*).

Since one's relationship to a cousin who is one's father's brother's son or daughter is very different from one's relationship to other types of cousins, it is necessary to distinguish between different types of cousins. In fact, the single English word "cousin," when translated into Arabic, must be reproduced by one of eight terms which are listed below:

ibn 'amm ('ammī) (my) father's brother's son	*ibn khāl (khālī)* (my) mother's brother's son
bint 'amm ('ammī) (my) father's brother's daughter	*bint khāl (khālī)* (my) mother's brother's daughter
ibn 'amme ('ammtī) (my) father's sister's son	*ibn khāle (khāltī)* (my) mother's sister's son
bint 'amme ('ammtī) (my) father's sister's daughter	*bint khāle (khāltī)* (my) mother's sister's daughter

Terms for first-degree relatives are as follows:[61]

abī, abū'ī	my father	*bintī*	my daughter
bābā	daddy	*waladī*	,, child (m.)
ummī, immī	,, mother	*ulādī*	,, children
māma	mummy	*'amm, ('ammī)*	,, father's brother
akhi, akhū'ī	,, brother		
ukhtī	,, sister	*'amme ('ammtī)*	,, father's sister
zūjī, jūzī	,, husband		
bint 'ammī, martī	,, wife	*khāl (khālī)*	,, mother's brother
maddāmtī	,, ,, (in the cities)	*khāle (khāltī)*	,, mother's sister
ibnī, bnayyī	,, son		

V. The Position of Women
and Sex Mores

MIDDLE EASTERN society is complex and mosaiclike. It is intricately structured both vertically and horizontally. In many parts of the huge land area of the Middle East lack of communications has favored the emergence of local differences beneath the over-all but often rather thinly spread veneer of Islamic culture. The strong traditionalism characteristic of the area has tended to perpetuate local variants. These conditions have resulted in the presence of a wide variety of sex mores ranging from the extreme of great strictness on the one hand to that of considerable laxity on the other.

The picture painted by travelogues and even by more serious studies of the area or of a region within it is often one-sided and distorted. Some writers emphasize the restrictions sexual morality places on women, others include titillating details as to socially sanctioned immorality of which they succeeded in getting a glimpse. Generalizations often follow, and the area as a whole is said to conform to one stereotyped pattern.

Islam has, of course, been the most important single factor in determining the traditional position assigned to women all over the Middle East. To this day, the foremost manifestation of the inequality of the sexes can be seen in the different moral standards applied by Islam to men and women. Official Islam countenances a considerable sexual laxity in men while imposing a rigid code of sex mores on women. In a traditional Muslim social environment men and women form two distinct and separate societies that do not mix or mingle. Only in the family circle can closely related men and women meet. Social life in the sense of several

unrelated families or couples periodically meeting in a private
home or in a public place (such as a café) does not exist, with a
few exceptions confined to the thin upper layer of urban society
in the countries close to the Mediterranean littoral. The Muslim
Middle East has been a man's world and its society a man's society,
and these they remained to a large extent to this very day.

VEILING AND SECLUSION

The official Muslim attitude toward sex is expressed in such
institutions as the veiling and segregation of women (often
referred to by the Indian term *purdah*). The two are usually
thrown together, although in fact they are two different and often
unconnected expressions of the position of women. A woman
may wear the veil without being secluded, or she may live in such
extreme seclusion that she rarely if ever has opportunity to use
the veil. Veiling is general or, more precisely, has been general
until the impact of Westernization, among townswomen only.
As recently as the beginning of the twentieth century, Muslim
townswomen wore the veil when leaving their homes for shopping
expeditions or for the purpose of paying a visit, and would rarely
if ever talk or show their faces to any man except their own
husbands and close male relatives.

"The outdoor costume of the Persian women—is made up of
three pieces: the big voluminous trousers which slip over the feet
and cling closely to the shape of the foot but above the ankle
fall full and baggy; over these are worn the large black chuddar,
the poor wearing black calico and the rich silk; and then, covering
the face, is the veil. This veil is a long strip of white calico with
open work for the part covering the eyes, and fastened together
at the back of the head by brass, silver, or gold and jewelled
clasps, according to the rank of the wearer. Through the open
work part of the veil the woman is able to find her way about,
and see all that there is to be seen, while no one can see the face
behind the veil."[1]

In traditional Turkey the townswoman, when leaving her
house, was bundled in her *çarşaf* and veiled beyond recognition.
The *çarşaf* was a loose, usually black, wrap that covered her

figure from head to foot, and one corner of which used to be drawn over the head and across the face, revealing only the eyes.[2]

In Afghanistan the *burqa* is worn, a covering that envelops the head, is gathered around the line of the forehead and falls to the feet, with two holes covered with netting for the eyes.[3]

The higher the social class to which the urban woman belonged, the greater was the strictness with which she observed the rules of veiling. Actually, veiling was a mark of class distinction rather than a mere Muslim religious tradition, as attested by the fact that the practice was observed by Christians and Jews as well as by Muslims.[4]

Also, the degree of seclusion to which a woman is (or was) subjected depends, within the general traditions of the locality in which she lives, on the social class to which she belongs. Among the women of the upper class, as recently as one or two generations ago, there were such who from puberty to death never left their quarters. As a result of this extreme form of seclusion it was found, in certain Muslim societies, that the incidence of tuberculosis was greater among the women who were never exposed to sunshine than among the men.

In a less stringent form of seclusion among the upper class, women were never supposed to go out to the street in the company of any man, not even in that of their own husbands, but only in the company of one or more elderly women, all of them, of course, heavily veiled.[5]

Nowadays, women of the middle class and to an even greater extent of the lower or working classes are free to go out on shopping expeditions, to visit friends, to go to the *ḥammām* (bath), and the like, veiled but alone. Since the great majority of townswomen belong to these classes, one can generalize and state that in most cases veiling is practiced even when the rules of seclusion are considerably relaxed.

Among the Jews of the Middle East, female seclusion is observed, as a rule, less strictly than among the Muslims.[6]

Among the fellahin of Syria, Jordan, Israel, and Iraq, in several of the oases of Northwestern Arabia, as well as in the smaller towns of these areas, the veiling of women is not practiced. Also, in many places in southern and eastern Arabia, including the small towns, the veil is absent. Only in the larger cities, for example, in Ṣanʻa, capital of Yemen, is veiling practiced. In southern Palestine it also was practiced, probably under Egyptian influence.[7]

Occasionally it is found among both Bedouins and fellahin that brides are veiled on the day of their wedding but otherwise veiling is not practiced, or that unmarried women go unveiled, but married women have to veil their faces.[8]

Among the nomads of northern Arabia, in Iraq, among the fellahin in Israel, and the seminomadic tribes of Jordan, women who wear no veil nevertheless frequently cover the lower part of the face with a sleeve or corner of the headkerchief when encountering or speaking to a stranger.[9] Sometimes they merely take a corner of the headkerchief in the mouth.[10] It also happens that, upon encountering a stranger, the unveiled woman turns away and talks to him with her face averted.[11]

In Egypt too, village women are always ready at a moment's notice to draw the edge of the headkerchief across the lower part of the face or at least to take a corner of it into the mouth, while in some places they cover the face with a long black veil, glossy or dull, when they go out. In the Qena district this veil is dark brown, while in the Sharqiyya province it is white.[12] No veiling of women is practiced among the Tuareg who regard the veil (*lithām*) as the prerogative of the free men.[13]

As we adduce more and more examples, it becomes increasingly clear that no hard and fast rules can be found as to the presence or absence of veiling in a certain region or group. The Rwala, one of the noblest tribes of the Syrian-Arabian Desert, practice no veiling, and girls are even free to let their tresses be seen.[14] Among several other tribes of the Arabian Northwest, such as the Benī Ṣakhr, Ḥwēṭāt, Benī ʻAṭiyya, veiling is absent.[15] In some of the other tribes north of the ʻAqaba-Kuwait line the women cover the lower part of the face up to the nose with a thin black veil (*milfa*), while several tribes south of this line, such as the Muṭayr, Ḥarb, Sbaʻa, Reshayda, Benī Hajir, ʻAwāzim, ʻAjmān, but not the Shammar and some of the Ḥijāz tribes) wear a longer or shorter black face mask (the so-called *burqa*) hanging down from the forehead and covering the entire face with the exception of

the eyes visible through two eyeholes. The Ṣolubba and other
low-status groups share with the noble Rwala the absence of
veils.[16] In some of the oases of Arabia, such as Teyma, the women
go about unveiled.[17] In southern Arabia, while veiling is practiced
in most of the towns,[18] occasionally with a *burqa*-like black face
cloth with a silver line stitched down the nose and two eye slits,[19]
among village women, the veil is rarer[20] and in some areas
completely absent.[21] Among a few tribes such as the 'Abida in
Hadhramaut, a *milfa*-type half veil is worn.[22] In the Bāṭina
district of Oman in some of the villages the women are unveiled,
in others they are veiled. In the interior of Oman veiling is more
general.[23] The generalization of Thomas,[24] "All the women of
the sands in Southern Arabia are veiled," is therefore question-
able. All that one can venture to say is that up to the twentieth
century veiling was the accepted practice in the middle and
upper classes of urban society; that among the lower class townspeople it was largely absent; and that among the villagers and
nomads it was (and is) only sporadically practiced.

This being the case, the laws and other efforts to abolish
veiling affect only a limited sector of Middle Eastern society;
although it has to be recognized that as a symbol of the emancipation of women the discarding of the veil is of great moment for
the area as a whole. The task the male and female reformers set
themselves is still far from being accomplished as the 1960's lead
us toward the end of the second third of the twentieth century.
In the Arabian Peninsula veiling and seclusion still survive in
practically unchanged form. In Iraq, Syria, Jordan, and Lebanon,
with the leading families showing the example, these old traditions
begin to give way. In these countries, "the real veil that covers
completely the whole figure is still carried either by a particularly
conservative class of people, or by the ignorant masses in the
cities; among the educated middle and upper class it is either
totally removed, or else symbolically represented by a scarf to
protect the hair, or by a thin veil on the face or on the hair. Yet
it should be admitted that the recent removal of the veil in certain
circles has not brought about the free association of men and
women. This is why marriage is still a family concern. It has to be
arranged by parents and to follow certain conditions and for-

malities, although a certain acquaintance could be made between the two parties in strictly liberal circles. Women are still treated with the utmost reserve, and the traditional respect of women and their chivalrous treatment have not been affected by their emancipation."[25]

In Egypt, the gradual and hesitant discarding of the veil, first by the upper class, then by the middle class Muslim women, serves as an example also for the Christian women of the same classes. The women of the lower class, who constitute the great majority of the female population, show themselves more reticent in this respect.[26] In Iran, the veil was largely discarded in 1936 by the Muslim townswomen;[27] but, following the abdication of Riza Shah in 1941, there was a certain resurgence of conservatism. Only in one country, Turkey, has the abolition of veiling been successfully carried out, at least in the towns;[28] in the villages in which veiling used to be practiced, the familiar female movement of pulling the edge of the headkerchief across the face was observed by this writer as recently as in the summer of 1959.

SOCIAL INTERCOURSE

Just as the seclusion and veiling of townswomen goes back to pre-Islamic times and even to ancient Near Eastern origins, so also the unveiled status and greater freedom of movement enjoyed by village and nomadic women are ancient traditions in the area. Veiling inhibits women in doing their chores and, accordingly, in societies where the women's outdoor work is an economic necessity they go about unveiled. This is the case in most agricultural villages in the Middle East where women help their husbands or fathers in tilling the fields and in the performance of other agricultural work, as well as among the nomadic tribes where the putting up and pulling down of the tents and the tending of the flocks is the women's task.

The absence of the veil and of seclusion makes for a freer demeanor of the women in their occasional encounters with non-related men. In ancient Arabia the women of the desert tribes went unveiled and associated freely with men. Much of this freedom of manners has been preserved to this day among the nomadic tribes primarily, but also among some of the village folk. Especially among the goat and sheep-breeding tribes of the Arabian Peninsula, where the flocks are entrusted to the care of women and young girls, the shepherdesses feel free to enter into friendly conversation with any wayfarer passing by, whether friend or stranger. Such chance encounters are often the occasion of some good-natured banter between man and maiden.[29] The same open and unrestrained friendliness is manifested by women of the oases[30] as well as of the villages of southern Arabia.[31]

At home, in the tent, in the absence of her husband, the wife is supposed to show hospitality to guests, to invite them to the part of the tent reserved for men, and to supply them with the utensils and wherewithal for preparing coffee. If she is acquainted with the guests, she joins them after supper, drinks coffee with them, and amuses herself in their company till midnight.[32] Occasionally, some bantering takes place in the tent as well, even in the presence of the husband, between a male guest and the wife of the host; the host takes no offense at such playful courting of his wife.[33] This actually is the same custom that Ibn Battuta found in the fourteenth century among the Berbers of North Africa and which he reported with considerable indignation.[34]

Among the Arabian nomads, girls have much premarital freedom in their relations with men. Although virginity is (with certain exceptions, about which later) as highly prized among them as among the villagers and townsfolk, Bedouin girls have many opportunities for meeting their lovers outside the camp, either during the day while the girl grazes her flock, or at night. On such occasions, although the traditional mores require of the girl to guard her virginity, flirting and petting take place, and incautious girls may even become pregnant. An unmarried pregnant girl must either try abortion, in which her female relatives help her, or persuade her lover to marry her at once, or run away from her tribe and seek refuge in the settled territory, or commit suicide. Should she be found out by her menfolk, they will be in honor bound to kill her. If she was raped, she may be spared, but her child will be killed.[35]

While among the Arabian nomads secrecy and decorum must be maintained, in nineteenth century Egypt it was "not uncommon to see females of the lower orders flirting and jesting with men in public, and men laying their hands upon them very freely."[36] Especially on the occasion of certain popular religious festivals, such as the 'Ashūra, the tenth day of the month of Muḥarram, men and women used to mingle freely in the mosques, and it was said by the people of Cairo that "no man goes to the mosque of the Hasanein on the day of Ashoora but for the sake of the women; that is to be justled among them . . . ."[37]

To the west of Egypt, among the nomads of the Libyan desert, seclusion exists only among the noble tribes. In the other groups, young men and girls mix freely, boys are allowed openly to court the girls, to visit them in their camps, and to sing to them of their love in verses of their own composition, as a preliminary to marriage.[38]

Only in isolated places does one find a definite relaxation of the strict rules of sexual morality. As an outstanding example, one may cite the Siwa Oasis on the western fringes of Egypt where, according to observers, extramarital relations, prostitution, and sodomy are rampant.[39]

Sharp distinction must be drawn between this kind of sexual liberty, which is regarded as immoral by the society itself in which it is practiced, and the traditionally regulated and accepted premarital freedom accorded to women in several places in the Middle East. Apart from a number of extreme cases in which exaggerated notions of hospitality resulted in the sexual accommodation of visiting strangers,[40] where premarital freedom is accorded to women the behavior pattern established shows a certain similarity to the modern Western habit of "dating and mating." Among the westerly neighbors of the Siwans, the Tuareg of the Sahara, ". . . Before marriage, which for oriental women occurs comparatively late in life, Tuareg girls enjoy a measure of freedom which would shock even the modern respectable folk of Southern Europe . . . it is common for a girl who is in love with a man to take a camel and ride all night to see him and then return to her own place, or for a suitor to make expeditions of superhuman endurance to see his lady . . . . Illicit love affairs inevitably occur: if they have unfortunate consequences the man is called upon to marry the woman, but infanticide is not unknown. Once married, the woman is expected to behave with decorum and modesty. Public opinion on these matters is strong. The married state, however, does not prevent a woman admitting men friends to an intimacy similar to that existing, perhaps, only among the Anglo-Saxon peoples."[41] It is easily recognizable that this Tuareg custom differs only in degree but not in kind from that of the Rwala and other noble Arab tribes of the Syrian-Arabian desert referred to above.

Among the Tuareg of Ahaggar in the Central Sahara, the pre-marital sex relations are given a more or less institutionalized form and are supposed to lead ultimately to marriage. Around the age of sixteen, both the young men and the girls of the tribes are admitted to the *ahals*, periodic meetings, taking place late in the evening outside the camp, and usually accompanied by *asri*, that is a considerable relaxation of the mores (literally: running with loosened bridles). The *ahal*, which attracts young men from neighboring camps, starts with playing the *amzad*, a one-string instrument played with a round bow, and group singing, but soon the young men and girls start rubbing noses, which is the parti-cular Targui form of kissing. Late at night, when the *ahal* ends, everyone is supposed to return to his or her own camp, but in actuality private trysts follow, either during the night or on later occasions. As a result of this institution, pre-Islamic in its origin, both girls and young men begin their sex life as soon as they reach maturity, and no value whatsoever is placed on virginity. Love affairs leading to marriages usually start at such *ahal* meetings. After marriage, however, the wife is supposed to remain faithful to her husband, who is expected to show no jealousy if old *ahal*-friends of his wife continue to court her in a Platonic fashion. The question whether marital fidelity of wives is merely an ideal or is actually adhered to is answered differently by different observers.[42]

At the extreme west of the Middle East, the Ouled Tidrarin, a nomadic Moorish tribe in the western central part of the Spanish Sahara, are reported "to celebrate exceptionally good harvests with a curious sort of strip-tease dance, a thoroughly pagan performance which begins with the young men and women lining up in two ranks facing one another. First a boy steps forward, places a present of sugar and tea or trinkets on the ground, and retires to his place. Then a girl steps out between the lines, lets her clothes fall to the ground, picks up the present, and goes back naked to her place. After this has been going on for a while, to the accompaniment of much whooping and yelling, self-restraint begins to crumble and eventually nature takes its course. Such doings make one wonder just what the day-to-day pre-marital relations between the sexes may be like, but so far no one who knows the Moors well—and there are few who do—has even mentioned the subject."[42a]

To the southwest of the Tuareg area, in the city of Timbuctoo, virginity, although valued in the eyes of Muslim law, is found upon marriage only among Arab girls, and is rare in the other ethnic groups.[43]

Also in the northeastern parts of the Middle East, tribal societies have preserved much of that ancient freedom of women that pre-vailed in pre-Islamic Arabia. Among the Kurdish and Lur tribes of western Iran, "young men and girls meet freely, they join in the old folk dances, and the courting of the marriageable girls goes on in the old forms, in which quick wit and repartee are combined with spontaneous or traditional poetical expression of feelings."[44]

In general, among both the villagers and the nomads the women's activities are largely confined to the home or the family circle. However, women help their husbands in certain types of work outside the home as well, such as gathering brushwood and dung, tending the flocks, fetching water, among the nomads; taking food to the menfolk working in the fields, helping them in field work, especially at harvest time, etc., among the villagers. They fatten sheep and dry the meat; pick lentils and spread them to dry; prepare crushed wheat, and bake their "handkerchief bread" in the courtyard oven fired with wood gathered by them. They make jams and tomato paste for use in stews during the winter. They carry water from the fountain, are busy with the harvesting and winnowing, and in the winter months spin with old-fashioned wooden spindles. To these activities must be added the participation of women in the traditional forms of hospitality in tent and house. All this has resulted in a considerable amount of traditionally sanctioned social contact between nonrelated men and women among the nomads and the villagers, and in the participation of both sexes in joint activities such as annual and family feasts. Nevertheless, it is a fact that men and women form two distinct and separate societies, with the family circle as the only locus for meeting on a day-to-day basis. It has been noted by one observer, for example, that three quarters of an hour before the sunset the young men of the village patrol up and down in front of the fountain, but when the girls approach to draw water, retire so as not to stand around oggling the women.[45]

This feeling of embarrassment in the presence of the opposite sex is characteristic of both men and women in many parts of the Middle East. Matters of sex, though discussed by men among themselves or by women among themselves, can never constitute a subject for public enjoyment or entertainment; sexual and physical modesty are the psychological concomitants of the strict moral code.

Aside from the exceptions referred to above, the standard for the Middle East is to regard premarital and extramarital sex relations of women with the utmost severity. In most nomadic tribes such a woman, if discovered, is put to death by her father or brothers (but not by her husband). No information as to the actual administration of such extreme punishment in villages is available, but the severity of the attitude toward female sexual laxity persists in them as well. Urban society is in a state of transition in this respect as in many other aspects of social intercourse. For lack of information all that can be said is a rough generalization to the effect that the higher the social class and the more advanced its Westernization, the less attention is paid by it to the traditional sexual code.

This being the situation, the majority of men and women have no opportunity for premarital or extramarital sexual activity, because this would immediately bring them into collision with the traditional guardians of female chastity: the women's fathers and brothers. There is an opinion, or suspicion, that this situation is favorable to the development of homosexual practices as well as sodomy, but for lack of data no statement can be ventured on this subject. In the towns, and especially in the port cities, prostitution

exists, in places in legalized form. During an Arab Women's
Congress in Cairo in 1944, a stand was taken against this legalized
prostitution, as well as against the white slave traffic.[46]

As to sexual relations in marriage, tradition allows complete
freedom to husband and wife, with the exception of the days
during and immediately after the menses and a longer period
after childbirth when relations are tabooed. To what extent these
prohibitions are actually observed by the various ecologic and
ethnoreligious groups in the Middle East is hard to say, because,
again, no data are available. Where a man has two wives, he is
traditionally expected to devote his attentions equally and
alternatingly to each of them.

The spread of education among the young men creates a
demand for the education of girls as well. The number of girls
receiving primary or secondary education is still much lower in
every Middle Eastern country than that of boys. One of the
results of this inequality is that a class of educated young men is
growing up which does not find equally educated women among
whom it could choose spouses. As can be expected, therefore, the
demand of the feminists for equal educational opportunities for
girls is seconded by the young educated males.

Typical of the change taking place at present in the Middle
Eastern urban society is the increasing freedom accorded to
women. Up to recent times, women in town as well as in country
were regarded as inferior to men. In the past, it was considered
a disgrace for a girl to work outside her home, but in recent years
girls have begun to seek employment in government offices,
schools, medical clinics, hospitals, and even in business. Nevertheless, even the educated urbanites, although consciously aware
of the equality of the educated woman, have not yet overcome the
feeling that she is weaker than man and that she requires help,
provision, and protection. Social life in the Western sense of
mixed public parties, etc., is only beginning to emerge. The girl
is always guarded by her family and chaperoned by her brothers,
sisters, or friends. She must always be at home before dark and is
never allowed to go home alone at night. A sign of the times is
that nowadays an engaged couple is occasionally allowed to walk
and talk together as long as they stay within the bounds of

morality, while not so long ago a fiancé was not supposed to see his betrothed until the wedding night.

A certain amount of separation between the sexes exists also among the conservative Christians in the Middle East. While the Maronites in Lebanon "do not segregate their women as do Muslims, and one may ask a man after his wife's health, a reserve is maintained in public or private, and one does not talk to a woman alone. Husband does not give his wife his arm when walking or talk familiarly with her in public. Men go with men, e.g. on Sunday to feasts, the women follow in a group. Even in church they sit separated by a wooden grill."[47]

TERM AND TRIAL MARRIAGE

Special forms of connubium that were practiced in pre-Islamic days and survived in certain parts of the Middle East down to the present time are the term marriage, usually referred to as *mut'ah*, or "enjoyment," and the trial marriage.

The first reports about term marriage in the Middle East are contained in Talmudic and Roman sources. The Talmud states unequivocally that among the Jews of Babylonia in the third century A.D. it was legal to marry a woman for a term as short as one day. After the expiration of the specified term the marriage was automatically terminated. In fact, even sages and rabbis when visiting in another town used to practice this custom. Of Rabh (third century A.D.) it is reported that when he visited the town of Dardashir (variant: Darshish) he used to have it announced: "Who wants to become my wife for one day?" Rabh Nahman (early fourth century A.D.) is reported to have done the same on his periodic visits to Shekansibh.[48]

Contemporary with the above is the report of the Roman historian, Ammianus Marcellinus (325–398 A.D.), who states (in Book XIV, Chap. 4, of his history of the Roman empire) that the Saracens of Arabia Felix (that is, Southern Arabia) "spend their lives in constant wanderings. They hire their women for money for a certain period according to agreement, and in order to make it a kind of marriage, the future wife offers the husband, under the name of a dowry (*dos*), a spear and a tent, so as to go away from him after the fixed day . . . ."

Term marriage seems to have been widely practiced all over Arabia in pre-Islamic days, and Mohammed therefore felt constrained to sanction it. The Koran (4 : 28) states, "such women as ye want to enjoy, give them their hire as a lawful due; for there is no crime in you about what ye agree between you after such lawful due." Nevertheless, term marriages were regarded as a lesser commitment than regular marriages and were, consequently, countenanced even with partners who were unfit for the latter. The story is told of a Ḥimyarite Sayyid who met a woman on the road and she offered him marriage then and there. However, when she found out from him that he was a Yemeni of the heretical Rāfiḍī sect, while she was of the rival Tamīmī tribe and of the Khārijite persuasion, she quickly withdrew her offer. But the Sayyid, who evidently got in the meantime keen on the idea, begged her: "Be of good sense and let your soul be generous toward me and let neither of us remember our ancestry or religion." She retorted: "When a marriage is made public, are not private concerns revealed?" The Sayyid then put forward a new idea: "I have a different suggestion to make to you ... namely *mutʿah*, of which no one need know anything." When the woman replied that term marriage is the sister of harlotry, the Sayyid reminded her that it was allowed according to the Koran, and the woman finally consented to this form of marriage.[49]

As to the payment a man had to render in order to enjoy term marriage with a woman, a piece of clothing was sufficient. Sabra, one of the companions of Mohammed, reminisced about such an experience he had shortly after the conquest of Mecca by the Prophet. "I went with one of my friends to a woman of the Bani ʿAmir, and we inquired whether she would be willing to contract *mutʿah*. She thereupon asked what we intended to give her, and we offered her our mantles. The mantle of my friend was finer than mine, but I was more handsome than he. When the woman looked at my friend's mantle, she was visibly inclined toward it; but when she saw me, I evoked her admiration. Thereupon she stated that she chose me, and that my mantle was sufficient payment. I remained with her for three days, and then the Prophet commanded all those who had women in *mutʿah* to send them away ...."

According to the same source, Mohammed's companions missed their wives during a military campaign to such an extent that they wanted to castrate themselves. This the Prophet forbade them to do, but he permitted them to contract term marriages.[50] Term marriage was regarded as a safeguard against immorality, and solicitous fathers ordered their sons to contract *mut'ah* while on pilgrimage to Mecca—at least according to one account describing such an event in the first half of the eighth century.[51]

Sunnī Islam nevertheless soon outlawed term marriages.[52] All the stringency of Sunnite jurisprudence remained, however, powerless to eradicate another variety of marriage closely related to, although not identical with, *mut'ah*. Many Muslim jurists agreed that only if a time limit is an expressly stated condition in the marriage contract is the marriage *mut'ah*, and thus forbidden; if a marriage is merely contracted with *the intention* that it should last only a definite period, it is valid and permitted. This type of marriage, in which both parties were fully aware that it was a temporary affair, was also widespread in pre-Islamic Arabia and has remained legal to this day.

The most famous of women practicing such provisional or trial marriages in the days of Mohammed was Umm Khārija. She was reputed to have had forty husbands from twenty different tribes. If a suitor came to her and said, "Will you marry me?" she answered, "It's a marriage," and the marriage could be consummated without any further formality or delay. It was the custom of the women who practiced these trial marriages that if they were satisfied with their new husbands they prepared for them food the morning after the wedding night; if not, they gave them no food, but sent them away. The mother of Mohammed's grandfather, it is said, was one of these oft-marrying women.[53]

In Arabia, including the holiest city of Islam, Mecca, these customs survived almost to the present time. In Ha'il and its environs in the Arabian Desert, temporary marriages little better than prostitution were common down to the 1860's. From other parts of the Peninsula their occurrence is reported as late as the beginning of the twentieth century. In many cases the temporary marriages were a concomitant of the pilgrimage to a holy city in which no hotels were available, but the pilgrim could find

5

accommodation in the house of a local woman provided he went through the formality of marrying her. The same situation obtained in connection with any other type of travel as well. As long as the man remained in the foreign city he thus had both a home and a wife. Before leaving, he pronounced the divorce formula, thereby ending all mutual obligations.[54]

In Egypt, a prohibition of prostitution (and of public female dancing) in 1834, with bastinado as the mandatory punishment for both culprits if caught, resulted in an increase in legal marriages of extremely short duration. The man would ask the woman, "Will you marry me?" and she would answer, "Yes." His next question would be, "For how much?" and she would name the sum. The man would give her the money and she would therewith become his lawfully wedded wife. Next morning he would pronounce the formula of divorce and go his way.[55]

Trial marriages of a usually somewhat longer duration are practiced to this day among certain tribes in Southern Arabia. The Say'ars told Ingrams "that they gave their girls to anyone who wanted them. After about a couple of months' trial the man might marry the girl, otherwise she would be returned with thanks and without ill-feelings."[56]

In contrast to Sunnī Islam, the Shī'ites retained term marriage as a legal institution to this day. Most of the reports term these *mut'ah* marriages—a form of legalized prostitution. It is especially in the holy cities of Shī'ite Islam that the *mut'ah* flourishes. Reliable travelers have observed in the course of the last hundred years that in the shadow of the Shī'ite sanctuaries many women contract this type of short-term union several times a day.[57]

However, the term marriage can serve also the opposite purpose: to make sure that a marriage does not end prematurely in divorce. To ensure this, some people contract *mut'ah* marriage for ninety-nine years. Since such a term marriage contract can be terminated prior to its specified expiration only with the consent of both contracting parties, it gives the wife a security she can never enjoy under a regular Muslim marriage. On the other hand, in a term marriage the husband has the right to refuse marital union which in ordinary marriage would give the woman the right to divorce. Children born of *mut'ah* marriage have all the right of the offspring of ordinary marriages, but the term wife (called *ṣīgha*), does not inherit from her husband, nor does he from her.[58]

FEMALE OCCUPATIONS

With regard to the occupations of women, the traditional situation all over the Middle East has been for them to be employed in the home and on the fields only. However, even the share of the women in agricultural work is but rarely reflected in statistical returns which, as a rule, do not count women as separate gainfully employed, or economically active, persons in case they merely help the male members of their families in the fields. It is for this reason that in the statistical returns of Egypt in 1937, only 896,950 women appeared as engaged in agriculture as against 5,198,032 men; or that among the Muslims in Palestine in 1931, only 8,451 women figured as engaged in "primary production" (mainly agriculture) as against 107,462 men.[59]

A true picture of the situation emerges from the Turkish census only, which in 1935 listed 2,734,025 women as against 2,843,752 men, as engaged in agriculture, and 3,096,799 women as against 3,383,269 men as engaged in "primary production."[60] The average Middle Eastern rural housewife undoubtedly takes her place in agricultural work at the side of her husband.

In addition to housework and fieldwork, the third traditional occupation of women in the Middle East is in the so-called "old industries," a term denoting the traditional and largely old-fashioned home industries, handicraft, rugmaking, and the like. In rural areas, the occasionally and sporadically practiced "old industries" are usually as much family undertakings as the tilling of the fields; they are taken up especially in the agricultural low seasons for the sake of augmenting the meager income of the family. In the towns, they are often carried out in small workshops in an employee capacity on a piece basis. The ratio of female to male labor employed in these "old industries" is exemplified by the results of an inquiry undertaken in 1937 in Syria and Lebanon which showed that 58,413 women were engaged in them as against 90,065 men (as well as 22,300 children).[61]

As to the so-called "new industries," that is, the recently established modern industrial undertakings, women have been much slower to take to them than men. The number of women employed in Syria and Lebanon in "new industries" in 1937 was 6,379 as against 24,007 men. The number of women employed in industry in Turkey (1935) was one fifth of the number of men, while in Egypt (1937) and among the Palestinian Muslims (1931) it was only one tenth.

The participation of women in commerce is even slighter. In Turkey 5 per cent, in Egypt 3 per cent of the total number of workers employed in commerce were women. It is only in domestic service that women are represented in some countries, for example in Turkey, by higher figures than men.

The meager participation of women in industrial work as well as in commerce as against their intensive participation in agricultural work means that the urban laborer, if he is a married man, has to earn enough to support his entire family, while the agricultural worker in the village is, as a rule, helped by his wife to make a living. The village-to-town migration and the exchange of agricultural work in favor of urban industrial labor therefore improves the economic conditions of a worker's family much less than would appear from the average income figures of family heads.

Another factor to consider in this connection is the difference between the ratio of female and male earnings in village and in town. While in the village the earnings of the women (as expressed in produce) can be as high as those of men, depending on the number of hours spent by each in the field, in urban industrial labor the wages of the women are in most cases much lower than those of men. In Syria and Lebanon in 1937, men earned in the old industries 10.50 francs, while women in similar types of work earned only 4.93 francs, that is, less than half. In new industries, men earned 13.40 fr., women 5.05 fr. In Iraq (1933), men earned 50 to 300 fils, women 25 to 50.[62] Similar differences between the wages of men and women exist in other countries.

THE EMANCIPATION OF WOMEN

Within the last forty-odd years Middle Eastern women of the leisure and educated class have been working actively toward raising the status of woman by studying her condition and agitating for reform. In Syria, "after World War I when the country became independent of Ottoman Turkey, women were still veiled but not inactive. However, the threats of traditionalists restricted them to rescue work and first-aid. Secondary schools for girls were opened by the Syrian government; some were sent to Europe for further study. The University of Damascus finally graduated two lady doctors from 'very good families' and two more as bachelors of law." A periodical, *El Arousse* (*The Bride*), was launched and dedicated to women by a woman authoress. A school for the daughters of Syrian war victims was opened by a woman, and patriotic and national associations for women were organized, among them the "Society of the Tree of Literature," led by a lady of the family of Prince Abd-el-Kader; the "Society of the Drop of Milk," which provides infants with milk; the "Society of the Red Crescent" (emulating the Red Cross), which has branches operated by women, and others.[63]

In Lebanon similar efforts were made by the Federation of Arab Women's Clubs (founded in 1921), an organization comprising 28 member societies with more than 2,000 members and representing the various creeds and institutions in that country.[64] In Turkey, the law of 1934 accorded political rights to women. In Iran, where the emancipation of women was proclaimed in 1938, the reform measures lost much of their vigor after the abdication of Riza Shah Pehlevi in 1941. In Egypt, feminist movements led by the Egyptian Feminist Association, have been organized for the purpose of obtaining general suffrage. In 1944, an Arab Women's Congress was held in Cairo. Delegations from several Arab countries participated and important resolutions concerning the status of women in the Arab world were passed.[65]

Among the things for which modern Middle Eastern women have been fighting has been the right to enter the professions, for while some women have gained entrance into medicine, dentistry, nursing, law, and education, most of them are still governed by tradition and custom. However, "the new generation is overcoming the old prejudice which 20 years ago thrust the woman doctor down to the level of a midwife and nothing else. Journalism has been attempted by one or two women. The difficulty there is that a woman is somewhat restricted in going about in search of copy. . . . Girls who wished to learn typing and shorthand and go into offices were warned by their parents and guardians that they would probably lose their character if they did anything 'so fast.' However, some more far-sighted people said that if they went to English or American offices they would be quite safe."[66]

VI. Cousin Marriage

T HE MIDDLE Eastern family has been characterized above as patrilineal, patrilocal, patriarchal, extended, occasionally polygynous, and emphatically endogamous. The first five of these six basic traits are found also in one or more of the culture areas contiguous to the Middle East. The sixth, endogamy, and especially its most conspicuous Middle Eastern form, which is marriage between a man and his father's brother's daughter (*bint 'amm* in Arabic), is practically nonexistent outside the Middle Eastern culture continent.

COUSIN MARRIAGE OUTSIDE THE MIDDLE EAST

Outside the Middle East the practice of marriage between children of two brothers is extremely rare. With the spread of Islam it was introduced into India where the Muslims have a definite preference for all types of cousin marriages, with marriage between the children of two brothers being the most common. The verbalized motivation is the one usual in the Middle East: cousin marriage keeps the family free from foreign blood and retains property within the family.[1]

In Madagascar marriage between the children of two brothers also is very common, and is looked upon as the most suitable marriage since it keeps the property in the family. Since descent is matrilineal, however, a man marrying his father's brother's daughter is not considered marrying a blood relative. Children of two siblings of opposite sex are allowed to marry after the performance of a rite whose purpose is to remove the impediment of consanguinity; but marriage between the children of two uterine

135

sisters is regarded with horror as incest.[2] Although there is a strong Arabic element in the language of Madagascar,[3] which is a clear evidence of the presence of Arab influences on the island, this marriage preference pattern is very different from the Middle Eastern one, in spite of the frequency of marriage between children of two brothers.

According to one authority, among the Bantu tribes of South Africa the natives of the mountains "of the interior" almost as a rule married the daughter of their father's brother, in order to keep property from being lost to the family.[4] For lack of more detailed information it is not possible to state whether this Bantu marriage pattern resembles the Middle Eastern or the Madagascan type.

In other parts of the world, cousin marriage means cross-cousin marriage; marriage between the children of two brothers is usually prohibited, or, in rare instances, grudgingly tolerated.[5]

HALF-SIBLING AND COUSIN MARRIAGE IN ANTIQUITY

In the Middle East itself the practice of cousin marriage and even of half-sibling marriage goes back to antiquity.

In ancient Egypt, the Pharaohs married their sisters or half-sisters, a practice continued by the Ptolemies.[6] In Roman Egypt, marriage between full siblings and half-siblings occurred frequently in the families of agriculturists and artisans.[7] According to Diodorus (i, 27), sibling marriage was a duty for Egyptians. However, it has to be taken into consideration that in ancient Egypt the wife was called "sister," and lovers called each other "brother" and "sister," even when they were not siblings.[8]

Whether there was brother-sister marriage in ancient Iran[9] is open to serious doubts in view of objections raised by both Parsi scholars[10] and Western students. According to these authorities, what the early Iranians practiced was marriage between first cousins, which is certainly the meaning of the modern Persian equivalent of the contested ancient term. In the Pehlevi texts, which in their present form date from the sixth to the ninth century, marriages between parents and children as well as between siblings are defended and advocated, as they are in the later period of the Sassanian dynasty and in subsequent centuries.

However, from the fifteenth century on, in the Persian writings called "Rivayat," references are found to marriage of first cousins only, with obscure allusions to marriage between closer blood relations as being long extinct.[11] The ancient Persians seem to have used the terms "sister," "mother," and "daughter" both in their proper sense and in a wider sense as did the ancient Egyptians, and great care is required to avoid confusion in interpreting them.[12] Similarly, among the ancient Hebrews, and the ancient and modern Arabs, these and other kinship terms were and respectively are used in a wider sense as well. Among the Phoenicians, King Tabnith married his father's daughter (by another mother), Am'ashtoreth, and at Tyre a man was allowed to marry his father's daughter down to the time of Achilles Tatius. The same thing occurred at Mecca; and a trace of this kind of marriage has survived to modern times at Mirbāṭ.[13]

Paternal half-sibling marriage occurred, and cousin marriage was the prevalent practice among the Hebrews in the patriarchal period.[14] Abraham himself married his half-sister Sarah (from the same father but from another mother; cf. Gen. 20 : 12). Isaac married his father's brother's son's daughter (Gen. 22 : 23; 24 : 47, 48). Nahor married a daughter of his brother, Haran (Gen. 11 : 27, 29). Esau married his father's brother's two daughters, Mahalath and Basemath (Gen. 28 : 9; 36 : 3). Jacob married his mother's brother's two daughters, Leah and Rachel (Gen. 29), who were also his father's father's brother's son's son's daughters.

Close in-family marriage was practiced by the Hebrews in later times as well. Amram married Jochebed, his father's sister (Ex. 6 : 20; Num. 26 : 59). Amram's son Aaron married his father's father's father's brother's son's son's son's son's daughter Elisheba (I Chron. 2 : 10; Ex. 6 : 23). Hezron (a grandson of Judah) married his father's father's brother's son's son's daughter (I Chron. 2 : 4, 21; Gen. 50 : 23). The sons of Kish married the daughters of his brother Eleazar (I Chron. 23 : 21–22). In the days of King David marriage betwen paternal half-siblings was still legal (II Sam. 13). Marriage between brother and sister was still practiced in Judah at the time of Ezekiel (sixth century B.C.), although the prophet strongly condemned it as an abomination (Ezek. 22 : 11).

5§

The hero of the Book of Tobit marries his father's brother's daughter, and according to the angel who accompanies Tobit, it would have been a mortal sin for Reuel (Tobit's uncle) to give his daughter to anybody else but to Tobit who had the right to inherit from his sonless uncle (cf. Book of Tobit 6; 1 ff. and 7 : 2, 10–12).

In the Arab world itself, while the right of a man to the hand of his *bint 'amm* goes back to pre-Islamic times,[15] marriage between half-siblings has disappeared following the spread of Islam. The only Muslim population that has countenanced it until recently seems to be the Mohammadan South Slavs.[16]

EXTENT AND FREQUENCY

The custom of cousin marriage has been confirmed and perpetuated by Muslim tradition and has remained alive down to the present day in all parts of the Middle East. According to the Hanafite school of legists, a man may give his daughter in marriage to his brother's son without her consent, and a young man may decide for himself whether he wants or does not want to marry his *bint 'amm*.[17] The fact that marriage between children of two brothers is regarded as the ideal marriage and is preferred in practice to all other unions is reflected in everyday linguistic usage. The common term a man employs in addressing his wife in Arabic is *bint 'ammī*, meaning "daughter of my father's brother"; while the wife addresses her husband as *ibn 'ammī*, son of my father's brother, whether the two actually stand in this relationship to each other or not.

The preference for cousin marriage is reflected in numerous proverbs and stories current among the Bedouins of Arabia and in the lands of the Fertile Crescent.[18] Marriage between the *ibn 'amm* and *bint 'amm* is well attested from all parts of the Middle East, and in several places the two are the usual marriage partners. In Turkey also marriages are arranged inside a large family circle.[19] In Iraq and all over the Arabian Peninsula, with few exceptions, marriage between children of two brothers is customary and preferred.[20]

The same custom exists in Iran as well. Ella C. Sykes reports that "if a girl is wedded to a cousin, which is constantly done to

keep the property of a family together, she will never have ex-
changed a word with him since childhood, save in the family
circle . . . ."[21] Although the author does not state whether the
cousin in question is the girl's father's brother's son, this seems to
be indicated by the reference to the contact between the two
young people in childhood, which would be possible only in case
they are the children of two brothers living in one household as
members of the same extended, patrilineal, and patrilocal family.
Also, the purpose of keeping the family property together is
achieved only if the bride and groom are the children of two
brothers, in which case the payment of the bride price is actually
nothing more than a financial transaction between two brothers
within the frame of one and the same extended family.

In fact, a Persian proverb states clearly: "The marriage of the
daughter of the father's brother with the son of the father's brother
is tied (i.e. decided upon) in heaven."[22]

This being the general view, "marriages between cousins are
very much sought after, and the children of such marriages are
if anything superior in physique to others."[23] The practice used
to be followed from the lowest to the highest ranks of Persian
society. In October 1867 the Crown Prince of Persia was married
to his cousin, both being sixteen years of age.[24]

Among the nomadic tribes of the Upper Helmand River in
Afghanistan "when a boy wants his first wife his mother selects a
girl for him, usually one from the same band."[25] The reference
here is probably to cousin marriage.

In Egypt, marriage between *ibn 'amm* and *bint 'amm* seems to
be even more prevalent than in Arabia. Lane observed in the
1830's that "It is very common among the Arabs of Egypt and of
other countries, but less so in Cairo than in other parts of Egypt,
for a man to marry his first cousin. In this case, the husband and
wife continue to call each other "cousin"; because the tie of blood
is indissoluble, but that of matrimony very precarious . . . . A
union of this kind is generally lasting, on account of this tie of
blood; and because mutual intercourse may have formed an
attachment between the parties in tender age; though if they be
of higher or middle classes, the young man is seldom allowed to
see the face of his female cousin, or even to meet and converse

with her, after she has arrived at or near the age of puberty, until she has become his wife."[26] To this day, in Egypt, "marriages between children of *'amm* and *khāl* are most common; others are concluded within the wider circle of the family."[27]

In Upper Egypt also the father's brother's daughter is the favorite marriage partner.[28] Similarly, among the Kabābīsh, a Sudan Arab tribe, the first choice is the father's brother's daughter, second choice the mother's brother's daughter, and third choice the mother's sister's daughter.[29]

Among the Copts of Egypt marriage between a man and his father's brother's daughter is as customary as among the Muslims.[30]

In the Oasis of Siwa also, close to the western border of Egypt, the Middle Eastern pattern of cousin-marriage is often followed.[31]

Only in a very few cases do we have any knowledge of the actual frequency of *bint 'amm* marriages in any period or any locality. In most reports in which mention is made of *bint 'amm* marriage, it is stated that these are "common" or "frequent" or "usual," but no precise data as to the percentage of *bint 'amm* marriages in relation to all the marriages is given. The more valuable are the rare studies that do contain such figures, although not in every case can one put equal reliance on them.

Remarkably enough, the first numerical evaluation of the frequency of in-family marriages refers not to cousin marriage but to brother-sister marriage. According to Erman and Ranke, under the Emperor Commodus (161–192 A.D.) two thirds of all the citizens of the township of Arsinoë in Roman Egypt had a sister as wife.[31]

Cousin marriage in the late pre-Islamic period in the Ḥijāz was much less frequent than the above figure. In Medina, in the days of Mohammed, and within one or two generations preceding him, marriage with *bint 'amm* was practiced but was not too frequent. Of 21 marriages reported by Muḥammad ibn Sa'd (167/8–230 A.H.) as having been contracted by men belonging to the clan of Banī 'Āmir ibn Zurayq, four were with daughters of their father's brothers. In the same period at Mecca, out of a total of 71 marriages contracted by Mohammed's own clan, 9 were *bint 'amm* marriages, 23 were within the clan, 21 were with other clans of the Quraysh tribe to which Mohammed's clan belonged, and only 18 were with other tribes. In another clan of the Quraysh, the Makhzum, out of 25 marriages two were with the *bint 'amm*, one was within the clan, 16 were with other clans of the Quraysh, and six men (and no women) married into other tribes. In late pre-Islamic Ḥijāz therefore of the 113 marriages recorded only 15 were between the children of two brothers, or 13.3 per cent of the total. This relatively low incidence seems to be contingent on the absence of one of the main motivations of such marriages, namely the inheritance of property by daughters that was introduced by Mohammed. It has to be considered also that in the period in question, the term *bint 'amm* was not confined to father's brother's daughter, but was used loosely with reference to second, third, etc., cousins, as long as the relationship could be traced to two brothers.[33]

In modern Egypt, according to Father Ayrouth, a lifelong student of the Egyptian fellahin, 80 per cent of all the marriages contracted by the fellahin take place between first cousins.[34] Another authority who in the 1870's lived for many years in Upper Egypt states that "in two thirds of the cases it has been previously settled that the young man is to marry his female cousin, and if he has none, more distant relations are applied to, and lastly strangers.[35]

In one Upper Egyptian Coptic family studied by Legrain, there were five brothers who among them had six married sons and seven married daughters. All the six married sons had a *bint 'amm* for wife, and only one of the seven married daughters had not an *ibn 'amm* but an outsider for husband.[36]

Barth, in his study of social organization of Southern Kurdistan, found that in tribal villages 57 per cent of all the marriages were cousin marriages (48 per cent *bint 'amm* marriages) while in a nontribal village (made up of recent immigrant families) only 17 per cent were cousin marriages (13 per cent *bint 'amm* marriages). The frequency of family endogamy in the tribal villages was 71 per cent, in the nontribal village 37 per cent, while that of village endogamy was in the tribal villages 80 per cent, in the nontribal villages 78 per cent.[37] In two normal-sized tribal villages in the Hamawand area Barth found that out of a total of 21 marriages nine were contracted between paternal parallel cousins.[38]

In the South Palestinian Arab village of Arṭās in the 1920's, of 264 marriages 35, or 13.3 per cent, were *bint 'amm* marriages; 69, or 26.1 per cent, were marriages with *bint 'amm* plus marriages with second cousin or first cousin once removed; 89, or 33.7 per cent, were all the marriages within the *ḥamūla* (clan); and 151 or 57.2 per cent was the number of all the in-village marriages.[39]

The Middle Eastern cousin marriage pattern extends from Egypt and the Sudan all across the northern one third of Africa. In the oasis-village of Sīdī Khāled, some 170 miles south of the port of Algiers, the ideal marriage is between children of two brothers. Further to the south, among the Mzabites, the preferred form of marriage is between children of brothers, among both the Muslims and the Jews. The same preference obtains also among the Chaamba, an Arab nomad tribe, and among the Moors of the extreme western Sahara.[39a]

In the town of Timbuctoo, a field investigator found that among the Arabs one third of the marriages are between cousins. "Half of these are with father's brother's daughters. Slightly fewer marriages are with mother's brother's daughters. The two other kinds of first cousins are taken to wife only rarely. . . . It is possible that the frequent marriage with mother's brother's daughter is the result of Songhoi influence."[40] Since the Arabs in Timbuctoo are immigrants from North Africa and their descendants, they must have brought along with them the Middle Eastern preference for *bint 'amm* marriage. The Songhoi consist of two groups, both speaking Songhoi only. One is the Gabibi, a group indigenous to the Sudan, among whom a preference for marriage with mother's brother's daughter and a definite dislike for marriage with father's brother's daughter is found. The other Songhoi group is the Arma, who are the descendants of sixteenth-century Moroccan Arab invaders and their Sudanese wives. Among these there is a preference for marriage with both father's brother's daughter and mother's sister's daughter. The third ethnic group inhabiting Timbuctoo is the Bela, who are Tuareg slaves, and among whom marriage between cross cousins is preferred in principle, while children of two brothers are considered "prime enemies." However, in spite of the stated preference for cross-cousin marriage, marriages between the children of two brothers were found to be as numerous as marriages with mother's brother's daughter. Marriage with father's sister's daughter did not occur and distaste for it was apparent. While Miner may be right in seeing Songhoi influence in the frequency of marriage with mother's brother's daughter among the Arabs of Timbuctoo, the data from Egypt, Palestine, etc., seem rather to indicate that it may ultimately go back to a general Middle Eastern pattern in which the right of the *ibn khāl* to marry a girl is second only to the right of the *ibn 'amm*. On the other hand, there can be little doubt that the greater frequency of marriages between children of two brothers "in spite of the stated preference for cross-cousin marriage"[41] must be the result of Arab Middle Eastern influence.

THE BRIDE PRICE

The preference of Middle Eastern society for cousin marriage is expressed in financial arrangements as well. All over the area it is customary for the bridegroom to pay a dowry or bride price to his bride. In effect, the bride price is as a rule paid by the father of the bridegroom to the father of the bride, and the latter is supposed to spend all or most or part of it, depending on the economic status of the family, on the outfitting of his daughter.[42] An additional provision is that the bride price agreed upon between the two fathers is not paid in full at the time or before the wedding. Part of it (in many cases one third) has to be paid only in case the husband divorces his wife, thus serving both as a deterrent against divorce (which can be effected any time and instantly by the husband) and as a trust fund for the divorced wife to draw upon.

The amount of the bride price varies greatly in different parts of the Middle East, as well as in different economic strata within the same locality. It may also depend on a number of additional factors, such as the beauty and age of the bride and, in exceptional cases, differences in status and prestige between the two intermarrying families. But, these other factors apart, the bride price is usually about twice as high if the bride is not a relative of the bridegroom as in the case of marriage between cousins or other close relatives. Among the better-off fellahin of Egypt, for instance, in the 1950's, the bride price of a cousin or other close relative varied from £E100 to £E150, while in the case of nonrelatives it ranged from £E200 to £E300.[43] Among poor fellahin (the overwhelming majority) the bride price paid for a cousin bride varied from £E15 to £E50.[44]

The custom of giving away the girl to her *ibn 'amm* for a reduced bride price is widespread in the Middle East.[45] Among the Rwala and other nomadic tribes of the Syrian Desert, the *ibn 'amm* may insist on paying a greatly reduced bride price for his cousin.[46]

Reduced bride price in the case of cousin marriage is the rule also among the fellahin of the Fertile Crescent.[47] Among the Kurds also "It is an agreed privilege for paternal cousins, to less extent also other near kin, to receive the girl at a reduced bride price. The normal bride price for village girls ranges between £30 and £100. Paternal cousins generally pay only wedding expenses."[48]

The considerable saving made possible by cousin marriage is a powerful factor in the eyes of the groom's family in favor of such marriages. Middle Eastern families in overwhelming majority are very poor, and cash expenditure is extremely difficult. Although the family of which the father is the head acquires, in return for the payment of the bride price, a new pair of working hands as well as a hopeful source of future sons, still the outlay requires an exceptional effort. This is the case not only in the settled sector of the population among whom the bride price is usually paid in cash, but also among the nomads who pay the bride price in valuables and especially in camels. And since under traditional circumstances the choice of the bride lies in the hands of the groom's father who is also expected to pay the bride price, it is easy to understand that the economic consideration of being able to save half of the bride price weighs heavily with him when making his choice. Thus it is in the economic interest of the father and of the bridegroom's family in general to choose his cousin for him as his bride.

As to the bride's family, they are expected to spend all or part

of the bride price on the outfitting of the bride, or to give her the
entire bride price or a considerable part of it.[49] Therefore, the
purely economic interest of the bride's father in a higher bride
price is not as primary as is the economic interest of the bridegroom's father in a lower bride price. Consequently, there is not
as strong a financial motivation in the case of the bride's father
against cousin marriage as there is in the case of the bridegroom's
father for it.

In the following sections we shall deal in greater detail with
what is probably the most significant aspect of Middle Eastern
cousin marriage: the compulsory nature of *bint 'amm* marriage as
manifested in the unwritten law that a man has the right to
marry his *bint 'amm* and that nobody else is allowed to marry a
girl until and unless her *ibn 'amm* (that is her father's brother's son)
gives his consent.

CENTRAL ARABIA

Let us begin our survey with the historical core of Middle
Eastern culture, the Arabian Peninsula. In all parts of the Peninsula (with a very few exceptions, of which later) a man's right to
his father's brother's daughter is upheld. This right is not voided
even by a great discrepancy in age. The force of this traditional
right is so strong that when it is infringed and then avenged by
the offended male cousin by bloodshed, this meets public appro-
bation.[50]

In the reports on the cousin's right, no difference in emphasis
can be discovered between the accounts of travelers and explorers
of the nineteenth century and of the twentieth century, which
seems to indicate that no relaxation of this traditional law has
taken place in the last one hundred or one hundred and fifty years.
One of the early nineteenth-century accounts is that of J. L.
Burckhardt. According to him, "All Arabian Bedouins acknowledge the first cousin's prior right to a girl; whose father cannot
refuse to bestow her upon him in marriage. ... A man has an
exclusive right to the hand of his cousin; he is not obliged to
marry her, but she cannot, without his consent, become the wife
of another person. If a man permits his cousin to marry her lover,

or if a husband divorces a runaway wife, he usually says, 'She was my slipper, I have cast her off.' "[51] Similarly Burton reports that "Every Badawi has a right to marry his father's brother's daughter before she is given to a stranger; hence 'cousin' (*Bint Amm*) in polite phrase signifies a 'wife'. "[52]

Doughty, on his way down to Medina, was told that marriage "betwixt brothers' children" was the most lawful. On one occasion he was asked by a petty shaykh whose wife, Hirfa, had run away, to persuade her to return to him. Upon undertaking this mission, Doughty was received by Hirfa's kinfolk, and her young cousin said to him: "I am her father (meaning, 'I have the *patria potestas* over her') and Hirfa is mine, Khalil; no! we will not give her more to Zeyd."[53] Wilfrid Blunt had a similar experience when he went to ask for the hand of a girl on behalf of a friend of his in the Nejd. While the negotiations over the bride price were in progress, a cousin "appeared on the scene and claimed his right to Muttra or an equivalent for her in coin."[54] William Robertson Smith, speaking of the township of Taif in Ḥijāz to the east of Mecca, states that "It must be understood that the preference for marriage between cousins, which exists also in Egypt, has here the character of a binding custom. A father cannot refuse his daughter to his brother's son, although another suitor offers a much higher dowry, unless the cousin is of weak intellect or notoriously of bad character. The cousin, if rejected for a rich suitor, can step in even at the last moment and stop the wedding."[55]

SOUTHERN ARABIA

The same rule holds good generally in Southern Arabia.[56] However, in the Qara Mountains (in the hinterland of the Ẓufar coast in Southern Arabia), the right of the *ibn 'amm* to marry his father's brother's daughter is insisted upon only among the Mahra, a seminomadic cattle-breeding tribe. Among the other tribes of these mountains the sole right of disposal vests in the father of the girl.[57] The probable explanation of this exception is that these relatively isolated mountain tribes have not been sufficiently exposed to Muslim-Middle Eastern cultural influences and therefore have retained different (and probably older) customs.

Also among the Jews of Yemen cousin marriages are frequently practiced and occasionally insisted upon by the *ibn 'amm*. Several cases are known in which the consent of the *ibn 'amm* to the marriage of his *bint 'amm* with another man had to be bought.[58] In the village of al-Gades in Lower Yemen, studied and described by Goitein, "the predilection for marriages among cousins had the actual effect of endogamy; the general tendency was to marry close relatives. ... It has been noted as early as the eighteenth century that Ṣan'a Jews regarded it a special blessing if a man had a great-grandchild from his own grandson and grand-daughter."[59]

NORTHERN ARABIA

The nomadic tribes of Northern Arabia represent in this respect (as in many others) true Arabian traditions. The foremost tribe occupying a large wandering territory in the western section of this area is that of the Rwala. Among them, the *ibn 'amm* has the right to marry his *bint 'amm*. His position in relation to her is so strong that if any other man wants to marry the girl, he has to come to the *ibn 'amm*, ask his permission, and pay him what he wants. Curiously, Musil makes the statement that the "eben el-'amm is generally a son of her (the girl's) father's *cousin*," whereas all that is known of this custom makes us expect the *ibn 'amm* to be among the Rwala as well the girl's father's *brother's son*. It would seem that the otherwise meticulous and accurate Musil made a mistake here. This becomes more likely if we read what Musil says in the same context, namely that if the girl has no *ibn 'amm*, she falls to the next nearest kinsman in the male line. This makes it the more probable that the *ibn 'amm* must be the nearest male relative with whom marriage is possible, that is the father's brother's son. If the *ibn 'amm* does not give his consent to the marriage of his *bint 'amm* to another man, the girl may be doomed to become an old maid. If the girl refuses to marry her *ibn 'amm* he may kill her without becoming liable to compensation. Only if the father of the girl gives her in exchange for a woman whom he himself wants to marry does this exchange marriage void the rights of the *ibn 'amm*.[60] Among other tribes also in the same area, if a man marries his daughter to another man without the consent of her *ibn 'amm* he risks his life, and there are many instances of blood revenge provoked by such acts.[61]

If the girl is in love with another man and the cousin gives her up, that is, foregoes exercising his right to marry her, this is regarded as a noble deed, worthy of praise and of being commemorated in song and story.[62]

FED'ĀN CASE HISTORIES

The right of the *ibn 'amm* to the hand of his *bint 'amm* is so strong that even a most powerful shaykh cannot prevail against it. Several case histories reported from the Bedouins of the Syrian Desert bear this out.

"Aisheh was passionately loved by two men, the brilliant chief shaykh Jed'ān [of the Fed'ān] and her cousin Shanteri for whom she had only contempt and aversion. This state of affairs continued for several years, and if Aisheh did not become the wife of Jed'ān this was not because of lack of consent on the part of her parents, but because Shanteri obstinately refused to give his consent, which was indispensable. A very rigorous law of the desert confers on the first cousin of a girl a right of preference to her hand, an exclusive right which he is free to use or not to use. His female cousin is not forced to marry him, but she cannot marry anybody else until he consents to renounce his right. . . .

"Shanteri was a fine young man but he was lazy and idle. He never wanted to participate in an act of war, not even in a raid (*ghazzu*). He was effeminate, afraid of danger and exertion. He loved to adorn himself with fine clothes and to strut in the shade in idleness, without any sense of shame; and all these are faults which make a man despised by our women. . . . His rival, on the contrary, had all the qualities which are esteemed in our nomadic society. The aversion Aisheh felt for the one and her passion for the other thus can be explained easily: these sentiments earned for her the honor and sympathy of all, but there was the law which had to be respected and obeyed in spite of all other considerations.

"Jed'ān made many efforts to make Shanteri give up his right. Persuasion, flatterings, menaces, rich presents, seductive promises, nothing succeeded. Shanteri knew well that he was despised and detested. But spite, jealousy, and hatred kept his passion alive and gained the upper hand over his greed, love of gain, luxury and idleness. . . .

"[Jed'ān could do nothing to force the issue, because there is in the desert] a sanction which is based on public opinion and on the solidarity of honor and interest among all without exception, and which is the foundation of nomadic life and its safeguard, and without which a terrible anarchy would reign in the desert. A man who does not respect the laws and customs and does not fulfil the duties imposed by them commits a dishonorable and contemptible act, the scandal and the consequences of which would spread from the individual to his family which accepts only rarely the solidarity [with a dishonest act], and from the family to the tribe which does never accept it. Hence there is a double pressure on the individual, a pressure to which he most often submits, or else he is forced to go to live with another tribe. . . . Jed'ān and Aisheh did not want to be in such a situation at any price. Also, an elopement does not lead to marriage. The consent of the cousin in this case is even more necessary for the validity of the marriage than that of the parents. Shanteri would have refused it without pity; he would have found his vengeance and Aisheh would have become merely the concubine of Jed'ān, a dishonor to which every noble 'Aneze girl prefers death. And for her family this would have been an opprobrium which it could not have left unpunished, even if this had resulted in bloody conflicts.

"Too proud and too superior ever to give herself to her odious and miserable cousin, the beautiful Aisheh, innocent and hopeless victim of an inflexible law, will probably remain an old maid."[63]

This story was recorded in 1866. Twelve years later Jed'ān again underwent a very similar experience. In the meantime he not only strengthened his chieftainship over the Fed'ān, but became the military leader (*'aqīd*) of the Sba'a, another 'Aneze tribe, as well. He was now a powerful leader of two of the greatest 'Aneze tribes. In 1878, when he was fifty-five years old, he contracted a marriage (his fifteenth) with a thirty-year-old girl from the Sirḥān, a small 'Aneze tribe to which also his mother belonged. Thirty years is, of course, quite an old age for a Bedouin girl. The reason for this particular pretty girl having remained unmarried until so late an age was that her cousin had claimed her for himself in marriage and then had kept her waiting year after year without either marrying her or setting her free. But since Jed'ān was a powerful shayh, the girl's father was persuaded to disregard the cousin's right, and his daughter's wedding with Jed'ān was duly cerebrated. However, from the very outset there was some doubt as to whether the marriage was legal, since it was contracted without obtaining the cousin's consent.

Soon after the wedding, the girl's cousin, a twenty-three-year-old man, brought action against Jed'ān for the recovery of his cousin, on the plea that he had not consented to her marriage. This case was of considerable interest, because the two adversaries were a powerful shaykh and a young man of no consequence, who was regarded by everybody as a hotheaded youth and who, in addition, was generally known to have behaved ill to the girl having put her off from year to year until the girl's father grew tired of waiting. Moreover, since he was twenty-three and the girl thirty, it was assumed that his only interest in the matter was a financial one. Jed'ān, on the other hand, seems to have had no knowledge of the existence of this cousin until after the marriage, and even then he thought that it would be merely a case of damages. But the cousin demanded the girl herself, or four other daughters in her stead: a claim which according to the local custom could be considered legitimate. The father of the girl offered him his only remaining daughter in place of the one married to Jed'ān, but the cousin did not want to hear of this, and, in order to show his anger and insistence, he ran one of the old man's camels through with his spear.

Thus the matter had to be referred for arbitration to Muḥammed Dukhi ibn Smeyr, shaykh of the Weld 'Alī (another 'Aneze tribe, friendly to the Sba'a), a man of about fifty, of considerable importance and influence. The deliberations started with a preliminary argument as to whether the case should be tried according to the Bedouin *'urf* (i.e., local traditional) law, or by the Muslim *sharī'a* law. According to the *'urf*, either the marriage of the girl with Jed'ān would have to be annulled or the entire dowry received by the girl's father from Jed'ān (the actual amount was 2,000 piasters) would have to be given to the cousin.

The cousin, of course, argued that the Bedouin law must apply. The argument for the other side was that the Muslim *sharī'a* law should apply; this would have held the offer of another daughter as a sufficient compensation for the cousin, on the principle that "an injured man, if replaced in the position held before injury, ceases to be injured." This idea, that the *sharī'a* law be applied, stemmed from a jurist from Aleppo who happened to be a guest of Jed'ān and his tribe. The attempt was doomed to failure, as everybody knew that the Bedouin *'urf* law must prevail.

While these preliminaries were in progress, Beteyen ibn Mershid, shaykh of the Gomussa section of the Sba'a, arrived in the camp in order to be present at the decision of this important suit. However, Muḥammed Dukhi shirked the responsibility of deciding such a weighty lawsuit himself, and the case was referred to three arbitrators chosen by the two parties. One of the three was objected to by one side. The second was objected to by the other side. The third, remaining alone and afraid of the responsibility, declared that he would be unable to bring a decision without reference to the shaykh of the Sirḥān, the tribe to which the girl and her cousin belonged. It was agreed to adjourn the case until the arrival of the Sirḥān who were encamped at a distance of several hundreds of miles in the Jauf, in the Lower Ḥamad in the desert, from where they came up north only rarely. When the Sirḥān finally arrived, the cousin of the girl brought his complaint to the shaykh of the Sirḥān. His decision was that since the girl had taken no steps prior to her marriage to Jed'ān to oblige her cousin to keep his promise and marry her, the cousin's rights remained valid. When this decision was announced to Jed'ān, he at once put his new wife on a camel and sent her to the shaykh of the Sirḥān. Thereupon a great wedding was solemnized between the girl and her cousin, Jed'ān being among the guests attending, "and no ill-will on either side marred the cordial enjoyment of festivities for three whole days."[64]

RWALA CASE HISTORIES

Even if a man is not in a position to marry his *bint 'amm* forthwith, for lack of funds to pay the bride price or for any other reason, he may "reserve" the girl for himself by making a public and formal declaration of his intentions to marry her at a future date. Although ordinarily such a reservation of the *bint 'amm* would not seem to be necessary, if it is done it clinches the cousin's claim, so to speak, and has the character of a formal engagement. Talāl and Saṭṭām were brothers, members of the princely family of the Rwala, the Sha'lān. Ṭalāl's son, 'Abdallah, reserved a daughter of Saṭṭām for himself, and "would not permit her to marry anyone else, asserting that as her nearest relative he had the first right to her."[65]

It can also happen that a man who is not the *ibn 'amm* of a girl, but a more remote relative, reserves her for himself soon after her birth, and in this case he acquires priority. Sa'ūd, son of Nūrī b. Sha'lān, emir of the Rwala, loved the sister of his mother, and she loved him, but he could not marry her because a more distant relative of her, 'Abdallah eben Ṭalāl (Nūrī's brother's son) had reserved her for himself a few days after her birth. Ever since then the girl belonged to him, and no one could marry her without his consent. To make the matter more involved, the brothers of the girls (her father seems to have died, and therefore her brothers had the *patria potestas* over her) did not permit her to marry 'Abdallah, but declared their readiness to give her to Sa'ūd eben Nūrī. Thus the girl was able to marry neither the man whom she loved nor the man who had the sole right to marry her. Prince Nūrī b. Sha'lān, when he told the story to Musil, remarked: "We could compel him ['Abdallah] to release her, but we do not wish to alienate him. . . ."[66]

A third case reported from the same princely family throws additional light on the rights and involvements of cousin marriage. Prince Nūrī had a brother, Fahad, with whose approval a certain Ṭrad al-'Arafa who posed as Fahad's son but who in reality was the son of Khalaf eben Iden, forced one of Nūrī's daughters into his tent intending to marry her. The girl, however, was able to jerk herself loose from him, and she fled into the desert where she was found by her brother Nawwāf. Nawwāf was greatly incensed at the injury done to his sister and persuaded Nūrī not to tolerate such a disgrace. Nūrī, although he was the paramount shaykh of the Rwala, felt it necessary to be assisted by three chiefs, and together with them went to Fahad to talk the matter over peaceably. After a long conference it was agreed that Ṭrad should not have Nūrī's daughter for a wife.[67]

JORDAN

The example quoted above (p. 150) shows that the *ibn 'amm* can lodge his complaint and obtain redress even after the consummation of the marriage of his *bint 'amm* with an outsider. Among the tribes inhabiting the area east of the Jordan and the Dead Sea (which in the past was variously called Arabia Petraea or Moab and most of which today forms part of the Kingdom of Jordan) the *ibn 'amm* enjoys similar rights. "In Arabia Petraea the *ibn 'amm* can interfere at the last moment with the marriage of his *bint 'amm* to another man. In order to circumvent the claim of the *ibn 'amm*, a man will carry off a girl and place her under the protection of another tribe, and then return to her father and enter into negotiations for the marriage."[68]

According to another observer, a man not only has the right to, but *must* claim for himself, to the exclusion of every other suitor, the hand of the daughter of his paternal or maternal uncle. It happens but rarely that a man renounces this right of his own free will. Even if the girl and her father do not want him, he as a rule insists, and they have to conform with the custom. If a man has any reason to suspect that his uncle wants to give his daughter to somebody else, he resorts to the following rite: He takes five camels and leads them to the tent of the tribal shaykh. There, in the presence of witnesses, he says: "Here are camels for my cousin; I claim her." The father of the girl answers: "Take them away; we do not want it [namely the marriage]." The suitor goes, but returns five days later with four camels, and says: "Here are my four camels for the girl; I want her." Again the father answers, "Take back your camels, we do not want it." After another five days the suitor presents himself at the tent of the shaykh or of the father with three camels, only to receive the same answer. The same encounter is repeated two more times, and then finally the youth brings a sheep or a goat to the shaykh's tent or to the father's tent, slaughters the animal and says: "This is the sacrifice of the girl." This act gives him the definitive right to take his cousin to wife, and he may even carry her away with him then and there. In particular, this right to the cousin's hand exists and is exercised among the following tribes: the Benī Ṣakhr, the Ḥwēṭāt, the Hajāya, the Catholic bedouins in the vicinity of Madaba (with the dispensation of the Church), and the Fuqarā. Differences in age, or the wishes of the girl are thereby completely disregarded.[69]

The actual working of the law can be illustrated by a number of examples taken from this area. A father arranged for the marriage of his daughter with an outsider, without obtaining the consent of her *ibn 'amm*. When the marriage procession progressed with the bride toward the house of the bridegroom, the *ibn 'amm* rushed forward, snatched away the girl, and forced her into his own house. This was regarded by all as a lawful marriage, and the father who originally objected to his nephew because the outsider agreed to pay a high bride price for his daughter now received no bride price at all.[70]

In some cases one and the same bride price acquires a girl not only for the *ibn 'amm* who actually marries her in the first place, but, should he divorce her, for his brothers as well. Jaussen reports such a case in which a man paid a she-ass as the *mahr* for his *bint 'amm*, married her, then divorced her, whereupon his brother took her in marriage by virtue of the same she-ass, then he divorced her too, and she was married in succession to the third and fourth brothers, and finally remarried the first brother, all for the one bride price of a single she-ass.[71]

In general, at the beginning of the twentieth century the situation with respect to the rights of the *ibn 'amm* among the tribes of the North Arabian and Syrian deserts was as follows: If a young man desired the hand of a girl who had cousins, one of the cousins who wanted to have the girl would caution the stranger to withdraw. If the latter persisted even after this admonition, it was his task to win, or rather to buy, the consent of the cousin who was the legal suitor of the girl. Otherwise, the stranger would have exposed himself to the enmity of the cousins and to mortal danger.[72]

A CHRISTIAN CASE HISTORY

Jaussen reports a case of which he heard among the Catholic bedouins of Madaba in Transjordan. One of them, Soleymān Shuweyḥāt, had a daughter, Ḥaḍra. In accordance with the cousin's right, his brother's son, Khalaf Shuweyḥāt, should have married the girl. But at the time when young Khalaf reached the age of marriage, Ḥaḍra fell ill: a pimple developed on her cheek, and she appeared to be attacked by a serious illness. Khalaf thereupon took another wife without either making any demand on the father of Ḥaḍra or informing him that he renounced his rights to her. Ḥaḍra remained in her father's house until the age of twenty-two. She recovered completely, and was demanded in marriage by another member of the tribe. Khalaf, hearing of this event, made immediate use of his cousin's right and claimed the girl for his younger brother. This was the Arab right. But Soleymān summarily rejected this demand saying that Khalaf had dishonored his daughter by refusing to marry her. His daughter was now promised to another man and would not be given to Khalaf's brother. Khalaf then made an appeal of protection to Shaykh Ya'qub, asking him to help him to make the cousin's right prevail. The shaykh could not refuse such a request. But being a relative of Soleymān Shuweyḥāt he used circumspection, lest Soleymān turn to another more powerful chief and he find himself involved in a serious conflict. After a series of discussions, Ḥaḍra was married to her suitor toward whom she inclined, and who was twenty-two years old, while Khalaf's brother was merely fifteen.[73]

PALESTINE

Among the Arabs of Palestine "a cousin is by custom the most eligible bride, and a youth has prior claim over all other suitors and their pretensions, if he chooses to demand her in marriage."[74] This right is alluded to in a number of proverbs. "Ibn al-'amm bitayyiḥ 'an el-faras"—"the *ibn* '*amm* may take down from the mare" (in another version: from the camel), that is he can take the bride down from the animal that carries her in the marriage procession to the house of the bridegroom, thus preventing her

from marrying an outsider, and marry her himself.[75] Another
proverb current among the Bedouins of Southern Palestine as
well as among the Rwala has it: "Her (i.e. the girl's) binding
and her release are in the hands of her *ibn 'amm.*" Still another
proverb warns: "The girl who is desired by her *ibn 'amm* is forbidden to a stranger." In the same sense it is also said: "The oil
which is wanted by its owner is forbidden to be given to the
mosque."[76]

If a girl has no *ibn 'amm,* or if the *ibn 'amm* renounces his right
to her, the second in line for her hand is the *ibn khāl,* her mother's
brother's son, who, in turn, is followed by the others in the family
and the brother of her sister's husband, each having a right of
priority in proportion to the degree of his relationship.[77]

Jaussen reports that among the inhabitants of Nablus in central
Palestine the right of a man to marry his *bint 'amm* "is religiously
respected" and "has an immutable value."[78] The same is true
elsewhere in Palestine in tradition-abiding circles.[79]

The present writer's observations among middle-class Muslim
Arabs in Palestine, and especially in Jerusalem, up to 1947,
showed the cousin's right in decline. There was no longer any
question of a suitor having to obtain the consent of the girl's
ibn 'amm. Only a vague sense of preference for *bint 'amm* marriage
was still noticeable here and there, but even this was disappearing
under the impact of the idea that cousin marriage may result in
sickly offspring.

The rural population, with its greater conservatism, evinced
no such change. The persistence of the cousin's right among the
Palestinian fellahin is reported by observers two generations
apart.[80] In the village of Arṭās, south of Bethlehem, the cousin's
right is verbalized in song and proverb. The songs often praise
the *ibn 'amm* as the ideal husband. If, however, he does not marry
his *bint 'amm,* but allows a stranger to take her away, he is blamed
and called a "heap of dirt." The obligation of an outsider to
compensate the *ibn 'amm* in money, in order to obtain his consent,
is a living custom in Arṭās. Among the proverbs alluding to the
cousin's right are found such statements as "The *ibn 'amm* comes
first," or "The *ibn 'amm* comes first in the eyes of the government
and of the fellahin."[81]

In an account of marriage preliminaries in the villages around Jerusalem, the father of the groom discusses the bride price with the father of the bride, and once this is settled the father of the bride says to him: "Now go and get the consent of her paternal uncle and cousins (" '*ammhā w'ulād 'ammhā*), buy clothes for her maternal uncle (*khālhā*). . . ." Thereupon the father of the groom goes to the paternal uncle of the bride and says to him: "How much do you want to let us get the girl?" The uncle thinks and then says: "I want 20 pieces of gold." Thereupon they discuss the amount until they settle on a sum. "The father of the groom can get the bride only if he has the consent of her *'amm* and his sons, and if he buys a robe for her *khāl* and shoes for his sons." After this, the father of the groom "makes efforts to get the consent of the girl's paternal cousins, but he has much trouble with them until he [finally] obtains their consent. . . ."[82]

ARṬĀS CASE HISTORIES

We have seen (pp. 150, 154) a few examples showing the complications that may arise when a father wishes to prefer an outsider as a son-in-law in order to secure a larger bride price than he would receive from his brother's son. The motivation of financial gain has caused conflicts between the father of a marriageable girl and his brother's son on several occasions in Arṭās.

Muṣṭafa Salem of Arṭās found a bride in Bethlehem for his son. They celebrated the betrothal feast, and he gave the girl's father about £P100 including presents. A year and a half passed, and they were about to go to the shaykh to conclude the marriage contract, when the bride's cousin appeared saying: "I come first." The girl herself said: "I want to have my cousin; he comes first." When the bridegroom's father heard this, he threatened saying: "There are judges" (i.e. there are fellah judges who will set the matter right). However, the betrothal was voided, and the bride's family had to compensate the groom's father for all he had spent on the girl.

Another case reported from Arṭās is even more instructive as to the rights of the *ibn 'amm*. Sma'īn Aḥmed, originally from Arṭās but living in Eḥbēle, had a daughter whom his cousin (his father's brother's son) 'Abdallah wanted to marry. However, an outsider offered £P150 as bride price for the girl, and thereupon Sma'īn refused to give his daughter to 'Abdallah who as a cousin would have had to pay a much smaller amount as bride price. Now Sma'īn's father and 'Abdallah's father (who were brothers) had another brother Mḥammad, and he arranged a *nidr*, or vow feast, to which he invited his brother from Eḥbēle, so that the relatives should be able to influence Sma'īn in favor of his cousin. "Far away . . . in . . . Eḥbēle, it was easy for him to refuse, but not so if he must do it before the whole group of relatives and villagers. . . ." When the evening meal was ready and about to be eaten, up rose Sma'īn's father, the oldest and most influential member of the extended family, and said: "I will not eat unless I know whether this is a betrothal feast or a vow feast." His son, the father of the girl, tried to hold his own by mentioning the high bride price offered to him by the stranger, but his father cut him short: "Nothing will come of that. We are relatives." An aunt of Sma'īn and 'Abdallah (their father's sister) also joined in the discussion and said to 'Abdallah: "I will not eat unless I know whether thou wilt give me a wedding garment." The resistance of the girl's father was thus broken down, he gave his consent, a Fātiḥa (the first chapter of the Koran) was read, and the meal began, it being understood that it was a betrothal feast. Next morning it was said: "This night Aḥmed Sma'īn [the girl's father's father] has instituted a new rule, that for a clan daughter only £P35 shall be given. So dear as it is now will not do."

In yet another case in the same village a girl's parents wanted to give her to her mother's brother's son (*ibn khāl*). But her father's brother's son (*ibn 'amm*) insisted on his rights, and finally got the girl.[83]

SYRIA

Moving up from Palestine into Syria, we find the same cousin right. Here too the girl's father's brother's son has the first right to her, followed by the right of more remote relatives in the male line. And here too the right can be renounced by the *ibn 'amm* for a compensation paid to him by the suitor of the girl who thus is a source of revenue for him. In Syria the right of receiving a compensation belongs to the *ibn ʿamm* alone, and not to the *ibn khāl* who has no special rights in his *bint ʿamme*. The proverb that refers to the cousin right and, as we have seen (p. 155) is current in Palestine, is also current in Syria in a somewhat different version: "*Inazzelhā min ʿala ḍahr el-faras.*" "He (the *ibn ʿamm*) can take her down from the back of the mare." Another proverb in the same sense is: "*Yakhtefhā min el-jalweh,*" "He can snatch her from the wedding ceremony."[84] Among the fellahin of the Hama, Homs, Aleppo, and Deir ez-Zor regions of Syria the *ibn ʿamm* asserts his right by referring to the traditional saying: "*Bent ʿammī, mā etlaʿ men ṭarīqhā,*" "She is my *bint ʿamm*, I shall not move out of her way." Among the Syrian bedouins they say: "*Bent ʿammī, mā futḥa,*" "She is my *bint ʿamm*, I shall not release her."[85]

In the entire Hawran district, as well as among the Syrian bedouins, and especially the tribes of Sulūṭ, Benī Khāled, and el-Weld, the custom of reserving the bride for himself is practiced by the *ibn ʿamm*. From the time a man reserves his *bint ʿamm* for himself and until such time as he actually marries her, she becomes "protected" *(majyūra)* by him, and nobody else has the right to marry her. But even if the *ibn ʿamm* has not expressly reserved the girl for himself, he has to be consulted before the girl can be given in marriage to someone else. This custom is followed not only in the rural areas and the smaller towns such as Homs, Hama, Deir ez-Zor, but, occasionally at least, even in the big cities of Syria, Damascus, and Aleppo.[86]

In the Syrian towns cousin marriage seems to be most frequent among the lower classes consisting of workers, artisans, and small employees. Here too the proverbs faithfully reflect the views of the people with regard to the rights of the *ibn ʿamm* and of the desirability of cousin marriage. "A tree is found near me; who has more right to it, my neighbor or myself?" asks one of these proverbs. Folk songs also assert the rights of the *ibn ʿamm*: "My *bint ʿamm* is for me, is for me. . . ."[87]

As in Arab Palestine, in Syria too the urban environment is not favorable to the preservation of folk traditions. In recent decades, especially in the big cities, a man could give his daughter in marriage to a stranger even if the girl had several patrilateral parallel cousins who demanded her hand, and concurrently compensation of the *ibn ʿamm* has also fallen into disuse. This development seems to be characteristic especially of the middle-class townspeople among whom cousin marriage has become much less frequent than among the lower classes. In the upper class, among the leading families, marriage between cousins is again frequent, and the *ibn ʿamm* has the right of preference, here motivated by the wish to preserve the property in the family and by a feeling of superiority to other families. For these reasons, marriage between maternal cousins is less frequent in these classes than marriage between paternal cousins; and more stress is laid on marrying a girl to a cousin than on finding an in-family match for a young man.[87]

Actually, as late as the 1930's there were still a number of leading families, especially in the small towns of Syria, among whom the old tradition of in-family marriage was faithfully preserved. In Homs and Hama, for instance, there were still certain families who would not give their daughters in marriage to an outsider, but insisted on their marrying members of the family itself. No such restrictions, however, existed with regard to their male members who were free to find wives for themselves outside their own family circle. In this respect too the Syrian town closely resembled the Palestinian Arab town. Recently, however, this rule has become weakened in many places. For instance, the rule of the K. family in Hama, according to which a K. girl was allowed to marry only a K. man, has been repeatedly infringed upon as early as the 1920's.

This rule was not confined to families of high standing, but could be found also among some fellah families. The ʿAbdallah family in Palmyra, for example, and several other families in the Hawran and Deir ez-Zor regions, adhered to it down to the 1930's. In the ʿAtasī family also husband and wife were almost always from the same family and this was the typical situation as far as the leading families were concerned.[89]

SYRIAN MINORITIES

The right of the *ibn ʿamm* is upheld also among the Syrian Turkomans, among whom also the payment of compensation to the *ibn 'amm* has been practiced. A story concerning the rivalry between two paternal cousins for the hand of their *bint 'amm*, who was the most beautiful Turkoman girl in Syria, was often heard a number of years ago. Both youths demanded the girl from her father, Ḥajj 'Alī, who, in order to suppress all rivalry between the two (since this would have weakened the family), refused her to both. However, knowing that two cousins had demanded her in marriage, nobody else dared to ask for the hand of the girl. She remained an old maid, and died unmarried.

The same customs are in force among the Syrian Kurds, both those of the Damascus area and those of Kurd Dagh. Among them, too, the *ibn 'amm* must be asked for his consent, if the girl is to marry somebody else, and has to be given compensation. The story is told of a certain 'Abdo, a Kurd of the village of Shikhut in the Kurd Dagh region, who has not received his *khul'a* (price of renunciation), and thereupon avenged himself by first killing the parents of his *bint 'amm* and later the girl herself. He was apprehended, condemned to death, and executed.

The cousin right does not exist among the Circassians in Syria. They hold marriages between a man and his *bint 'amm* or *bint khāl* absolutely forbidden, because these cousins are regarded by them as siblings. The same type of family exogamy is practiced also among the Circassians in the Caucasus, the original home of the Syrian Circassians.[90]

IRAQ

In Iraq as well as in northeastern Arabia, "first cousin marriage is the rule invariably. A girl belongs of right to the son of her father's brother (*ibn 'amm*) unless he expressly renounces his right to marry her. Even in this case she may not marry without his permission. If the girl breaks this rule or her parents prevail on her to marry someone else, her rightful lord will murder her if he can. This is the cause of most of the tribal killings of women, especially in Iraq."[91]

This custom is frequently reflected in Iraqi folk stories. In one of these, Harun al-Rashid's brother's son does not let Harun marry his daughter to anybody else, until finally Harun gives her to him in marriage. In another story, a father from the country of

6

Waq-waq does not want his daughter to marry her *ibn 'amm*, and therefore flees with her to Iraq. Later, however, the father returns with his daughter to Waq-waq land, whereupon the marriage feast of his daughter with his brother's son is begun. However, the girl's lover arrives in the last minute, kills the *ibn 'amm*, and then flees with the girl back to Iraq.[92]

Among the Jews of Iraq, if a man wants to give his daughter in marriage to somebody, he must first persuade the girl's cousin to renounce his right to her. If the cousin does not listen to persuasion, the girl's father pays him a sum of money to buy his consent. This is done in order to prevent enmity and tension within the family.[93]

In Northern Iraq also the *ibn 'amm* has the right to marry his *bint 'amm*. This is "the principal rule of marriage. . . . If they do not care for each other, however, the man will usually accept a present from the outside suitor, and in return will forego his right to his cousin."[94]

An Iraqi Case History

The following account, which contains all the elements of the cousin's right, is given by H. R. P. Dickson. The heroine is Binniyah, a sixteen-year-old girl of the al-Gharri tribe, headed by Shaykh Manshad al-Habayib. "Her people lived at Batha, a village on the Euphrates, some twenty miles from Nasiríyah, and she lived happily with her father and mother in their black tent until a short time previously, when they had told her that she was to marry her *ibn 'am* (first cousin) and that the wedding was to be solemnized on the new moon. The news had come as a terrible blow to her, for she loved another boy of the tribe and he loved her, and had told her of his love for her. In great distress she had told him that her father proposed giving her to her cousin on the new moon, and begged his advice and help. She would die, she had told him, rather than be the wife of anyone but him. The youth had received this calmly, but had been deeply angered, with murder in his heart. He had told Binniyah that he must have time to think out a plan, and would return on the third day and tell her what this was. They had arranged to meet on the river bank where she was accustomed to fetch water at midday, and he would find an opportunity of talking to her.

"Binniyah had passed three long days in misery and despondency. What chance had her lover, and what hope had she of getting out of the marriage arranged by her powerful father? Moreover, by Arab custom, her cousin has the right to marry her, and she could take no one else in this world unless he waived that right. She knew also that if, in spite of everyone, she married someone other than her cousin, her life would be forfeit and her cousin would be the one to kill her. Her only chance—and it was a very, very slender one—was to run away with her lover, but then she would have to flee far from her home and people and abandon all hope of ever seeing them again. If they ran away there would be an immediate pursuit, and woe betide her and her boy if the pursuers came up with them. Tribal law never forgave in such matters.

"Three days later she had been at the rendezvous by the riverside. Other women had been drawing water also, but her lover had managed to get private word with her as he had walked part of the way home. He had only one plan to offer: to run away, and on that very night. He would appear behind her tent at midnight with a fast mare and, on his giving the cry of a jackal three times, she was to slip out from under the tent curtain, join him at the back, and together they would fly away to Suq ash Shuyúkh and take refuge with the Mujarrah tribes. There they would get married, and if they could not find safety they would flee farther to distant Basra. . . .

"Midnight had arrived, and Binniyah had crept out quietly to the rear of the tent on hearing the jackal cry. Silently they had got through the sleeping camp unnoticed and then, mounting one behind the other, had sped away into the open country, their objective the palm belt opposite Nasiríyah town. Alas, someone or some dog must have given the alarm. Binniyah could not tell me how it had happened. Suffice to say, when dawn had broken the fleeing pair had seen in the distance behind them a party of horsemen, obviously following hard on their trail. . . . They had thrown off their pursuers for a moment, and Binniyah had been almost happy. Then what disillusionment! The young man had apparently decided that, handicapped by Binniyah, he would never escape, but that he might get away alone. He had suddenly told her he was leaving her. It was useless, he had said, for them both to get killed, when he could escape to Suq and reach Basra by way of the Hamár Lake. He had not given Binniyah time to argue or even plead. He had just disappeared into the darkness. Life was sweet, so why throw it away on a *bint*?"

Thereupon Binniyah fled into Dickson's house. Somewhat later Shaykh Manshad too arrived and demanded that Dickson hand the girl over to him. But Binniyah pleaded for her life: "He is only concerned with getting me out of your hands and the *hakúma's* protection. Afterwards he will hand me over to my *ibn 'am* and tribal justice."

Turning to Manshad she said: "I cannot, I dare not go back with you, Yá Manshad," she sobbed in a way that touched the heart. "You know the tribal law; it is utterly unforgiving in the case of erring girls like me, and you know full well that you must hand me over to my father and brethren, since they will demand me of you. I am afraid to die, for I am young."

So Binniyah remained for a while with the Dicksons: "In my predicament as to what to do with her, I sought the help and guidance of Dhári Beg al Fahad Al Sa'dún. I told him the whole story, and he advised me that the only hope for the girl was to have her married to some worthy citizen of Nasiríyah town. According to Dhári, if she were once properly married and settled down in the town, her tribe would no longer attempt to molest her, and in due course her *ibn 'am* and parents might forgive her, especially if her husband were to pay over a sum of money by way of compensation to the *ibn 'am* who fancied himself injured. Binniyah herself approved this step, so I acted on Dhári's advice and, after some days, found a very respectable man who ran a coffee-shop a few doors away from my house, and he agreed to marry Binniyah. The wedding was a quiet one and turned out very happily. As my contribution to the happy event I gave the bride-groom six hundred rupees to be paid over to Binniyah's cousin."[95]

KURDISTAN

The same rule prevails in the Kurdish area of Northern Iraq as well. It is the tribal law among the Kurds that the cousin "has the first refusal of a lady's hand,"[96] in other words it is he who can either take her for himself or dispose of her if he so wishes. In the sedentary Hamawand tribe (in the Kirkuk Liwa of Iraq) "paternal cousins have first rights to a girl, and where the father of the girl contemplates giving her in marriage to anyone else, the paternal cousin must first release her by renouncing his claim." In the southern Kurdish feudally organized territory, neighboring on the Hamawand area, the "first rights of paternal cousins are not as strongly emphasized." Barth, who made a special study of this problem among the Kurds, recorded in the course of his field work cases of violence resulting from a breach of the father's obligation to obtain his brother's son's consent to the marriage of his daughter to somebody else. In one case, an outsider who asked for the hand of a girl was refused by her father on the grounds that (as he said), "I am afraid my brother's sons will kill me if I give her to you."[97]

One Kurdish case history should suffice to show that murder can actually result from the refusal to let a girl marry her *ibn 'amm* (or *amoaza* in Kurdish). In 1920, in a village called Kapanak Resh, on the eastern slope of the Qara Choq Dag in the Arbil region of Iraqi Kurdistan, under the protection of the village headman, named Khālbekr, lived his widowed sister, Amīna Khanum, and her beautiful daughter, Fāṭima. In a village on the other side of the hill lived Fāṭima's cousins, Farhān the Lame and Raḥmān Agha. Farhān sent his brother several times to ask Khālbekr for the hand of his niece, but was each time refused. Finally, one of the three big Dizai chiefs, Ḥajji Pīr Daoud Agha, secretly approached Khālbekr and offered him a large bride price for his niece whom he asked in marriage for his son Ma'ruf. Khālbekr gave his consent and the preparations for the marriage started but with utmost secrecy. So as to prevent the occurrence of any legal hitch, even the consent of the Muslim judge of Arbil was obtained. However, as was to be expected, these plans could not for long remain secret, and Raḥmān Agha planned revenge. One night Fāṭima was sleeping with her mother and her maid in a booth of branches just outside their house, when suddenly two men appeared and stabbed the girl and her maid to death, the mother narrowly escaping with her life. The bloody deed horrified

the whole tribe, because the traditionally correct thing would
have been to carry off the girl by force, or to kill her bridegroom.
Since the girl herself had nothing to say in the matter of her
marriage, to kill her was a crime by tribal standards. Raḥmān
Agha was imprisoned, but no proof of his guilt could be found,
and he was finally released.[98]

IRAN

In Persian Azerbaijan the same right is accorded to a man with
regard to the hand of his *ämün gyzi*, father's brother's daughter.
In an account of Azerbaijani marriage customs reported by an
informant from Tabriz, the fourteen-year-old boy says to his
mother that he wants to marry, whereupon the mother answers:
"Wait until your cousin (*ämün gyzi*) Aliye grows up, I shall take
her for you as wife . . . she is your property. . . ."[99]

If among the Papis of Iran, a Lur tribe, a girl is married to a
stranger, he has to compensate her cousins by giving each one of
them a goat.[100]

SINAI AND EGYPT

The Sinai Peninsula forms the connecting link between the
Asian and the African halves of the Middle East. Ethnologically,
the nomads of the Peninsula are the connecting link between the
peoples of the Arabian and Syrian deserts on the one hand and
the tribes of Egypt and North Africa on the other. Two firsthand
reports a hundred and twenty years apart attest to the prevalence
of the cousin's right in Sinai. John Lewis Burckhardt, traveling in
the Sinai Peninsula prior to 1816, observed that "The Arabs of
Sinai . . . sometimes marry their daughters to strangers in the
absence of the cousins. This happened to a guide whom I had
taken from Suez. When we arrived at his encampment, one day's
journey from the convent of Sinai, he expected to marry a cousin
of his own, and during the whole journey he had extolled to me
the festivities which I should witness on that occasion. He, too,
had brought with him some new clothes for his intended bride;
and was therefore exceedingly disappointed and chagrined on his
arrival, when he learned that three days before the girl had been

married to another. It appeared that her mother was secretly his
enemy; and had contrived matters in such a manner as to render
him ridiculous in the eyes of his companions. He bore his misfortune, however, like a man; and, instead of evincing any signs
of displeasure, soon turned the tide of ridicule upon the mother
herself, and her son-in-law. To prevent similar occurrences, a
cousin, if he be determined to marry his relation, pays down the
price of her as a deposit into the hands of some respectable
member of the encampment, and places the girl under the protection of four men belonging to his own tribe. In this case she
cannot marry another without his permission, whether he be
absent or present; and he may then marry her at his leisure, whenever he pleases. If, however, he himself break off the match, the
money that had been deposited is paid into the hands of the girl's
master. This kind of betrothing takes place sometimes long before
the girl has attained the age of puberty."[101]

The nonchalant manner in which Burckhardt's guide reacted
to the marriage of his cousin to another man, as well as the
institutionalized method of preventing "similar occurrences,"
which is different from the mere reservation of the girl practiced
elsewhere (p. 152), seem to indicate that no great emphasis was
placed on cousin right in those days. In the course of the subsequent century the attitude to the cousin's right must have become
considerably more rigorous, since Murray in the 1930's reports
that this right is generally respected among the Bedouins of
Sinai as well as among those inhabiting the desert of Egypt
stretching between the Nile and the Red Sea. Among the
Egyptian Bedouin "every youth has the right to marry his *bint
'amm*. . . . The right is absolute, and if her father wishes to dispose
of the girl otherwise, he must first obtain (and pay for) his
nephew's consent. The vast majority of first marriages (every
Bedouin marries several times) are of this nature, and consequently a high proportion of the population are the offspring of
first cousins. So also an 'Abadi or Bishari usually marries his
bint 'amm, but the Hadendowa are not so patrilineal and when
choosing a bride give no special preference to that lady."[102]

As to the Bisharin, C. G. Seligman reports that among those in
the neighborhood of Aswan in Upper Egypt whom he studied,

the *bint 'amm* "is the best [wife] and a man would consider that he had prior right to the hand of his *bint 'amm*."[103]

SUDAN

Moving down south into Sudan, we find that among the Kababish, an Arab tribe, marriage with the *bint 'amm* predominates. The Seligmans found that "it was clear that no other alliance for a girl would be considered if there were an *ibn 'amm* available for her. Further, if a lad were betrothed to his *bint 'amm* who was considerably younger than himself, he could not take another wife while waiting for her to grow up. A *bint 'amm* could not be second to any other woman unless she, too, were *bint 'amm* to the husband. This rule was demonstrated in the case of the shaykh of the Kababish himself: he married his *bint 'amm*, then later he married a second wife who was not his *bint 'amm*. Then he wanted to marry another *bint 'amm* of his, but before being able to do so he had first to divorce his second wife, so that he should have no wife preceding a *bint 'amm*.[104]

NORTH AFRICA

Thanks to the researches of Westermarck and of a number of French scholars we have ample information as to the prevalence of *bint 'amm* marriage in Morocco, the westernmost outpost of Middle Eastern culture. Both among Arabs and Berbers, marriages between children of two brothers are not only common, but a man is held to have the right to marry his father's brother's daughter.

In Andjra, Westermarck was told that the cousin has to be asked before a girl can be given away to another man, and that if this step is omitted, the cousin is entitled to prevent the marriage even on the very day of the wedding by forcibly removing her from the bridal box. Among the Uled Bu'Aziz, a man who has contracted marriage with another man's *bint 'amm* can be compelled to give her up, if he is compensated for his expenses and if he has not yet settled down with her. In the Rif instances are known in which a man who has married his daughter to an outsider has been killed by his brother's son.[105]

Also "A Mohammedan Hausa has the right to marry the daughter of his father's brother," but he has no such right to the hand of any of the other cousins, whom he can marry only if her father agrees.[106]

POSITIVE MOTIVATIONS

Several cogent reasons have been advanced for the marriage of paternal cousins by the peoples practicing it. One of the earliest of these was given by the Persian king Ardeshir who advised his lawyers, secretaries, officers, and husbandmen to "marry near relatives for the sympathy of kinship is kept alive thereby."[107] Although the meaning of marriage between "close relatives" is not defined more fully, it must have referred to brother-sister and/or cousin marriages.

The same motivation, namely the strengthening of the kinship ties, is given in ancient Arabic sources referring to the practice of marriage between paternal cousins prevalent in pre-Islamic Arabia.[108]

We read in the *Kitāb al-Aghānī* that Qays ibn Dhariḥ, of the stock of Kinānā, fell in love with Labna, a beautiful maiden of the Quḍā'a tribe, and when he implored his father for permission to marry her, the father objected saying that he (the father, Dhariḥ) was indeed a rich and wealthy man and he did not want his son to take the side of a stranger.[109]

A related consideration in favor of paternal cousin marriage is the assumption that a man who grows up together with his *bint 'amm* within the intimate framework of one extended family knows her and develops a liking and a love for her, which in turn augur well for the happiness and stability of the marriage.

In the Middle Ages in Arab lands, a cousin (father's brother's daughter) was "often chosen as a wife, on account of the tie of blood which is likely to attach her more strongly to her husband, or on account of an affection conceived in early years."[110] Speaking of Egypt of the early nineteenth century, Lane remarks that "a union of this kind is generally lasting, on account of this tie of blood; and because mutual intercourse may have formed an attachment between the parties in tender age."[111] In Syria also in middle-class urban society, although "marriages between

6§

cousins are less frequent than in the families of high society," if they occur, "they are dictated more often by feelings of affection which develops easily between male and female cousins who in the town can see each other and talk to each other."[112] According to a Syrian proverb, "Ill luck which you know is better than good luck with which you get acquainted,"[113] that is, it is preferable to marry a cousin whose faults you know rather than a strange girl who seems to be better but with whose true qualities you will get acquainted only later. A Palestinian Arab proverb expresses the same feeling: "Follow the circular (that is, normal, or regular) path, even if it is long, and marry your *bint 'amm* even if she is a miserable [match]."[114]

A Meccan proverb encourages the young man not to be ashamed of his *bint 'amm*: "He who is ashamed of his *bint 'amm*, will get no boy from her."[115]

Several Moroccan Arabic proverbs likewise emphasize the desirability of marrying a *bint 'amm* because of the advantages of familiarity with her: "He who marries his *bint 'amm* celebrates his feast with a sheep from his own flock"; or "Marrying a stranger is like drinking water from an earthenware bottle, but marriage with a *bint 'amm* is like drinking water from a dish": that is, you can see what you drink.

The Persian proverb quoted above (p. 139) expresses the view that marriages between paternal cousins are made in heaven, that is, are preordained by God.

Another important motivation of marriage between paternal cousins is the endeavor to preserve the property in the family. This motivation comes into play as a result of the traditional Middle Eastern system of inheritance, which conflicts to some extent with the rule of patrilineal descent. Under this rule, a woman's children belong to the family (and larger kin-group) of her husband only. Whatever property a woman inherits from her father, and, in turn, leaves to her children, thus passes from her father's family into that of her husband. The marriage of a daughter with an outsider therefore ultimately results in the alienation of part of the family's property. On the other hand, if paternal cousins marry, their children are the offspring of the same grandfather through both their father and their mother, and thus whatever a daughter inherits from a man is passed on by her to her children who are also the patrilineal grandchildren of the same man. In this case, therefore, even that part of the family property that is inherited by the daughters remains in the family.

In fact, in one of the earliest Middle Eastern documents relating to this subject the inheritance of daughters is made contingent upon their marrying members of the in-group, and, as it eventually transpired, all the five female heirs in question married their father's brothers' sons (Numbers 36 : 1–12).

Although *bint 'amm* marriage was practiced in Mecca and Medina in pre-Islamic days, it can be assumed that when Mohammed reformed the laws of inheritance, allowing the daughters a share in the father's estate, this resulted in an increased frequency of *bint 'amm* marriages.[116] The basic Koranic legislation in this respect is found in Surah iv : 11, where it is said: "Allah chargeth you concerning your children: to the male the equivalent of the portion of two females, and if there be women (only), more than two, then theirs is two thirds of the inheritance, and if there be one (only), then the half."

This Islamic law is by no means adhered to by all Middle Eastern tribal and village societies, who in many cases still follow their old, pre-Islamic customary local law. In general it can nevertheless be said that some portion at least of the father's estate is inherited, as a rule, by his daughter, and thus passes on from her to her children. Therefore, the preservation of the property in the family becomes an important motivation for the preference for paternal cousin marriage, and is stated to be one of its purposes in many parts of the Middle East.[117]

In many Middle Eastern societies people are conscious of several of the motivations for cousin marriage. In Kurdistan, for instance, "Giving one's daughter to a brother's son is . . . considered thoughtful and proper. The father knows his daughter's spouse well, and will also be able to exert some control over his actions toward her after marriage; marriage should be between equals, and no one is closer in status and sentiment than a paternal cousin. The small child is pleasantly embarrassed when teased for being "in love" with a paternal cousin. The importance of endo-

gamy in maintaining family property is also recognized, though
the problem only arises with any degree of gravity where Koranic
laws of inheritance, giving stipulated fractions of the estate to
female descendants, are strictly followed, and this does not
generally seem to be the case. ... Such a pattern of father's
brother's daughter marriage plays a prominent role in solidifying
the minimal lineage as a corporate group in factional struggle.
Marriages of this type thus serve to reinforce the political implications of the lineage system. ... relative to the first potential
lines of fission and segmentation within the minimal lineage
itself."[118]

To sum up, in the Middle Eastern patrilineal kinship system it
is of extremely great importance for the head of the family to be
assured of the unwavering support of his brothers and their sons.
The greater the number of the male kin on whose unquestioning
loyalty he can count, the greater his influence, power, security,
and prestige. One of the time-proved methods of strengthening
the ties of kinship and of common interests between the head of a
family and his patrilineal kinsmen is to give them his daughters
in marriage. These considerations in most cases outweigh by far
the loss of money resulting from the reduced bride price paid by
a brother's son. The same considerations hold good also from the
point of view of the young man about to choose a wife. If the wife
is from a different family, and even more so if she is from a
different village or tribe, the husband cannot be sure that the
interests of his father-in-law will always harmonize with his own.
Contrary interests, especially if they lead to mutual raiding or
warfare, put the wife in a difficult and at times tragic situation
whereby the inner coherence in the nuclear family of the husband
and also in the extended family of which he is a member may be
weakened. If on the other hand his wife is a *bint 'amm*, a daughter
of his father's brother, the likelihood of the occurrence of such
a conflict of interests is greatly reduced, and in general the
harmonious community of interests between a man and his father-
in-law is enhanced.

Close in-group or in-family endogamy is to this day the prevalent
practice in all social strata of the Middle East with the exception of
those exposed to modern Western influences. Endogamy still seems

to satisfy most young men and women, because young people who grow up in the large and protective environment of the extended family seem to be conditioned by their upbringing to have a preference for continuing their lives in the same environment and atmosphere; given this preference, such close in-group marriages as between a man and his father's brother's daughter have all the advantages as against marrying a nonrelated outsider. Two young people who grow up in the same extended family (or at least in two closely related extended families) have in general a pre-existing community of interests and a similarity in outlook and personality determinants, and can therefore look forward to a much smoother adaptation to each other, adjustment to the larger frame of the extended family, and further growth within it, than can be the case in an out-group marriage.

OPPOSITION TO COUSIN MARRIAGE

Occasionally opposition to cousin marriage arose among those who practiced it, and was expressed in the form of good advice or proverbs. al-Maydānī (ii : 250) makes the following exhortation: "Marry the distant, but not the near [in relationship]." The reason given for the advisability of avoiding cousin marriages is most frequently the belief that the offspring of such marriages will be feeble. In Jauharī's Arabic Dictionary a *Ḥadīth* (an oral tradition going back to the Prophet Mohammed) is quoted to the effect that by marrying strangers one will not have feeble posterity. Another early Arab author, Ibn 'Abd Rabbihi, in his *Kitāb al-'iqd al-farīd* (iii : 290) says in praise of a hero: He is a hero not borne by the cousin (of his father), he is not weakly; for the seed of relations brings forth feeble fruit."[119]

The weakness of such offspring may be manifested in their small stature. It is said of Omar that when he once asked why were the Qurayshites so small of stature, he was told that this was the result of their frequent cousin marriages. Thereupon Omar is said to have prohibited the continuation of this practice. The same idea is expressed in a verse quoted in Bajuri's Commentary to Ibn Qasim (ii : 153): "If you want nobility of descent (i.e., physical excellence) marry a stranger and do not enter into a tie with relatives." According to Bajuri, a man's desire for a closely related woman such as his *bint 'amm* is weak, and therefore the child born of such a union will also be weak.[120]

Abu Hamid al-Ghazali (1059–1111) in his principal ethical work, the *Iḥyā 'ulūm al-dīn* ("The revivification of the religious sciences"), devotes a section to the properties and characteristics required of a wife. One of these is that "the woman should not be a near relative of the husband, because near relationship diminishes the sensuous desire. 'Marry not near relations,' says the Blessed One (Mohammed), 'otherwise one must expect a weak (*ḍāwī*) progeny.' *Ḍāwī* means *naḥīf* (thin, weakly). The reason for this is that this circumstance results in a weakening effect on the sensuous desire. This latter, namely, is aroused through sensations of sight and touch, and these are especially strong in the case of a new and strange object. If, however, the object in question is familiar, and has been in front of one's eyes for a long time, then the sense becomes dulled so that it can no longer completely perceive it and be impressed by it. Therefore also the libido will not be excited by it."[121] The same feeling was expressed in modern Morocco as well as by a Berber informant of Westermarck's: "How can a man love a woman with whom he has grown up from childhood?"[122]

Another stated reason for the dislike of cousin marriages was that they might lead to quarreling and disharmony. The ancient Arabic poet, 'Amr b. Kulthūm, said: "Do not marry in your own family, for domestic enmity arises therefrom."[123] This fear too is expressed in modern Moroccan proverbs. One of these says: "Your father's brother will make you blind, and your mother's brother will make you destitute, and keep away from your blood that it shall not visit you with misfortunes." Girls in Fez when wishing to get married go to ask help at the shrine of the saint Sīdī Mbārak ben Ababū, and address him: "O Sīdī Mbārak, give me a husband who has no friends." This they do in order to avoid being given in marriage to a cousin, since cousin marriages are supposed to lead to quarrels between the husband's and the wife's families, both of whom want to interfere in the married life of the couple.[124]

In Syria also there is a proverb that speaks about the inconveniences of cousin marriage, which may lead to quarrels between the two families: "Do not approach your relatives, their scorpions ✓ will bite you."[125]

CONCLUSION

A comparison of the distribution data of the cousin's right with those of preference for *bint 'amm* marriage shows that there are ethnic groups in considerable numbers within the limits of the Middle Eastern culture continent whose marriage pattern includes preference for *bint 'amm* marriage without, however, according to a man the *right* to marry his *bint 'amm*. The cousin's right to marry his *bint 'amm* does not and cannot exist without preference for *bint 'amm* marriage; while preference can and does exist without the right, having apparently a wider distribution. The fullest form of *bint 'amm* marriage appears to be the one in which a man has the right to marry his *bint 'amm*. On the other hand, the existence of the preference for cousin marriage without this right can be taken as an indication of an incomplete, partial form of the institution of cousin marriage. The incomplete variety of cousin marriage (preference without right) may be contingent upon one or more of the following factors and circumstances:

a. The geographic location of the ethnic group in question may be marginal to the Middle Eastern culture continent and the pattern of cousin marriage may therefore not exist in it in the full form developed in the Middle Eastern core culture (example: the Timbuctoo area, or the Fulani in Nupe). This assumption is predicated on the known existence of cousin marriage among the Biblical Hebrews and pre-Islamic Arabs; on the known increase in incidence of cousin marriage in Arabia after Mohammed; and on its incorporation into Muslim tradition, which secured its acceptance by all (or nearly all) Islamized peoples. It also implies that the cousin's right was a later development in the Middle Eastern core culture, and that therefore it has not yet reached marginally located ethnic groups that have already absorbed the earlier form of Middle Eastern preference for cousin marriage.

b. Ethnic groups located geographically well within the central sector of the Middle Eastern culture continent may yet occupy a position of cultural marginality. Such a group may be influenced by the older and less stringent preference for cousin marriage and may have subsequently resisted or remained unaffected by the later specific and strict Middle Eastern formulation of the cousin's right (example: the Copts in Egypt).

c. As a result of modernization and Westernization, a distance may develop between the actual culture of a sector of the population in a locality and the traditional culture of the ethnic group of which the local aggregate is part. In such cases, which can be observed, for example, in the middle-class population of many Middle Eastern cities, the most stringent feature of the traditional cousin marriage complex, namely the man's right to marry his *bint 'amm*, may be discarded because it is felt that it contravenes Western ideas that are being consciously absorbed. The preference for cousin marriage may at the same time persist, insofar as both parties, now allowed their free choice of marriage partners, may still feel that cousin marriage has, after all, some of those advantages that tradition ascribes to it. In this transitional stage, the frequency of cousin marriage may still testify to a continued preference for it, while the cousin's right may be ridiculed as obsolete.

d. An external circumstance must also be taken into consideration. This is the specific nature of the sources from which the data concerning the Middle Eastern marriage pattern (and Middle Eastern culture as a whole) are derived. Work in Middle Eastern anthropology on an over-all area basis, and especially attempts at distribution studies, still have to rely to a considerable extent on accounts of travelers, officials, residents, and other nonanthropologists. These writings, while often containing valuable firsthand observations, often fall short as far as detail and completeness are concerned. The absence of any reference to the cousin's right in a given ethnic group may therefore mean not only that the cousin's right did actually not exist, but also that the author of the account failed to notice it or was not even aware of its possible existence. At least part of the distributional discrepancy between the cousin's right and the preference for cousin marriage is probably due to this circumstance.

VII. Dual Organization

STUDENTS OF culture in general and of certain world areas in particular have repeatedly devoted their attention to the form of social structure commonly referred to in anthropological literature as *dual organization*. The definitions of what constitutes dual organization vary.[1] One of the most comprehensive analyses of the characteristics of dual organization throughout the world is that of Josef Haekel, published in the 1950 volume of *Anthropos*.[2] These can be subsumed as follows:

A Sociological Dichotomy. A division of local aggregates, tribes, or clans into two; an extension of the dual division to larger territories; a dichotomy of the men's clubs, the ceremonial houses, the age groups, classes, or ceremonial groups. The existence of the two groups (usually referred to as "moieties") can be overtly manifest or present only in the consciousness of the people, or expressed in certain modes of behavior. It can be either permanent or temporary.

Occasionally there is also a tendency to *further dual subdivisions* within the moieties. In these subgroups a combination with totem clans is frequent. On the other hand, the dual system can be present without any further subdivision of the moieties.

Regulation of Marriage. The dual organization either is or is not accompanied by moiety exogamy. When there are two marriage classes they are, as a rule, the moieties of villages or tribes. Secondarily, exogamy may be lost.

Descent. Descent is counted within the moiety in general most frequently in the maternal line, but patrilineal descent occurs also in connection with dual organization.

Ideology and Symbolism. Pairs of opposites, often expressed in names, figure in the *ideology and symbolism* of the moieties, such as the symbolic division of natural objects into two groups. There are also associations with districts and directions, or with opposites such as sky—earth, above—below, male—female; or with opposites of colors; with war—peace, with contraposited animal pairs (totemistic or totemizing dual systems); with heavenly bodies such as light and dark moon or sun—moon. Often a competitive brotherly pair or some other ancestral pair figures in the moiety.

Naming. The two moieties are called by opposite names.

Antagonism and Rivalry. Symbolic or fictional enmity usually obtains between the two moieties, sometimes degenerating into serious strife. Jealousy, mutual ridiculing, joking designations, competitive fights and games are common.

Reciprocity. This is expressed in mutual services at feasts and funerals.

Evaluation and Status. There is a higher evaluation of one moiety, which is partly a practical utilization of existing ethnic stratification.

The presence of all or most of these characteristics, with differing emphases, is attested by data from the following world areas: India, the Ugric peoples of Central Asia, Indonesia, Oceania, North America, and Negro Africa.[3] Woelfel, Jeffreys, and Haekel also refer to the presence of the dual system in North Africa among certain Berber groups.[4] As far as could be verified, no attempt has been made hitherto to establish the presence of the system in the Middle East in general.

In the course of the author's researches in Middle Eastern social structure it has become apparent not only that dual organization is present in many parts of the Middle East but that, up to its present decline as a consequence of the impact of modern Western sociopolitical forms, it was a highly significant factor in the traditional social organization as well as in the political life of the area as a whole. Specifically, among the following Middle Eastern peoples were traces of dual organization observed: The nomadic and the settled population of the Arabian Peninsula from pre-Islamic days to the present, including the major tribes and tribal federations of Southern and Central Arabia as well as of the Syrian Desert. The tribes of Iran and Afghanistan. The tribal elements and the settled peoples of Iraq, Syria, Lebanon, Palestine, and Transjordan, including the urban population, and Muslims as well as Christians. The Druzes of Syria and Lebanon. The urban population as well as the villagers of Egypt. The settled and nomadic, Arab and Berber, groups of Libya, Tunisia, Algeria, and Morocco. The peoples inhabiting the oases of the Sahara, down to the deep south.

Data indicating the presence of the dual organization in the Middle East are so abundant that one may be justified in assuming that this form of social structure is one of the general character- istics of Middle Eastern culture.

GENERAL CHARACTERISTICS

Pride in descent forms one of the most significant traits in the ethos of Middle Eastern peoples. Emphasis on noble ancestry is greatest among the nomadic elements, while in the settled popu- lation, both villagers and townspeople, it appears to be weakening in recent decades.

The nomads, among whom ancient traditions have survived in greater force than among other segments of Middle Eastern society, accord the highest prestige not to the richest or most war- like families or tribes, but to those who have the oldest and most noble genealogy and the most famous men among their an- cestry.[5] "To know this pedigree is of practical value to any one who has to deal with Arab nomads, owing to the value which they themselves attach to genealogy, the social distinctions which they base upon it, and the estimation in which they hold those expert in its intricacies."[6]

Since among the Arabian nomadic and seminomadic tribes a knowledge of tribal genealogy has remained to this day such a highly prized accomplishment, every older tribesman has, as a rule, at least some rudimentary idea as to his tribal ancestry and can give some account of his genealogy. Folk memory, however, tends to simplify the complex family trees of both individuals and tribes, with the result that several links, representing a generation

each, are often omitted and several centuries of tribal history telescoped into a few brief generations.[7] This reduction in depth is
paralleled by a reduction in breadth, that is, by a simplification
of the complicated structure of tribal relationships, and notably
by a parallel arrangement of tribal groups into coequal elements,
although originally the actual relationship may have been that
of subordination of the one to the other. In this manner a complicated vertical structure is transformed by popular tradition
into a relatively simple horizontal one.[8]

In addition to this simplified tribal genealogy, the more complete and probably more faithful tradition of the origins and
relationship of the tribe is also as a rule preserved by one or two
individuals in each tribe who are specialists in tribal lore. Since
genealogic knowledge is of special importance for the families of
shaykhs, whose main claim for chieftainship rests in many cases
solely on their descent, these genealogical specialists, called
nassāba, usually are members of shaykhly families.[9]

A recurrent feature of these genealogic traditions, whether
popular or learned, is that in all parts of the Middle East they
group the tribes, and in many cases the settled population as well,
into two factions or moieties. Both the specialists and the laymen
in every tribe know to which of the two locally prevailing groups
their tribe belongs. An additional characteristic of this genealogic dichotomy is that frequently it has developed into a political
bisection and that often tribes or tribal groups belonging genealogically to one moiety have become politically attached to and
incorporated into the other. A third, even more remarkable
characteristic is that in spite of the all-pervading importance of
religion in Middle Eastern culture as a divisive force, groups
belonging to different religious sects or even to altogether different
religions are often parts of the same moiety, and conversely, that
members of the same sect or faith belong to both moieties. Finally,
moiety adherence also cuts across the omnipresent threefold division of Middle Eastern populations into nomadic, agricultural,
and urban aggregates. The political-genealogic dichotomy of
Middle Eastern society must therefore be regarded as a social
phenomenon independent of and at cross purposes with all the
other classificatory developments of the area.

A further general characteristic of this dichotomy is its re-
appearance on various levels of traditional Middle Eastern social
structure, beginning with the largest social units produced by
Middle Eastern society and down to the *hamūla*, the genetic kinship group or lineage. The prevalent pattern is that of continued
bifurcation, dividing the largest unit into two, and so forth, until
the smallest group comprising only a few extended families is
reached.

With regard to the nomadic and seminomadic tribes of the
Arabian Peninsula (including the Syrian Desert), a preliminary
count showed that this type of dual tribal structure is at least
twice as frequent as all the other nondual (unal or plural) tribal
structures together, or that at least two thirds of all the Arabian
tribes possess a dual organization.

The dual system itself is at least several centuries older than
Islam. The sixth-century Byzantine historian Procopius mentions
that the Homeritae (Himyarites, a subdivision of Qaḥṭān) were
the overlords of the Maddeni (i.e., the Maʿaddites), a northern
people.[10] The Arab tradition therefore has a solid historical basis
in speaking of the early wars in which the Maʿadd strove to
throw off the Ḥimyarite yoke.[11] As to the other Islam-dominated
countries, one cannot at this stage answer satisfactorily the question of whether the dual organization was introduced into them
by the spread of Islam or whether it had existed before and was
ultimately derived from an ancient Near Eastern, possibly
Egyptian prototype. The fact, however, remains that local dual
organizations exist all over the Middle East, from the Golden
River to the Golden Road, and that the Arab genealogists of the
Middle Ages unhesitantly assigned every Arab, Arabicized, or
Islamicized tribe to one of the two Arab ancestral stocks.

Genealogic Traditions

As to the Arabian tribes themselves, the efforts of the Arab
genealogists of the first Islamic century were directed toward
two goals: first, to assign every Arabian tribe to either of two
ancestral lines converging ultimately in two eponymous ancestors; and, secondly, to identify these two ancestors as sons or

descendants of early heroes mentioned in the Bible, in the Book of Genesis. Although much of the resulting genealogic structure must be regarded as an artificial device resorted to in order to carry through consistently a preconceived rigid genealogic scheme, there can be no doubt as to the actual division of the early Arabian population into two great stocks, nor as to the persistence in later Arabian popular thought of the tradition of the dual descent.[12]

Orientalists and Islamists have devoted much attention to the question of whether the present patrilineal descent, whose prevalence is well attested since the beginnings of Islam in the seventh century, was preceded by an older matrilineal system. This problem, however, has no direct bearing upon the subject dealt with here, for by the time the popular Arab genealogies became crystallized, there was an overwhelming consensus that every tribe was composed of the descendants in the male line of one single man: the eponymous tribal ancestor. Two related tribes were (and are to this day) generally regarded as the patrilineal descendants of two brothers, whose father, in turn, was the brother of another eponymous hero, the progenitor of one or more additional tribes, not quite as closely related to the first one. The logical conclusion of this speculative genealogic penetration farther and farther back into early legendary history was to arrive at two individuals, the first ancestors of the two all-Arabian moieties. The first of these was Qahṭān, ancestor of all the South Arabian tribes, and the second ʿAdnān, ancestor of all the North Arabian tribes.

Qahṭān was identified with the Biblical Yoqṭan (Gen. 10 : 25), son of ʿĒbher (in Arabic ʿAbar), son of Shelah (Shalakh), son of Arpakhshad (Arfakhshad), son of Shēm (Sām), son of Noah (Nūḥ) (Gen. 10 : 1, 21–25). Although there is no further correspondence between the sons of Yoqṭan as enumerated in Genesis and as appearing in the traditional genealogy of the South Arabian tribes, it is interesting to note that Biblical exegesis identifies several of the Yoqṭanides with South Arabian tribal or regional names.[13]

A tribal federation, called Qahṭān or Yaman (meaning south) actually existed in pre-Islamic times, and still occupies a considerable area southeast of Mecca. Early in the Muslim period,

Qaḥṭān was divided into two parts: the one, called Kahlān, was the larger group, comprising mostly nomadic and seminomadic tribes, while the other, called Ḥimyar, was a smaller group, consisting mostly of settled peoples.[14]

'Adnān, the father of all the North Arabian tribes, is regarded by Arab genealogists as the son of Ishmael (Ismāʿīl), son of Abraham. Of the ten sons of 'Adnān,[15] Maʿadd, through his son Nizār, became the progenitor of the North Arabians. Two of Nizār's sons, Rabīʿa and Muḍar, are regarded as the ancestors of most northern tribes, that is, the tribes who inhabited in pre-Islamic days the northern half of the Arabian peninsula as far south as the 22nd or the 21st parallel N. Probably the most famous and noble of the northern tribes were those known collectively as Qays, after the name of their eponymous ancestor varyingly called Qays 'Aylān, son of Muḍar, or Qays son of 'Aylān, son of Muḍar.[16] The totality of northern tribes is called either 'Adnān, in which case the southern group as a whole is referred to as Qaḥṭān, or Qays, in which case the opposite moiety is called Yaman (Yemen). The northern tribes, in addition, are also referred to as Maʿadd, or Nizār, or Muḍar tribes.

Since Qaḥṭān belonged, according to the Bible, to the fifth generation after Noah, while 'Adnān lived in the 12th generation after Noah, the Qaḥṭān or southern tribes were regarded as constituting the older or true aboriginal Arab stock (al-'Arab al-ʿāriba), while the northern 'Adnānis were considered as the younger group, as merely Arabicized (al-'Arab al-*mustaʿriba*) peoples.[17]

ETHNIC MOVEMENTS AND POLITICAL DUALISM

Whatever the historical kernel of this tradition of dual descent, it seems certain that 'Adnān (northern) and Qaḥṭān (southern) tribal groups were "separated even in pre-Islamic times by racial hatred, perhaps originally mainly based on the opposition between the desert and the sown."[18] The original home of the southern tribes was Southern Arabia, and more specifically its south-western corner, roughly corresponding to the area occupied today by the Kingdom of Yemen. Emigrations of southern tribes from this corner of the Arabian peninsula took place at an early date. Toward the end of the third century A.D., when the famous dam of Ma'rib was destroyed, a Yamani tribe fled the country and settled in the Hawran and al-Balqa districts of Syria. Even earlier than these, several other Yamanī tribes settled in the fertile region west of the Euphrates (modern Iraq), and some of these later moved on to southern Lebanon where their descendants profess to this day the Druze religion.[19]

While these examples illustrate the pre-Islamic establishment of southern tribes in the very midst of northern regions, the ethnic movements of the northern tribes can also be followed back to almost as remote a period. Arab tradition has it that the Qays tribe itself, the main prototype and protagonist of the northern division, originally inhabited the low parts of the Tihāma district in southwestern Arabia and was thus a close neighbor of the Yamanī tribes. In the sixth century, however, Qays tribes were already found spread over vast areas in northern and central Arabia. Mohammed (570–632) himself belonged, with his tribe, the Quraysh, to the northern group, although not to the Qays, but to its el-Yās branch. The people of Medina (north of Mecca), however, who were the first supporters (Anṣār) of Mohammed after his flight from Mecca (the so-called Hijra, in 622), were of Qaḥtānī southern origin whose readiness to rally behind Mohammed may well have been motivated by the traditional rivalry between them and the northern Qurayshites of Mecca who originally opposed Mohammed. This historical accident undoubtedly played a significant role in sharpening the conflict between the two groups, for each felt that it had a valid claim to superiority: the northerners on account of their genealogic relationship to the Prophet, and the southerners on account of the incontestable merit of having been his first supporters.

Although Islam brought in many places a tremendous superiority to the 'Adnān (northern) faction, tribal rivalry became more pointed as a result of political developments in the first few decades after the death of Mohammed; and after the battle of Marj Rāhiṭ (in 65/685) the tendency to form tribal federations became even more intensified. This was a period of calculated re-alignments. The powerful tribal groups of Tamīm (in Khurasan,

Iran), Qays, and Muḍar joined forces and constituted the northern faction, while the Azd, the Yamanīs, and later the Syrian Quḍāʿa (or Kalb) lined up against them as the southern moiety. The effects of this dual grouping of the most powerful tribal federations was to bisect the entire Arab world, and to wipe out, temporarily at least, other local antagonisms.[20]

The spread of Islam and the great social and political upheavals that accompanied it resulted in the uprooting of many tribes and in forced or voluntary migrations. These ethnic movements effected a further throwing together and mixing up of northern and southern tribes. Under the early Caliphs, considerable numbers of southern groups were found throughout Syria, in Mesopotamia (including large factions of the population of al-Kūfa and al-Baṣra), in Bahrein, in Isfahan. From Baṣra they penetrated even distant Khurasan where the Azdites and the Rabīʿa (Bakr) were included among them.[21]

Hand in hand with actual dislocations and ethnic movements went the fictitious assignment of northern or southern genealogy to newly conquered or converted populations. In general, all the native peoples of the northern provinces, such as the Nabateans of Idumea, as well as the inhabitants of the northernmost oasis outposts such as Palmyra, came to be regarded as sons of ʿAdnān, that is, as belonging to the northern stock.

While geographically the distinction between southern and northern tribes lost its meaning as a result of such ethnic movements and countermovements, the traditional Arab emphasis on nobility of descent kept the memory of the dual origin alive down to the present time. As late as the end of the nineteenth century all the noble Arab tribes regarded themselves as the descendants of either Qaḥṭān or Ishmael,[22] that is, as either southerners or northerners.

Under the Umayyad Caliphs, who took wives from both factions, the hostilities between the two led to intermittent and often extremely bloody strife. The reigning Caliph was constrained to rely alternatingly on either the Qays or the Kalb (Yaman) for support. In the latter part of the Umayyad period especially, the Caliph appeared to be "rather the head of a particular party than the sovereign of a united empire."[23] Between 719 and 745, that is, within 26 years, the actual control of the government passed five times from one faction to the other.[24]

The repeated alliances of the Qaysite Umayyad dynasty with the Yamanīs shows the diminishing importance of the genealogic as against the political factor in the constitution of the two parties. Moreover, it repeatedly happened that individuals and groups, and even the reigning monarch himself, changed party allegiance for material or political reasons. Thus the Caliph Hisham was at the beginning of his rule a Yamanī but later declared himself to be a Qaysite for what seemed to be purely pecuniary reasons. In 734, he appointed a Qaysite governor of Africa, who, upon finding only two small Qaysite tribes in Egypt, promptly imported 1,300 poor Qaysī families, thus to strengthen his popular support.[25]

In general, however, party allegiance was a serious matter that often led to hostilities and bloodshed in all parts of the expanding domains of Islam. The district of Damascus became the scene of relentless warfare for two years because a Ma'addite (northerner) had stolen a melon from a Yamanite's (southerner's) garden. In Murcia in Spain blood is said to have flowed for several years because a Muḍarite (northerner) picked a vine leaf from the yard of a Yamanite. The beginning of the ninth century saw a seven-year war fought between the Yamanites and the Ma'addites. Toward the end of the same century, in the province of Elvira in Spain, the rivalry between the two parties almost cost the Arabs their rule of the entire province.[26] "Everywhere, in the capital as well as in the provinces, on the banks of the Indus, the shores of Sicily and the borders of the Sahara, the ancestral feud, transformed into an alignment of two political parties, one against the other, made itself felt. It proved a potent factor in ultimately arresting the progress of Moslem arms in France and in the decline of the Andalusian caliphate."[27]

OMAN AND THE EAST COAST OF ARABIA

The preponderance of the political over the genealogic factor characterizes the dual organization of the 118 tribes of Oman, in the southeastern part of the Arabian peninsula, at the present time. The Oman tribes belong to either of two factions, called

Hināwī after the powerful Benī Hinā tribe, and Ghāfirī, after the strong Benī Ghāfir tribe, respectively. These names have been current in Oman for at least two hundred years. Prior to that time, the Hināwīs used to be known for centuries as Yamanīs, and were identified as southerners, while the Ghāfirīs were known as Nizārīs and northerners. The Hināwī faction, which is the more powerful of the two, comprises, generally speaking, tribes of southern or Qaḥṭānī genealogy; while the majority of the Ghāfirī tribes are of 'Adnānī or northern origin. Of the 111 Oman tribes whose party affiliation and traditional origin are known, 61 belong today to the Hināwī party. Of these, however, only 53 are of traditionally southern (Qaḥṭānī) origin while the remaining eight tribes, although at present belonging to the Hināwī faction, are known to be of northern ('Adnānī) descent. Conversely, of the 50 tribes making up the present strength of the Ghāfirī party, only 44 are of northern origin, while the remaining six are of southern origin. These figures show that in the case of a considerable percentage of the tribes political considerations have overridden traditional ties of descent and resulted in a switch of allegiance.

The following particulars will contribute to our understanding of these relatively frequent changes of factional allegiance in Oman. The larger and more powerful tribes of the same faction are mostly in alliance or in league with one another in each district. The purpose of these alliances, called in Arabic *ṣuff*, is primarily political: they are defense alliances with mutual commitments to come to the aid of one another if attacked. The weaker tribes living in the proximity of these powerful allied tribes have no choice but to place themselves under their protection in a client-master relationship known also from other regions of the Middle East. Whatever the original descent of such weaker tribes, they must ally themselves politically with the powerful *ṣuff* in whose shadow they dwell, and ultimately affiliate themselves with their political faction. In other cases the reason for affiliating oneself with the opposite faction lies in internal quarrels between two sections of a tribe, as a result of which the weaker section is constrained to seek the help of its traditional enemies against its brother tribe.

The district alliances of tribes belonging to the same faction constitute a country-wide coalition of the Hināwī and Ghāfirī factions respectively. In spite of the obviously political coloring of these two factions, in the popular thinking of the tribes themselves they are held together by the ties of kinship.

The relationship between the two factions is that of traditional hostility and undisguised antagonism, "keeping the country in perpetual turmoil and disruption through their jealous feuds and hatreds, and this undying enmity is the key to the internal history of the land." [28]

The enmity between the two factions is so keen that a stranger wishing to travel among the tribes must take along both a Hināwī and a Ghāfirī guide to serve as guarantors of his safety.

There is no clear-cut geographic division between the two factions, although the Hināwī predominate in the southeast including the Bāṭina coast, and the Ghāfirī in the northwest, as well as in the central tribal block. The intermingling of the two factions throughout the country usually takes the form of groups of villages belonging to one of them and maintaining a constant state of feud with a neighboring group of villages belonging to the other. Often a single town or village is split into two by allegiance to the two factions, and the tension and hostility between the two are intensified when, owing to its location, one of the two moieties is able to control the water supply of the whole settlement.

The town of Nizwa, for example, which formerly was the capital of Oman, was torn for a long time by the strife between the Benī Hinā who inhabited the lower town and the Benī Riyām who occupied the upper town and were able to cut off the water supply from the lower town. [29]

The religion of the majority in both factions is the Ibāḍī sect of Islam. But among the Hināwī almost three quarters of the tribes are Ibāḍī and only one quarter Sunni Muslim, while among the Ghāfirī some 60 per cent are Ibāḍī and 40 per cent Sunni. A few Ghāfirī tribes (notably the Benī Rasib and Benī Bū 'Alī) follow the puritanistic Wahhābī creed of Central Arabia.

The Hināwī and Ghāfirī division cuts also across Trucial Oman, where, however, the Hināwī are Mālikī Sunnīs, and the Ghāfirī virtually Wahhābīs. [30]

In the eighteenth century there was a civil war and a dynastic squabble over succession in Oman between the Hināwī and the Ghāfirī factions, but the existence of the dual division and the tension still characterizing the relationship between the two, cannot be attributed to this cause alone.

Interesting are the instances in which traditions contrary to the generally prevalent belief in the tribal origin of the dual organization of Oman have remained alive in certain tribes. The Daru' and the Manāhil, for instance, although belonging to opposite moieties, maintain a tradition of common origin.[31]

The South Coast of Arabia

While the eastern section of the south of Arabia forms part of Oman, the central and western regions constitute the Eastern and Western Aden Protectorates respectively. This entire region is inhabited by both settled agriculturist and nomadic pastoral populations, both organized on a tribal basis. The typical South Arabian social organization is a tribal confederation, headed by a sultan, and consisting of nomadic tribes, agricultural villages, as well as a few towns. Very often these tribal confederations have a dual character.

The two over-all parties to either of which the individual confederations belong are called in the Hadhramaut (Ḥaḍramawt; the central part of the South Arabian coastal region) Yafa' and Ḥamdān. All the free tribes boast of belonging to one of these two factions, and only the lower classes of society such as the low-caste inhabitants of Shihr and other nontribesmen are not directly involved in this dichotomy.[32]

Both the Yafa' and the Ḥamdān belong to the southern division, that is, regard themselves as the descendants of Qaḥṭān. Saba (who was the son of Yashjub son of Ya'rub son of Qaḥṭān) had two sons, Ḥimyar and Kahlān by name.[33] These two are claimed to be the ancestors of the Yafa' and Ḥamdān respectively. The ultimately common origin of the two sections does not, of course, prevent them from continuing in a state of unceasing rivalry, enmity, and open hostility.

The most powerful group of the Ḥimyarī Yafa' confederation

is the section that has retained the original name of Yafa'. The powerful and warlike Yafa' confederation, comprising more than one hundred thousand souls, occupies a considerable tract of land to the northeast of Aden town, just south of the frontier of the Aden Protectorate. It consists of two sections: the Upper Yafa' in the north, and the Lower Yafa' in the south. The chief tribes of the Upper Yafa' are the Mausata, Dhūbī, Maflaḥī, Bo'sī and Da'ūdi; those of the Lower Yafa' are the Kaladī, Yaharī, Sa'dī, Yazīdī and Banī 'Afīf. Other tribes belonging to the Yafa' group include the Ahl Arḍī.[34]

Schematic Genealogical Table of the
Tribes of Hadhramaut

To the northeast of Aden town lies the port of Shaqra or Sughrah, which is the center of another confederation of tribes of Ḥimyarī descent constituting the Sultanate of Faḍlī. The Faḍlī are divided into numerous sections, one of the largest of which, the Merākash (sing. Merkāshī) was known for the loose morality of its women and the survival of several matriarchal or matrilineal traits.[35]

To the north of the Faḍlī is the 'Awdhalī Sultanate, named after the 'Awdhilla tribe. It includes the Dathīna district, inhabited by two great tribal confederations, the Ahl al-Sa'īdī and the 'Olah ('ölah, 'Ulah). The 'Olah again are divided into two groups: the 'Olah al-Kōr, inhabiting the Kōr (Kawr) Mountain, and the 'Olah al-Baḥr, or Sea-'Olah. The former comprises five, the latter eight tribes. According to the genealogic traditions of the 'Olah, they all are the descendants of 'Olah who was the grandson of Madḥij, and who had two sons, Sa'īd el-Buqeyrāt, from whom three of the 'Olah tribes are descended, and 'Alī el-Buqeyrāt, who became the ancestor of all the other 'Olah tribes.[36]

To the north of the 'Awdhalī Sultanate, and separated from it by an eastern tongue of Yemen, is the independent territory of Bayḥān in the Western Aden Protectorate. This territory comprises two parts: Bayḥān al-Asfal (with four districts), and Bayḥān al-Qaṣāb, inhabited by the tribe of al-Muṣ'abayn. As the name indicates ("the two Muṣ'abs"), this tribe consists of two moieties, descended from the two sons of the original progenitor, Muṣ'ab: Aḥmed, vulgarly called Ḥomeyd, became the ancestor of the Āl Aḥmed, and 'Arīf the father of the Āl 'Arīf. Each of the two sons, in turn, had four sons, to whom the eight subtribes trace their descent.[37] The accompanying diagram shows the structure of the Muṣ'abayn.

To the northeast of the Faḍli is the ʻAwlaqī tribal confederation consisting of Yafaʻi Himyarite tribes. It is divided into two sultanates: to the north is that of the Upper ʻAwlaqī, called ʻAwlaqī el-Niṣāb or ʻAwlaqī al-ʻAliyu, and to the south, on the coast, that of the Lower ʻAwlaqī, called ʻAwlaqī ʻAli Nasir or ʻAwlaqī Bā Kāzim. The Upper ʻAwlaqī are again subdivided into two parts, the Benī Maʻan (or Maʻam; comprising 18 tribes) in the southeast, and the Maḥājir (23 tribes) in the north, each with a separate ruler of its own, but both claiming Yafaʻi descent. The Lower ʻAwlaqī also fall into two sections, each with many subdivisions, called Bā Kāzim and Laqmush (or Qumūsh) respectively.[38] The Ḥammām of the Wādī Ḥammām and Wādī Markha are an ʻAwlaqī tribe who do not acknowledge the suzerainty of the ʻAwlaqī Sultan of Ansāb (Niṣāb). The ruling family of Niṣāb claims descent from a Jaufi ancestry.[39]

To the east of the ʻAwlaqī on the coast is another Himyarite confederation, the Dheaybī (or Dhiaybī, Dhiĕbī), or Ḥimyar; they used the word "ḥimyar" as their war-cry. This tribal confederation, which regards itself as kin to the Laqmush (Qumūsh), is divided into two factions: the Great Ḥimyar (*Ḥimyar al-kubra*), whose territory touches upon the Yafaʻ to the west, and the Little Ḥimyar (*Ḥimyar al-ṣughra*) who inhabit the Wādī Ḥalbān and its vicinity, and who, in turn, are subdivided into five tribes.[40]

The eastern neighbor of the Dheaybī or Ḥimyar is one of the most powerful Yafaʻī tribes, the Qaʻaytī, which occupies the seashore around the towns of Mukallā and Shiheir (Shihr), as well as the hinterland as far north as Shibam and Haurah. All these townships, as well as the towns of Hojarein and Qatan and the entire intervening territory belongs to the Qaʻaytī and constitutes the Qaʻaytī sultanate of Mukallā.[41]

East of the Qaʻaytī, on the coast, the Mahra, a large tribe numbering several thousands, occupies an extensive steppe area. This tribe does not speak Arabic, but retains its ancient Ḥimyarite dialect, as well as several archaic customs (such as taking their mothers' names instead of their fathers'), and prides itself on the antiquity of its genealogy claiming descent from ʻĀd ibn Aws ibn Irem ibn Shām (Shem) ibn Nūḥ (Noah).[42] This genealogy is, of course, a strongly abbreviated or telescoped version of a fuller tribal family tree that has been reconstructed as follows: Mahra b. Heydan b. 'Amr b. el-Hafi b. Quḍā'a b. Mālik b. 'Amr b. Murra b. Zeyd b. Mālik b. Ḥimyar.[43] The Mahra tribal confederation consists of four divisions called *'uṣebāt*: Bin Gesūs, Shehshihī, Bin Sār, and Bin Boqi bin Aḥmed, each one of whom comprises numerous tribes. The Mahra confederation is ruled by the Bin Afrar family (claiming relationship with the Benī Alif of the Lower Yafa') which is divided into two branches: the senior branch, called Sa'd bin Towar, residing in Soqotra, and the junior branch, 'Āmr bin Towar, ruling for the sultan in Mahraland itself.[44]

While the western part of South Arabia, including the Western Aden Protectorate, is thus found to belong traditionally to the Ḥimyar moiety of Qaḥṭān (with a few exceptions to be noted later), the predominant element in the central and eastern parts of the Eastern Aden Protectorate is the Kahlān moiety of Qaḥṭān, or more precisely, the Ḥamdān elements of Kahlān. According to the traditional genealogy, Ḥamdān, who was a sixth generation descendant of Kahlān,[45] had two sons, Kathīr and 'Amr.[46] The descendants of Kathīr are the Kathīrī, the powerful eastern neighbors of the Himyarite Qa'aytī in the Hadhramaut,[47] who occupy not only the greater part of Central Hadhramaut including the Hadhramī towns of Seyyūn (or Saiūn), Terim, and Ghurfa, but also the entire coastal district of Ẓufar. The boundary between the two groups runs in a southeasterly direction between the Qa'aytī town of Shibam and the Kathīrī town of Seyyūn, the seat of the Kathīrī sultan. These two towns are located at a distance of a mere ten miles from each other. These two tribes "are extremely hostile to each other."[48]

The Kathīrī themselves fall into two sections, the western of which, inhabiting Central Hadhramaut, is headed by the Kathīrī Sultan of Seyyūn (whose traditional rival is the Qa'aytī sultan of Mukallā), while the eastern section, located around the Ẓufar coast, is ruled by the governor of Ẓufar who is a representative of the Sultan of Oman.[49] The Kathīrī Sultanate of Seyyūn consists, in addition to the towns and villages of Seyyūn, Tarim, Taris, al-Ghurfa, Mariama, and Al Gheil, also of a confederation of a considerable number of tribal groups, the Kathīrī, the

7

'Awāmir, the Jabirī, and the Bajrī.[50] The Eastern Kathīrī are
again subdivided into two divisions, both of whom are represented in seven villages of the Zufar coast and are called 'Omar
bin Kathīr or al-'Umar and 'Amr bin Kathīr or Āl 'Amr, respectively. The same two tribes inhabit also al-Ghurfa and Ahl
Fās (two villages between Shibam and Seyyūn) and are constantly at feud with each other.[51]

The traditional rivals of the Kathīrī are the Qara who are
wedged in between them and the al-Rashīd, an independent
section of the Kathīrī. Al-Rashīd occupies a territory contiguous
to the central portion of the Kathīrī country. The traditional
enemies of al-Rashīd are the Sa'ar (or Say'ar) in the northern
Hadhramaut, to the west of al-Rashīd and to the northeast of the
town of Seyyūn. Another independent section of the Kathīrī is
the Bayt Imānī.[52] So much for the Kathīr moiety of Hamdān.

The 'Amr moiety of Hamdān claims descent from 'Amr ibn
Hamdān. The main representative of this moiety is the 'Awāmir
confederation located in three separate areas: (1) al-Qaff, from
the Wādī Hadhramaut as far north as the southern edge of the
Rub' al-Khālī; (2) al-Zafra between Qaṭar and al-Buraymī; and
(3) Oman. Although the three parts of the tribe have little
contact with one another, a twofold division into Āl Badr and
Āl Lazz runs through all of them.[53]

The genealogic affiliation of the other Hadhramī tribes is not
clear, but one can assume that they too belong to the Ḥimyar
or Kahlān moieties of Qaḥtān. This country lies close to the
Oman border and the typical Oman dichotomy into Hināwī
and Ghāfirī is found in it as well. Thus the Harasī, Afar, Manāhil,
and the 'Awāmir and al-Kathīr themselves are said to belong to
the Hināwī, while the Daru', the Ālbū Shamis, and even the more
distantly western Say'ar are regarded as Ghāfirī, their avowedly
Qahtānī descent notwithstanding. Here, however, as distinct from
Oman proper, these labels have no political significance, and
instead of the factional solidarity that is supreme in Oman,
allegiance follows genealogic lines.[54]

The Say'ar, probably identical with the Ausaretae mentioned
by Pliny, claim to be ultimately descended from the Qahtān
tribe through an ancestor named Mighdad al-Aswad, who is

said to have been a Companion of the Prophet. One of the Say'ar tribes is the al-Junaybir which moved from the Hadhramaut to the Najrān area within Saudi Arabia. The main tribal area of the Say'ar lies to the east of that of the Dahm and to the north of the Hadhramaut valley. The Hadhramaut Say'ar are divided into two sections, a semisettled element (of which the Āl 'Abdullah bin 'Aun are a constituent tribe) called Ahl Ḥātim, centering around a scattered group of hamlets called Raydat Ahl Ḥātim, and ruled by two leading chieftains; and a purely nomadic section called Ahl bil-Layth whose chieftain has his semipermanent head-quarters, called Raydat Ahl bil-Layth, at wells located some 25 to 30 miles east of Raydat Ahl Ḥātim. The two village groups together are known as Raydat al-Say'ar in the Wādī Makhya. Another Say'ar tribe is the Al Baqī Msellem one of whose two chiefs resides in Ba Rumeydan due north of Wādī Hadhramaut.[55]

To the east of the Say'ar stretches the territory of yet another dual confederation, that of the Mishqas. The southern Mishqas confederation embraces all non-Kathīrī elements south of the eastern section of the Hadhramaut valley. The Humūmī are one of these tribes, with the Bā-Aḥsan as one of its clans. The northern Mishqas comprise the Manāhil, 'Awāmir, and Tamīm tribes.[56]

YEMEN

The available information on the tribal organization in the Kingdom of Yemen is very fragmentary. *The Handbook of Arabia* enumerates 74 tribes or tribal confederations in Yemen, but it states only occasionally how these units are structured, that is how many and what kind of subdivisions they comprise. As to the tribal genealogy—this is mentioned in two or three cases only. Nor is information available as to the presence or absence of the dual organization.

Among the tribes claiming a definitely southern origin are the following: Bekīl, Ḥamdān, Ḥāshid, Khaulān, Benī Murra. As against these, the following seem to be of northern extraction: Al 'Absī or 'Absiyah, 'Anaza, Benī Ismā'īl, Benī Qays.

Dual division within each of the two moieties is found among several tribes. The most important of these is that of Ḥāshid and

Bekīl. According to tribal traditions, Ḥamdān begot Jusham who
begot Ḥāshid el-Akbar who begot Bekīl. Another version of the
tradition has it that Ḥāshid and Bekīl were the two sons of
Babroshām and his wife, the princess Nejema, who came from
Anatolia to Yemen. The Ḥāshid tribes counted 22,000 armed men
in the first quarter of the twentieth century, while the Bekīl at
the same time counted 80,000. Both the Ḥāshid and the Bekīl
follow the Zaydī sect. They live in the area called Balad Ḥamdān
(to the north of the capital, Ṣanʿa), the eastern part of which
belongs to the Bekīl and the western to the Ḥāshid. In spite of
the traditional close relationship between the two groups, their
attitude toward each other has been that of enmity which occasionally erupted into fighting, as, for example, in 1885, when
there was a bloody war between the two.[57]

It is interesting to note that among the Ḥāshid a threefold
division is found, instead of the more common dual one. The
whole of the Ḥāshid is divided into three groups: al-Khārif,
Benī Ṣuraym, and al-ʿUsaymāt. Al-Khārif again is subdivided
into three subgroups, the tribes of Jubar, Kalbīyīn, and al-Ṣayad.
The Benī Ṣuraym is subdivided into nine (three times three)
groups, called *tsiʿe* or ninth; and the ʿUsaymāt are subdivided
again into three groups. These threefold divisions are called
thulth, third.[58]

Among several other Yemenite tribes the usual dual division
is found. The Ahl ʿAmmar, the ʿAnaza, the Ḥamdān, the Khaulan,
and the Benī Saʿfan are each subdivided into two groups. In two
cases at least this subdivision has a geographic connotation: the
two subdivisions of the Ḥamdān are called Ḥamdān esh-Shām
(Ḥamdān of the North) and Ḥamdān el-Yemen (Ḥamdān of
the South), respectively. The two subdivisions of the Khaulān
are called Khaulān el-Ṭawal (Long Khaulān), and Khaulān
esh-Shām (Khaulān of the North) respectively.[59]

ʿAsīr

North of Yemen on the west coast of the Arabian peninsula lies
the province of ʿAsīr. In the southern part of ʿAsīr the main
tribal elements are comprised in a tribal confederation that falls
into two main groups: ʿAsīr al-Ḥijāz and ʿAsīr al-Tihāma, the

former occupying the main range, the latter the transverse ranges
and valleys between it and the coastal plain (Tihāma). According
to information obtained by Philby from the elders of the village
Suda in the highlands of 'Asīr, the 'Asīr al-Ḥijāz comprise the
following four tribes: 1. Banī Mughayd; 2. 'Alkam; 3. Rabī'a
wa-Rufayda; 4. Banī Mālik. The 'Asīr al-Tihāma comprise seven
tribes: 1. Banī Zayd; 2. Ahl Tha'lab; 3. Banī Juna; 4. Al-Qays;
5. Banī Qutba; 6. al-Shaba; and 7. Banī Dhalim. Each of these
eleven tribes has a shaykh of its own and comprises several
subdivisions.[60] Although Philby does not specify the genealogic
claims of these tribes, we know that the Banī Mālik are of Qahṭān
stock as are the Rabī'a wa-Rufayda.[61]

The Banī Mālik Tribes

According to popular tradition, the Banī Mālik are the descendants of an eponymous ancestor called Mālik. This Mālik is

said to have had two sons, Mughāmir and Kathīr, who became the progenitors of the two main branches of the present Banī Mālik. Mughāmir again had two sons: Khālid, father of the present Khālidī, and Saʿīd, father of the present Saʿīdī sections of the Banī Mālik. The other son of Mālik, Kathīr, had four sons, ʿAlil (father of the present Ahl ʿAlil), Yaʿla, father of the present Ahl Salma and Ahl Habs), Haris (father of the present Benī Haris) and Raym. Raym again had three sons, of whom Yahya became the ancestor of the present Yahyawī section, Zaydān that of the present Zaydānī section, while the third, Nukhayf, seems to have had no descendants. The Benī Haris are divided into a southern and a northern branch, called Haris al-Yamanī and Haris am-Hashr, respectively. The southern Benī Haris have two main sections: Akāwīn and Ahl ʿAmr.

Mālik himself belonged to the Khaulan group, and therefore all the Benī Mālik are simply a branch of Khaulan. The Khaulan are descended from Khaulan ibn ʿAmir. Both the Khaulan and the Qahtān tribes are jointly regarded as Banī ʿAmir.

The Khaulan themselves are divided into two groups: one is the so called Yahanīya group (descended from Yahnawī, son or descendant of Khaulan), which comprises the Banī Mālik, Banī Jumaʿa, Ahl Fayfā, as well as a number of additional tribes. The other Khaulan group is the al-Furūd, which comprises four tribal confederations: the Bal Ghāzī, Banī Munabba, Ashar, and Nasīfa. According to the medieval Arab genealogists, Khaulan ibn ʿAmr was a descendant of Kahlān and the eponymous ancestor of a large tribe that spread from Yemen to Syria and then to Egypt.[62]

To the north of this group is the territory of the Shahrān tribes, a large and independent group that seems to derive ultimately from Qahtān stock. This large tribal confederation, which is headed by a titular shaykh, is traditionally hostile to its northwestern neighbors, the highlanders of ʿAsīr. The Shahrān tribal confederation consists of a large number of tribes, most of which are again subdivided into several sections. Philby mentions the following Shahrān tribes: Muʿāwya, Banī Sulum, Banī Munabba, Wahib, Kud, Nahas, Rushayd, Banī Bijad, Banī Hamudh, Ahl Tindaha, Ahl al-Shām (comprising the Maʿraj, Maʿjūr,

'Askar, Wayla, and other subsections), 'Abs, as well as a related Banī Shihr tribe.[63] The Shahrān have both settled and nomadic sections.

Although no mention of a bisection of the Shahrān group is made by Philby, there are certain indications that seem to point in this direction. First of all, one group of the Shahrān are called Ahl al-Shām, that is, people of the north, and said to be the offshoot of the Banī Shihr of northern 'Asīr. This would indicate that other Shahrān tribes may be regarded as belonging to a southern section of the confederation. Secondly, several Shahrān tribal names (for example, Banī Sulum, 'Abs) reappear farther to the east as tribes of the Qaḥṭān confederation, which is definitely divided into a southern and a northern moiety. The partial affiliation of one and the same tribe with two larger units is a familiar phenomenon also in other parts of Arabia. Thirdly, dual division is the basic form of social organization among all the tribal units of the area (Murra, Qaḥṭān, 'Asīr, and others) and it seems therefore probable that it also existed or still exists among the Shahrān.

Another descendant of Kahlān, Ḥamdān, who, as we have seen, is regarded as the eponymous ancestor of one of the two moieties of the south Arabian tribes, reappears in the genealogic traditions of the tribes of 'Asīr and the contiguous section of the Rub' al-Khālī to the east. Ḥamdān was the son of Mālik who was the son of Zayd, but in popular 'Asīrī tradition he is known as Ḥamdān ibn Zayd.[64] In the Jauf area near the Yemen-Saudi Arabian border are the Dahm tribes, while the Wada' hold the Dhahran district just north of the Yemen-'Asīr frontier. Both these groups are large independent tribal confederations belonging to the Ḥamdān stock.[65]

Another and very widely dispersed branch of the Ḥamdān stock is that of the Yām. According to 'Asīrī tradition, Yām was the son of Yusba' who was the son of Ḥamdān. Yām himself had two sons, Jusham (popularly pronounced Chām), and Madhkar, who were the progenitors of the two great branches into which the Yām tribes at present are divided. To the Chām (Jusham) group belong the Rizq, Sulum, Ahl al-Ḥārith, and Ahl al-Hindī groups, as well as the very widespread Murra group of eastern

Rubʿ al-Khālī. The Madhkar group falls into two parts, the
Mawājid, of which the Beni Nusayd are a subsection, and the
Ahl Fāṭima, comprising the descendants of Fāṭima, the second
wife of Madhkar. The Ahl Fāṭima again are subdivided into two
groups, called Hisham and Wasil. No information seems to be
available of the Wasil, but Hisham is again subdivided into two
groups, called ʿAjaym and Wuʿayl. Nothing is known of the
ʿAjaym, but the Wuʿayl comprise the following tribes: al-ʿArja,
al-Rashīd, al-Fahhād, al-Muṭliq, al-Futayḥ, al-Ḥasan, Ibn ʿĪsa,
al-Zayid, al-Waʿla, Ahl Ḥamad ibn Fāḍil, as well as the large and
important ʿAjmān tribal federation.[66] The Ahl Fāṭima also comprise the Nisiyīn, Dhayban, and Ahl Hushaysh sections whose
nearer affiliation is not known.

The Yām Tribes

With regard to the 'Ajmān (or 'Ujmān) it should be noted that since the eighteenth century they have lived in the Ḥasa region near the central part of the east coast of Arabia,[67] at a distance of some 500 miles from Najrān, and yet the tradition of their Najrān home and Yām descent has been preserved to this day not only in 'Asīr but also among the 'Ajmān themselves in Ḥasa. According to 'Ajmān tradition the Yām tribes comprise in addition to themselves also the Murra, Manāsir, Manāhir, 'Awāmir, Rashīd, Say'ar and Karab.[68] Such recurrences of basic-ally identical tribal traditions in widely separated areas, and going back to several generations, are calculated to increase our trust in the existence of a historical kernel underlying them. The al-'Arja and the al-Rashīd, who according to Philby's 'Asīrī informant belong to the Ahl Fāṭima,[69] appear as two actual tribal groups related to the 'Ajmān, living in southern Tuweyq, and still preserving the memory of the Najrānī origin.[70] Other 'Asīr tribes subdivided into two moieties are the following:

'Air (or Bal-'Air), divided into the nomadic Āl 'Amr, and the sedentary al-Nawāshirah sections, a total of about 35,000 persons.

'Alkam (or 'Alkam al-Haul), north of Abha, divided into 'Alkam al-Sāḥil and 'Alkam al-A'lūn, a total of about 20,000 persons.

Ghāmid, between Abha and Taif, subdivided into the settled al-Ḥadr and the nomadic Āl Ṣiyāḥ sections, at odds with each other.

Hilāl, divided into a western part along the coast and an eastern part along Halī, a total of about 35,000.

Qarn (or Bal-Qarn), from southwest of the Bishah valley to the mountain slopes, divided into a settled coastal group and a partly nomadic mountain group, a total of about 40,000.[71]

Before leaving the 'Asīr district for a glance at the interior of Southern Arabia, which is the present home of the large Murra division of the Yām, of the Qaḥṭān, and of the tribes that retained the name Yām itself, a word must be said about Zayd, the father (or grandfather) of Ḥamdān, ancestor of this large tribal group. According to Philby, this Zayd was identical with Zayd al-Hilālī, the most famous legendary hero (also called Abū Zayd al-Hilālī)[72] of the Benī Hilāl, about whom many colorful legends

7§

are still told in Southern Arabia.[73] From Philby's wording it does
not become clear whether this identification is his own or was
done by his 'Asīrī informants, in which case it would be a good
example of that merging of different historical or legendary
figures into one that is characteristics of the working of popular
fancy and tradition.

The Benī Hilāl, who in the early Middle Ages left the Yemen-
'Asīr region, invaded Egypt, and spread all over North Africa,
were a northern, Qaysī, tribal confederation.[74] Their tribal
genealogy is still remembered in Arabia in the usual abridged
form as Hilāl b. Hawāzin b. Qays,[75] while the fuller form according to the medieval Arab genealogists is Hilāl b. 'Amir b. Ṣa'ṣa'a
b. Mu'āwiya b. Bekr b. Hawāzin b. Manṣūr b. 'Ikrima b. Khaṣafa
b. Qays.[76] Obviously therefore Zayd, the progenitor of the
important Ḥamdān section of the Qaḥtān, cannot be identical
with Zayd, leader of the Benī Hilāl, an important Qaysī tribal
confederation.

THE RUB' AL-KHĀLĪ

Under this heading will be treated briefly the tribes inhabiting
the entire southern half of the interior of the Arabian Peninsula.
In contrast to the large number of small groups with their intricate interrelationship, characterizing the social structure of the
coastal sections of Southern Arabia, the interior, most of which is
taken up by the Rub' al-Khālī, the Empty Quarter, the great
South Arabian Desert, is but sparsely peopled by a few tribes
(with several subdivisions, of course), each one of which is undisputed master of a very large if inhospitable tribal area.

The entire southern part of the Rub' al-Khālī, from Yemen
in the west to Oman in the east, a territory of roughly 150,000
square miles of sandy desert, is held, as far as one can judge from
the scarce data available, by the Murra confederation of tribes
who trace their descent to 'Alī al-Murra.[77]

As to the genealogic connections of the Murra, we have already
seen that they are one of the Jusham groups. According to a native
authority quoted by Fu'ād Ḥamza, the Jusham comprise four
groups: Āl Dimnān, Āl Hetēle, Āl Murra, and Āl Hindī.[78] Of
these four we have already met the Al Hindī of the Najrān dis-

trict. The Āl Dimnān and Āl Hetēle, although in the traditional
genealogy offered by the native informant they appear as brothers
of the Murra, that is, non-Murra tribes who have a common
ancestor with the Murra, are today two small subgroups of the
Murra, still headed each by a shaykh of its own, but numbering
only 60 and 50 tents respectively.[79]

This change of status of a tribe or subtribe in relation to the
larger unit of which it forms a part is characteristic of the vertical
mobility of tribal organization. Popular memory retains the older
order of several generations ago with which the actual situation
may be at wide variance. In connection with the Murra, the
shifting of the position of individual groups within the entire
tribal structure can be shown clearly in several cases.

The accompanying illustration shows the traditional tribal
organization of the Murra with its characteristic preponderance
of the dual divisions and subdivisions.[80]

Let us compare with this the actual organization of the Murra
as found by Philby: [81]

A comparison of the two genealogies enables us to make several observations with regard to the changes that took place in the structure of the Murra in the course of the last few generations. First of all the over-all division into two groups (Āl 'Alī and Āl Shebīb in the first table) disappeared. Secondly, the vertical structure has been changed into a horizontal one: the Āl Fheyde and Āl Edhbe, for instance, which traditionally figure as subdivisions of the Āl Fāḍel subgroup of the Āl Beshīr subtribe of the Āl Sa'īd tribe, now appear as full-fledged tribes occupying the same rank as the other Murra tribes, and independent of the Āl Sa'īd tribe.

An additional change is the breaking up of groups into subgroups, as a result, no doubt, of their growth: Āl Edhbe, originally a subordinated subgroup, is now a tribe consisting of two subtribes, the Āl Manṣūr and the Āl Jfeysh. Again, some tribes, formerly independent, became subordinated to another tribe as one of its subtribes, probably as a result of a shift in the power relationship: of the two tribes el-Ghiyāthīn and el-Jerāb'a, who formed the Āl 'Alī moiety of the Murra, the Ghiyāthīn today appears as merely one of the two subtribes forming the el-Jerāb'a tribe.

It also happens that both a tribe and one of its own subdivisions become two subtribes of equal status of another tribe; this was the case with the Āl Sa'īd and the Āl Breyd, who today form parts of the Āl Beḥēḥ tribe of the Murra. That all this is not merely a local and isolated phenomenon will be seen when similar shifts in the North Arabian 'Aneze confederation of tribes will be considered.

The western neighbors of the Murra are the Qaḥṭān, occupying the somewhat less unfriendly region between ʿAsīr (Shahrān) and Riyāḍ. These tribes retained the proud ancient name of Qaḥṭān, although their actual genealogic connection with the pre-Islamic Qaḥṭān is, to say the least, doubtful.[82] Qaḥṭān today is one of the strongest confederations of tribes in Central Arabia, and as to its prestige in the desert, according to Doughty it is "the noblest blood of the South Arabians," while Philby remarks that it is "the most famous and still possibly the greatest of all the Arab tribes—the Joktan of Genesis" and is "the very cream of Arab tribal chivalry."[83]

No satisfactory information on the Qaḥṭān is available. In Oppenheim's *Die Beduinen*, basing on an older list made by J. J. Hess, the Qaḥṭān are divided into three groups: the first, ʿAbide, comprising 14 tribes; the second, Āl Muḥammed, comprising seven tribal confederations (with the number of individual tribes in each varying from three to eight), and two single tribes; the third, Āl el-Jimel, comprising three tribal confederations (with three, two, and two tribes) and two single tribes.[84]

A more detailed picture of the western Qaḥṭān can be pieced together from many scattered remarks contained in Philby's *Arabian Highlands*. First of all, it appears that the Qaḥṭān of the ʿAsīr district and its eastern outskirts (merging into the Rubʿ al-Khālī), are divided into two great groups, the *Southern Qaḥṭān* with a paramount chief of its own, residing in the village of Qauz, and the *Northern Qaḥṭān* with their paramount chief residing in the Kharj district. As the chief tribal confederations belonging to the southern Qaḥṭān Philby mentions the ʿAbida and the Sanḥān, the latter comprising the Zahra, Ahl Hirran, al-Jabara, and possibly also the Shurayf tribes. Another group of the Qaḥṭān, the Jaub, claims to be the parent stock of the ʿAbida, Shurayf, and Banī Bishr, so we can also take the Jaub and the Banī Bishr as belonging to the southern Qaḥṭān. To the Jaub belongs a subsection, Ahl Ḥasan. The general name of the northern Qaḥṭān is Jahādir. Philby refers to a number of additional important, Qaḥṭān tribal confederations such as the Benī Kalb or Uklab, the Saʿd, the Benī Sulum, the Rufayda, the Juhādil, the al-Sariʿ, and others, each with a number of tribes and subtribes, but

unfortunately he fails to mention whether these belong to the
northern or southern Qaḥṭān.[85] Although the information is far
from being satisfactory, the by now familiar picture of a bisected
tribal organization emerges, with each moiety further subdivided
into two or more sections.[86]

South of the Qaḥṭān, in the southernmost part of Saudi Arabia,
is the territory of a tribal confederation that has retained the
ancient name of *Yām*. The Yām tribes of the Wadi Dawāsir and
the Western Rub' al-Khālī offer one of the few examples of a
tribal confederation bifurcated along religious sectarian lines.
At present this division is no longer clear, but until recently the
Yām tribes were divided into a Biyādhiyya and a Rufadha half.
The Biyādhiyya persuasion is a schism that has something in
common with the Wahhabi doctrines, and is of Omani origin.
The various sections of the Mahshil, including the al-Rashīd and
al-Fahhād, belong or have belonged until their recent conversion
to Wahhabism to the Biyādiyya, which apparently dispenses
with the *adhān* and congregational prayer. The Rufadha, a variety
of the Ismā'īlī sect of the Shī'a, is the persuasion of the Fāṭima and
Madhkar groups of the Yām, including the Rizq and the Sulum
section of the Madhkar.[87]

NORTHERN ARABIA AND THE SYRIAN DESERT

Under this heading will be discussed the tribes of the northern
half of Saudi Arabia, as well as those tribes whose wandering territories lie wholly or partly in Jordan, Syria, or Iraq. In this area,
too, the dual division is the prevailing form of tribal structure on
various levels.

All the tribes, in general, relate themselves either to Qays or
to Yaman. In the Syrian Desert and as far south as the Ḥijāz, in
addition, the name-pair *Ahl el-Shemāl* ('People of the North') and
Ahl el-Qeblī ('People of the South') also are in vogue.[88]

The dual division can also be found in each locality or tribal
group.

Let us begin with the Ḥijāz area. One of the most powerful
tribes between Mecca and Medina is the Ḥarb, who are of
southern origin; they came in Islamic times from Yemen to
Ḥijāz.[89]

The Ḥarb tribes fall into two groups: an eastern group, ranging about 'Ayn Ibn Fuhayd and the Ja'la plain, Asyah, and the Dahna to the east of Qasim; and a western group ranging west of Qasim in the western Nejd around Nafi, Haid, and Dahna. The eastern group comprises three tribes, each headed by a chief shaykh: I. Banī 'Alī (subdivided into five subtribes); II. Āl Wuhub (six subtribes); III. Āl Farda (or Frida, Froda, six subtribes). The western group comprises two tribes, neither of which is headed by a chief shaykh: Benī Salim and Benī 'Amr. The Benī Salim again comprise two subgroups, the Mēmūn and el-Merāweha.[90]

Another Ḥijāzī group, that of the Jehēne, or Juhayna, is composed of two moieties: the Benī Mālek with fourteen tribes, and the Awlād Mūsā with nine tribes.[91]

The Hudhayl, an important Ḥijāzī tribe numbering about 50,000, is divided into a northern group located east and south of Mecca, and a southern group.

The Quraysh, descendants of the tribe of Mohammed, consists today of two weak branches, one around 'Arafāt, the other near Ṭaif. They are shepherds, numbering about 9,000.

The 'Utaybah is a powerful nomadic tribe east of central Ḥijāz and west of central Nejd, divided into al-Rūqah (12,000) and Barqah (18,000) sections.[92]

Turning now to the Syrian desert, we find that the dual alignment of the nomadic tribes along the Qays and Yemen division is characteristic also of this area.

In the past, since the Benī Kalb was the leading tribe among the Yemenī moiety in Syria, the two parties were known by the names Kelbites and Qaysites.[93]

In the Syrian Desert, politically divided among several states, the Qays-Yaman rivalry is as alive today as it was in past centuries. Of the two most powerful tribal confederations of true or camel nomads, the 'Aneze (18,000 tents or 72,000 persons) and the Shammar, the first belongs to the Ma'add (Qays) and the second to the Yaman or Qahṭān.[94] Up to the consolidation of governmental power in the Syrian Desert, which took place only in recent years, these two great tribal confederations were constantly feuding with one another as behooves traditional enemies. Since

World War II, however, raiding has become increasingly difficult, and the tribes have become used to living without this activity, which was both a source of income and a pastime.

In addition to the over-all division into Qaysī and Yamanī tribal confederations, most of the tribal confederations are in themselves divided into two moieties, which in their turn fall into successively smaller subdivisions, with a diminishing amount of intergroup hostility down the scale.

The 'Aneze themselves fall into two mutually hostile groups, the Danā Bishr and the Danā Muslim, the last flare-up between whom was quelled by the French in 1929.[95] According to the traditional tribal genealogy as elicited by Oppenheim from old members of the tribes, the Bishr comprise four tribes, the Sba'a, Fed'ān, el-Jebel, and el-Dehāmeshe, the first two forming the 'Obēd group and the latter two the 'Ammār or 'Amarāt group. In addition to these four, a fifth tribe, the Weld Suleymān, is now traditionally held to belong to the Bishr group, although originally, in the Nejd, the Weld Suleymān did not belong to the 'Aneze but to the Ja'āfera. Small parts of the tribe merely attached themselves to the 'Aneze and became politically dependent on these more powerful tribal groups in the course of their wanderings, which led them from the Nejd up into the Syrian Desert in the eighteenth century. To the other 'Aneze moiety, the Danā Muslim, traditional tribal genealogy attributes eight tribes whose names are as follows: Weld 'Alī, el-Ḥesene, el-Mesālikh, el-Ḥajjāj (these four together forming the Benī Wahhāb section of the Muslim moiety); el-Sewāleme, el-Ashāje'a, 'Abdelle, and el-Rwala (these latter four forming the Mejlas of Jelas section of the Muslim moiety). In the actual tribal organization as observed by Oppenheim in the early part of the twentieth century, both moieties of the 'Aneze lost from their original number of tribes, leaving the Bishr with three and the Muslim with six tribes.[96]

The dual organization is evident on the subtribal level as well. Of the nine actual tribes (*qabā'il*, sing. *qabīla*) of the 'Aneze, four are subdivided into two subtribes (*'ashā'ir*, sing. *'ashīra*) each. The Fed'ān (approximately 5,000 tents) comprise the Weld and el-Khrese (or Khro a) subtribes; the Sba'a (approximately 2,200 tents) the Qemesa (or Gmosa) and the 'Ebede subtribes; the 'Amarāt (approximately 5,000 tents), the Jebel and Dehāmeshe subtribes; the Weld 'Alī (approximately 650 tents), the Ibn Sumēr and el-Ṭayyār subtribes. Of the remaining five tribes four are very small (150 to 700 tents each), and the last, the powerful Rwala (variously estimated at 4,000 to 5,000 tents), is divided into five subtribes.

The Dual Organization of the
'Aneze Confederacy

Level   I the eponymous ancestor
Level   II the main moieties
Level   III the secondary moieties
Level   IV the tribes (qabā'il)
Level   V the subtribes ('ashā'ir)
Level   VI the afrāq "thighs")
Level   VII the ḥamā'il (clans)

A word may be said here as to the relationship of chieftainship to the dual organization, which can be illustrated by examples drawn from the 'Aneze confederacy. The confederacy as a whole recognizes no paramount chief, nor do the two moieties. On the tribal level, the bifurcated tribe may either recognize the shaykh of one of the two subtribes as the head of the entire tribe (in which case the shaykh of the other subtribe is subordinated to him, as in the 'Amarāt tribe); or each of the two subtribes may have an independent shaykh of its own, in which case the tribe has no paramount chief (as in the Fed'ān, Sba'a, and Weld 'Alī tribes). When the tribe is divided into more than two subtribes (as in the case of the Rwala), all the subtribes recognize the shaykh of one of them as their paramount chief and as the head of the entire tribe.

In the remaining tribes of Syria the following are bifurcated: the el-'Amūr (in the Palmyra-Homs-Damascus region) into 'Amūr el-Dīre and Mehāreshe; the 'Arab el-Lejāh (also known as al-Sulūṭ, in the same area, into the Benī Ḥamad (or al-Sulūṭ al-Qibliyīn, i.e., southern Sulūṭ) and the Benī 'Amr (or al-Sulūṭ al-Shimāliyīn, i.e., northern Sulūṭ); the 'Arab el-Jebel (in the Hawran region) into the Zubēd and the Wessāmet el-Bāhel; the Mawālī (in the Aleppo region, approximately 2,000 tents), into el-Shemaliyīn (northerners) and el-Qibliyīn (southerners).

The subtribes (*'ashā'ir*) are usually further subdivided into subsubtribes (*firaq* or *afrāq* or *afāriqah*, sing. *firqah*); these again into "thighs" (*afkhādh*, sing. *fakhedh*); the "thighs" fall into clans (*ḥamā'il*, sing. *ḥamūla*); and the latter into extended families (*ahāl*, sing. *ahl*, also meaning house or tent).[97]

The Shammar, the hereditary enemies of the 'Aneze, are also divided into two groups: the Western Shammar whose tribal territory is in Syria, and the Eastern or Northern Shammar of Iraq. The Western Shammar group comprises three tribes: the Thābet (with 1,600 tents, consisting of six subtribes); the Feddāgha (with 1,500 tents, eight subtribes); and the el-'Amūd (800 tents, three subtribes). The Iraqi Shammar also are divided into three tribes: the Khreṣe (1,650 tents, five subtribes); the Sāyih (3,500 tents, two subtribes); and the 'Abdeh (3,000 tents, five subtribes).

Among the Northern Shammar of the Northern Jazīrah in Iraq dual division is in evidence in several of the Jarbah tribes:

The Dughayrāt are divided into D. al-Badwa (or Desert D.) and D. al-Ḥaḍar (or settled D.).

The Āl 'Ulayyāh are divided into Āl 'Ikāb and Āl Subayyah.
The Haḍabah are divided into Āl Jad'ān and Āl Funayfin.
The Āl Burayj are divided into al-Aḥāsinah and Āl Buhaymān.
The Ṭauqah division is as illustrated.

The following Kurdish tribes in Iraq also are subdivided into
two sections: Bacelhan, Zengene, Hewramy (into H. Teḥt and
H. Lihon), Shiwan, Pijderiy, Berwariy (into B. Bala and B.
Zer).[98]

The Ṭayy confederation, located east of Niṣibin in northern
Syria, also consists of two tribal groups: the Ṭayy of Niṣibin
(with one paramount shaykh with eleven tribes) and the Ṭayy
of Shemāmik (under another paramount shaykh with four tribes).
In the past, the Ṭayy were divided into el-Ghauth and Jadila,
who were constantly fighting one another.[99] The Ḥadediyyīn
(2,000 tents) of Syria are divided into two sections, each with a
chief of its own: the al-Kwame (four clans), and the al-Ghanātṣe
(six clans).[100]

The Baqqāra, between Aleppo, Dēr, and Mosul, fall into two
groups: The Baqqārat el-Zōr (with a paramount shaykh, six
tribes, divided into numerous subdivisions); and the Baqqārat
el-Jebel (with another paramount shaykh, eleven tribes, also
divided into many subdivisions).

The Nu'ēm are divided into the Nu'ēm of Iraq and the Nu'ēm
of Syria. The Nu'ēm of Iraq again are subdivided into two groups,
the Nu'ēm of the Jazīrah (four tribes) and the Nu'ēm of Jebel
Ḥamrīn (one tribe). The Nu'ēm of Syria are divided into three
groups: the Nu'ēm of Homs (one paramount shaykh, five tribes);
the Nu'ēm of Ghūṭa (no paramount shaykh, four tribes); and the
Nu'ēm of Jōlān (one paramount shaykh, three tribes).

The Benī Jirius and Benī Zaydān in the Jebel 'Ajlūn Nāhīya in Jordan claim descent from two brothers, Jirius and Zaydān. They are Christians (Greek Orthodox and Latin Catholics).

The Beni Sa'īd of Irjan (in the Jebel 'Ajlūn Nāhīya) claim descent from Sa'īd, whose brother, Sa'ad, went to Hebron where he became the ancestor of the Benī Sa'ad.

The Maqātīsh and Oweysāt in the same Nāhīya are the descendants of two brothers, Miqtish and Oweys, who came from Wādī Mūsā. They are Greek Catholics, although some of the Oweysāt follow the Latin faith.

The Bashātwa, living on both sides of the Jordan, are composed of two sections: the Shiheymāt of Kurdish origin, and the Bakkār of Nu'ēmāt extraction.

The Abābna in the Benī Juhma Nāhīya are divided into two sections.

The Bsūl and Kawāfha in the same nāhīya claim descent from two brothers: the Bsūl from Huseyn, and the Kawāfha from Shihādeh. The father of the two brothers, Ibrāhīm, came from the al-Khazāla section of the Benī Hasan tribe.

The Benī Hamd and Benī Irshēyd clans in the Kura Nāhīya are said to be descendants of two brothers, Hamd and Rashīd, who came from Khanzīra in the Kerak District.

The Falahāt and Lawāhma are two clans in the Marad Nāhīya of the Ajlun District of Transjordan; both claim descent from Ibrāhīm, a man who came to their village, Nebī Hūd, more than two hundred years ago.

The Benī Hasan, one of the largest tribes of Jordan, derive their descent from Mishqib ibn Hasan who is said to have come from Turba in the Hijāz. His two sons, Amsh and Mishqib, became the ancestors of the original two divisions of the tribe, the Imūsh and the Mashāqba. At present, the Benī Hasan are still divided into two large groups, called Hulēl (or Benī Hilayil) and Thebte (or al-Sabta). Each of the two has a paramount shaykh of its own and is subdivided into three tribes.

The Shuyāb and the Atāmna are two small tribes in the Benī 'Obeyd Nāhīya of the Ajlūn District in Transjordan who claim descent from a common ancestor who originally lived at Hebron.

The Saqarāt of the Remtha Nāhīya in the same district are

divided into two: the Saqarāt proper, and the Diyābāt; both live in al-Remtha.

The 'Abbād, a confederation of tribes in the Belqa District having no common ancestor, is divided into two great divisions: the Jbūriyya, and the Jrūmiyya, also known as al-Qdēriyye.

The Akrād, thus named after the Wādī al-Akrād quarter in al-Salṭ in which they live, are divided into two large sections: al-Akrād (three tribes) and al-Basābsa (eight tribes).

The Qawāqsha of al-Salṭ, a Greek Orthodox tribe that traces its descent to an ancestor who came from Salkhad in the Jebel Druze, are divided into two sections: al-Nuweysir and al-Ya'qūb.

The Ghawārna in the Kerak District are divided into those living in Ghōr al-Mazra'a and those of Ghōr al-Sāfī. The former are again divided into two: al-Aḥlāf (six sections) and al-Khanāzra (three sections). The inhabitants of Ghōr al-Sāfī are also divided into two sections: al-Awāysa (six subtribes) and al-Miḥlaf (six subtribes).

The Akasha and the Ḥijāziyyīn are two sections united to form one tribe in the Kerak District.

The Maayta in the same district are also divided into two large sections: al-Rashayda and al-Zaqayla. The former is again divided into two: al-Sahir (composed of two subtribes: al-Jubrān and al-Rashīd) and al-Ṭālib (composed of two subtribes: Awlād Id and Awlād Khalīl). The Zaqayla are also divided into two: al-Ibrāhīm and al-Salīm (the latter again composed of two subtribes, the Awlād Ayād and Awlād Muṭlaq).

The Majālī, the largest tribe in Kerak, are divided into two: the Suleymān (three sections) and the Yūsef (eight sections).

The Mdānāt, in the Kerak District, are divided into the Dabana of al-Salṭ and the Amāmira or Amayra of Ḥusn.

The Benī Hamīda in the same district are divided into al-Da'ajna and al-Matārfa. Another Benī Hamī dagroup lives in the Belqa to the north.

The Nu'ēmāt of the Kerak District, probably related to the Nu'ēm of Iraq and Syria, are divided into two subtribes: the 'Abābda (divided into al-Awasa and al-Ja'āfra) and el-Aḥāmda (divided into four subgroups).

The Qatāwna of the Kerak District, said to have come originally from Qatia in Sinai, are divided into two sections: the Awlād 'Alī and Awlād Salameh.

The Sarāyra, in the same district, are divided into Āl 'Alī and Āl Da'ud.

The Tarāwna in the same district, who came from Wādī Mūsā, are divided into 'Ayāl Jibrīn and 'Ayāl Jubrān.

The Town of Ma'an in the district of the same name in southern Jordan is composed of two quarters: Ma'an al-Shāmiyya (Northern Ma'an) inhabited by the 'Ayāl Maḥmūd, and Ma'an al-Ḥijāziyya (Southern Ma'an), inhabited by the 'Ayāl Aḥmed. The 'Ayāl Maḥmūd and 'Ayāl Aḥmed are said to be the descendants of two brothers, Maḥmūd and Aḥmed, who lived in the sixteenth century and quarreled over the possession of the fort of Ma'an. The 'Ayāl Maḥmūd are composed of three tribes, while the 'Ayāl Aḥmed comprise four tribes.

The 'Obeydiyyīn, one of the tribes of Wādī Mūsā in the south of Jordan, are composed of two tribes, the Hilālāt who claim to be true Layāthna, that is indigenous to Wādī Mūsā; and the Ḥasanāt who claim descent from the Billī of Ḥijāz.

The Sa'idiyyīn of the Wādī 'Araba (the boundary between Jordan and the Negev district of Israel), fall into two main groups: the Eastern Sa'idiyyīn who live in Jordan, and the Western Sa'idiyyīn who used to live west of the Wādī 'Araba, in the Negev. The Eastern Sa'idiyyīn are composed of two groups: the Srūriyyīn and the Onāt. The Western Sa'idiyyīn comprise four tribes.

The Nu'ēmāt of the Shera Mountains in southern Jordan are divided into two large groups: the Manājda and the Sleymāt. The Manājda claim descent from Manṣūr and their further dual subdivisions are shown in the accompanying chart.

The Sleymāt are divided into al-Arāqda and al-Sbu. The ancestor of the Arāqda is said to have been a slave by the name of Ireyqed, and because of their base descent the Manājda do not intermarry with them.

The Benī Ṣakhr, the largest camel nomad tribe in Jordan, are divided into two groups: al-Ṭūqa or Ṭwāqa (four tribes) and el-Ka'ābene or al-Ka'ābna (pronounced Cha'ābna; two tribes). All the six Ṣukhūr tribes recognize one single paramount shaykh.

Before leaving the tribes of Jordan a word may be said about a supertribal confederation that played an important role in the history of the area. About 1650 the Sirḥān tribe moved down from the Hawran and occupied the area on the present borderline between Jordan and Saudi Arabia called after them Wādī Sirḥān. Shortly thereafter, however, the great movement of the 'Aneze tribes from the Ḥijāz up to the North Arabian Desert took place. The 'Aneze forced the Sirḥān and their allies, the Benī Ṣakhr, to move up into the Belqa. The 'Aneze pressed after them and came in conflict with the Muḥāfuẓ, as the paramount shaykh of the Sardīya was called whose followers were known collectively as Ahl al-Shamāl (People of the North). The 'Aneze defeated them too, but soon the Ahl al-Shamāl confederation was reconstituted under the leadership of the Benī Ṣakhr and with the participation of the Sardīya, 'Īsā, Fheyli, and Sirḥān tribes. By the beginning of the nineteenth century the Ahl al-Shemāl were strong enough to engage the 'Aneze and forced them successively eastward until at the end of the nineteenth century the Wādī Sirḥān area was held alternatingly by the Ahl al-Shamāl in the winter and the 'Aneze during their annual wanderings to and from their summer grazing grounds in Syria.[101]

There are two tribal groups divided between the Negev and the Sinai: The Terābīn and the Tiyāha. The Terābīn of the Sinai Peninsula comprise three tribes, while the Terābīn of the Negev have eight tribes. The Tiyāha of the Sinai have five tribes, the Tiyāha of the Negev twelve.

On the Saudi-Iraqi border is located the al-Zafīr tribe, a large camel-breeding tribe, divided into two sections: the Wahhābite al-Buṭūn in Nejd, and the Ṣumudah, mostly in Iraq.[102]

The Muṭayr of the Kuwait—el-Ḥasa region are subdivided into three major groups, called al-Dushān, al-'Ilwah, and al-Burayh. The last two of these comprise each three tribes. The Dushān show a definite tendency toward a bifurcated structure.[103]

The Zubēd of Iraq are divided into three groups. The first of these is called el-Jebūr and is divided into two groups: the Jebūr of Khābūr (with one paramount shaykh and sixteen tribes) and the Jebūr of the Tigris (with fourteen tribes). The second group is that of el-Dulēm with one paramount shaykh at its head. The main group of el-Dulēm is that of the Ālbū Rudēnī, consisting of thirteen tribes and several attached subgroups. In addition, five more small tribal groups belong to the Dulēm (and owe allegiance to its paramount shaykh), counting from 200 to 800 tents each. Finally, the third group belonging to the Zubēd is el-'Obēd, under whose paramount shaykh are six tribes.

A similar threefold division is shown by the Ālbū Sha'bān group. These live in the upper Euphrates valley, and are divided into three divisions: the Welde, consisting of three subgroups, each with a paramount shaykh of its own: (1) Welde of Bāb-Menbij, six tribes; (2) Welde of Shāmīye, two tribes; and (3) Welde of the Jazīrah, eight tribes. The second group is that of the 'Afādele under whose paramount shaykh are seven tribes; and the third is el-Sabkha whose paramount shaykh commands a single tribe.[104]

The above listing exhausts the major tribes of the Syrian Desert. Of the tribal confederations enumerated the great majority is found to have the dual system as the basis of their tribal organization, with only two showing a threefold division. As to smaller groups, these generally are not subdivided into two main groups, but fall directly into three to twelve (or more) tribes, with or without a paramount shaykh to head the tribes that make up one larger unit. The dual division is thus found to be, if not the exclusive, the dominant and characteristic structural form of the nomadic tribes of the Arabian and Syrian deserts.

The Negev of Palestine on the fringes of the Syrian Desert also was the home of nomadic tribes aligned into two moieties. Toward the end of the eighteenth century the Qays moiety was here headed by Emir Ḥasan el-Waḥaydī, surnamed el-Daymī, who was followed by the Jabārāt, Qalāzīn, Sowāreke, and 'Amadīn tribes. Interestingly, the rival Yamanī moiety also was headed by a Waḥaydī, a close relative of Emir Ḥasan: Emir Ayash el-Waḥaydī. This moiety consisted of the Tiyāha, Terābīn, Ḥwēṭāt, and Billī tribes. Tradition has it that in one of the battles between the two Waḥaydī chieftains and their followers, 2,800 men were killed. After Napoleon left Palestine in 1798, the feuding between the two factions increased in intensity. In the first quarter of the nineteenth century, the son of Ḥasan, Salīm el-Daymī, who inherited the chieftainship of the Qays faction from his father, repeatedly attacked the Tiyāha and Terābīn tribes.

It is remarkable that the followers of the two chieftains saw no contradiction between their own traditions, according to which membership in the Qays and Yaman factions was genealogically determined, and the fact that two scions of one and the same family headed both factions. The same eighteenth-century source that tells of the feuds between the two factions also contains a brief account of the traditions concerning the origin of the two factions. According to the Negev tribes of the times, the two factions were the descendents of two brothers called Qays and Yemen, both of whom had large families.[105] Can it be that this tradition, which is at variance with the tradition about the origin of Qays and Yemen prevalent in Arabia itself, was influenced by the actual situation in which two kinsmen (in popular parlance two "brothers") headed the two factions?

In the nineteenth century the tribal line-up in the Negev and Transjordan was as follows: Qaysī tribes: Benī Ṣakhr, Shararāt, Benī ʿAṭiyye, Benī Ḥumeyda; Yamanī tribes: Tiyāha, Terābīn, ʿAzāzme, Ḥanājra, Wheydāt, ʿAdwān, Mjallī.[106]

SYRIA, LEBANON, PALESTINE

In Lebanon and Palestine the Qays-Yaman rivalry remained a living issue until modern times. Pitched battles were fought between the two parties as late as the early part of the eighteenth century,[107] and sporadic fighting continued well into the twentieth.

In this area an entire town or village may belong to one faction while a neighboring town or village may belong to the opposite faction; or else, one and the same locality may be split up between both factions. The village of Bīr in the vicinity of Jerusalem was the scene of a fight between the two factions inhabiting it, as late as a short time before World War I. Each faction tried to offend the flag of the other. A Yamanī woman took a red cock and beat it within the sight of Qaysīs (red being the Qaysī color). Thereupon Qaysī women did the same thing with a white cock (white being the Yamanī color).

Bethlehem (today in Jordan) is a Yamanī town, while Hebron (in Jordan), a mere twelve miles to the south of it, is Qaysī. A tree on a hilltop used to mark the boundary between the territories under the sway of each.[108] The factionalism was so strong that these inimical towns had to keep considerable contingents of armed men in constant readiness for defense and retaliation. Hebron had in the eighteenth century 800 to 900 armed men, and bloody fights between them and Bethlehem were common occurrences.[109]

Jerusalem, as the largest town in the neighborhood, was divided between Qaysīs and Yamanīs. In 1838, Robinson found that the majority in the Jerusalem district were Yamanīs.[110] The two foremost families in Jerusalem, who competed for leadership not only in the city but also in the whole of Arab Palestine down to the very end of the days of the British Mandate (1948), were the Yamanī Ḥusaynīs and the Qaysī Khālidīs.[111]

The village population in this area of the Judean hills and as far north as Ramallah is also divided between Qays and Yaman. Bitter wars between the two continued here as late as the nineteenth century. The enmity between the two factions was so keen that the Qaysī headman of the 'Āmar family, the shaykh of Durrah village, had all strangers who came into his village questioned: "For whom are you? For Qays or for Yaman?" If he answered, "Qays," he was honored; if "Yaman," he was put to death.[112]

Just as in the days of the Umayyads, the dual organization of the population in the eighteenth and nineteenth centuries was a factor to be reckoned with by administrative officers and military leaders as well. The military expeditions and punitive actions of governors were more than once frustrated because local levies would not fight against rebels of their own factions. An outstanding example was the experience of Othman Pasha el-Sadiq at his attack on the township of Nablus in Palestine in 1764.[113]

In Ramleh in the Palestinian coastal plain, fellahin of rival factions used to destroy each other's valuable olive groves, and in general it became a point of honor to ruin the rival town's crops, to injure its fruit trees, and, on the other hand, to guide, support and, in case of threatened retaliation, to protect the Bedouin raiding parties of one's own faction. As Volney remarked, "This discord which has prevailed throughout the country, from the earliest times of the Arabs causes a perpetual civil war. The peasants are incessantly making inroads on each other's lands, destroying their corn, dourra, sesamum and olive trees, and carrying off their sheep, goats, and camels. The Turks, who are everywhere negligent in repressing similar disorders, are the less attentive to them here, since their authority is very precarious; the Bedouins, whose camps occupy the level country, are continually at open hostilities with them, of which the peasants avail themselves to resist their authority, or to do mischief to each other, according to the blind caprice of their ignorance, or the interests of the moment. Hence arises an anarchy, which is still more dreadful than the despotism which prevails elsewhere, while the mutual devastations of the contending parties render the appearance of this part of Syria more wrecked than that of any other."[114]

During the last few decades of Turkish rule in Palestine much was done to subdue the rival elements or, at least, not to let the antagonisms emerge into the open. While as late as the second half of the nineteenth century the Qays and Yaman factions, headed by shaykhs and aided by Bedouins, waged feuds and rendered commerce and travel precarious or impossible, by the end of the century this state of affairs was a thing of the past. The squabbles, while they lasted, were not confined to Qays *versus* Yaman strife; they broke out, frequently enough, even between groups belonging to one and the same moiety. In the second half of the nineteenth century, for instance, a feud of some seriousness arose between the Christian Arab villagers of Ramallah and the Christian Arab villagers of neighboring el-Bire. The Ramallah Christians were helped by the Ramallah Muslims, while the el-Bire Christians were supported by the el-Bire Muslims. All the inhabitants of both places belonged to the Qays faction, and normally the relationship between them was amicable enough.[115]

In addition to the Qays and Yaman factions there were in Arab Palestine a number of other village organizations, more localized in their character, the common feature of all of which was their duality. The villages around Jerusalem, for instance, were divided into a group of Benī Ḥasan villages, and into a rival group of Benī Mālek villages. In the Ramallah district there were Benī Ḥārith villages (with the village of Bir Zeyt as their center), and Benī Zayd villages (with Deyr Ghassāneh as their center). Information on this subject is far from being adequate, and it is impossible to tell whether these village groupings appeared only in the dual form, or whether single and triple groupings also existed.[116] Neither is it clear in most cases what, if any, was the connection between these local groupings and the wider Qays and Yaman factions.

In the town of Ramallah itself, however, the connection is clear. The entire population of Ramallah has remained split into two opposing factions down to the present time. One is called Ḥaddādeh or Sharaqa (Eastern), the other Ḥamāyel. Each is subdivided into four clans (*ḥamūla-s*). The story goes that a shaykh or emir of a Christian Bedouin tribe, named Sabra el-Ḥaddādīn, a Qaysite who lived in the Shobak Karak district of Transjordan, was the original ancestor of all the ḥamūlas of Ramallah. His eldest son was Rashīd whose first wife bore him a son Ḥaddād, and died. He married a second wife, a widow who had a son by her first husband, a Yamani. Rashīd adopted this boy, Shukayr and had three more sons by his second wife. These four sons of Rashīd's second wife became the ancestors of the four ḥamūlas of the Ḥamāyel moiety in Ramallah; while Ḥaddād, his son by his first wife, became the ancestor of the four Ḥaddādeh ḥamūlas of the town, through his four sons. Thus the peculiar situation obtains in Ramallah that all the four ḥamūlas of the Ḥaddādeh moiety and three ḥamūlas of the Ḥamāyel moiety are Qaysites, while the fourth ḥamūla of the Ḥamāyel moiety is Yamanite, and is still referred to as "Yaman." They display the white color and the white flag at weddings and on all formal occasions, in contrast to the red of the Qays ḥamūlas.[117]

Among the Druzes in Lebanon, the Qays-Yaman duality completely overshadowed all other divisions. They were caught by the feuds between the two factions to such an extent that their entire history was modified by it. In the course of several centuries the constant feuding between the two factions depleted the manhood not only of the Druzes, but of the Lebanon as a whole. In 1698, the Shī'ite Mutawālīs, who inhabited the mountainous country between the Sea of Galilee and Sidon (Arabic: Ṣayda), revolted under the leadership of a Yamanī shaykh. The Druze Emir Bashir I of the Qays party, in alliance with the Pashas of Sidon and Tripoli, put down the revolt and installed the head of an influential local Qaysī family as shaykh of Safed.[118] In 1711 a decisive battle took place between the Qaysīs and the Yamanīs at 'Ayn-Darah, which resulted in the utter defeat of the Yamanī faction. Many Druzes who belonged to this faction thereupon emigrated to the Hawran region and laid the foundation of a new Druze concentration in that south Syrian district.[119] Among the Druzes, the Qaysī faction used to carry a red flag and is known to the present day under the name Reds, while the Yamanī faction had a white flag and is still known as Whites.[120]

Forthwith, however, two new competing factions emerged in the Lebanon and continued the feuds of the old Qaysī and Yamanī moieties. These were in Yesbek and Jumblat factions which, as heirs to Qays and Yaman, rallied the support of the population of these regions in the elections during the mandatory period of the country (1921–1936).[121]

In Palestine, many if not most Arab villages were divided into two ḥamūlas, although small villages had often only one ḥamūla, while large ones had three or even more. The ḥamūla is a group of families tied together by actual or assumed genetic relationship. A ḥamūla usually inhabits a special quarter in the village, called ḥāra, so that a typical two-ḥamūla village consists of two ḥāras. Each ḥamūla is headed by an unofficial head whose office is hereditary within the leading family of the ḥamūla, though it does not necessarily pass from father to son, and can also be acquired by a powerful member of another family belonging to the ḥamūla. In villages whose lands belong to absentee landlords or which are in a status of economic dependence on outside moneylenders, merchants, or others, the headship of the ḥamūla is usually occupied by men who have the confidence of the landowner or the economic potentate. The usual relationship between the two ḥamūlas is one of strife, squabble, and enmity. Every individual difference that is bound to arise from time to time in the course of the social and economic relations between two individuals belonging to two different ḥamūlas becomes immediately a concern of the ḥamūlas in their entirety, and thus a cause for renewed fighting. Most of the ḥamūlas are endogamous, and marriages between two ḥamūlas of the same village are much less frequent than those contracted within one and the same ḥamūla.

The ḥamūlas are in most cases subdivided into sub-ḥamūlas which fall into a number of extended families. Most of the ḥamūlas preserve a tradition according to which their ancestors came and settled in the village as a compact group of immigrants. In villages inhabited by members of more than one sect, such as Muslims, Druzes, Greek Orthodox, etc., the religious community takes the place of the usual ḥamūla-structure.[122]

IRAN AND AFGHANISTAN

Several volumes exist in Persian on the tribes of various provinces in Iran. However, of the books available to the author only one contained information on the internal structure of the tribes. This was a volume on the tribes of Kūh-Gīlūyē, a small district in the province of Kuzistan, at the northern tip of the Persian Gulf.[123]

It appears that bifurcation is the rule among the Kūh-Gīlūyē tribes. Almost half the entire district is the domain of the Bovīr-Aḥmad tribe, which is divided into Bovīr-Aḥmad Garmsīri and Bovīr-Aḥmad Sardsīri. This name pair, Garmsīri and Sardsīri (meaning "of the warm place" and "of the cold place" respectively) occurs repeatedly in Kūh-Gīlūyē as well as in its vicinity, as a designation of two moieties. The Bovīr-Aḥmad Sardsīri is again subdivided into two, the Bovīr-Aḥmad S. Bālā (Bovīr-Aḥmad of the upper cold place) and the Bovīr-Aḥmad S. Pā'in (Bovīr-Aḥmad of the lower cold place).

The central part of Kūh-Gīlūyē is the home of the Ṭayyibī tribe, subdivided into T. Garmsīri (warm Ṭayyibī) and T. Sardsīri (cold Ṭayyibī). Just to the north of the Kūh-Gīlūyē district is the tribal area of the Jānekī tribe, subdivided into J. Garmsīri (to the northwest of Kūh-Gīlūyē) and J. Sardsīri (to the northeast).

Yet another name pair, in addition to warm—cold, upper—lower, is "of the mountain" and "of the plain." The Līrāvī tribe is subdivided into Līrāvī Kūh (mountain Līrāvī) and L. Dasht (plains Līrāvī). The entire Līrāvī tribe forms one of the two moieties of the Jākī tribe, the other being the Chahār Benīche, which, in accordance with its name ("Four B.") falls into four tribes.

Tribal Structure of the Jākī

The Līrāvī Kuh is subdivided into four groups, one of which, the Līrāvī Kūh Bahma'ī, is in turn subdivided into two, the Bahma'ī Aḥmadi and the Bahma'ī Muḥammadi. The former is again bifurcated into Bahma'ī Aḥmadi Pusht-i-Kūh (transmontane Bahma'ī Aḥmadi), and Bahma'ī Aḥmadi Zīr-i-Kūh (cismontane Bahma'ī Aḥmadi).[124]

From other parts of Iran only the most general kind of information is available. Of the Bakhtiyārī, one of the largest tribal confederations in western Iran, it is known that they are divided into two groups, the Haft Lang (or Seven Tribes, comprising 55 subtribes) and the Chahār Lang (or Four Tribes, with 24 subtribes). Various traditions are current in the tribes themselves in explanation of their dual division. According to one, they are the descendants of two brothers, one of whom had seven sons and the other four. According to another, Bakhtiyār, the eponymous ancestor of the tribe, had two wives; by one he had seven sons, who became the progenitors of the Seven Tribes; by the other four, from whom are descended the Four Tribes. The Bakhti-yārīs seem to have migrated in the tenth century from Syria to Iran, and the dual division may have been brought along by them at that time. As was pointed out above, the dual faction-alism penetrated Iran and reached even distant Khurasan as early as the first century of Islam.

The Lurs, another huge tribal confederation in western Iran, are divided into Lur-i-buzurg (Big Lurs) and Lur-i-kuchek (Little Lurs).[125] The Jākī, mentioned above, is a Lur tribe.

The third large tribal confederation, that of the Qashqais, is divided into two parts, or one nomadic and one settled.[126]

Crossing over into Afghanistan, we find that the old Afghan traditions as to the origin and structure of the Afghan tribes were collected and put into writing by Ni'mat Allah in his *Makhzan-i Afghānī* (completed in 1613). These traditions regard the Biblical King Saul (Ṭālūt or Sārūl) as the original ancestor of the Afghans. He, they say, had a daughter, Iramiah, whom he married to King David. Their son was Afghana who helped his father build the Temple in Jerusalem. He had forty sons with whom he trekked to the hills of Ghur, and thence to Afghanistan. One of Afghana's descendants was Qays 'Abd al-Rashīd, who became converted to Islam by Khalid, and had three sons: Sarban, Baṭan, (Biṭan) and Ghurghusht. Each of these three became the ancestor of a dual grouping of tribes. Sarban's two sons, Sharkhbūn and Kharshbūn, are regarded as the progenitors of a considerable number of tribes, among them the most powerful of all Afghan tribes, the Durrānīs, formerly called Abdālī. Biṭan's two sons, Warspūn and Kajin, are regarded as the joint ancestors of the Biṭanī tribe, while his daughter Matō (married to Shāh Ḥusayn Ghūrī) is the mother of the Mati tribes, among whom the Ghalzay were for a long time the traditional rivals of the Durrānīs. Ghurghusht's two sons, Dānay and Mandū, are the ancestors of a third set of dual tribal groups.

Dual division occurs on all levels of tribal organization. The Durrānīs, for example, comprise two principal clans, the Popalzay and the Bārakzay (to whom the present royal family of Afghanis-tan belongs). The Kharshbūn moiety of Sarban falls into three

8

groups. One of these, the Kand, is bifurcated into two tribes, the Ghori or Ghura, and the Khakhay or Khashay. One part of the latter is the Yūsufzay tribe, which is subdivided into five subtribes. One of these, the Akōzays, are again subdivided into several sections, including the Rānīzays. The Rānīzays comprise five clans; one of the latter is again subdivided into four subclans. One of these, the Ghaybī Khēl, comprises two subgroups, one of which, the Nūr Muḥammed Khēls, are again subdivided into Gharīb Khēl and Dwar Khēl.

In the eighteenth and nineteenth centuries the two foremost rival groups were the Bārakzay and the Sadōzay tribes, both of whom supplied the country with dynasties of rulers, and whose feuding kept Afghanistan in a constant state of turmoil for most of the past two centuries.

The Kāfirs of Afghanistan (now called the Nūristānīs or Jadīdīs that is, new converts to Islam) are divided into two groups: the Siyāh-pūsh or black-clad, and the Safīd-pūsh or white-clad.

The Tājīks, as the Persian-speaking population of Afghanistan is called, fall into two principal groups: the mountain Tājīks (in the high mountain valleys of Badakhshān and in Wakhan, the east tongue of Afghanistan); and plain-dwelling Tājīks, also known as Pārsiwāns.[127]

The Brahuis who inhabit the central area of Balujistan are organized into two main groups, the Sarāwān and the Jahl-āwān.[128]

EGYPT AND SUDAN

Egypt was the classical example of dual organization in antiquity. In the fourth millennium B.C., the king of Upper Egypt conquered Lower Egypt, and since that time the country is always referred to as Upper and Lower Egypt. The ancient Biblical name of Egypt, *Miṣrayim*, has the dual ending " . . .*ayim*," thereby indicating the duality of the kingdom. The Crown of Upper Egypt was white and that of Lower Egypt red, the two colors that symbolize to this day the two moieties in some Middle Eastern lands. The white and red crown together formed the characteristic double crown of the Pharaohs, well known from innumerable pictorial and plastic representations.

We may begin the tracing of the presence of the dual organization in Muslim Egypt with the Mamluks who ruled Egypt from 1250 to 1517. During the later Mamluk rivalries the population of Egypt, and especially the artisan guilds, were divided into two competing factions, called Sa'd and Ḥaram. The rivalry was so keen and so general that even the 'ulamā', the learned religious leaders and authorized expositors of Muslim law, took sides for and against Sa'd and Ḥaram. The division between the two factions continued after the conquest of Egypt by the Ottomans (1517) and even spread into the Egyptian army, which became divided into two rival camps, the Fikarites and the Kassemites.

Jabarti (1754–1822), to whom we are indebted for this information goes on to describe the original popular tradition attributed to this dual division of the Egyptian army. There was, he says, an old Circassian Emir by the name of Sudun, who lived at the time Turkish Sultan Selim conquered Egypt, and he had two sons, named Kassem and Zulfikar, both of them great heroes. At the command of the Sultan, the two brothers engaged in a bout, and after a wonderful fight the Sultan divided his army between the two, giving to Zulfikar the greatest part of the Turkish cavalry, while to Kassem he gave most of the brave Egyptian warriors. Furthermore, he gave the Fikarites the white color as their emblem, and to the Kassemites the red color. The two groups engaged again in a fight, but this time the bout degenerated into a real combat, until finally the Sultan gave the signal for retreat. Ever since that day these two parties continued to exist in the Egyptian army, each of them preserving the color that its chief received as their emblem, showing repugnance toward the color of the rival party, down to table ware and kitchen utensils.

Soon the Fikarites declared themselves for the Sa'dite party and the Kassemites for the Ḥaramites. The division grew in significance from day to day. It passed from masters to slaves, from fathers to sons, and became the cause of many crimes, massacres, pillages, rapes, and arsons.

Another tradition as to the origin of this dual division in the Egyptian army is also recorded by Jabarti. According to this second version, the Kassemites were the partisans of Kassem Bey el-Daftardar, and the Fikarites were the followers of Zulfikar Bey el-Kebir. This tradition places the origin of the division into the year 1050 H. (the middle of the seventeenth century). The Fikarites excelled by their generosity, while the Kassemites distinguished themselves by their riches and their avarice. When in arms, the Fikarites carried a white flag whose shaft was surmounted by a globe, and the Kassemites a red flag surmounted by an iron ring.

Carrying on the story of this dual division, Jabarti records that at the beginning of the twelfth century H. (eighteenth century), the Emirs of Egypt were divided into Fikarites and Kassemites.[129]

In the eighteenth century, Lower Egypt was constantly torn by party strife between the Sa'd and the Ḥaram factions. Each of these two factions was composed of both villagers and nomadic Bedouins. The shaykhs of the rival villages used, on the slightest pretext, to arm their peasants against one another, and supported the Bedouins of their own factions in their plundering raids on the villages of the other faction. Horses, too expensive to be employed as draught animals in agriculture, were a highly valued possession because in these intervillage feuds success usually went to the side that had the greatest number of horsemen. In the flood season rival irrigation interests also further embittered these factional strifes and gave opportunity for the display of strength, often resulting in bloody disputes, there being no police to intervene.[130]

Interesting details as to the factional affiliation of Egyptian tribes in the eighteenth century are contained in Chabrol's study on the mores of the inhabitants of Egypt, which forms a part of the monumental *Description de l'Egypte* initiated by Napoleon. In the province of Bahyreh (Buḥeyra), Chabrol states, the Namiady tribe belonged to the first class (or faction) and the Awlād 'Alī tribe to the second. Both tribes were tent-dwellers, and they were the most redoubtable and most powerful tribes in the whole of Egypt. They were inimical to each other, separated by the hatreds of religion, and dominated between them the entire province. One of them followed the opinions of a shaykh named Sa'd, while the other believed in the infallibility of his antagonist, Ḥaram. They nourished a deep antipathy toward each other, and the origin of this feeling as well as the origin of the twofold division itself were known to go back to antiquity. But not only the

Bahyreh province, says Chabrol, the whole of Egypt was divided by the same schism. The partisans of Sa'd and Ḥaram attributed such importance to their opinions that they condemned each other to eternal damnation. The government of the celebrated 'Alī Bey put an end to these fanatical furors. As a result of this Sa'd and Ḥaram became largely forgotten, but the names of these two chiefs of sects continue to cause discord among the free people of the desert.

PROVINCE OF SHARQIYYA
Nomadic Tribes

First Class	Second Class
Billī	Gomayleh
Refā'at	Benī Ayyūb
Samdānī	Jomeylah
Awlād 'Alī	
Hiwan	

Sedentary Tribes

First Class	Second Class
Qassāsīn	Awlād Zehera
Samākīn	Motwalli
Suwalyeh	Bawārsheh
Ayd	Warāwra
Zomly	
Awlād Mūsā	
Lakkam	

PROVINCE OF QELYUT

First Class	Second Class
Swālheh and Geheynī	A'yadyah
Ḥweiṭāt	Terābīn

After remarking that the same two factions reappear in Syria under the names of Qays and Yaman, and that in all the countries of the Orient these two factions play an important role with their mutual hatred and passion, Chabrol lists the Egyptian tribes, and other groups that belonged to each of them.[131]

Another French scholar whose work forms part of the *Description de l'Egypte*, M. P. S. Girard, supplements the above information with observations of his own. He states that most of the inhabitants of the Nile delta form two inimical parties, known

under the names of Sa'd and Ḥaram, who constantly harm each
other by all possible means.

> When asked about the origin of this division, they tell ridiculous
> stories, or admit that they are ignorant of it. Moreover, this origin
> interests them the least; the hostilities are never suspended, and
> each party has always recent injuries to avenge.
>
> Although the existence of these two parties is generally known,
> the shaykhs of Cairo, who are regarded as knowing best the
> history of their country, are not in agreement as to the circum-
> stances which gave birth to them. The opinion which I hold to be
> the most reasonable boils down to the following:
>
> During the civil wars which ruined Arabia under the Calif
> Yezid ibn Hayweh, about the year 65 of the Hegira (685 A.D.),
> the two armies took as rallying cries in one nocturnal combat the
> names of Sa'd and Ḥaram, by which their respective chiefs'
> families were known. These names the fighters and subsequently
> their descendants applied to themselves. In this manner the discord
> was perpetuated and became an insurmountable obstacle to
> their reconciliation. The Arabs who in various ages came to estab-
> lish themselves in Egypt brought along, together with the name
> of the faction to which their ancestors belonged, their inveterate
> hatred against the opposite faction, and this hatred has perpetu-
> ated itself down to the present from generation to generation.
>
> It is to this internal division that one must attribute the influence
> of the Bedouin Arabs and the terror they inspired in the interior of
> the Delta: a small number of horsemen could carry off ordinarily
> without resistance the flocks of a considerable population . . . .
>
> These Arabs, always sure of being welcomed and saved by the
> villages of the party opposing the one they despoiled, and not
> preserving the liaison with one party longer than dictated by the
> exigencies of their momentary interests, exercise their brigandage
> with impunity in the whole province.[132]

The Sa'd-Ḥaram feuding remained notorious well into the
nineteenth century, when Edward William Lane, making his
firsthand observations of Egyptian life in the 1820's and 30's,
wrote: "In many instances, the blood-revenge is taken a century
or more after the commission of the act which has occasioned it;
when the feud, for that time, has lain dormant, and perhaps is
remembered by scarcely more than one individual. Two tribes in
Lower Egypt, which are called 'Saad' and 'Haram,' are most
notorious for these petty wars and feuds, (like the 'Keys' and

'Yemen' of Syria), and hence their names are commonly applied to any two persons or parties at enmity with each other."[133]

The Egyptian Bedouins are divided into two great groups, Se'ādī and Salāleme, who trace their descent to Sa'de and Dhīb respectively. Most of these became sedentarized in 1898 and some of them migrated to Syria.[134]

As examples of tribes with a dual division among the Bedouins of the Sinai Peninsula the Muzayna and Suwārka can be mentioned. The Muzayna, one of the Towara tribes who inhabit the southern tip of Sinai, claim a certain 'Alwān as their original ancestor. His two sons, 'Alī and Ghanim, became the progenitors of the two moieties of the tribe. The Suwārka, the largest tribe in Sinai (approximately 4,000 persons) claim to be the descendants of two brothers, Nuṣayr and Manṣūr, whose original ancestor was Okasha. The progeny of Nuṣayr are the 'Aradāt, also called Ghōz el-'Arab, who have the reputation of exceptional cleanliness in food and dress. Manṣūr's progeny, twelve sections, are nicknamed Awlād el-Tharwa, "children of the gray-haired woman," because Manṣūr is supposed to have married a gray-haired woman and she became the mother of his children.[135]

The dichotomy into two opposing factions was a characteristic feature of society in Upper Egypt as well. Here, just as in Lower Egypt, a number of villages belonged (and do belong to this day) to one faction, while a similar number belonged to the opposing faction. In the urban sector, on the other hand, and again as in Lower Egypt, members of the two opposing factions lived in one and the same town. The earliest mention of the dichotomy of towns in Muslim times in Upper Egypt is contained in the famous travel accounts written by Ibn Battuta (1304–1368/9), who visited the town of Aydhāb in the summer of 1326. Today the town of Aydhāb is merely a site of ruins, 12 miles north of the town of Halayb on the shores of the Red Sea, just south of the Egyptian border. But in the fourteenth century it was a populous town, inhabited by Beja camel-breeders. The town was divided into two parts: one part, comprising one third of the town, belonged to the Sultan of Egypt, while the other part, comprising two thirds of the town, belonged to the Beja king, al-Ḥudrubi. Just at the time of Ibn Battuta's visit the two factions were

engaged in warfare against each other, and the Bejas routed the
Egyptian troops.[136] Al-Ḥudrubi was the head of the Ḥadārib,
the dominant Beja tribe of southern descent (from the Hadhramaut). A more numerous servile class, the Zanāfij, acted as their
herdsmen.[137]

Fights between two opposing villages were common in Upper
Egypt as late as the 1920's. According to Winifred Blackman who
lived in an Upper Egyptian village in those years, intervillage
fights were frequent, the two feuding parties often representing
two villages on the opposite sides of a canal. The typical form of
these brawls was that a group of men, armed with *nabbuts* (stout
and heavy sticks), and sometimes with even more dangerous
weapons, would enter the market place of the "enemy" village
and start a fight. On the next occasion the visit would be repaid
by the men of the "attacked" village.[138]

More information concerning dual organization of villages in
Upper Egypt became available recently with the publication of
Hamed Ammar's fine study on *"Growing Up in an Egyptian Village."*
According to Ammar, "apart from the towns 'where people are
mixed,' " most of the villages of the Aswan Province of Upper
Egypt are inhabited by members of two factions: the G'āfra and
the 'Abābda. The G'āfra consider themselves the descendants of
G'afar al-Ṣadīq whose great-grandfather was the grandson of the
Prophet Mohammed, while the 'Abābda regard themselves the
descendants of 'Abdullah ibn al-Zubayr, a member of the
Quraysh tribe to which also Mohammed belonged but which was
"not so close in kinship or favour to the Prophet." Both the
G'āfra and the 'Abābda are farmers at present, but farming is
considered as the occupation typical of the G'āfra, since the
'Abābda were originally camel-drivers. The G'āfra consider
themselves more hospitable than the 'Abābda.

No information is given by Ammar as to the internal subdivisions of the 'Abābda, but he deals in some detail with the
G'āfra. We learn that they are divided into two parts: the villages
of the eastern bank of the Nile are regarded as descendants of
Baḥr, while those on the western bank of the Nile are regarded as
descendants of Baḥr's brother, Buḥayr. (Bahr means sea or river,
and is used in Egypt specifically to denote the river Nile; Buḥayr

is the diminutive form of Baḥr.) The two brothers "were not in agreement."

A group of ten villages, officially known as Silwa, belongs to the Baḥr division of G'āfra. Silwa falls into two groups: Silwa Baḥarī (Northern Silwa) comprising five villages, and Silwa Qiblī (Southern Silwa) also comprising five villages. All the ten villages together have a population of approximately 11,000. The five villages of Silwa Baḥarī consider themselves as descendants of two individuals, called 'On and Mūsā, sons of Baḥr; while the five villages of Silwa Qiblī consider themselves as descendants of 'Ayyāsh, another son of Baḥr.

One of the five villages of Silwa Baḥarī is the village of Silwa proper, which is the administrative center of all the ten Silwa villages. In this village the population belongs to either of two sections called in Arabic *ḥiṣṣa*. One of these two sections comprises the descendants of 'On and is accordingly called 'Onāb, while to the other belong descendants of 'On's brother Mūsā, and this section is therefore called Mūsiāb. The 'Onāb section is divided into five clans, called *qabā'il* (in sing. *qabīla*), namely: Diābāb, Hasaballāb, M'alliāb, Waznāb, and Gharamāb. The Mūsiāb *ḥiṣṣa* comprises four clans whose names are Marāzīk, 'Atamnī, 'Amrāb, and Brahimāb. It should be noted here that the suffix *-āb* is common among the Beja tribal names, and seems to have nothing to do with the Arabic *āb*, father.[139]

Each of these clans is composed of several extended families (called *'ayla* or *bayt*). It is the prevalent belief that each of the two sections represents half the population of the village. The majority of the Mūsiāb live in the northern part of the village, while most of the 'Onāb reside in the southern part.

Members of the two sections are supposed to be distinguished from one another by certain physical and mental characteristics. The Mūsiāb are supposed to be heavily built, inclined to boasting and self-pride, while the 'Onāb have the reputation of being comparatively stingy and much inclined to gossip.

Each of the two sections of the village elect one of their members to function as "*Shaykh ḥiṣṣa*" or sectional chief. These two shaykhs are not paid, and each one of them is primarily concerned with the problems of his *ḥiṣṣa*. They, together with the *'Omda*, the

official head of the village whose office is both elective and hereditary as well as appointive, form the village leadership whose task
is to settle disputes that arise in the village.

The participation of the villages in the wider political life of the
country is channeled entirely by the dual division into G'āfra
and 'Abābda. The G'āfra villages traditionally vote for a candidate who belongs to their group. The 'Abābda, of course, have
their own candidate. On one recent occasion, the 'Abābda en-
couraged a second G'āfra candidate to run against his own
clansman, and as a result of the splitting of the G'āfra vote
between the two G'āfra candidates, the election was lost by them.
Political views have little if anything to do with the elections.[140]

The Bishārīn, a Beja tribe in northeastern Sudan, are divided
into two main classes: the Umm 'Alī and the Umm Nājī. They
seem to have a genealogic connection with the Awlād Kāhil
(or Kawāhla), an Arab tribe that lived near 'Aydhāb in the
fourteenth century.[141]

NORTH AFRICA

The main problem in connection with the dual organization in
North Africa is whether its prevalence among the Berber tribes
is due to Arab influence or goes back to pre-Islamic times. No
satisfactory answer can be given to this question, which has
received much too scanty attention on the part of historians.

The dual organization of the *Arab tribes* in North Africa, so
much seems to be certain, was brought along by them from the
east. Of the two main tribal groups, the Benī Sulaym and the
Benī Hilāl, the former is the senior branch. Both came from the
Nejd and are of Muḍarī (Qaysī) stock. According to tradition,
Sulaym, who lived in the third century A.D. and Hilāl in the 5th
had as their common ancestor Manṣūr who was the grandson of
Qays. The Sulaym tribes are spread today from Egypt to Tunisia
and are divided in Cyrenaica into two main branches, the
Jibārna and the Harabī. The Benī Hilāl settled in the western
part of the same territory; tribes claiming Hilālī descent are found
today mainly in Tripolitania and Tunisia. Client or vassal tribes
as well as noble or free tribes are grouped under the same dual
genealogy. The secondary tribes have attached themselves to the

dominant tribes and by a process well known also from the tribal life of the Syrian Desert have grafted their branch of descent onto the family tree of the noble tribes. The term used by the Bedouins of Libya to describe this process is *laf* (to connect, to wrap).[142]

It is not intended to discuss here the extremely intricate problem of the origin of the North African *Berber tribes*. For our present purposes it will be sufficient to summarize briefly the popular traditions which, just as in Arabia proper, assign a dual origin to the Berber tribes.

These popular traditions are reflected in the genealogic speculations contained in the writings of medieval Arab historians and summarized by Ibn Khaldun (1332–1406). The traditions are contradictory and confusing, as popular traditions often are, but they all agree on one basic point: that, namely, all the non-Arab North African tribes belong to either of two groups, called *Beranes* and *Botr*, respectively. According to information obtained by Ibn Hazm from the son of Abu Yezid, chief of the Zenāta (one of the Botr tribes), and reported by Ibn Khaldun, the descendants of Madghis el-Abter, that is the Botr tribes, "did not belong to the Berber race."[143]

A number of other genealogists of the Berber people (Sabeq ibn Soleyman el-Matmati, Hani ibn Masdur (or Isdur) el-Kumi, Kahlān ibn abi Lua) quoted elsewhere by Ibn Khaldun (i : 168) projected further back the fictitious ancestry of the Berbers and connected them with Biblical figures. According to them, the Beranes were the children of Berr, who was the son (or descendant) of Mazigh, the son of Canaan, the son of Ham, the son of Noah. The Beranes tribes, therefore, are represented as laterally related to the South Arabian Yamanī tribes, whose ancestor, Qahṭān, was the great-great-grandson of Shem, brother of Ham. According to the same genealogists, the Botr tribes were the descendants of Berr (not identical with the first Berr) who was the son of Qays, a descendant of Ishmael. In this manner the Arabian theory of dual descent was deftly applied to the Berbers.

The appearance of the name Berr in the traditional lineage of both North African groups of tribes is explained by other traditions as referring to one and the same person. Ibn Hazm, while faithfully recording the Zenāta tradition of separate ancestry, was himself of the opinion that Bernes and Madghis el-Abter were brothers, the sons of Berr, who was a descendant of Mazigh, son of Canaan, son of Ham, son of Noah.[144] This tradition, therefore, assigns to all the Berbers a "Hamitic" origin, and makes them cousins to the South Arabian Yamanī tribes. Since, according to the Biblical genealogy (Gen. 10) Canaan was the ancestor of the people who inhabited the Land of Canaan before its occupation by the Hebrew tribes, as well as the coastal districts to the north of it, the assumption that the ancestry of the North African tribes was of Canaanite origin may be a legendary or traditional reflection of the historical fact that North Africa was colonized by Canaanite (Phoenician) tribes.

This assumption is supported by a tradition reported by the Arab historian Abu 'Obeyd Allah 'Abdallah el-Bekrī in his *Kitāb el-Mesālik*, to the effect that the Berbers originated in Syria where they inhabited Palestine ("Filistin"). They left Palestine after their king Thālūt killed Jālūt (Goliath), crossed Egypt, and settled in the Maghreb.[145] The tradition of the Syrian-Phoenician origin of the Berbers was still prevalent among the Saharan tribes in the beginning of the twentieth century.[146]

It would thus seem that all genealogists up to the fourteenth century agreed that the Beranes were true Berber tribes of Hamitic origin and therefore related to some extent to the South Arabian tribes, while the Botr tribes were, according to some, of the same origin, and, according to others, of Ishmaelitic origin and thus related to the Northern or Qaysī Arab tribes.

No unanimity is found in the traditions assigning the individual Berber tribes or tribal groupings a Beranes or a Botr affiliation. Again according to Ibn Khaldun, most genealogists agreed that the Beranes formed seven big tribes: Azdaja, Masmuda, Aurēba, Ajīka, Ketama, Ṣanhāja, and Aurigha; and that the Botr formed four big tribes: Addaṣa, Nefuṣa, Darīṣa, and the children of Lua the Elder, all the four the descendants of Zahlik (or Zejjik), son of Madghis el-Abter. To the Botr group were counted also the Zenāta, who were regarded as the descendants of Yaḥya, son of Dari, son of Zahlik (Zejjik), son of Madghis el-Abter.

Not all the genealogists, however, agreed that all the seven tribes enumerated above have to be assigned to the Beranes. According to Ibn el-Kelbi, quoted by Ibn Khaldun, two of them, the Ketama and Ṣanhāja tribes, did not belong to the Berber race, but were "branches of the Yemenite population whom Ifriqos ibn Sayfi established in Ifrīqiya (that is, North Africa) with the armies whom he left behind to guard the country. . . ." This version, therefore, did not regard the Ketama and Ṣanhāja as "Hamites," but rather as "Semites," descended from Sem through the South Arabian, Qahṭānī, or Yamanī lineage.

To the Azdaja branch of the Beranes tribes were counted the Mestaṣa (or Mesettaṣa), the Masmuda, and the Ghomara.

The North Arabian descent and affinities of the Zenāta tribes seem to be supported by the great similarity of their way of life to that of the Arabs of the Arabian and Syrian deserts. As Ibn Khaldun points out, "In our days, one can notice among this people (the Zenāta), many usages proper of the Arabs: they live in tents; they raise camels; they ride horses; they transport their dwellings from one locality to another; they spend the summer in the Tell (the northern mountainous area of North Africa) and the winter in the desert; they raid the inhabitants of the cultivated land and they reject a just and regular government."

The Zenata were the most powerful group of the Botr. Their traditional enemies, the Ṣanhāja (or Ṣenhāja), were counted, as we have seen, by most genealogists among the Beranes. Bloody wars between the Zenata and the Ṣanhāja were a constant feature of North African history in the Middle Ages.[147]

The Ṣanhāja, however, fought with the same bitterness and persistence also a Beranes brother tribe, the Ghomara, a subdivision of the Azdaja branch of the Beranes. The Ṣanhāja-Ghomara wars took place in pre-Islamic times, that is, long before the Ṣanhāja-Zenāta fights, but they left an indelible impression on popular tradition and imagination to this day. "It seemed that the whole world joined in, every tribe of the Rif belonged to one side or the other, and now even inanimate objects are sometimes divided into Ṣenhāja and Ghomara."[148] It seems possible that the uncertainty in the traditions as to the genealogy of the Ṣanhāja tribes had something to do with these prolonged struggles of the

Ṣanhāja, first with the Ghomara and then with the Zenāta. Those who were familiar mainly or only with the Ṣanhāja-Zenāta wars, the bulk of which took place only a few centuries before the times of Ibn Khaldun, were inclined to assign a Beranes status to the traditional enemies of a Botr tribe. Those, however, who remembered also the much earlier Ṣanhāja-Ghomara fights, excluded the Ṣanhāja from the Beranes stock and attributed them a Yamanī (or Qaḥṭānī) descent.

In modern times, the social organization in North Africa still reflects the historical and traditional forces that molded it for the past fifteen hundred years. The dichotomy of tribes into two mutually hostile groups still characterizes the area, although under European (French) influence the importance of these traditional rivalries is today definitely on the decline.

An alliance of tribes is called in North Africa *leff*, while a smaller alliance, composed of related families, is called *ṣoff*.[149] As a rule, two competing *leffs* are lined up against each other in any larger area of North Africa. In Northern Morocco the two *leffs* are still called by the traditional name pair, Senhāja and Ghomara.[150] The political tension between the two notwithstanding, in both of these groups of tribes as well as in the Ktama (Ketama) group (all the three of whom belong according to "most genealogists" quoted by Ibn Khaldun to the Beranes group), Senhajan and Jebalan cultural traits predominate; while in the eastern part of Morocco and especially among the Benī Bu Yaḥyī (let us recall that Yaḥya figures as an ancestral name in the genealogy of the Zenāta) and the Metalsa tribes, Zenātan nomadic cultural traits predominate. In between the two areas there is a territory in which both the Zenatan and the Senhajan traits are absent and which has been designated as the center of a Central Riffian culture.

The Ṣenhāja and the Ghomara are distinguished from each other by certain differences reminiscent of the differences in custom between the Qays and the Yaman villages in Palestine. The Ṣenhāja leave food in the bowl, for shame of taking the last bit, and also in order to keep the *baraka*, the blessing of plenty, in the house; the Ghomara leave none. The Ṣenhāja are hospitable to strangers, the Ghomara are cold to them.[151]

In Ibala and the Rif the dual groups of tribes who are constantly at war with each other have curious totemistic relations to animals and food prohibitions: the Ṣanhāja are connected with quadrupeds, the Ghomara with birds.[152]

The claim of ancestry is, of course, not an infallible guide to the actual descent of North African tribes. Some of the Rifian tribes, for instance, claim Ṣanhāja, others Zenāta ancestry; still others claim that their ancestors were the indigenous heathens of North Africa; and yet others claim foreign, western ancestry. It is interesting that in one and the same tribe various subdivisions sometimes claim different ancestries.[153]

But to return to the dual division of North African tribes. In the Anti-Atlas region of Southern Morocco the two *leffs* are called Igezzulen (in the west) and Isuktan or Ahoggwa (in the east); in the Western Atlas Ait Atman and Ait Iraten; in the Atlantic plains of Morocco Sofian and Benī Mālek; in the Jurjura Kabylia up to the end of the eighteenth century there were two *ṣoffs*, which however were organizationally similar to the *leffs* in other places, named Ṣoff Ufella and Ṣoff Bu-Adda.[154] Among the Masmuda, sedentary Berbers of the Moroccan High Atlas, there are, in addition to strong alliances in the form of *leffs*, also larger local organizations grouped into *tagbilt*-s or cantons, each with a name of its own, engaged pair-wise in keen rivalry with each other and playing an important part in political life. A similar situation prevails in the Aures Mountains.[155]

When neighboring villages are lined up against each other in two competing and hostile moieties, these groupings may be called either *leff* or *ṣoff*. When a village is internally divided into two parties these are usually called *ṣoffs*. Whatever the name, the two parties are usually about equal in strength, and in case of intermoiety hostilities the moiety solidarity overrides everything else, the entire *ṣoff* (or *leff*) rallying to the support of a menaced member. Only when the interests of the village or of the tribe as a whole are menaced by a common danger is the partisan spirit of the *ṣoff* or of the *leff* attenuated for a while In some places a group may be broken up into three *ṣoffs*. Generally, however, there are two *ṣoffs* in a village, although *ṣoff*-allegiance of individual families is often changed[156]—a situation resembling the one met with in Oman.

The two *ṣoffs* may be called after the names of their leaders or, in accordance with their geographical location in the village, they may be called by such name pairs as Upper Ṣoff and Lower Ṣoff; Eastern Ṣoff (Ṣoff Sherqī) and Western Ṣoff (Ṣoff Gherbī); Central Ṣoff and Outer Ṣoff.[157]

The same dichotomy of villages into moieties is found also outside Morocco all over North Africa. In Algeria, for instance, the town of Laghuat is divided into two sections or quarters, the one inhabited by the Ouled Serghina, the other by the Ouled Hallaf. The constant feuding and bloodshed that marked the relationship of the two tribes is suppressed today, but the hatred persists, and each tribe still sticks closely to its own quarter.[158]

Occasionally the two quarters of the village are so completely separated from each other that they give the impression of twin villages rather than two sections of one and the same village. Barth in his travels passed through several such Berber villages in Libya. About one of them, Mizda, a hundred miles due south of Tripoli (probably identical with Masti Roma of Ptolemy), he reports: "... So we proceeded, passing between the widely separated quarters of villages distinguished as the upper 'el fok' and the lower 'el utah.' ..." Elsewhere he mentions a couple of villages distinguished as *Bega el-Fōka* and *Bega el-Utlīyah*, that is Upper and Lower Bega.[159]

Much the same conditions prevail in the most thoroughly studied spot in the Libyan desert, the Siwa Oasis, just inside the western frontier of Egypt. The chief settlement within the oasis is Siwa town, which is divided into two antagonistic factions sharply localized within the Eastern and Western halves of the town and called accordingly *el-Sharqiyin* or Easterners and *el-Gharbiyin* or Westerners.

According to native tradition, the division of the town resulted from a quarrel about a narrow street that separates the two quarters and took place in 1807. However, in view of the common occurrence of the dual division of towns and villages, one will be inclined to assume that much older traditional rivalries must have underlain that event. The Easterners comprise five distinct patrilineal groups, usually tracing their origin to different male immigrants by whose names they are often called, thus closely corresponding in structure to the ḥamūlas of the Palestinian fellahin. Some of these gentes are undivided, others are subdivided into as much as four sections, believed to be descended from the sons, grandsons, etc., of the supposed ancestor of the whole gens. Similarly, the Westerners are divided into three gentes.

Until recently, the most trivial events sufficed to precipitate a battle between the two factions. According to Cline, who studied Siwa in 1926–27, all the Westerners belong to the Senussi sect and order of Islam, while the Easterners in addition to some adherents of this order have many members in the sect called Madaniyah, and this difference in creed has accentuated the conflict between the two. Formerly no intermarriage took place between the factions, but more recently, since the Egyptian government took full control of the oasis and put an end to open strife, marriages between East and West have become frequent. However, even today, preferred marriages are those contracted within the faction, more particularly within the gens, and often they follow the Arab custom of marriage with the first cousin.[160]

In the Saharan urban centers in general dual groupings, referred to here as well by the term *sof*, are a striking feature of political organization. The basis of the dichotomy is usually economic, but it is mostly couched in cultural or political terms: one *sof* is formed by the more conservative citizens, the other by the more progressive elements. However, not infrequently, two different ethnic groups are lined up against each other in the two *sofs*. To this should be added that the openly avowed reason for the dual system is almost always said to be a matter of theological disagreement.

The geographical factor, by now thoroughly familiar to us, appears frequently in the Saharan towns as well. At Laghouat, for instance, on the extreme northern edge of the desert in Algeria, the oasis is cut into two by a high ridge of bare rock; one *sof* occupies the northwestern, the other the southeastern half of the settlement. At El Atteuf (pronounced El Atf) in the Mzab, local tradition has it that the people quarreled over a point of religious doctrine, the question of the conjugal fidelity of Mohammed's wife Aisha, and, unable to agree, broke up into two groups, the Sheraga (easterners) and Gharba (westerners). The presence of

two mosques, belonging respectively to the two, gives concrete
expression to the dichotomy.

In the town of El Oued (or El Wed), some seventy miles to the
east of Touggourt, and among the Hassaouna of the Fezzan, the
main dividing line between the two parties is ethnic, with the
Arabs forming the one, and the Berbers the other group.

A characteristic of the Saharan dual organization is that it is
generally based on the socially predominant groups, with the
exclusion of the lowest rungs of society. Some minority groups,
however, reproduce, on a small scale, the dichotomy characterizing the ruling classes. The Jews of Ghardaia (some 300 miles
south of Algiers), for instance, although numbering only 1,200
souls, are split into two bitterly opposed factions that disagree
violently on nearly all questions of general policy. In their relations with Muslims or Christians they are united, but in internal
matters, social or economic, the two parties have as little as
possible to do with each other.

The dual organization seems to be most highly developed in
the commercial centers of the northern Sahara, and apparently
fades out gradually toward the south as the commercial function
of sedentary settlements in general becomes more attenuated.
Membership in the moieties is, like other social affiliation, hereditary, but members can, and sometimes do, change sides with
bewildering suddenness—a phenomenon which, as will be
remembered, is not confined to this part of the Middle East.[160a]

Among the tribes of Cyrenaica the al-Ḥasa can serve as an
example of dual organization, as is shown. In fact, the structure
of this tribe closely resembles that of the 'Aneze, insofar as the
tribe is divided into two subtribes, each of whom is again subdivided into two groups.[161]

Occasionally the dichotomy of a village or the traditional hostility of two neighboring villages survive today only in cere- monial fights in which two halves of the population are lined up against each other and which at times have prognostic significance. The Berber Shlöh tribe of the Imejjat in the southwestern corner of Morocco celebrate in October the feast of Sīdī Ḥamad u-Mūsā. After a ceremonial meal "all the people divide into two parties, a northern representing the Gharb and a southern representing Sus, and a fight with slings ensues, which, though only a game, is often attended with serious accidents. It is believed that if Sus wins in this contest the year will be good, and if the Gharb wins, bad."[162]

Dual division is a characteristic feature of the social organiza- tion of the Arab nomads of the Sahara of whom the Chaamba (Shaamba) can be taken as an example. The Chaamba area lies in central Algeria, north of the Tuareg territory. They used to have a well developed *sof*-like dual system which has by now lost much of its former force but clear traces of which still persist. The tents of a single camp, for instance, are usually pitched in two more or less distinct clusters; the two groups are known as Sheraga (easterners) and Gharba (westerners). The Sheraga are traditionally progressive in all things; the Gharba, conservative. The two still retain a spirit of profound rivalry. The men form two distinct groups in the traditional ceremonial *fantasiyas* (gym- khanas). The boys form two opposing teams in their informal hockey games. Combat teams of warriors usually include men of one party only.

As to descent traditions, we find the familiar picture of origin from two brothers. The Berazga division of the Chaamba, for instance, are divided intwo two tribes based on Metlili, the Ouled Allouch (Wled Allush) and the Ouled (Wled) Abd-el- Kader. The first, numbering about 4,000, is divided into seven clans, of which the most noble is the Ouled Touameur (Wled Twamr), the supposed descendants of Twamr, the mythical founder of Metlili. Hanich (Hanish), Twamr's younger brother, is believed to be the ancestor of the Ouled Hanich, the leading clan of the Ouled Abd-el-Kader which number about 3,300 and is divided into five clans. The Wled Allush tribe belongs to the eastern party, while the Abd-el-Kader is divided between the two, as is the sedentary clan of the Beni Merzoug.

Dual structure characterizes also other Chaamba tribes.[162a]

In Mogador, on the eve of the 'Ashūra (the Moslem New Year's Day, celebrated on the tenth day of the first month, Muḥarram, called in Morocco *Shar de l'Ashūr*, month of 'Ashūr), the people divide into two camps that engage in sham battles sometimes assuming a serious character.[163]

In Mequinez this sham fight used to take place two days later, on the twelfth of the month, in the afternoon, between the young men and boys, likewise divided into two parties.[164]

Ceremonial fights between two villages take place frequently in Morocco on the 'Ashūra-day; or on the day of the 'Id el-kebīr, the Great Feast, celebrated on the tenth day of the twelfth month, Dhu el-ḥijjah; or in the form of a tug-of-war, or racing, on the day of the solar New Year (January 1) or the day preceding it; or on Midsummer's day (in the form of pouring water on one another in many places of the country; or in the form of other two-party fights, or on the fourth day before Midsummer (in Salli, a town on the Atlantic coast, in the form of a fight between two parties composed of young men and boys), sometimes with the express purpose of making the rain fall.[165]

In introducing the subject of the traces of dual organization among the Tuareg of the Central Sahara, we have to refer again briefly to Ibn Khaldun. According to this Arab historian, four of the six Beranes groups, namely the Lemta, Ṣanhāja, Ketama, and Aurigha, formed the Muleththemīn, or the people of the veil,[166] the ancestors of the present-day Tuareg. This tradition thus assigns a Beranes genealogy to the Tuareg tribes, and any subdivision of the Tuareg would therefore have to be regarded as intramoiety fissions.

The Tuareg of the Central Sahara were up to the sixteenth century divided into two groups, the north and the south. The Northern Tuareg, also called Saharan Tuareg, were the Ihaggaren; while the southern or Sudanese Tuareg were called Tademaket and inhabited initially the Adghar (mountain range) of Ifoghas. In the sixteenth century, the Saharan Tuareg broke up into two groups, the Kel (people) Ahaggar, who retained the

original name of the group (Ihaggaren is the plural of Ahaggar)
and the Kel Ajjer or Azger. These two tribal confederations are
close neighbors to this day (the Azger live to the north and to the
east of the Ahaggar), and the tradition of their common ancestry
is strengthened by the presence to this day among the fourteen
tribes of the Ahaggar of the Kel Ahamellen group, which as
recently as the beginning of the nineteenth century still belonged
to the Azger confederation.[167] The Ahaggar and the Azger form
to this day the two great sections of the Northern Tuareg. Each
of the two is subdivided into tribes, both noble (*ihaggaren*) and
vassal (*imghād*).[168]

The break-up of the Tademaket moiety began a century later.
In the seventeenth century the Aulimmiden group moved from
Ifoghas southwestward and established itself to the east of the
great bend of the Niger river, in the region of the township of
Menaka (Meneka). Subsequently, several subdivisions of the
Tademaket became dependent on the Aulimmiden: the Tuareg
of the Ifoghas Range, and the Tuareg of the interior of the great
knee of the Niger. In the eighteenth century a subdivision of the
Aulimmiden broke away from the main body, moved to the east,
and established itself under the name of Kel Dinnik as a semi-
independent subgroup of the Aulimmiden, in the region of Tahwa,
some 250 miles to the east-southeast of Menaka.[169] At about the
same time also the Ifoghas Tuareg obtained practically complete
independence from the Aulimmiden. The direct descendants of
the Tademaket are the Tengeregif, who moved to the east of
Timbuctoo, established themselves all around the shores of
Lake Fagibin, and at one time were the rulers of the city of
Timbuctoo itself. By the middle of the nineteenth century the
importance of the Aulimmiden in relation to the other tribes of
the Tuareg southwest grew to such an extent that the whole
group, including the Tademaket, was designated by the name of
Aulimmiden.[170] The Kel Geres tribes living south of the Air
mountains came at a late date from the north and are composed
of the same stock as the Ahaggar tribes. The Kel Owi of the Air
or Azben Mountains seem to be the descendants of a group of the
Tademaket.[171]

It appears, therefore, that in spite of the present-day multiple groupings of the Tuareg, they all can be reduced to two original groups, the Tademaket and the Ahaggar.

Evidence of Tuareg dual organization can be found also in the following details: The noble Kel Rela were also called Kel Ahem Mellen (People of White Tents), in contrast to another tribe, the Issetafenin, the ancestors of the present-day Aulimmiden, who were called Kel Ahen Settefet (People of Black Tents). At the present time, the Kel Rela are also called the "upper people" because they inhabit the elevated center part of the Ahaggar; while their cousin tribe, the Taitok, are also called the "lower people," because they inhabit the lower western part of the Ahaggar. These two, the Kel Rela and the Taitok, had prolonged fights over the *tobol*, the large drum that is the symbol of paramount chieftainship of the Ahaggar Tuareg. Although today there is a third noble tribe in the Ahaggar, the Tēgēhē Mellet, who also claim descent from a daughter of Ti-n-Hinan, there are conflicting traditions as to the origin of this tribe, and if one gives credit to the one that attributes Shamba extraction to it, the Ahaggar nobility is left with a clear-cut dual division.

The over-all organization of all the Tuareg thus gives the following picture:

    I. Northern Tuareg
        1. Ihaggaren
            a. Kel Rela
            b. Taitok
        2. Kel Ajjer
    II. Southern Tuareg
        1. Aulimmiden
        2. Tengeregif
    III. Kel Air or Kel Azben or Southeastern Tuareg
        1. Kel Geres
        2. Kel Owi[172]

CONCLUSION

To sum up, the main characteristics of Middle Eastern dual organization along the lines indicated by Haekel's study appear to be as follows:

1. Middle Eastern dual organization is characterized by a dual division of tribal federations and of settled populations inhabiting extensive territories, as well as of single tribes and villages. The dual division is present in

a. Overtly manifest groupings, as well as in

b. The consciousness of the people;

c. Expressed occasionally in differences in mode of behavior and attributed character traits; and is

d. A permanent phenomenon.

An additional ethnologic characteristic of Middle Eastern dual organization is that it does not as a rule contraposit one major ethnic group as against the other, even where the ethnic stratification would be favorable to such a development. In North Africa, for example, it is not the Berbers on the one hand and the Arabs on the other who form two moieties. The Berbers among themselves are divided into two moieties, as are the Arabs among themselves. Within one and the same ethnic group, however, the dual division transcends other social, cultural, and religious groupings. In Lebanon and Palestine, for example, each of the two moieties, here called Qays and Yaman, is composed of nomads, villagers, and townspeople, as well as of Muslims, Christians, and Druzes.

2. Middle Eastern dual organization is characterized by a very frequent subdivision of each of the moieties into secondary and tertiary groupings. Of the two most powerful tribal confederations of the Syrian Desert, one, the 'Aneze, belongs to the Qays moiety, while the other, the Shammar, belongs to the Yaman or Qaḥṭān moiety. Both the 'Aneze and the Shammar are divided into two submoieties: the 'Aneze into Ḍanā Bishr and Ḍanā Muslim; and the Shammar into the Eastern (or Northern) Shammar and the Western Shammar. Again, the Ḍanā Bishr is divided into four (today only three) tribes. Each of these tribes is further subdivided into subtribes, and each of the subtribes into still smaller groups.

3. In the emphatically endogamous Middle Eastern society, the dual organization cannot play a significant role with regard to the regulation of marriage. A man's preferred wife is his father's brother's daughter, or failing this, another next of kin in the male

line. On the whole, however, the dual system tends to reinforce
this endogamous trend, marriage with the opposite moiety being
regarded with varying degrees of disapproval.

4. Since Middle Eastern society in general is patrilineal, moiety
membership is inherited in the male line. The prevalent belief is
that there is an unbroken genetic connection between the present
membership of the two moieties and the original two groups or
two individuals who are believed to have been their first ancestors.
This traditional or mythical ancestry often goes back to pre-
Islamic times. Actually, however, historical evidence shows that
there has always been a considerable amount of shifting between
moieties or changing of allegiance, of switching of families or
larger groups from one moiety to the other. In such cases as a rule
very soon genetic connection is assumed between the group in
question and the ancestor(s) of the moiety on which it has grafted
itself.

5. With regard to ideology and symbolism evidence is scanty.
In the central area of the Middle East, the Qays moiety has been
associated with the red color and the carrying of a red flag, while
in the Yaman moiety white has played the same role. Among the
Tuareg and in Afghanistan, the name pair black and white
occurs.

The distinction between southern and northern moieties or
between eastern and western ones in the Middle East is a reflection of actual geographic location which either prevails to this
day or which characterized the two moieties in the past.

There seems to be some sporadic evidence as to the association
of different kinds of animals with the two moieties in North
Africa, but pending additional data this cannot be considered as
conclusive.

The tradition of the descent of the two moieties from two
brothers, on the other hand, is found repeatedly in places as
distant from each other as Iran and Morocco.

6. As to the presence of name pairs with opposite meanings,
only the following preliminary statement can be made at present:
In many cases the two moieties have no special names, but are
distinguished from each other by names of the localities that they
inhabit. For example, the Nuʿēm of Iraq are divided into the

Nuʿēm of Jazīrah and the Nuʿēm of Jebel Ḥamrin. Sometimes the two moieties are distinguished only as the eastern and western branches of the same group; or as upper and lower; cold and warm; transmontane and cismontane; mountain and plains.

When, in addition to the common name of the tribal federation or over-all group, the two moieties have separate individual names, only thorough linguistic and historical studies could in most cases elucidate the original meaning of these names; even their present-day connotation could only be established by carefully questioning members of the groups themselves as well as of neighboring groups. The author has no knowledge of such studies having been made to date. If one can rely on a superficial impression gained from a cursory examination of a few name pairs that can be relatively easily interpreted, it would seem that the tendency to denote opposites can be discovered in them. (The Yaman-Qays name pair, for example, can be interpreted as meaning fortune and misfortune).

7. The relationship between the two moieties is, as a rule, hostile. Hostility is present from the highest down to the lowest levels of the dual divisions. The hostility is at best latent, but very often leads to open fighting, pitched battles, and even massacres. A major part of the wars that took place in the history of the Islamic East was fought between opposing moieties. Only scanty traces have been found of the more harmless ceremonial type of rivalry that according to some students is characteristic of the dual organization.[173] The prevailing serious nature of the rivalry, enmity, and intermoiety warfare in the Middle East does not seem to bear out the expectation of Murdock that "opposing factions should be more characteristic of peaceful than of warlike communities."[174]

8. No traces of reciprocity or mutuality in services at feasts and funerals have been found in connection with Middle Eastern dual organization.

9. Likewise, no traces of an assigned superiority of one moiety and a corresponding inferior status of the other have been found in the modern Middle East.[175] On the contrary, the two moieties appear everywhere as equals in rank. It is this circumstance precisely that makes the two moieties the most suitable opponents.

No noble Arab tribe, for instance, would stoop to fight another tribe that is inferior to it in status. How the distinction between noble and vassal tribes fits into the dual organization pattern is not quite clear at present. But it seems certain that it never happens that a noble tribe, or noble tribes, should form one moiety, with a vassal tribe or tribes forming the other. The inferior tribes in general are vassals of a noble tribe that belongs to one of the two moieties but they do not as a rule participate in the intermoiety fighting, which is a strictly noble affair.

VIII. Noble and Vassal Tribes

A CHARACTERISTIC OF Middle Eastern social organization is the presence among the nomadic population of superior or noble tribes on the one hand and of inferior or vassal or client tribes on the other. As far as geographic location is concerned, this distinction between noble and vassal tribes is also found in practically every part of the Middle East inhabited by nomadic tribes. The noble tribes generally show a much greater organizational coherence than the vassal tribes. A noble tribe, though subdivided into several divisions and wandering units, will generally be found to inhabit a definite geographic area that is regarded as its tribal territory, and under normal circumstances its movements will be confined to the boundaries of this area. The typical vassal tribe, on the other hand, is broken up into many splinter groups, widely scattered over large areas, without cohesion and often without contact among them.

One of the best-known and –studied vassal tribes, the Ṣolubba (variants: Ṣulubba, Ṣleyb, Ṣalib, Ṣulaba, Ṣoliba, etc.) are dispersed all over the northern half of the Arabian Peninsula, and further to the north in the Syrian Desert and the adjoining territories, while according to some observers they can be found as far south as Yemen.[1] Ṣolubba splinter groups are attached to practically every tribe within this wide area, and while they all go under the name of Ṣolubba, they can be identified more closely by the name of the tribe of which they are the clients. Thus there are in the Syrian Desert Shammar Ṣolubba, ʿAmārāt Ṣolubba, Rwala Ṣolubba, Muṭayr Ṣolubba, etc.[2] The Muṭayr, in addition, have two serf tribes, the Rashayda and their cousins, the Hirshān [3]

The same is the case with another vassal group, the Hteym (variants: Hiteym, Hutaym, Heteym, etc., pl. Hitmān) of whom John Lewis Burckhardt observed in the beginning of the nine-teenth century that "of the innumerable tribes who people the deserts of Arabia, none is more dispersed, nor more frequently seen in all parts of that country, than the Heteym. In Syria, in Lower and Upper Egypt, along the whole coast of the Red Sea down to Yemen, in Nedjd and Mesopotamia, encampments of the Heteym are always to be found. . . ."[4]

In fact, the name Hteym has become a mere generic descriptive term, something like "serf" or "vassal," and the several Hteym tribes are each called by a name of their own. In the Syrian desert the Ṣleyb, al-Ḥawāzem, al-Fheyjāt, Shararāt, 'Āzem, are all Hteym tribes.[5] The Sharārāt themselves are scattered among the Rwala, Benī Ṣakhr, Ḥwēṭāt, and Shammar. The 'Awāzim, too, are widely scattered.[6] In the Sinai Peninsula the Hteym are called Rashayda, at Qatira they are called Dawāghra, in Jebel Hilāl among the Tiyāha, Orenat; in Egypt, Muṭayr, 'Azaza, Qizayz and 'Aqeyl.[7] The 'Azayre of Upper Egypt were also regarded as a Hteym group.[8]

Yet another type of vassal tribal group does not possess any tribal name of its own but is called simply ṣāni', that is, artisan or tinker, or in plural ṣunnā' (variant: ṣana'). The ṣunnā', just as the Ṣolubba or the Hteym, are found at one time or another with each noble tribe, and are called by the name of their protector tribe, for example, Ṣunnā' al-Muteyr, the smiths of the Muteyr.[9]

In Southern Arabia, especially in Muscat and Yemen, vassal tribal groups referred to as *Akhdām* ("serviles"), are scattered among all the other tribes. In the Aden Protectorate the main vassal tribes are the Zatut (sing. Zutti), a kind of gypsy caste, and the Shahara, who were once the lords of the land but are today the vassals of the Qara.[10]

In Libya, among the tribes of Cyrenaica, both the vassal and the noble tribes are called by collective group names. The vassal tribes are called Marabṭīn (or Murābiṭīn), the nobles Sa'adī.[11] Among the Tuareg in the central Sahara, the noble tribes are called Imoshar, Ihaggaren, or Imuhagh, and the vassals Imghad, singular Amghid.[12]

There are no generally valid criteria of the relationship between the vassal and noble tribes. However, in most cases the vassal tribe is tied to a noble tribe (or to several noble tribes) in such a manner as to leave no place for doubt with regard to the status of the two.

The most common expression of the inferior status of the vassal tribe is the payment of a tribute, called *khuwwa*, or "brother-hood," to a stronger superior or noble tribe. Up to World War I, most seminomadic tribes on the outskirts of the Syrian Desert paid *khuwwa* to the big and powerful nomadic tribes.[13] The superior tribe that receives the *khuwwa* undertakes in exchange not to attack or raid the vassal tribe, to protect it from other tribes in case of attack or raid, to restore any property of the vassal tribe taken by a member of the protecting noble tribe, and, occasionally, to allow the vassal tribe to sojourn permanently within the boundaries of its (the noble tribe's) tribal territory and to use its water and pasture.

The rendering of such a *khuwwa* payment in itself is sufficient to stamp a tribe with the mark of inferiority, to make *khwān*, "brothers," that is brotherhood money-payers, out of it. Usually an inferior tribe (or a section of an inferior tribe) pays *khuwwa* to a single superior tribe and therewith becomes its protected client. Only occasionally does one and the same group pay *khuwwa* to several protectors. The Rwala collect *khuwwa* from all the Hteym tribes, such as the Ṣleyb, al-Hawāzem, al-Fheyjāt, Shararāt, and 'Azem, as well as from several villages lying on the outskirts of their tribal territory, such as the Qaryatayn, Tadmor, Sukhne, Kawm, Ṭayyibe. Each tributary tribe and village has among the Rwala its "brother" (*akh*) to whom it pays directly a certain annual sum (which in the early 1900's amounted to about 25 Mejidiyyes). For this payment the *akh* gives protection and is bound to restore all property that fellow-tribesmen may have taken from the vassal tribe or village.[14]

The stigma of inferiority attaches to a tribe long after it has ceased to pay the *khuwwa*. In the first half of the nineteenth century the Ḥwēṭāt and Benī 'Aṭiyye tribes paid *khuwwa* to the Shararāt tribe that belonged to the Hteym category and camped with them as their *quṣarā* or protected neighbors; consequently, more than two generations later (in the beginning of the twentieth century) the Rwala still regarded the Ḥwēṭāt and the Benī ʿAṭiyye as inferior tribes and refused to intermarry with them.[15] Similarly, the Hteym between Medina and Hail used to pay *khuwwa* some generations ago, and although of recent years they fight like any Bedouin tribe, they cannot change their inferior social status.[16]

Conditions imposed by a victorious tribe upon another tribe defeated by it in war also can stamp the latter with an inferior status. About the same time when part of the Ḥwēṭāt tribe paid *khuwwa* to the Shararāt, another part of the Ḥwēṭāt defeated the Beni ʿUqba in battle and imposed upon them the following six conditions: (1) The Beni ʿUqba, having lost their rights to the land, become *khwān*. (2) They give up the privilege of escorting the Ḥajj-caravan to Mecca. (3) If a Ḥwēṭī were proved to have plundered a pilgrim, his tribe was to make good the loss, but if the thief escaped detection, the Beni ʿUqba have to pay the value of the stolen property in cash or kind. (4) The Beni ʿUqba are not allowed to receive as guests any tribe at enmity with the Ḥwēṭāt. (5) If a sheikh of the Ḥwēṭāt fancied a camel belonging to one of the Beni ʿUqba, the latter must sell it to him under cost price. (6) The Beni ʿUqba are not allowed to wear the *ʿabā*, the cloak of the Bedouin.[17]

The Ḥwēṭāt occupy an exceptional position insofar as they are superior with regard to one tribe and inferior in relation to another. The general pattern is that a vassal tribe is inferior in relation to all noble tribes, and the only groups inferior to them are gypsylike splinter tribes and small scattered groupings of the ṣunnāʿ, the tinkers and blacksmiths.

Some of the noble tribes hold themselves to be superior to other noble tribes and frown upon intermarriage with them, for example, the Rwala and the ʿAneze in general, or the Shammar.[18] Even the Hwēṭāt regard themselves as superior not only to the fellahin, but also to all the nomadic, tent-dwelling Bedouin Arabs.[19] This can be explained by the generally prevailing ethnocentrism that is narrowly localized among the nomadic people within the tribe or, occasionally, within a subsection of the tribe.

A more remarkable feature is the consensus of opinion among both the noble and the vassal tribes with regard to the general dichotomy of the tribal population into these two over-all groupings. The attitude of the noble to the vassal tribes is expressed in certain phrases of institutionalized conduct. In addition to the prohibition of intermarrying with them, which has been referred to above, they are regarded as weak and unwarlike and therefore not a suitable object of attack or raid according to the unwritten code of Bedouin chivalry. "Paying to all men a petty tribute, they are molested by none of them. No Beduwy, they say, will rob a Solubby, although he met him alone, in the deep of the wilderness, and with the skin of an ostrich in his hand, that is worth a *thelul* (a good riding camel)."[20] "By the unwritten Bedouin laws, they [the Ṣleyb] are outside the pale but inviolate. . . . They have no allies and no other Bedouin tribe is permitted to raid or attack them. . . ."[21] For this inviolateness the Ṣleyb have to pay with suffering insults and contempt: "They have never taken part in the wars and feuds which have occupied the greater part of the Bedouins' lives for centuries. A Sulubbi, like a woman, was a creature with whom it was too inferior to fight. . . . Beduin travelers or raiders invariably called at Sulubba tents if they could find them and demanded food and hospitality. The Beduin, who is normally a model of sedateness and reserved decorum among strangers, exhibited the worst aspects of his character in a Sulubba camp. He shouted, bullied, cursed, and swaggered in a manner sometimes shameful. He demanded the best of food, cursed his host, complained of everything, ate all he could and then demanded more food to take with him as supplies for his journey. . . ."[22]

According to another observer, "When raiding tribes pass through their territory and chance to stop where their tents are pitched, they can demand water of the Salib, and coffee, but not food."[23]

On the other hand, if the Ṣolubba come to the camp of a noble tribe, they are not received hospitably. One of the features in the stereotype of the Ṣolubba is that they will shamelessly beg for food.[24] Doughty records that if a Ṣolubbi asks for sour milk at the tent of a noble Bedouin, "the housewife will pour out leban

from her semila [skin], but it is in their own bowl, to the poor
Ṣolubba: for Beduins, otherwise little nice, will not willingly
drink after Ṣolubbies. . . ."[25] More liberal-minded noble tribesmen may invite the Ṣolubba to take water and coffee in their
tents, but they will sit apart from the rest of the guests, and for
the night they will pitch their own little tent where they will
prepare their own meal and spend the night.[26]

It is in accordance with this general attitude toward the
inferior tribes that the penalty for injuring or killing one of
them is especially severe: "In Southern Sinai, the penalty for
hitting or killing a Hiteimi used to be greater than that for a
man, i.e. they were put in the category of women, slaves and the
like."[27]

Although the vassal tribes are thus held in general contempt,
members of the noble tribes usually admit that the inferior tribes
surpass them in certain accomplishments that are very useful in
the desert. According to the Bedouins of northern Arabia, the
Ṣolubba are excellent hunters who can at will choose the wild
game that they wish to fell on a certain day, or that they will
keep in reserve for themselves to be hunted in the future.[28] It
is also acknowledged by the noble tribes that the Ṣolubba know
the desert better than they, and members of noble tribes therefore
often employ the Ṣolubba as guides in the desert or consult them
regarding routes and grazing or camping grounds.[29] Also the
Hteym are regarded as the best hunters in the Ḥijāz, as well as
excellent camel-breeders,[30] and the Shararāt as expert guides.[31]

The attitude of the inferior tribes toward themselves and
toward the superior tribes clearly reflects their low social position.
The name Hteymī has been used as an insult by superior tribes
to such an extent that even the Hteym themselves came to regard
it as such. "To call a man a Hiteimi is an insult even if he is one;
and if he is not, it is a serious slander to be expiated by a fine
and the building of white cairns."[32]

In their approach to members of superior tribes the Ṣolubba
exhibit an exaggerated humility. "Sulubba men are in general a
miserable, fawning lot, affecting endearing and diminutive Arab
terms of address, and are cringing in their manner."[33] Other
authors us even stronger terms in describing their behavior.

Glubb describes an encounter he witnessed: the "Sulubba cowered and whined. Long oppression has indeed made them very low class. The ingratiating whine in which they address the Beduin as 'Ya Amaimi,' 'Oh my little uncle,' makes one ashamed of human nature."[34]

The same attitude can be observed among the Hteym in their relations to members of other tribes: "... when the Fellahs say, *Tatahattim* (=*tatamaskin* or *tatazalli*), they mean, "Thou cringest, thou makest thyself contemptible as a Hutaymi." Moreover, they must pay the dishonoring *Akhāwat* or 'brother-tax' to all the Bedouin amongst whom they settle."[35]

Just as a noble tribe can lose its superior status by being forced into payment of *khuwwa* to a more powerful tribe, an inferior, *khuwwa*-paying tribe can move up on the social scale and can become independent if its increased strength enables it to throw off the overlordship of the tribe of which it is a client. This upward social mobility is illustrated by the recent history of the 'Awāzim tribe whose strength is approximately 4,000 fighting men, excluding those who live in Kuwait and environs, and which possesses some 100,000 camels and 250,000 sheep. This tribe, which ranges from the northeastern corner of Arabia (Kuwait town) as far south as Ras Bidiya in the Ḥasa district, is divided into some 20 sections, each with 40 to 150 tents. The 'Awāzim (sing. 'Āzimī) were looked upon as the vassals of the powerful and noble 'Ajmān tribe whose tribal territory is to the south of that of the 'Awāzim. In order to weaken the 'Ajmān who were un-friendly to him, King Ibn Saud of Saudi Arabia honored the 'Awāzim with the title of an independent tribe, armed them with modern weapons, and distributed much ammunition amongst them. During 1929–30, the years of the Ikhwān rebellion, over 1,500 new British rifles were thus distributed among the 'Awāzim. Today the 'Awāzim are nominally independent, apart, that is, from the allegiance they owe to Ibn Saud, and they regard their former overlords, the 'Ajmān, as their hereditary enemies.[36]

In a similar manner other tribes, too, succeeded in shaking off the yoke of *khuwwa* payment and in establishing themselves as free fighting tribes; for example, some of the Ṣolubba in 1919–22 and the Hteym.[37] Total equality with the old noble (*aṣīlīn*)

9

tribes, however, could not be achieved by them. While the noble
tribe was not powerful enough to prevent its former vassal from
attaining independence, it still had one means left at its disposal
of which it could not be deprived and by which it continued to
assert its superiority over its newly liberated vassal. This means
was the prohibition of intermarriage, which has already been
referred to earlier.

Bedouin society is most sensitive with regard to sex mores in
general and marriage regulations and restrictions in particular.
Among the settled peoples of the Middle East, and especially the
townspeople, marriage restrictions are stringent only as far as
women are concerned; while no special stigma is attached to a
man marrying lower than his class, the marriage of a woman to
a man of lower status would not only be resented but would be a
cause justifying forced intervention. This difference does not exist
in nomadic society in which neither the marriage of a man with a
girl from a lower tribe nor the giving of a girl in wedlock to a man
from an inferior group is tolerated. Consequently, the continuation of the marriage prohibition against any tribe on the part of
a superior tribe is a much more effective social barrier than it
could ever be in a settled community.

Thus, although the 'Awāzim with the help of Ibn Saud have
emancipated themselves completely from the 'Ajmān, the latter
will still not intermarry with them, which means that the social
distance has not appreciably diminished between the two. The
Ḥwēṭāt and the Benī 'Aṭiyye are still regarded as inferior by the
Rwala, who will not intermarry with them. Marriage between a
noble tribe and a Ṣolubba tribe is quite out of the question. "No
Arab can marry a Ṣolubba girl. He would be killed by his people
if he did, and she also." If a young man from a noble tribe
nevertheless loses his head over a Ṣolubba girl, the two have to
flee their tribes and seek safety in distance. When the Emir
Fawāz of the Rwala took a pretty Ṣolubba maiden into the desert
and kept her there as a mistress (without formally marrying her,
which would have been impossible even for a prince or chief
shaykh of the powerful tribe), he was "roundly cursed by all good
Badawin."[38] A Rweylī or any other noble Bedouin cannot marry
a girl from the Hteym or Ṣunnā' tribe just as he cannot marry a

slave. If he were to disregard these prohibitions he would be killed by his own next of kin.[39]

In fact, the prohibition of intermarriage with an inferior tribe is so general among all the Arab tribes that it can be taken as one of the chief criteria of tribal inferiority. This tradition is so strong that it is carried over from the desert into the town, as illustrated by the following occurrence: In 1931 'Abdullah Beg al-Ṣanaʿ who, though of Ṣāniʿ origin, attained the high position of Director General of the Ministry of Interior in Iraq, married in Baghdad a girl from the noble Saʿdūn tribe. Both the girl and her mother had agreed to the marriage. Shortly thereafter 'Abdullah was killed by the girl's kin because he was admittedly of servile origin. At the subsequent trial several ministers of the state were called in by the defense to show that the murder was no crime according to the traditional Arab standards. When the murderer, a shaykh, was nevertheless condemned to death by an Iraqi court, his sentence was commuted to 15 years of imprisonment, and after only 19 months King Fayṣal pardoned him.[40]

Details of the marriage restrictions make one aware of differences in status within the vassal groups themselves. The Ṣolubba, Hteym, and other vassal tribes, although despised, are still regarded as free Arabs (*ḥorr*). As such, they stand higher in the social scale than the slaves who are as a rule black (*'abd*), and even than the *ṣunnāʿ*, the blacksmiths who, although white, are not independent, and therefore inferior to the other vassal tribes. Consequently, no intermarriage is countenanced by the vassal tribes with the slaves and the blacksmiths. Freed slaves marry among the freedmen groups in the towns, or the daughter of a blacksmith.[41]

In this connection it may be mentioned that the women of vassal tribes generally enjoy more freedom than the women of the noble tribes. Among the noble tribes there are several who veil their women. The women of the vassal tribes, however, do not wear any veil, and therefore, especially in places where the noble women are veiled, are easily recognizable. The Ṣolubba women, for instance, never veil and rarely wear a *milfa* (a face or head veil as opposed to the *burqa*, face mask). Among the Ṣolubba, who are very fond of dancing, it is moreover customary for men and

women to dance together—in itself a highly disgraceful and un-
seemly thing in the eyes of the noble tribes—and, what is even
more shocking for them, in the course of the dance the men
occasionally kiss their partners on the mouth before the audience.
Also, some Ṣolubba husbands tolerate that their wives prostitute
themselves.[42] The Hteym, "inhabiting the seaboard about
Yambu', are taxed by other Badawin as low and vile of origin.
The unchastity of the women is connived at by the men; who,
however, are brave and celebrated as marksmen. . . ."[43]

Vassal tribes usually but by no means always engage in occupations different from those of the noble tribes. Sometimes, as in
the case of the 'Awāzim, the Hazim, the Sulaylāt, they pursue the
same occupations as the noble tribes, breeding camels and
sheep.[44] In most cases, however, members of vassal tribes or
splinter groups engage in all kinds of works and tasks that the
noble tribes disdain. The Ṣolubba, for instance, are hunters,
tinkers, trackers, guides, coppersmiths, leatherworkers, wood-
workers, cattle surgeons, doctors for men, women, and beasts;
while their women are washerwomen, preparers of poisons and
love potions, casters of the evil eye, versed in witchcraft, and even
engage in prostitution.[45] Some Shararāt live with members of
noble tribes, perform the menial tasks of servants and herdsmen,
and are excellent guides.[46] The Ṣunnā' are ironworkers, farriers,
swordsmiths, gunsmiths, they shoe the horses, beat out the tent
stakes of their hosts, etc.[47] The Zatut in Southern Arabia are
circumcisers, barbers, bloodletters, auctioneers, ironworkers. The
Shahara in Southern Arabia hew wood and draw water for their
Qara overlords.[48] The 'Aqeyl are merchants controlling the camel
trade between Kassala and Egypt, and agents among the tribes
of wholesale merchants who have their establishments in the
larger towns on the borders of Arabia, as well as in Egypt and
India.[49] The Jebeliya in the Sinai Peninsula engage in gardening
and some of them are employed as servants of the monastery of
Sinai.[50] The Kauliyah or gypsies in Iraq are fortune tellers,
palmists, and thieves, while their women perform the female
circumcision practiced in Southern Iraq, and among the Muntafiq
tribes of the Euphrates and Banī Tamīm Arabs.[51] The Hteym in
Arabia "make, eat, and sell cheese, for which reason that food is

despised by the Ḥarb. . . . The Khalawiyah (pl. of Khalawī) are equally despised; they are generally blacksmiths, have a fine breed of greyhounds, and give asses as a dowry, which secures them the derision of their fellows."[52]

The following traits are thus found to distinguish the vassal tribes from the noble ones:

1. The noble tribes exhibit a coherent tribal structure; the vassal tribes are fragmentized and scattered.

2. The noble tribes are strong enough to protect themselves against enemies; the vassal tribes are unable to do this and pay *khuwwa*, brotherhood money, to a noble tribe whose clients they thus become, or to an individual member of such a noble tribe who is then in honor bound to protect them.

3. The noble tribes do not intermarry with the vassal tribes on account of the latters' inferiority.

4. The only occupation befitting a member of a noble tribe is tending the herds. The noblest of the noble tribes are camel-herders, the second-class noble tribes have mostly sheep and goats. The vassal tribes, though they too may possess these animals, engage mainly in handicraft, as well as in hunting.

5. A favorite pastime (under traditional conditions) of a noble tribe is raiding and warfare, undertaken either for the sake of booty or as a point of "honor." The vassal tribes, as a rule, do not fight, not only because they are weak, but also because they have no comparable "honor" to defend.

6. The women of the noble tribes conform, in general, to a more stringent code of sex mores than the women of vassal tribes. Women of vassal tribes go unveiled.

At the present stage of our knowledge of Middle Eastern social structure it is impossible to answer the question concerning the origin of this division of the nomadic peoples into noble and vassal tribes. All that can be done at present is to adduce some data as to the ideas current among the tribes themselves with regard to this social dichotomy. Since Middle Eastern tribes in Southwest Asia as well as in North Africa are extremely conscious of origin and descent, it will come as no surprise that the noble or vassal status of a tribe is, as a rule, attributed to a noble and a servile descent respectively.

The Ṣolubba, whose name resembles the Arabic word for cross, are regarded by many tribes, as well as by several European students of the Middle East, as descendants of Crusaders, or Crusaders' mercenaries, or their camp followers.[53] The theory of the non-Arab ancestry of the Ṣolubba is supported by the non-Arab language that they use among themselves (with non-Ṣolubba they speak of course Arabic), and in which some observers thought to have recognized traces of French or Latin roots.[54] Others regard this explanation of the descent of the Ṣolubba and of the frequency of a blond type in their midst as "a modern European fantasia,"[55] and believe that they are the "oldest inhabitants of the desert."[56]

Equally little is known of the actual descent of the Hteym, concerning whom there is not even such a plausible theory current as about the origin of the Ṣolubba.[57]

As to the Ṣunnāʿ, according to some they are of Negro origin[58] while in other tribes they are regarded as of white blood, but nevertheless not independent or free. Still others maintain that the Ṣunnāʿ are of inferior descent simply because nothing is known of their genealogy, and because they themselves have no pride of descent, and marry any newcomer, whether from town or tribe, whether free, vassal, or slave.[59]

Of the ʿAwāzim it is stated that "they are not of pure descent." The Sulaylāt are said to be descended from an ʿAneze man who married a Ṣolubba woman. According to another version of this explanation of their inferior status, it was Ibn Ghafil, the grandfather of the present chief of the Sulaylāt, who married a Ṣolubba gipsy woman, and therefore his entire tribe lost status.[60]

Nothing derogatory is known or circulated about the descent of the ʿAqeyl. The Jebeliya are believed to be descendants of Bosnian and Wallachian serfs who were given by Justinian to the Monastery of St. Catherine in the Sinai Peninsula in the sixth century and who were, of course, originally Christian.[61] The Shahara, the most ancient tribe in the Qara mountain district of Southern Arabia, were vanquished and subjugated by the Qara.[62]

The Marsh Arabs of Southern Iraq are regarded as inferior by the surrounding desert tribes not on account of inferior descent but simply because of their settling down and becoming marsh dwellers.[63] Similarly, the still seminomadic riverain Ajwān on the Euphrates around Nasiriyah are regarded with contempt by the true Bedouin.[64]

In Cyrenaica, the Marabṭīn (or Murābiṭīn) tribes, although nominally vassals of the Saʿadī tribes, maintain in actuality a much higher status than the typical vassal groups in the Asiatic part of the Middle East. They constitute larger tribal units, that is, they approximate even in this respect the Saʿadī tribes. These larger groups live, in fact, independently and pay no *khuwwa* or any other dues to the Saʿadī tribes who are the nominal owners of the land. According to a Senussi leader, the Marabṭīn tribes are the descendants of the Yemeni (South Arabian) tribes who colonized North Africa after the first invasion of the continent by the Arabs. In the eleventh century they were subjugated by the Benī Sulaym who conquered the country and continued in it their nomadic mode of life.[65]

A division into noble and vassal tribes is characteristic of the social organization of the Tuareg. According to the traditions of the Ihaggaren, the Tuareg of Ahaggar, some two or three hundred years ago two Berber women came from Morocco to the Sīlet oasis. One was noble, Ti-n-Hinan by name, and the other was her serving-woman, Takama (or, according to others, Temālek). Ti-n-Hinan settled in Abalessa and gave birth to three daughters: about the father or fathers of these daughters the Targui legend has nothing to say. From the first daughter, Kella, descended all the Kel Rela; the second daughter became the ancestress of the Taitok, and the third, named Tahenkot, became the progenitress of the Tēgēhē Mellet. These three are the noble tribes of Ahaggar, whose chiefs have *tobol*-s, large drums that are the symbol of chieftainship.

The servant girl, Takama, also gave birth to two daughters, one of whom became the ancestress of the Ihadanaren, a second-rank tribe; while the other became the mother of the two vassal tribes, Dag Rāli and Ait Loaien. Ti-n-Hinan gave the oases of Sīlet and Ennedid to the two daughters of Takama, and their descendants still own them to this day.

The Ti-n-Hinan legend is an interesting illustration of the

Middle Eastern tendency to "telescope" history. Excavations carried out at Abalessa unearthed the tomb of the Tuareg queen whom tradition regards as the ancestress of the tribes and calls Ti-n-Hinan. But the archaeological evidence shows beyond doubt that the tomb was pre-Islamic, and that the real Ti-n-Hinan must have therefore lived in a much more remote period than attributed to her by popular tradition.[66]

However that may be, descent from Ti-n-Hinan is as much a part of living tradition among the Tuareg as is their division into noble and vassal groups. The Tuareg themselves commonly speak of "noble clans" and "vassal clans." When the warriors of a noble clan go raiding, they often take along the fighting men of one or more of their vassal class, who subsequently receive a substantial share of the plunder. It is said that vassals also have an obligation to fight at the side of their noble masters in intertribal wars. If this be true, it would constitute an interesting deviation from the general Middle Eastern custom, which keeps vassal groups out of any fighting.

The vassals of the Tuareg pay annual tribute to their tribal chiefs or to the Amenokal, the paramount chief of the Ahaggar confederation, or to both. These payments consist, as a rule, of dates, millet, melted butter, young camels, sheep and goats, as well as all kinds of manufactured articles. Also shares are paid from profits the vassal groups make on imported articles and on their caravan commerce. If they go out independently of their masters on raiding expeditions, about one half of the booty is paid over to the nobles. In addition, each vassal family used to contribute toward the upkeep of a particular noble family. A peculiar development of this relationship was that the noble men and women used to go begging from their vassals who could hardly afford to refuse them. "But if this systematic begging became unbearable, as it often did, the vassals would simply pull up stakes and move quietly out of reach of their noble parasites." In recent years, however, the Amenokal and his whole camp has been supported by the French Government, so that these higher nobles are no longer in need of support by their vassals.

Traditions and environment combined have evolved a division of labor and responsibilities between the noble and vassal Tuareg.

"The nobles of a tribe, together with the headmen of the vassal clans, ride out in search of new pastures and at the same time act as military scouts, always on the watch for enemy raiders as well as for potential victims, alien camps or caravans which they can raid themselves. The vassals in their turn are responsible for the daily management and immediate protection of the flocks and herds, most of which belong to them anyway; and they contribute an armed reserve that can be called up quickly in case a battle becomes imminent or a good opportunity for a quick raid presents itself."[67]

A somewhat similar situation prevails among the Teda, to the east of the Tuareg, in the Tibesti massif of the southeastern Sahara. They are divided into some forty clans, headed by the noble clan of the Tomaghera (or Tomagra), the Gunda and the Arna. Beneath them rank the commoners and the vassals, between whom there is little if any status difference. The lowest ranks comprise, in descending order, the Azza (hunters, smiths, and artisans), the negroid serfs (*Ḥarrāthīn*), and the Negro slaves. Many vassal clans are divided into two or more fractions, each attached to a different noble clan. The tribal chiefs of the noble clans are chosen usually by a council of clan leaders, but, "curiously enough, it is said that they are named sometimes by the council of family headmen of the vassal clan supposed to have been longest resident in the tribal territory."[68]

Among the nomadic Arab Chaamba (or Shaamba) tribes in central Algeria, each tribe contains noble clans and vassal clans. One of the noble clans in each tribe is usually considered as more noble than the rest, its rank being based on its assumed descent from an early and famous or holy ancestor, but clan rank can be changed rapidly if a group is outstandingly successful or the reverse. Below the nobles are the tributary vassal clans which, however, are relatively few in numbers.[69]

The Moors, the pastoral nomadic tribes of the Spanish Sahara and of the adjoining, formerly French, Saharan territory, too, comprise both noble and vassal clans. Vertical mobility is considerable here, too, but sheer numbers and consequent group strength are not always decisive factors in determining rank; in some of the most powerful tribes one finds vassal clans that are twice as big as the noble ones. Wealth in livestock does not seem to be the deciding factor either, for some vassal tribes are far richer than their noble masters. As Briggs has observed, "it looks as though an efficient fighting organization, together with the strong leadership and rigid discipline which this implies, is the only thing that can surely raise a nomadic Moorish community above others of its kind."

Rank status is greatly influenced by tribute payment. The rule is that the receiver of tribute ranks higher than the payer. But the situation is complicated by the variety of reasons for which tribute is paid. Thus not only do weaker groups pay tribute to stronger ones for armed protection or for economic assistance in times of hardship; also, rich groups pay tribute to poorer ones if the latter are more warlike and therefore useful as mercenaries. Even some Maraboutic clans, whose holiness is, as a rule, sufficient to protect them, pay for protection; these are known as "Marabouts of the shade" in distinction from the independent "Marabouts of the sun."

The tribute payment is usually rendered by the headman of a vassal family to the headman of a noble family; in other words, the client-patron relationship is established between families rather than entire clans. The right to such tribute can be sold by the headman of the noble family to the head of another noble family, but this is done only in extreme and sudden emergency. Otherwise, the nobles prefer to go begging to their vassals in a manner similar to the one usual among the Tuareg.[70]

IX. The Middle Eastern Town

In the Middle East are located the most ancient towns of the world. Sites occupied continuously or intermittently for four thousand years or even longer are nothing exceptional in this world area. Throughout this long period the towns were of central importance to their respective hinterlands, a position they hold to this very day, and therefore the primary goals of all conquerors. A change of hands in them often meant a considerable shift of population, the elimination of the leaders and of the articulate or otherwise important elements either by ruthless liquidation or by exile, and their replacement by new settlers with a view to political reliability and loyalty.

The fate of the towns was thus always characterized by more frequent and incisive changes than that of the villages. The villages, among which too there are many with a history of millennia, have remained largely the same throughout their history, with basically the same way of life carried on largely by the same ethnic group, generation after generation. The towns, on the other hand, have often experienced catastrophic ups and downs, they changed rulers, were destroyed and rebuilt, or evacuated and resettled. Their importance increased in one period and decreased in another, depending on their position within the empire to which they happened to be annexed. These great political, social, and cultural upheavals notwithstanding, the towns remained the undisputed centers of every cultural achievement in their areas of influence.

Town and Village

The concentration of all cultural and civilizational achievements in the towns means that in the Middle East there is a considerable contrast between the rural and the urban varieties of culture. Without attempting to probe into the historical origins of this situation, it can be stated briefly that whatever differences had existed between town and country in the Middle East in pre-Islamic times were greatly accentuated by Islam, itself a religion of townspeople[1]—that turned town and country into veritable opposites.

The contrast which exists between the rural community and the city in every society was rarely more striking than in the medieval Islamic world. Here it was not merely a contrast between isolation and congregation, between the dispersed economy of the village and the concentrated economy of the town, between oppressed poverty and relative freedom and wealth, between producer and consumer. It was a contrast of civilizations. The medieval Moslem culture was above all an urban culture. While Islam but lightly touched the secular life of the countryside, it rebuilt and refashioned the cities from their foundations, and stamped them with an individual impress which has persisted even to the present day. Between the Egyptian or Syrian city and its country districts there was little or no tie but the economic one—indeed, the possibility of any stronger tie was all but ruled out by the contempt with which the townsman regarded the peasant—while the cities of widely distant countries shared a common culture, a common order of life, a common disposition of mind, and a sense of unity fostered by these joint possessions and traditions, even when physical intercourse between them was relatively limited. There is a marked change of spiritual atmosphere in the cities; though they share in the general decline of the eighteenth century, there is something of independence in the bearing of the townsmen, a conviction of their dignity as citizens of Islam, and a readiness to assert their rights, even though it might degenerate into mere rioting and mob demonstrations.[2]

The contrast between the town and the country outlined in this passage persists to this day. In fact, the first outcome of Westernization was an augmentation of the disparateness between the city that showed a relative readiness to absorb Western influences and the village that was not reached by this outside force. Although this initial stage has now been largely left behind, inasmuch as urban influences, and with them Western cultural traits, tend nowadays to spread more and more into the rural areas, resulting in a diminishing of the age-old gap between city and village, the very persistence of this gap for hundreds of years is a noteworthy fact that has to be understood and appreciated in trying to evaluate the role of the town in Middle Eastern culture.

For it is remarkable indeed that in the Middle East as a whole, where more than three fourths of the population lives in rural areas, the village should have contributed so little to the culture of the country. Broadly speaking, the role of the rural population has been confined to providing food and taxes, and some raw materials and folklore. Everything else originated in the towns.

Only on the lowest economic level is the rural population self-sufficient in the sense that it satisfies all its needs in producing simple utensils, apparel, and housing in accordance with age-old methods of home craft. As soon as a village raises itself over the barest subsistence level, it becomes dependent on wares and merchandise produced in the towns. The higher the standard of living of villagers, the more they rely on the town even for the satisfaction of primary needs such as food, clothing, housing, utensils, and all kinds of consumer goods. In exchange for this the country has only its agricultural products to offer, bought up by the town through a series of middlemen at advantageous prices.

In addition to being the economic, trading, manufacturing (and more recently industrial), commercial and financial center, the typical Middle Eastern town is also the seat of all the administrative, political, judicial, religious, and educational institutions, and concentrates within its confines all those elements who devote themselves wholly or partly to occupations pursued in these institutions, or to literary, journalistic, or artistic work, or, in fact, to any other field outside food production. During the last few decades, as a result of Westernization, such institutions as modern universities, hospitals, libraries, academies, scientific and other societies, as well as amusement centers and the like, have been added to the cultural features that are all concentrated in the towns.

A particular feature of Middle Eastern social structure has facilitated this development. This feature has been (and is to this day) the preference for urban residence (and, in particular, residence in the capital city) by the owners of landed estates. The actual supervision of these estates has traditionally been entrusted to managers, while the landlord and his family lived in the city and had no direct contact whatsoever with the people whose work made it possible for him to indulge in leisure and luxury. The residence of these landed proprietors in the towns meant a concentration in them of all those trades, crafts, and arts that depended on the existence of a class of wealthy connoisseurs. In this manner the congregation of absentee landlords in the towns became a powerful factor in the development of a specific, refined, and sophisticated urban culture, separated by a wide gulf from the simple folk culture of the villages.

A more recent outcome of the concentration of the wealthy landlord class in the towns was that this same class began to utilize some of its accumulated capital for investment into new economic enterprises such as commercial, financial, and industrial undertakings. Furthermore, when in the wake of continuing Westernization Western forms of government were adopted, it was again this same class whose presence and availability in the capital and district centers enabled it to become the foremost element in the formation of governments, ministerial and other administrative offices, and representative bodies. Thus, while a visitor to the capital at the turn of the century would have found the upper class comprising chiefly great landowning families, half a century later he would have found the upper class still consisting largely of the same families but this time also as leaders in many economic, administrative, and political fields.

The outcome of this deep cleavage between town and country has been that the town has been regarded by all those who knew about its existence and had some knowledge of it even though only from hearsay, as the place where one can live a good life, attain status, prestige, satisfaction, and enjoyment, in short, as the seat of everything desirable. The village, in contrast, and especially in the eyes of the townspeople, has become the symbol of backwardness. The attraction the town exerted on the villagers in the past explains at least partly the constant flow of migrants from village to town, a process that has become greatly accelerated as a result of Westernization and the greater employment opportunities offered by the industrial plants established in the towns. A result of this internal migration from village to town has been a faster increase of the urban than of the rural population. The village-to-town movement has gathered additional speed during the Second World War as a result of war conditions. In some places it was easier to obtain supplies in the towns than in the rural areas; in others, industrial development spurred by wartime demands attracted unemployed or underemployed agricultural workers; and again elsewhere the villagers were attracted by work provided by the Allied forces. These developments reinforced the general tendency to prefer urban life and employment with its higher prestige to agricultural activities in the rural districts. After the war, there was in some cases a movement back to the countryside, but this was merely a temporary reversal of the general trend which by and large continued.

One of the results of Westernization and industrialization is the rapid growth of cities. The largest city of the entire Middle East, Cairo, had only 240,000 inhabitants in the 1830's, according to Lane's estimate.[3] In a century their number increased tenfold, and by 1947 it was more than two and a half millions. Three more cities passed the million mark in recent years: Teheran, capital of Iran (1,500,000 in 1956), Istanbul, former capital of Turkey (1,215,000 in 1955), and Alexandria, the second largest city in Egypt (1,157,000 in 1947). Two more cities were in the half million to million range: Baghdad, capital of Iraq (730,000), and Casablanca, the most important port city of Morocco (700,000). Eleven additional cities had inhabitants whose numbers ranged from one quarter to a half million: Ankara, the new capital of Turkey (453,000); Beirut, capital of Lebanon (450,000); Tunis, capital of Tunisia (410,000); Tel Aviv-Jaffa in Israel (400,000); Damascus, capital of Syria, and Aleppo in northern Syria (400,000 each); Algiers, capital of Algeria (361,000); Oran in Algeria (299,000); Izmir in Turkey (286,000); and the Iranian cities of Tabriz (290,000) and Isfahan (254,000). Another thirty cities had populations ranging from one hundred thousand to a quarter of a million. Thus, of the 156 million people living in the Middle East, only about 15 million or 10 per cent, lived in the middle of the twentieth century in cities of more than 100,000.

Nevertheless, the influence of urban civilization in the Middle East as a whole is considerable. Especially in the vicinity of the cities and towns is their presence strongly felt. The inhabitants of villages within walking distance and, where good transportation is available, within easy traveling distance, are frequent visitors to the town. There they transact business or spend their leisure time sitting in coffeehouses, attending a motion picture performance, or listening to the litigations in the law courts. They familiarize themselves with the ways of the townspeople, become influenced by their clothing habits, their speech forms, their outlook. Some of them will spend some time working in the town or even find permanent employment there and either take up residence in the town or become commuters.

The urbanizing influence of the town radiating into its environs is manifested, among other things, in such external changes as the adoption of urban styles of architecture, the installation oj street lights, the introduction of water supply, the erection of a bus station, a coffeehouse, etc. The proximity of the town also brings about certain economic advantages for nearby villagse, such as easier marketing of their products, additional income derived from urban employment, etc. All these effects of the town make a village situated close by very different from a remote village, the urban influences diminishing with the increasing distance. Cultural standards of the town also affect the villages in its vicinity. Schools are built, or children are sent for schooling to town. Interest in political events taking place in the town begins to engross the villagers, and so forth.

Until now we spoke of village and town as though they were two clearly distinguishable disparate entities. In fact, however, it is not always easy to distinguish between village and town in the Middle East because the size of the local aggregate does not always provide a reliable criterion.

A careful scrutiny of the constant and most outstanding differences between village and town discloses that they boil down ultimately to distinctions in occupational structure. The village is characterized by a largely homogeneous occupational structure: most of the people in the village are engaged in agriculture, with merely a sprinkling of individuals engaged in service occupations, such as a shoemaker, tailor, carpenter, watchman, barber, religious functionary, etc. In the town, on the other hand, one finds a heterogeneous occupational structure, with the majority, moreover, engaged as a rule in nonfarming occupations.

The heterogeneous occupational structure of the Middle Eastern town is contingent on a number of factors. The concentration in the town of the landed proprietors, already referred to above, attracts a considerable number of specialists in trades, crafts, arts, and professions to cater to the needs of this wealthy upper crust of society. Since antiquity the town has been a place of exchange, a *sūq* or bazaar, where the villager and the nomad come to sell their surplus products and to buy the town-produced goods. This position of the town as the central place of commerce enables a sizable merchant class to make a living here. The town is usually the administrative center of a province or district or a subdistrict seat, depending on its size and importance. It has a mayor and a municipal council, a district governor or a district officer, law courts of first or second appeal, a police force, some military post, a telegraph and post office, and other paraphernalia of government; consequently in it live numerous government employees, officials, clerks, soldiers (if it is a garrison town), and similar personnel. These, in turn, give work and employment to many more people engaged in service occupations. In contradistinction, the village may or may not have a small police force; otherwise, the only symbol of government is the headman who acts as a representative of both the government and the people.

As to the public institutions found in Middle Eastern cities, it is difficult to generalize. The number and character of these institutions seem to show a direct correlation to the size of the city and a reversed correlation with its distance from the Mediterranean littoral. In other words, the larger the city and the closer to the Mediterranean it is located, the more public institutions are found in it and the more Western the character of these institutions. This observation would seem to hold good with reference to such institutions as hospitals, clinics, secondary public or private schools, colleges, museums, newspapers, societies, men's clubs, literary and sports clubs, motion picture theaters, cafés and restaurants, dance halls, night clubs. The same holds good with regard to the availability of electric current and piped water. The general rule is that the larger the town the more Westernized it is, and probably the higher the percentage in its population of the Westernized and semi-Westernized elements. In the largest towns there are whole sections that have a completely Western character; no comparable quarters can be found in the small towns.

Under traditional circumstances town life was the culminating refinement of which the local subcultures of the Middle East were capable. One of the most typical examples of this was Damascus with its bazaars filled with the finest products of Syrian craftsmanship, with its great concentration of wealth and luxuries on the one hand and of intellectual, artistic, and literary activity on the other. The tenor of life in a city such as Damascus, although surpassing by far that of the countryside, was nevertheless part and parcel of one and the same cultural *genus*. With the impact of Westernization, urban culture in the large Middle Eastern cities has begun to absorb more and more of the traits introduced from a very different cultural *genus*, that of the modern Western world, and consequently an increasing distance began to develop between urban and rural culture. In fact, increasingly large proportions of the urban population, especially in the coastal towns of North Africa and in the largest cities of Egypt and the Levant, are adopting a way of life which in its external forms consciously copies the West. A villager from the remote hinterland feels almost as lost in the modern sections of Casablanca, Algiers, Alexandria, or Beirut as he would in Rome or Paris. Only in the most recent years, as indicated above, has this distance begun to diminish again, owing to the fact that the influence of the new Westernized urban culture radiates more and more powerfully into the surrounding countryside, gradually drawing closer to itself the still largely tradition-bound culture of the rural communities.

TOWNSMAN AND PEASANT

Whatever will be the outcome of this most recent trend, for the time being the situation is that the disparate cultures of town and country endow the townsman and the peasant with two greatly differing social personalities. To be a true townsman means not only to live in a town, but also to adhere to a definite way of life, to enjoy a certain social status, and to engage only in certain types of occupations, to the definite exclusion, in the first place, of agriculture. An urbanite may own land and make a living from income derived from the land, but under no condition will he personally engage in agriculture. On the other hand, it is not an indispensable prerequisite for the maintenance of an urban status to reside in a town or city. A townsman may move to a village, spend decades there, acquire property, conduct his business, raise his children there, contribute to the welfare of the village, and even participate in its social life, yet he will still remain regarded as a townsman both by the villagers and by himself, a man distinct from the villagers (fellahin) and, in a certain sense, an outsider.

In Middle Eastern society one of the surest manifestations of status differences is the marriage barrier. Consequently, there has always been a strong tendency for the children of townsmen and of villagers not to intermarry, even though they may be next-door neighbors, play together every day, and grow up together. Only recently, with the general changes in traditional mores, are these restrictions somewhat relaxed. Another characteristic feature distinguishing the townsman from the villager even after a life-time spent in a village, is that when the townsman retires from active life, he moves back to the town rather than live out his last years in the village.

The fellah, although secretly he may be envious of urban life, dislikes certain qualities that he believes characterize the towns-man. He regards the urbanite as soft, pampered, and dissipated. Conversely, the latter despises the fellah and regards him as ignorant, backward, primitive, and uncouth.

Among the traits that have traditionally differentiated the townsman from the fellah, in addition to occupation, are his clothes, his food, his house, and his social life. The townsman may or may not wear European clothes; the fellah, never. Once he does so, he has ceased, strictly speaking, to be a fellah. (This statement does not apply to some minority groups such as the Circassians who do wear European clothes, and have their own special village and social organization.) The difference in dress is even more pronounced among the women. Fellah women, as has been pointed out, do not wear the veil; whereas many urban Muslim women traditionally do. The *fellāḥa* (peasant woman) wears a simple black garment of durable cotton material, in some areas with an embroidered front. Urban women wear a conglomeration of European clothes, and the Muslim among them, when leaving the house, were usually covered by a black overdress.

The fellah's food is generally very simple. It consists mostly of bread, ground wheat (burghul), lentils, olives and olive oil (depending on the region), some rice, sour milk (leben), some butter, and rarely meat. Very few vegetables are eaten with the exception of onions. Milk is used generally for babies only, although a pudding is made of it sometimes. Goat meat is generally preferred to mutton.

A townsman's food is much more varied and more luxurious. Vegetables and fruits are fairly extensively used. Mutton is preferred to goat meat, but beef is also consumed. Some of the well-known Middle Eastern dishes, such as stuffed grape leaves, stuffed chicken, stuffed squash, kibbeh, various broiled meats, ḥummuṣ, etc., are strictly urban foods seldom indulged in by the fellah. While pastries are fairly common among the townsmen, the fellahin seldom have them.

Traditionally, the house of the fellah is a one-room structure that shelters his family and sometimes his animals. It is generally devoid of even the simplest amenities. The urban house is a stone structure of two or more rooms constructed, until recently, with the seclusion of women in mind. It may be surrounded by a high-walled courtyard. Today, it may have running water, electricity, and a kitchen and bathroom inside the house.

As far as social life is concerned, contact between men and women is less restricted among the villagers than among the townspeople. Urban women until fairly recently were completely secluded, restricted to taking care of the home and the children. Village women, in addition to doing their household chores, work side by side with their menfolk in the fields; they are freer, and have a limited amount of social intercourse with men.

The relative inactivity of townswomen often results in a tendency to become fat and flabby. The village woman, on the other hand, is active, works hard, and walks gracefully, being able to carry a heavy water jar on her head without holding it.

The ageing process in village women is often accompanied by loss of weight.

The differences in style of living between the fellah and the townsman amount to almost a class difference. The lines, however, are not rigid, and the fellah can and frequently does pass into the urban group. Furthermore, education, village to town migration, and Westernization are closing the gap at an increasing rate.

SOCIAL ORGANIZATION

With regard to social organization, a distinction has to be made between old and new towns respectively, between the indigenous established population of a town and the newcomers. Little can be said here about the social organization of the newly settled groups or elements: these, to some extent and for a certain length of time, tend to retain the social organization that they brought along from their home locality. In many cases, however, under the impact of the changed conditions, their social organization, and even their family organization, disintegrate to the extent that they appear as an amorphous population aggregate.

The old sections of the towns are characterized by a tendency toward a mosaiclike clustering of population elements. The tangible manifestation of this age-old tendency is the quarter. The most important basis of the formation of these quarters may be the *ḥamūla* (lineage or clan), or else the religious or ethnic group. Thus the typical east-Mediterranean town has a Christian (for example, Greek Orthodox) quarter, an Armenian quarter, a Jewish quarter, a Kurdish quarter, etc., and, of course, several Muslim quarters inhabited by Sunni Muslim Arabs who form the majority of the population.[4]

This structure of the Middle Eastern town is an inevitable outcome of a number of factors characteristic of society. Among these can be mentioned the religious-community basis of social organization, recognized and stabilized by the Turkish millet system and the great coherence of minority groups living in the midst of an unsympathetic majority, feeling secure only among themselves and suspicious of every outgroup.

The result of this quarter system in traditional circumstances has been to confine social contact within each town largely to the inhabitants of one and the same quarter. This in turn greatly facilitated the preservation of the social identity of the ethnic or religious group as a separate minority. In recent decades considerable changes have begun to manifest themselves in this respect. With the penetration of Westernization, modernization, and industrialization, the separateness and socioeconomic self-reliance of the quarters is gradually giving way to a greater and greater interdependence of the various sections and their inhabitants.

While the minorities thus are being brought closer to the dominant majority of the town they inhabit, one must not lose sight of the fact that, compared with the percentage of the minorities in the country as a whole, they constitute a much higher proportion among the urban population. Statistical data are not available, but the concentration of minorities in the towns is apparent to every visitor. In most cases, moreover, the urban minority groups surpass the Muslim Arab or Muslim Persian or Muslim Turkish majority in economic standing, literacy, skills, professional accomplishments, etc. Occasionally the minorities engage in occupations not practiced by the Muslim majority, and conversely, there are occupations engaged in only by the Muslims but not by members of the minority groups. In Damascus, for example, only Christians are engaged in meat-drying and the manufacture of alcoholic beverages.[5]

Up to the end of the First World War the Middle Eastern towns were characterized by a two-class system. A small number of rich people on the one hand and a large number of artisans, small shopkeepers, workers (including many agriculturists who lived in the smaller towns) on the other—this was the prevalent social structure of the towns. The life of the first or upper class was a life of opulence, ease, and luxury, while the second or working class exerted itself laboring many hours a day, seven days a week, hardly earning enough to make the barest living on the most meager subsistence level.

In spite of this great inequality in standard of living between the few rich and the many poor, and in spite of the spatial proximity of the two groups, there was a certain balance between the two and an acquiescence manifested by the poor with regard to their own position. Two factors were mainly responsible for the existence of this attitude among the working classes: first, tradition and religious influence; all situations in which a person finds himself are predestined by Allah, and it is the duty of man to submit himself to the will of God. Only God knows what is best for man, and by submitting to His will in this world man acquires merits that will be rewarded by Him in the Beyond. The second factor was the informal, almost egalitarian character of all contacts between people of different social classes. The forms of relationship between superior and inferior (such as between employer and employee, master and servant, ruler and subject, etc.) were patterned after those of father and son in the traditional Middle Eastern patriarchal family. The equation of all superior statuses with the paternal status and of all inferior statuses with the filial status made it easier for people in inferior positions to subordinate themselves to those in superior positions; the situation presented itself merely as an extension of the family situation in which the individual developed and in which his personality received its first and most decisive molding influences.

Many of these attitudes still persist to this day, although, of course, with the emergence of large cities interpersonal contact between the upper and the working classes tends to shift more and more from the personal to the impersonal level. Wealth and leadership still show a high correlation: ownership of landed property, of commercial, industrial, and financial enterprise on the one hand, and political, social, and cultural leadership on the other are still frequently concentrated in the hands of single individuals or of members of one family. The power and influence of the great families, however, have been severely challenged and are on the decline.

As a result of incipient industrialization in the Middle Eastern towns the urban working class is undergoing a considerable transformation not only with regard to the objective conditions and circumstances in which it performs its tasks, but also with reference to its attitudes toward the employer-owner class. The paternal-filial relationship between these two classes is rapidly becoming a thing of the past, to be replaced by an impersonal relationship in which the regulative influence of laws and rules becomes more and more necessary. The improvement of the working conditions and the impersonalization of the employer-employee relationship are probably the two most important changes that characterize the transformation of the Middle Eastern working class.

The middle class is the most recent accretion to the Middle Eastern urban class structure. It is still relatively small in numbers, although not insignificant in weight. The emergence of a middle class is a direct outcome of Westernization, in the sense that most individuals who belong to this class and are conscious of it are engaged in occupations that emerged as a result of Westernization. Other persons or families who on the basis of their economic level would have to be counted with the middle class (such as merchants, house owners, workshop owners, lower officials of the traditional type, etc.), are actually people not identified with the middle class but aspiring to rise into the ranks of the upper class. The true or new middle class therefore comprises in the main members of the professions (doctors, lawyers, teachers, social workers, writers, journalists, etc.). In this connection it must be remembered that much of the traditional urban upper-class attitude of disdain toward manual labor still survives even in the modern town, and that consequently there is a hesitancy in engaging in occupations such as mechanics or engineering. There are fewer persons engaged in these specialties than needed by the country and those who are engaged in them are counted by public opinion as members of the working class rather than of the middle class.

An interesting question of more than theoretical significance is, from where are the members of this new urban middle class recruited? A satisfactory reply to this question would have to be based on statistical studies concerning the occupations of the fathers of those individuals who today form this new class. In the absence of such studies all one can do is make a cautious surmise as follows: seemingly the members of the new middle class come from three main sources: the rural areas, from relatively well-to-do fellah families who have the means to educate their sons, enabling the more ambitious and more talented to continue in high school in the town and ultimately to become professional workers; the urban working class, as a result of a similar process; the urban upper class, most of whose scions have the opportunity for high school education that leads some of them into the professions. According to the prevailing social values, however, these professional individuals who belong to the "great" families are counted as members of the upper class.

CULTURE CHANGE

Innovations and resultant cultural changes emanate as a rule from the urban centers toward the peripheries. In the cultural exchange between a country and the world at large, it is the centrally located urban aggregates that first receive the impact of new cultural traits introduced from abroad in the technological, organizational, or ideational fields. The rural sector receives these changes in a secondhand form, as it were, after their adaptation by the city to the requirements of the urban variety of the local culture.

While the above holds good in a general way for the world at large, it is doubly true in the Middle Eastern culture continent. In world areas contiguous to the Middle East the rural sector has played a relatively larger role in the cultural interchange between town and country than in the Middle East itself. In the Middle East, even in most ancient times, the urban centers were practically the sole carriers and advancers of culture. Even in our present day the Middle Eastern village is a more or less passive recipient of cultural changes, improvements, and modernizations, all of which radiate from the town.

With the possible exception of Ottoman soldiers in Turkey's imperial days and of a few isolated instances of recruitment of rural labor for modern industrial work (as in the case of Aramco), only the town population of Middle Eastern countries has had the opportunity for firsthand acquaintance with Western culture, or at least with some of its more conspicuous traits. Within the town itself, more than a fleeting and superficial familiarity with what the West has to offer is limited to the members of the upper and middle classes.

Western culture penetrates the Middle Eastern town in a great many ways: through the offices, business and industrial premises, educational and other institutions, and the homes of the upper and middle classes. Members of these classes therefore function as the sieve through which must pass all Western influence before reaching the working classes in the towns and the people in the rural areas.

Since foreign influence, in most cases Western, reaches the town first, and only later emanates from it to the rural areas, there is as a rule a considerable time lag between a stage reached in the process of culture change in the town and the corresponding stage in the rural areas. There is, moreover, also a definite differential in intensity: in the town, and especially in the upper and middle classes of its population, culture change reaches a peak not found in rural areas. Furthermore, corresponding to the heterogeneous social and cultural structuring of the town (in contrast to the much more homogeneous village), the degree and extent of culture change show a much greater diversity; in other words, in the town the different sectors and classes of the population manifest a wide difference with regard to culture change, ranging from the almost completely Westernized element on the one hand to sectors very little touched by Westernization on the other.

One more factor must be mentioned: Since the town is the locus of the almost exclusive concentration of Middle Eastern intellectual life, it is only in the town that we expect to find, and actually do find, a variety of consciously formulated attitudes toward specific and concrete manifestations of culture change, toward the total trend of Westernization as a whole, and toward traditional Middle Eastern culture. The average villager is more inclined to follow the lead of those whom he respects and holds in authority. Therefore, the village aggregate as a rule will be found to be characterized by one typical attitude, or at the utmost by a very narrow range of attitudes, toward the problems of culture change. In the town, on the other hand, the heterogeneity of the consciously propounded and advocated attitudes may become a dividing factor and the basis for headlong clashes.

Another problem has now to be touched upon, albeit briefly.

It has repeatedly been observed that culture change, that is, the adoption of Western culture traits, is inevitably accompanied by a rejection or disappearance of traditional Middle Eastern culture traits. In some cases we understand *a priori* that this must be so. If somebody desires to have his house furnished in the Western manner, he can carry out his decision only after he has discarded the old furniture to make place for the new. But here the question arises: why must one make the complete switch to Western furniture? Instead, why does one not introduce only some pieces of Western furnishing, primarily those of undoubted utility, while at the same time retaining some pieces of the traditional Middle Eastern furnishings, primarily those of undoubted beauty, thus accomplishing in the house a combination of the good and desirable features of this facet of both cultures? This simple example conveys some idea as to the problems of culture change in such varied fields as architecture, clothing, food consumption and cuisine, family life, social organization, manners and morals, aesthetics, religious outlook, and *Weltanschauung*.

The extent to which Western influence has changed the life of the upper and middle classes in the Muslim towns, and especially in the big cities, can best be gauged by comparing the present-day life of these social groups in a large urban center such as Cairo with the detailed and admirable account given of the same city by Edward William Lane some three generations ago.[6] Living in Cairo in the twenties and thirties of the past century, Lane felt, and with a masterly pen conveyed the feeling to his readers, that he was moving in a world essentially different from his own English background both in basic mentality and the minutest manifestations. Cairo of today—or at least large sections of it—is much more similar culturally to London than Lane would ever have dreamt was possible.

This cultural change in the town itself affects directly the town-country relationship. Even in traditional circumstances, the Middle Eastern town always attracted the country population and its growth was partly contingent upon a slow but steady village-to-town migration. This influx has become immensely augmented as a result of the Westernization of the town itself with its concomitant industrialization and rapidly increasing employment opportunities. Although the natural increase of the Middle Eastern town population is smaller than that of the villagers, the village-to-town movement results in a proportionately much greater increase of the urban than of the rural sectors. A country-wide result, therefore, of the technologic aspect of culture change in the towns is a definite gradual shift from the traditional Middle Eastern pattern of rural-urban population distribution toward the Western pattern with its typical half-and-half division between rural and urban population.

The accelerated processes of culture change that the Middle Eastern town undergoes today confront it with a large number of taxing problems. Leaving aside for the moment the administrative, educational, medical, sanitational, economic and technological aspects of these problems, I wish briefly to dwell only on that aspect that touches upon social psychology in its relation to the changing cultural background.

The over-all effect of the cultural innovations introduced from the West into the towns of the Middle East is one of a general rise in the urban standard of living. The almost proverbial scourges of the Middle East: disease, poverty, and ignorance are slowly being forced to loosen their deadly grip. But these highly desirable developments are all too often accompanied by evils that all but cancel out their intrinsic value. Freya Stark, one of the few Westerners who has acquired true insight into the Arab psyche, has stated: "Discontent with their standards is the first step in the degradation of the East. Surrounded by our mechanical glamour, the virtues wrung out of the hardness of their lives easily come to appear poor and useless in their eyes; their spirit loses its dignity in this world, its belief in the next."[7]

It must be assumed that there exists a causal connection between the penetration of Westernization, and especially of Western technology, on the one hand, and the deterioration of the satisfactions derived from traditional culture on the other. This is borne out by a number of disquieting social phenomena, including the lure of Communism for certain elements. The why and the how of these undesirable and potentially dangerous concomitants of Westernization have not yet been satisfactorily studied and understood. Nor have the processes of Westernization in the

Muslim town in general been sufficiently investigated. To mention only a few of the problems falling under this general heading: What are the processes of adjustment of Middle Eastern villagers to urban life? What are the cultural effects of industrialization on the working classes in the Middle East? What is the correlation between the adoption of Western culture traits and rejection or disappearance of traditional Middle Eastern culture traits? The great practical significance of research into these and similar problems for the cultural future of the Middle East needs no elaboration.

X. Religion in Middle Eastern, Far Eastern and Western Culture[1]

I N THIS chapter an attempt will be made to examine the role of religion in the three cultural archetypes of the Middle East, the Far East and the modern West. Geographically, the Middle East will be taken as delimited in Chapter One;[2] the Far East as composed of the Indian subcontinent, Southeast Asia, China, and Japan; and the modern West as including all the countries in which Western civilization has reached its typical development, notably Western Europe and America north of the Rio Grande.

In trying to outline within the confines of a brief chapter the differential roles religion plays in the cultures of these three major world areas, generalization and disregard of detail will be inevitable. Only an attempt at a rough and over-all preliminary typology can be essayed to the neglect of extramodal variants. Nor will particular doctrines and practices be emphasized. Whether divinity is conceived in polytheistic, trinitarian, dualistic, or unitarian terms would appear irrelevant in relation to such a more basic question as: Is the religion centered around a personal deity or not? Similarly, rules of religious ritual must seem unimportant when interest is focused primarily on the degree of influence religious ritual as a whole exerts upon everyday life.

The role religion plays and the position it holds in a culture can be discerned by examining various aspects of religion in their relationship to the total context of culture.

In the first place, religion functions as a normative force regulating customary behavior, inasmuch as it has both positive and negative commandments with which the individual is expected to comply. The extent to which religious rules and teachings influence human activities and modes of thought varies from one culture to another. *The normative function* of religion can therefore be recognized as one of the variables in the relationship of religion and culture.

Another aspect of the relationship between religion and culture is reflected in *the psychological effect* of religion on emotional life. The quality as well as the intensity of this psychological effect of religion can vary from culture to culture and thus supply us with a second variable.

A third variable can be seen in the character of the general orientation of the teachings of religion concerning supernatural beings, forces, or things. As a rule religions deal to some extent with the supernatural and possess certain theologies and metaphysics. An examination of the general character of the religious teachings concerning *the supernatural component* yields the third variable.

Each religion also has a definite outlook on its own value in relation to that of other religions. Its relationship to other religions may range from complete toleration to the complete lack of it, with a corresponding range of self-evaluation. This variable, best called *religiocentrism* (on the analogy of ethnocentrism), can serve as an additional avenue of approach to the study of our subject.

Lastly, religions channel human ambitions towards different goals, and especially in adversity and suffering hold out to man comforts of varying types. This *teleologic or purposive orientation* of religion will serve then as the fifth and last variable in examining the role of religion in Middle Eastern, Far Eastern, and modern Western cultures.

THE NORMATIVE FUNCTION

In a study dealing with the general cultural characteristics of the Middle East, the religious component of Middle Eastern culture has been characterized as permeating the totality of life and as holding supreme sway over performance, thinking, and feeling: in brief, over life as a whole. Religion is the fundamental motivating force in most phases and aspects of culture, and is in evidence in practically every act and moment of existence. The observance of the traditional forms and rites, whether of the "official" or of the popular kind, is an integral part of everyday life.

A close connection exists between religion and other aspects of culture in the Middle East. Art in its entire scope is closely circumscribed by religion, and all the arts serve primarily religious purposes.

All custom and tradition are basically religious; for whatever is old and customary and traditional is hallowed by religion. Religious practice itself is mainly tradition and custom, so that practically every act and every activity is either in conformity with or contrary to religion.[3] These observations hold equally good for Islam, which is the religion of about 90 per cent of the population of the Middle East, for the Eastern Christian churches, and for Judaism in its Middle Eastern form. In brief, religion in the Middle East is the main normative force.

In these traits Middle Eastern religion closely approximates Far Eastern religions.

Hinduism, the closest major eastern neighbor of Islam, "deals directly with the Hindu's total life, including morals, economics, politics, and even music, medicine, military science, architecture, phonetics, grammar, astronomy and ceremonial. Hindus may include all these in what they call religion."[4] "Correct caste behavior is enforced largely by the weight of religious sanction. . . . Religion enters into all phases of Hindu life. Washing oneself in the morning, preparing and eating meals, sowing the fields take on sacramental quality when performed with the appropriate ritual. Religious merit is acquired as much by simple adherence to one's caste conventions and family obligations as by any special act of worship. . . . The cultural life of the village is almost completely bound up with religious observances and religious holidays. . . . Hinduism and Islam . . . provide the sanction which gives each individual his place in society, his code of social relations, and his guide to personal behavior. . . ."[5]

Similarly Buddhism, the dominant religion of southeast Asia, Ceylon, and Tibet, which is highly influential also in India, China, Korea and Japan, is "a pervasive influence shaping men's attitudes towards life and their ultimate aspirations and hopes far more than appears on the surface of things." The Buddhist teachings extend into such fields as the relationship of parents and children, teachers and disciples, husbands and wives, friend and friend, masters and servants, laymen and monks, and include such details as for example the recreations and luxuries a master should provide for his servant.[6]

In China in general, "religion and conduct belong together. . . . Religion in China is connected with politics. It expresses the emotional and esthetic aspects of life while conduct and politics express the active aspects."[7]

Taoism, the Chinese philosophical religion, contains, in addition to its mystical element, a set of political principles, a philsosophy of government, a number of economic principles and moral precepts, and gave rise to a large number of societies or brotherhoods that were a powerful ethical force elevating the moral tone of the community, ministering to the wounded, the refugees, and the needy, and often robbing the rich to help the poor.[8]

Confucianism, several centuries older in China than Taoism, has ethical teachings close to those of Buddhism. Its relationship to the arts can be gauged from the following saying contained in the Confucianist Book of Rites: "Poetry is what gives the first stimulus to character; ceremonial is what gives it stability; music is what brings it to full development."[9] Confucian doctrines are replete with detailed rules (in the form of good advice or "wisdom") with regard to conduct, the attainment of happiness, and the ordering of life.[10] The "New Life Movement" established by Chiang Kai-Shek at Nanchang in 1934, which has a close kinship with Confucianism, advocates that "life should be artistic"; that "the people are to be trained to take a new attitude toward nature as revealed in modern science"; that "tidiness and truthfulness should be emulated" and the like.[11]

These few instances suffice to show that basically common features characterize the normative function of religion within the totality of culture in the Middle East and in the Far East. In both areas religion is a major factor, if not the major factor, in directing and regulating life.

Religion in the Western world differs from both Middle Eastern and Far Eastern religion insofar as since the onset of the industrial

10

revolution it has been on the retreat. The dominating religion of the West, Christianity, although originally born in the same region that was the cradle of Judaism and Islam, the central part of the Middle East, and partaking of the same general characteristics that these two creeds have or had in common with the religions of the Far East, has profoundly changed its character since the emergence of modern Western civilization. The function of religion, as it can be observed today in the modern Western world, is restricted to a rather narrowly delimited field of its own. Its ritual and its practical precepts have little to do with the everyday pursuits of Western life, and its credos and tenets are equally divorced from the essentially secular goals and values of modern Western culture. Even in the lives of those religiously observant, an hour or two a week set aside for the satisfaction of the traditionally persisting religious needs are deemed sufficient.

Furthermore, while both in the Middle East and in the Far East the great majority of the people are religious, and with the exception of those regions where the impact of Westernization has considerably altered the situation, persons whose lives are not dominated by religion are few and exceptional, in the modern West (and especially in the highly urbanized areas) the majority of the population does no longer possess deep religious attachment but is religiously either lukewarm or indifferent.[12]

Religion in the Middle East and the Far East thus appears as the dominant normative force, while in the modern West it has largely ceased to be a significant normative factor.

THE PSYCHOLOGICAL EFFECT

In the Middle East, religion is an asset the psychological value of which cannot be overestimated. It is a psychological factor of first-class magnitude, lending unfailing spiritual sustenance to all true believers, that is to the overwhelming majority of the population. The religious Middle Easterner appraises life with all its adversities and vicissitudes from a wider angle, from a long-range perspective as it were, in which sojourn on this earth with all its possible gains and losses appears as merely the lower and lesser half of the great totality of existence, the essentials and ultimates of which lie in the Beyond. Spiritual outlook thus moves along a higher plane, beyond the reaches of discomfort, pain, anguish, and privation. Hence that composure, that peace of mind even in the face of great adversity which in the Middle East ever and again gives rise to wonderment in the Western observer.[13]

Rebecca West noted this phenomenon as far west as among the Muslims of Bosnia. Comparing her Christian Bosnian guide with his Muslim neighbors, she observed: "The lad was worse off for being a Christian; he had not that air of being sustained in his poverty by secret spiritual funds that is so noticeable in the poverty-stricken Moslem."[14]

In the Middle East proper, no such distinction between Islam and other faiths is apparent with respect to what can be termed the spiritual sustaining power of religion. The different rites of Islam, the semi-Muslim sects (such as the Druzes, the Nusairis, etc.), the various Christian churches, and the Oriental Jewish communities all share this basic characteristic of being able to generate a psychological certainty of possessing the Truth, of following the Right Path, and of wielding the Perfect Key to the gates of the Great Beyond. Among them is the feeling that one does what is right because one observes the commandments of one's religion, and that one is inwardly protected from serious harm because God in whom one trusts keeps an eye on each individual and ultimately metes out just retribution. These convictions give the true believers of every faith, creed, and sect an extraordinary sense of security, an ability to preserve their calm and dignity and detachment, without depriving them of the ability to seek and enjoy whatever pleasures can be wrung from this world.

The same psychological effect of religion can be observed in the Far East.

In India, where as we have seen religion pervades all aspects of life, it constitutes, just as in the Middle East, a sustaining force of matchless effectiveness. Religion functions as a sort of protecting caul that envelopes the human on his way from birth to death, leaving him psychologically unscathed by the poverty, ill-health, misery, and suffering that are the inevitable concomitants of life for the great majority of Indians. No matter what his religious group, his total life is a religious life, and in its pursuit he attains security and self-confidence.

The "liberated living man" who has attained spiritual perfection is characterized in the *Yogavisistha* as follows: "Pleasures do not delight him; pains do not distress. There is no feeling of like or dislike produced in his mind even towards serious, violent, and continued states of pleasure or pain. . . . He rests unagitated in the Supreme Bliss. . . . He is full of mercy and magnanimity even when surrounded by enemies. . . ."[15]

Farther to the east, the same religious mentality characterizes the followers of Buddhism, Taoism, and Confucianism. Younghill Kang, describing his native Korean village, says: ". . . my family did not seem to mind their helpless poverty, since most of them were indulging in the mystical doctrine of Buddhism, or in the classics of Confucius, who always advocated that a man should not be ashamed of coarse food, humble clothing, and modest dwelling. . . . The sage said: "Living on coarse rice and water, with bent arm for pillow, mirth may yet be mine. . . ." My grandmother . . . was a true Oriental woman. The quietism of Buddha, the mysterious calm of Taoism, the ethical insight of Confucianism all helped to make her an unusually refined personality. . . ."[16]

Speaking of Asia in general, Kurt Singer remarks: "Oriental harmony . . . is a mood in which Oriental man accepts both peace and strife as he accepts the change from light to darkness, summer and autumn, life and death. . . ." Therefore, ". . . life in the Orient is happier and more harmonious than in the West. . . ."[17] Similarly, Northrop notes "the equanimity, the poise, the steady, sure peace of mind, and all-embracing calmness and joy of the Oriental. . . ."[18]

Compared with this gift bestowed by religion upon Middle Eastern and Far Eastern man, Western religion must indeed seem pallid and impotent. The Bosnian observation of Rebecca West can be generalized, for the impression that religion in the West has remained a sustaining force only in rare cases thrusts itself even upon the most casual observer. In a society in which religion is detached from the chief interests and pursuits of everyday life, in which the principle of separation of church and state is upheld, and where the desire to attain purely secular aims is the main incentive in human life, religion evidently must have lost any spiritual sustaining power it may have had in the past. Toynbee speaks of "the spiritual vacuum which has been hollowed in our Western hearts by the progressive decay of religious belief that has been going on for some two-and-a-half centuries."[19]

Minor undulations in the psychological influence of religion can, it is true, be observed. In times of stress and strain there is a certain religious resurgence. But these waves even when at their peak remain far below the high and steady level maintained by the powerful outpour of psychological sustenance emanating from religion in the Middle East and the Far East.

The Supernatural Component

The supernatural component of religion has to be dealt with on two levels: the doctrinary or official level and the popular level.

The official doctrines about the supernatural are contained, in all the three world areas examined here, in voluminous religious literatures the composition of which was effected in the course of several centuries, and the older layers of which have acquired a character of sanctity. The degree of conformity evinced by the actually maintained beliefs as to the supernatural depends as a rule on the extent of the individual's absorption of the traditional literature of his religion. On the popular level, that is among the great masses of the people, where the familiarity with the traditional literature is minimal, the conformity of the concept of the supernatural with that of the official doctrine is very slight.

Middle Eastern religions in their supernatural aspect occupy an intermediary position between the religions of the Far East and of the modern West, inasmuch as on the popular level their typological affinities definitely lie with the Far Eastern religions while on the official doctrinary level they and the Western religions belong to one group.

That the popular religious beliefs and practices of Judaism, Christianity, and Islam in the Middle East are practically identical did not escape the keen eye of Lane well over a hundred years ago. "It is a very remarkable trait," he wrote in the 1830's, "in the character of the people of Egypt and other countries of the East, that Muslims, Christians and Jews adopt each other's superstitions, while they abhor the leading doctrines of each other's faiths."[20] Likewise, a more general similarity can be observed, not in the concrete details, but in the over-all type of popular religious beliefs and practices of the Middle East as a whole on the one hand and of the Far East as a whole on the other.

Popular religious belief in both world areas can best be described as polytheodemonistic, with complementary practices carried out at innumerable shrines, temples, and sanctuaries. A large plurality of gods, godlings, heroes, demons, ancestors, and patron saints are believed in, sculpturally or symbolically represented, and served in a great variety of rites in Japan, China, Indonesia, Indo-china, and India. In China, ancestor worship added considerably to the number of the available deities, while in India to the hosts of gods and goddesses are added sacred animals, rivers, and the like. In the Middle East, the worship of holy or merely haunted spots marked by springs, trees, and stones, or of shrines supposed to be the tombs of saints, is the popular institutionalized and formalized expression of a polydemonistic belief in spirits, ghouls, afrits, jinns, and other demons whose numbers are legion and who constantly interfere with the lives of men. Formless powers and forces such as the much-sought-after *baraka* or holiness or the greatly feared evil eye round up the picture of popular Middle Eastern religion.

Little of this type of popular religiosity has survived in the modern West. To be sure, in countries or regions where old local folk cultures still linger on, as for instance amid the agricultural peasantry of Europe, the popular veneration and worship of saints as well as the belief in demons and spirits, in the evil eye, and other supernatural powers, are the truly forceful elements of religious life. The spiritual distance between this type of religion and that of the official exponents of the faith can be visualized if one thinks of the Christianity of an Italian fishing village in comparison with that of the Vatican. In the urban population of industrialized Western Europe or in America north of the Rio Grande, however, this type of popular religion is practically extinct or is on its way to becoming so, and the chief difference between the religion of the people and that of the official religious leadership is one of degree rather than one of kind. It is only the religious leadership whose life is mainly concerned with religion, while in the life of the simple people religion plays, as has been pointed out above, a negligible role. The average individual, even if he is a member of a church or a religious community, will know very little of the officially sanctioned religious doctrines of his faith; but he will as a rule not hold beliefs or practice religious rites contrary to those of his church (as this is the case in the Middle East). He will simply neglect out of ignorance or indifference the rites of his church, and will have little knowledge of and even less interest in the doctrines of his church concerning the supernatural.

While with regard to the popular side of the relationship to the supernatural in the three world areas the line of demarcation thus clearly runs between the West and the Middle East, the official doctrine concerning the supernatural shows a basic typological homogeneity in the West and the Middle East setting both apart from the religions of the Far East.

Far Eastern religions, with the exception of Japanese Shintoism which, however, need not concern us in this context, are basically *nontheistic* in their original unadulterated doctrines, while Middle Eastern and Western religions in the official formulation of their tenets are *theistic*, or more precisely *monotheistic*. Theism in religion, as defined by Northrop, "is the thesis that the divine is identified with an immortal, non-transitory factory in the nature of things, which is determinate in character. A theistic God is one whose character can be conveyed positively by a determinate thesis. His nature is describable in terms of specific attributes."[21]

Monotheism, therefore, is the doctrine of *one* theistic God whose nature is describable in terms of specific attributes. The belief in such a God, as characterized by his determinate attributes, is the basic creed of the theistic religions.

Students of Far Eastern religions (again with the exception of Shinto) are unanimous in describing them not merely as nontheistic but also as noncreedal. John Clark Archer has commented upon the noticeable absence from Hinduism of formalized creed and characterized it as "theologically non-creedal."[22] Of the six recognized Hindu religiophilosophical systems only one, the Vedanta, is concerned with the concept of the divine. According to the Vedanta doctrine, however, Brahman (God) is indefinable, since every predicate, even the most general and indefinite, implies a contrary, an opposite, and besides Brahman there is non-else; he is all-pervading, all-comprising. In Shankara's formulation of the Vedanta there seems to be no place left for "faith" as a positive experience,[23] or a positive belief in some eternal that is determinate in character.[24]

It is difficult to reduce to a common denominator the teachings of the numerous schools of thought of Buddhism in the several countries in which they developed. Reischauer states that "there are a good many of the better educated and liberal leaders [of Buddhism] who claim that the very essence of true Buddhism is not a fixed or unchanging doctrine but rather a certain attitude of mind, a spirit of free inquiry and passion for truth."[25] This noncreedal character of modern Buddhism is completely in keeping with the original noncreedal and nontheistic formulation of Buddha's teachings. As a Japanese authority on Buddhism put it, "Buddhism teaches that there is no personal creator or ruler of the world."[26]

Confucianism, although it enjoins the worship of Heaven and Earth, of Confucius himself, of imperial and other ancestors and heroes, has never attained a theistic quality, and does not concern itself with the supernatural. It recognizes the divine, but as the divine is not determinate, it cannot have a concept of it, only a name for it. Moreover, it can realize it in experience but not say what it is in terms of determinate qualities.[24] Taoism centers around "the physical concept of the way of the heavens in relation to earth, transfigured and deepened by the mystic trance. The Tao is universal but not transcendent.[27] It produces all and yet is not above all. It is not a person or an individual. It is the basic, cosmic energy which informs all."[28]

The numerous religious societies that spring up in China to meet critical situations, "have no creed but they have a ritual."[29]

Hinduism, Buddhism, Confucianism, and Taoism are thus in their uncorrupted form nontheistic and noncreedal, all of them holding that the divine is indeterminate and that no specific attributes can be ascribed to it. In contrast to them the religions of the Middle East and the West are both theistic and creedal.

The chief source of Muslim religious doctrine, the Koran, as well as later theological writings, is replete with divine appellatives and attributes the study of which developed into a formidable science at a relatively early date in the history of Islam. The determinate attributes of Allah are grouped under the seven headings of Life, Knowledge, Power, Will, Hearing, Seeing, and Speech,[30] in addition to which he is described as merciful, gracious, the guardian over all, the reviver, the deliverer, and other such terms totaling ninety-nine in number.

Similarly in Christian theology God is described as a supreme being whose attributes include, to mention only a few, infinite power, wisdom, goodness, who has an inscrutable will and holds sovereign dominion over the world.[31]

Much of both the Muslim and the Christian doctrines of God goes ultimately back to the Hebrew Bible in which God is described by a rich variety of moral excellencies, including power, wisdom, foresight, righteousness, love, mercy, and loving-kindness. Post-Biblical Jewish literature repeatedly contains lengthy enumerations of these and other divine attributes.

With regard to the supernatural aspect, Far Eastern religions are thus found to be polytheodemonistic on the popular level and nontheistic on the higher doctrinary level; Middle Eastern religions, polytheodemonistic on the popular level and monotheistic on the higher doctrinary level; Western religions, polytheodemonistic on the folk-culture level, indifferently monotheistic on the modern popular level, and exclusively monotheistic on the official religious level.

THE RELIGIOCENTRIC ASPECT

One of the significant characteristics of the Far Eastern nontheistic religions is the high degree of toleration they display toward other religions. This trait is usually accompanied by a merging or fusion of different religions. Religious jealousy or exclusiveness, the conviction that one's own religion is the only valid and true one and that all other faiths are necessarily erroneous, is rare and is frowned upon.

While Europe (and the West as a whole) is predominantly Christian, and the Middle East is equally predominantly Muslim, no such exclusive and homogeneous religious characteristic exists in the Far East. Religious pluralism is the rule, however narrowly one tries to define the geographic unit subjected to scrutiny. Members of the same family, or even single individuals, often belong to two or more religions simultaneously, or, in other cases, alternatingly. Not only is there no stigma attached (as there is in the West and the Middle East) to such religious changeovers; they are taken as manifestations of a commendably sincere quest for the Truth.

Seekers for truth are likened in an ancient Oriental parable to people setting out from different starting points to climb a high mountain. The peak is too steep for the climbers to aim directly upward, so each of them begins spiraling the slopes in different directions. When two of the climbers meet somewhere, both may be convinced that the other is on a false track since he is going in an opposite direction. But actually, of course, though following different paths, both and all aim toward the same truth symbolized by one and the same lofty summit.

Just as Far Eastern religions are noncreedal and nontheistic, they are also nonaggressive, tolerant, and nonproselytizing. They do not require of their adherents, as Western and Middle Eastern religions do, to believe that their own teachings are the embodiment of the only true and perfect faith and that all other religions are bogged down in ignorance and error. They freely borrow from one another, and incorporate even substantial teachings taken from different schools.

In India, "Hinduism . . . is as much Buddhist as it is Brahman. The Tantric doctrines . . . appear as much in the Buddhism of Tibet as they do in the Hinduism of India. Recently, Surendranath Dasgupta, the leader of the contemporary Indian philosophical and religious thought, has proposed an actual practical unification of Buddhism and Hinduism."[32]

As a modern Indian philosopher has put it, "Every seeker of truth and perfection is allowed in Hindu society to pursue his own method freely, and nobody is expected to interfere or meddle with it. . . . This tolerance of differences of opinion and creed within its own fold and even outside itself is an essential characteristic of Indian culture."[33]

The same open-minded receptiveness characterizes the Hindu approach to Western religions. As Max Weber already has pointed out, a Hindu could accept the most specifically Christian sectarian doctrines without ceasing to be a Hindu. In fact the extreme religious "tolerance" characteristic of Hinduism appeared to Weber to have reached such a level as to make him conclude that "Hinduism is something different from 'religion' in our sense of the word."[34]

In Indo-China, in Annam, Cochin China, and Tonkin, "a peculiar combination of Confucianism, Taoism and Buddhism prevails. . . ." The official religion of the Annamese empire included Confucianist, Buddhist, and Taoist elements all intermixed, yet it remained essentially a combination of magic, animism, and ancestor worship.[35]

Passing on to China, we again find that "religion in China does not follow the pattern of interreligious exclusiveness of the West. . . . The temples are dedicated to a variety of gods. . . . There is one temple in this region which houses Confucius, Lao-tze (Founder of Taoism), and Buddha. This mixture is seen everywhere in China. . . .[36] Individual Chinese or Korean families are often composed of Confucians, Taoists, and Buddhists . . . and even single individuals accept all three religions at once."[37]

Some of the numerous religious societies the emergence of which in times of crisis is characteristic of China "placed above their old gods the God of all religions. Christianity, Islam, Buddhism, Confucianism and Taoism were viewed as ways of salvation under the direction of the God of all Religions."[38]

The same is reported of Japan. "Japanese . . . rarely accept one religious sect to the exclusion of others; almost everyone considers himself at once a Buddhist, a Shintoist, and a Confucian. Individuals worship any deity regardless of cult affiliation. . . ."[39] Or, as observed by another student of Far Eastern religions: ". . . in countries like China and Japan many of the adherents of Buddhism at the same time give allegience to the original national faiths. . . ."[40]

All this sounds as alien to anyone brought up in one of the three monotheistic religions that originated in the Middle East as the monotheistic religious exclusiveness and aggressiveness appears "narrow, intolerant and provincial"[41] to Far Easterners reared in one or more of their nontheistic religions. As Krishnalal Shridharani wrote, "It is forgivable to insist on *one* God, but to insist upon *The* Prophet and *The* Law is intellectually wrong. The assertion of Louis XIV that 'I am The State' is quite innocent compared to anyone's assertion that 'I am The Law.' ... This exclusiveness is antispiritual inasmuch as it is overweening in the light of the limitations of human perception."[42]

Western observers as well noted the "enormity of intolerance and persecution [which] has shown its hideous countenance, almost without fail, whenever and wherever a higher religion has been preached,"[43] such as Biblical Judaism and its daughter religions, Christianity and Islam. In Christian Europe, religious conformity was a matter upon which the local secular power felt called upon to rule, if necessary by armed force. "In Central Europe ... the secular princes did successfully use their power to force down the throats of their subjects whichever of the competing varieties of Western Christianity the local potentate happened to favour."[44]

Speaking of the theistic religions of the Middle East and the West, Northrop observes: "All the theistic religions are aggressive, all except recent Judaism are dominated by a missionary zeal, and all tend to regard religious views other than their own as heathen, erroneous, or inferior. Each tends to have a provincial self-righteousness which assumes that its doctrine is completely perfect, and consequently that its adherents are divinely commissioned and by duty bound to replace all other religions with 'the one perfect religion.' "[45]

The basically different self-evaluation of theistic religions in relation to other religions from that of nontheistic religions explains the significant difference in geographic distribution between the two types of religions. Since theistic religions are by their very nature doctrinary, creedal, aggressive, intolerant, and proselytizing, each one of them as occasion arose tended to establish itself as the only religion in the territory or region in which it won for itself a majority position or in which it attained the physical ability of doing so. Adherents of other religions were either expelled, or forcibly converted, or, in exceptional cases, allowed to remain as "tolerated" and "protected" peoples, in residentially and socially segregated, despised and disliked groups. As a result of this, Europe and America became compactly Christian continents, all the natives of the former (with the exception of a small Muslim island in the Balkans) and practically all the latter having been converted to one or another variety of Christianity. The fate of the Jews in Europe, as a group stubbornly adhering to an alien religion, at times persecuted and at times tolerated, is too well known to need more than passing mention.

To the south and the east of Christian Europe, Islam established itself in a similarly compact and definite block. The Islamization of the entire Middle East from Morocco and Río de Oro in the west to Turkestan, Afghanistan, and what is today Pakistan in the east was a rapid process accomplished in a phenomenally short time. In close analogy to the Christian *Ecclesia militans*, the spread of Islam by force was made a principle: *Dīn Muḥammad bissayf*—the religion of Mohammed with the sword. The result was a geographic region as exclusively Muslim as Europe became Christian. Where the two met, they fought, until one of them was completely defeated and had to retreat, as best exemplified by medieval Spain, or the flow and ebb of Turkish power in Hungary in the sixteenth to eighteenth centuries. After the Muslim retreat from those European countries no trace was allowed to remain of its long rule: no Muslim community or group was left behind; the population as a whole reverted to Christianity or was replaced by Christians. In the south and the east, on the other hand, Islam was more successful than Christianity in its proselytizing activities. In the twentieth century its boundaries are still pushing southward across the Sudan belt into Negro Africa, and are being strengthened in Indonesia and other parts of the Far East. What is happening to Islam's Central Asian outpost is little known; the Iron Curtain guards its secrets well.

While the traditional adherent of Judaism, Christianity, and Islam remains to this day convinced that only his religion or, more narrowly, only his own particular sect is the sole holder of the truth, including the only true ritual, the general attitude towards religious and sectarian differences, at least as far as

Golden River to Golden Road

Christianity is concerned, underwent a decisive change since the
second half of the seventeenth century. "In this half century the
Catholic and Protestant factions . . . seem to have become aware
that they no longer cared sufficiently for the theological issues at
stake to relish making any further sacrifices for their sake. They
repudiated the traditional virtue of "enthusiasm" (which by
derivation means being filled with the spirit of God) and hence-
forth regarded it as a vice."[46]

This toleration of religions in Christian Europe, however, was
based on "disillusionment, apprehension and cynicism. It was not
an arduous achievement of religious fervour but a facile by-
product of its abatement."[47]

We thus recognize that in the Far East religious toleration is a
result of the deep religiosity characteristic of its cultures, while
in the West, and to some extent in the Middle East as well, religious tolerance emerged as a result of a general and successive
liberation of the cultures from the grip of religion. In the Far
East, the more religious a person is the more tolerant he is of other
religions, the more ready he is to concede that other religions also
have their values, their truths, and their "paths." In the Middle
East and the West, tolerance of other religions stands as a rule in
reverse ratio to the fervor with which an individual follows the
precepts of his own religion.

THE TELEOLOGIC ORIENTATION

The last aspect of religion to be considered here is its teleo-
logical or purposive orientation, with respect to which it again is
found that Middle Eastern religion has close affinities with
Western religion, while both differ greatly from Far Eastern
religions.

The ultimate aim of religion is to satisfy certain spiritual needs
of which man is aware at varying frequencies, and to help him
in the crises and other difficulties that he inevitably meets as he
makes his way from cradle to grave. In the three world areas under
scrutiny we find that this basic purpose is served either by supply-
ing psychological satisfaction to this-worldly aspirations of man,
or by giving his ambitions an other-worldly orientation, or by a
combination of both.

Confucianism exemplifies the first of these three ways. Although in every other respect it belongs closely together with the other Far Eastern noncreedal and nontheistic religions, "it has almost no other-worldly content, confining itself to practical maxims on the sensible conduct of life in this world."[48] Confucianism offers its followers a satisfactory cosmology, and detailed ethical doctrines, concentrating especially on the duties and obligations of people standing in certain social or familial relationship to one another. A worship of Heaven and Earth, of imperial ancestors and heroes with appropriate and well ordered ritual rounds out the picture.[49] This is a religion eminently suited to human needs as channeled by Chinese culture: as long as things are more or less in good order. Chinese observers themselves noted, however, that when confronted with tragedy and death, their compatriots tend to become Buddhists[50] or Taoists. In funeral processions, for example, Confucianist families often employ a group of Taoist and/or Buddhist monks.[51] Moreover, it can be stated that Confucianism pure and undiluted is a relatively rare phenomenon; in most cases it is merely one of the threads that go into the texture of religious life in China.

With the exception of Confucianism (and Shintoism, which on account of its theistic content and aggressive character is not considered in this paper among the Far Eastern religions), Far Eastern religions typically satisfy human psychological needs by giving them an other-wordly orientation. This world is regarded as a vale of tears into which man is born against his will. The ultimate goal that man can obtain and that he therefore should try to achieve lies in the Beyond, in a remote state of peace that man can reach either directly upon his death, or, in accordance with most teachings, after a series of rebirths and reincarnations in various human or other forms.

This other-wordly orientation given to life by religion goes in the case of Hinduism hand in hand with a basically pessimistic attitude toward this world. According to Shankara, only the spiritual has reality, all else is sheer illusion, or *maya*. Life goes on by karmic repetition; deeds and rebirth are causally related. Man has to accept his lot, and "live at best within it in the distant hope that the round would eventually be broken and his spirit would escape to another, agreeable portion of the fixed universe, whence he would not come back again to birth."[52] Only if one is able to find the true self can one escape karma and yet remain in the world bringing spiritual equanimity into it.[24]

The same idea is further developed in Buddhism. Buddha is told to have said: "I have obtained emancipation by the destruction of desire. . . . I have obtained coolness (by extinction of passions) and have obtained *Nirvana*. . . ."[53] Human life is predominantly an existence of suffering. Conditions of individual existence are painful; whatever pleasures and satisfactions may exist in life are overshadowed by pain and sorrow. The best in life is fleeting and impermanent. This is the first of the "Four Noble Truths" of Buddha. The second is that the cause of human suffering is human desire and cravings. The third and the fourth truths state that man can conquer his craving thirst by following the "Noble Eightfold Path," which includes the renunciation of the life of pleasure, the nurturing of the spirit, moral conduct, peaceful occupations, the suppression of evil states of mind, strict self-discipline, a concentration of mind and meditation, until an understanding of the nature of the self is achieved, with a complete freedom from all passions and fetters binding one to this life. Thus prepared, the enlightened self can enter a state of peace, or *Nirvana*, and thus "gain release from 'rounds of existence' in this evil world." *Nirvana*, however, remains a distant hope. In the meantime, man's efforts should be directed toward attaining a more favorable rebirth into this world. This can be effected by following certain ideals of conduct, namely the "five precepts" forbidding the destruction of life, theft, unchastity, falsehoods, and strong drink.[54]

Also according to Taoist doctrine, the sensuous world is a mere appearance. "Long life was not in the tradition of Taoism. The ancient Taoists regarded the body as not worth preserving. . . ." Under the influence of Buddhism, also in Taoism a "moral relation was established between this life and the condition of the soul beyond this life by the theory of karma, the equivalence of deed and reward. This proved a great boon in easing the tensions of life. Poverty and wealth, sickness and health, happiness and misfortune were not only explained by this formula, but were made endurable."

The northern school of Taoism in modern China "emphasizes meditation, and metaphysical speculation, and practices breathing."[55]

For all these religions Kurt Singer's generalization holds good: "It is a basic tendency of the Asiatic mind to keep aloof from every thought that hinders him in his great movement of withdrawal from the world, an illusory veil to be cast off by him who is awakened, a tiny shore which must be left in order to reach the infinite expanses of the Great Void."[56]

No such other-worldliness, no such exclusive concentration on spiritual or meditational detachment characterizes the three theistic religions of Judaism, Christianity and Islam. These three Middle Eastern and Western religions emphasize more or less equally the material well-being of the individual in this world, and the spiritual well-being or salvation of his individual soul after the death of the body. They therefore represent a combination of this-worldly and other-worldly orientations. While spiritual and moral values are stressed, these are underlined or reinforced by concretely formulated and tangible promises of rewards in the future life for good conduct, or alternatively, punishments for rebelliousness and disobedience. The amount of stress put in Judaism, Christianity, and Islam, as well as in the different sects of the latter two, on the belief in Paradise or Heaven for the good and on Purgatory or Hell for the evil, varies; but common to all is the accent on divine justice tempered with mercy that measures out reward and punishment to each individual according to his deeds which after death are carefully weighed and evaluated. It is, therefore, in the well-conceived self-interest of every individual (inasmuch as he is a believer) to pay as much attention as he can to the salvation of his soul. This can be achieved by following the precepts of one's church or religion or sect with regard to one's duties toward fellow-men and toward the deity. The duties toward one's fellow-men are mainly deedal, that is, consist of do's and don't's, while the duties toward God are both creedal and deedal in varying combinations.

Simultaneously, however, both deed and creed aim at a second, and often more important, end: to assure and secure the material well-being of the individual and his society in this world. One must believe in the particular credos of one's religion or sect and fulfill the various do's and don't's in relation to both God and fellow-men in order to be blessed as a reward by God with all the material benefits that are valued in this life and are striven for also in other, more direct ways. This is expressed succinctly in the Christian supplication for the daily bread contained in the "Lord's Prayer" (Matthew 6 : 11). It is dwelt upon in greater detail in the Jewish "Shema" in which material blessings are made directly contingent upon the observation of God's command-ments (Deut. 11 : 13–25), and in the "Eighteen Benedictions," the main portion of every Jewish service, in which God is asked, among other blessings, for forgiveness, redemption, health, good crops, the rebuilding of Jerusalem, the coming of the Messiah, etc. This prayer is repeated by observant Jews three times every weekday and four times on Saturdays and holidays.

The Koran, too, is explicit with regard to Allah's reward of those who pray to him:

O ye who have believed when proclamation is made for the prayer on the day of the assembly [Friday] endeavor to come to the remembrance of Allah, and leave off bargaining; that is better for you, if he have knowledge. Then when the prayer is finished scatter abroad in the land and seek the bounty of Allah, but call Allah frequently to mind; mayhap ye will prosper (Koran 62 : 9–10).

In the popular religion in the Middle East manifested in saint worship and the institution of the *Ziyāra* (visitation of shrines), the quest for material blessings is even more predominant.

These three theistic religions, therefore, are oriented toward two goals: to secure immediate material blessings in this world and to hold out the promise of the Beyond, the happy life after death.

With regard to teleologic orientation, religion in the Far East is other-worldly, while in the Middle East and in the West it is equally concerned with this world and with the Beyond. One of the factors that militate against religion retaining its influence in the modern West is the definite this-worldly orientation of modern Western culture in which religion with its promise of a life in the Beyond seems out of tune. But as far as religion is still alive or again comes alive in the Western world, it displays the same orientation toward the same two foci of well-being in this world and rewards in the other world that is the common heritage of all religions that originated in the ancient Middle East.

In summary, the function of religion within the total cultural context of each of the three world areas considered can be characterized as follows:

1. In the Far East and in the Middle East religion is the dominant normative force regulating behavior; in the West it has largely lost its normative function.

2. Psychologically, in the Far East and in the Middle East religion is a powerful sustaining influence; in the West it has also largely lost this function.

3. On the popular level of the supernatural aspect, in the Far East and in the Middle East religion is polytheodemonistic; in the West this character of religion is on the wane with the decline of folk cultures.

3a. On the higher doctrinary level of the supernatural aspect, in the Far East religion is nontheistic and noncreedal; in the Middle East and in the West it is both theistic and creedal.

4. Religion in the Far East is characterized by the absence of religiocentrism: there is a marked toleration of other religions and a mutual borrowing and influencing; in the Middle East and in the West there is a high degree of religiocentrism, with intolerance and scorn of other religions: each religion is exclusive and regards itself as the "one and only" true faith.

5. As to teleologic orientation, in the Far East religion has a distinctly other-worldly orientation often accompanied by a definitely negative attitude toward this world; in the Middle East and in the West religion is characterized by a dual orientation toward both this world and the other world.

The place of Middle Eastern religion in this scheme is intermediary. Religion is the dominant normative force in Middle Eastern culture as it is in the Far East. It has a powerful psychologic influence as it has in the Far East. On the popular level its supernatural component is polytheodemonistic as in the Far East. On the other hand, on the higher doctrinary level, it is theistic and creedal as is religion in the West. It displays a high degree of religiocentrism as does religion in the West. And it shares with the West a dual, this-worldly and other-worldly teleologic orientation.

XI. Social and Cultural Determinants of Middle Eastern Nationalism

WESTERN AND MIDDLE EASTERN NATIONALISM

T HE STORY of the penetration of the Western-born idea of nationalism into the Middle East has attracted considerable attention on the part of European and American scholars. Following the pioneering study of Hans Kohn, *A History of Nationalism in the East*, originally published in German in 1928 and in English in 1929, the history of Middle Eastern nationalism has been studied from various angles. Its origins, going back to the Napoleonic occupation of Egypt in 1798, have been unraveled, and its place within the context of the general process of Westernization duly noted. Attention was given also to the way in which nationalism transformed communal and political life in the major and even minor states witin the area. Similarly, the historical sequence of nationalistic developments in the Middle East, from the first emergence of parliamentary governments in emulation of the West to their decline in certain countries and replacement by dictatorial rule, has been investigated.

On the other hand, certain important aspects of Middle Eastern nationalism have received lamentably scanty attention. The writer, for instance, knows of no exhaustive or detailed study of the specific traits that characterize Middle Eastern nationalism, nor of a probing into the question of which of these features can be found also in the Western world and which of them are specific to the Middle East or to some countries in it. When we come to the problem of the causes, the motivating factors that gave Middle Eastern nationalism its specific flavor, we find not only no answers but, in most cases, not even questions raised. The present chapter will attempt to deal with at least part of these issues. It will try to isolate some of the social and cultural determinants that went into the making of modern Middle Eastern nationalism and gave it its special character.

To begin with, it should be stated that even within the immediate geographic vicinity of its European birthplace, nationalism has manifested a wide range of variations in orientation, emphasis, and general character. It is, of course, possible to give a generally valid definition of nationalism, such as "a state or condition of mind characteristic of certain peoples with a homogeneous culture, living together in close association on a given territory, and sharing a belief in a distinctive existence and a common destiny."[1] However, to any such general definition one must unfailingly append, as was in fact done by the author of the one quoted, the caution that nationalism "varies all the way from the healthy patriotism of the Swiss nation to the fanatical intolerance of Nazi Germany."[2]

Nationalism is generally regarded as a "healthy patriotism" when the positive, affirmative elements predominate in it, and when it is coupled with democracy and liberalism. It is branded as "fanatical intolerance" when it appears in the company of exclusivism, racism, fascism, or any form of totalitarian dictatorship, and when its emphasis is largely negative, expressed in *anti*, rather than *pro*, policies, aims, and slogans, directed primarily against other peoples, ideas, and endeavors. In Europe, generally speaking, liberal nationalisms emerged in the nineteenth century; fascist or totalitarian nationalisms were the product of the twentieth century, following World War I. This observation leads directly to the formulation of the first problem that arises in a consideration of the characteristics of Middle Eastern nationalism.

The Middle East was reached by the nationalist tide well before the onset of its second period in Europe, that of fascist or totalitarian nationalisms. One would, therefore, have expected that, when emulating the Western example, the Middle Eastern peoples would develop their own brand of nationalism in keeping with the general trend of "healthy patriotism" of the period.

Yet this was not the case. Quite on the contrary, the Middle Eastern nationalist movements started out with a strong *anti-*emphasis. This is what happened with early Turkish nationalism, which had a clear-cut aim in opposing the rule of the Sultan but a much hazier idea as to what it was to strive for. As for the Arabs, Hazem Zaki Nuseibeh, a keen analyst of Arab nationalism, and himself an Arab, pointed out "how predominant the negative element was" in the early phases of their nationalism, which lasted roughly until the eve of World War I; "the impelling force," according to Nusiebeh, "was either fear of an advancing European imperialism and the inability of the state to withstand it, or distrust of the Turkish intentions and designs."[3]

Following the above observation, one could go on to isolating additional important specific characteristics of Middle Eastern nationalism until one felt that one had a more or less complete portrait of it, and then reviewing the factors in traditional Middle Eastern culture that would seem to explain these characteristics. Such a procedure, however, would be too cumbersome and complicated, since it would have to deal with two sets of extremely complex phenomena, and attempt to establish a correlation between them.

Let us, instead, switch our attention at this point to those aspects of traditional Middle Eastern culture and society that can be assumed to have had an influence on the development of the first trait of Middle Eastern nationalism discussed above. After having dealt, albeit briefly, with these aspects, we can go on to a discussion of the traditional determinants of a second, and then a third, special feature of modern Middle Eastern nationalism. In this manner we shall deal with only one trait at a time, a procedure that should prove both simpler and clearer. In sum we shall nevertheless arrive at an over-all view of Middle Eastern nationalism *in toto* with its manifold determinants anchored in traditional Middle Eastern society and culture.

Such a national trait as xenophobic dislike and distrust of foreigners must evidently be a resultant, among possible other factors, of those forces which in the past molded traditional ingroup-outgroup attitudes among the peoples of the area.

There are, in particular, two ruling institutions in traditional Middle Eastern culture that not only shaped the traditional ingroup-outgroup attitudes but, more than that, were of basic importance in the very process of group formation itself. Both are heavily value-laden, closely interrelated, and mutually support and reinforce each other. Both are, in fact, more than institutions; they are ideologies, powerful motivations, and ends in themselves. They are phenomena nonexistent in modern Western culture whose designation requires the coining of new terms: religionism and familism.

"RELIGIONISM" AND NATIONALISM

Religionism can be defined as the domination by religion of life as a whole, on all levels, individual, familial, social, cultural, and even national and political.

To what extent politics were dominated by religion down to the last years of the Ottoman Empire can be shown by adducing as an example an event that took place as late as 1913. In that year a revolt broke out in Macedonia against the Sultan, who wanted to dispatch troops to suppress it. But this would have amounted to a war of Muslims against Muslims, which is forbidden by religion, and can be undertaken only if a special *fetwa*, religious decision, is issued by the Shaykh ul-Islam, the chief religious authority in the Empire. The Sultan, Abdul Hamid, could not obtain the *fetwa*, and thus was unable to order his troops to Macedonia. Once the impotence of the Sultan became thereby manifest, his ministers were able to pressure him into granting a constitution. This was the effective end of the Sultan's rule in Turkey.[4]

A concomitant of the religion-centered outlook is the conviction that only one's own religion, that is to say the religion of one's own family, tribe, or larger social aggregate is the right one, while other faiths are, with equal sincerity, regarded as inferior, mistaken, and wrong. As far as Islam is concerned, it teaches that Mohammed was the last and greatest of prophets, that the Koran is the ultimate revelation of God's will, and that not to accept Islam is a sinful shortsightedness, for which idolators have to be punished by death and the *ahl al-kitāb*, the monotheistic People of the Book, by subjugation and reduction to the quasi-vassal status of *dhimmis*.

For centuries Islam almost unfailingly helped the true believers to victory after victory over the infidels in the three continents of the old world. The march of history appeared to the Muslims to fall into a clear pattern: infidels were defeated by the Sword of Islam and converted to the true faith. Thereupon, having become Muslims, they in turn achieved victories over other infidels. In this way the *Dār al-Islām*, the pacified House of Islam, continued to expand, and the *Dār al-Ḥarb*, the House of War, to recede. These circumstances engendered in the Muslims a feeling of contempt for the unbelievers which, with the passage of generations, became an ingrained and organic part of Muslim religionism.

Of the many facets of the Muslim outlook on the infidels the one that most directly influenced the formation of the antiforeign component in Middle Eastern nationalism was their attitude to the *dhimmis*, the subject People of the Book. The Muslim, to put it succinctly, viewed the *dhimmi* dimly. The less able the Muslims became, from the seventeenth century on, to withstand the onslaught of the Christian world, the more unkind their attitude became to the *dhimmis* who continued to live in their midst. Since the traditional conviction that the infidel was inferior could no longer feed on new victories over him, it had to be maintained instead by a constant reassertion of Muslim superiority over the *dhimmis*. If this was the case among the Turks and the Persians who, in spite of the rising tide of Christian power, remained independent and masters of their own destiny, it had to be even more so among the Arabs who themselves had become the subjects of the Ottoman Turks and were treated by them as *ra'īya*, flocks, as human cattle, to be shepherded for the benefit of the conqueror, to be milked, fleeced, and allowed to live their own lives so long as they gave no trouble.[5] For these Arabs it was a psychological necessity for the maintenance of their self-esteem and for at least a partial fulfilment of the expectations of their traditional religionism to have, near at hand, another human group to look down upon, to pity, to distrust.

Religionism had yet another important effect on Middle Eastern nationalisms. In spite of certain superficial resemblances between the *Fuhrer*-centered nationalism in several Arab countries and the European Fascist-type nationalisms, there is one significant difference between the two: Fascism, Nazism, and Communism all felt constrained to turn against religion and to try to break or at least to weaken the hold of the church on the people. The new nationalist ideology, with its own brand of *ethos* and *mythos*, was supposed to supplant the Christian teachings and ethics. Not so Middle Eastern nationalism which, in spite of its alien origin and nonautochthonous nature, knew how to build on the old religious foundation of Middle Eastern culture, and to appear as the genuine offspring of the local, indigenous tradition.[6] In this manner the simple, average Middle Easterner was spared the dilemma into which the totalitarian nationalist movements forced the European Christian who had to choose between Catholicism and Fascism, between Lutheranism and Nazism, between Pravoslavism and Communism. Instead, the new nationalism sought to convince the Middle Easterner that the more enthusiastically he followed his particular national leader, the better a Muslim he would be; or, if he happened to be a Christian Arab, the better a Christian Arab he would be. Thus, under the quasi-charismatic leadership of a military *Führer*, Middle Eastern nationalism has become a new religious creed, a new stage in the development of the faith, imbued with all the attributes of a religiocentrism of which there is more today in the Middle East than in any Western, Westernized, or semi-Westernized world area.

FAMILISM AND NATIONALISM

Closely related to Middle Eastern religion is familism. Familism can be defined as the centrality of the family in social organization, its primacy in the loyalty scale, and its supremacy over individual life. All the six basic characteristics of the Middle Eastern family have a close correlation to familism: a family that is patriarchal, patrilineal, patrilocal, endogamous, polygynous, and extended must needs be central, primary, and supreme in both social and individual life.[7] Negative and in the larger sense disruptive correlates of this type of familism are interfamilial tension, competition, and enmity which, in the centuries of Arab and Muslim history, have repeatedly caused protracted and far-flung blood feuds, and have occasionally developed or, if you will, degenerated, into large-scale bloody internecine wars sapping the strength of the people in many a part of the Middle East.

One of the numerous proverbs that express with admirable succinctness basic features in the Arab self-stereotype reflects on both sides of the old Arab coin of familism. Variants of this proverb are current in the non-Arabic speaking areas of the Middle East as well, and it has more than once been quoted by Western writers as a Kurdish, Persian, or Afghan saying. It states: "I and my cousins against the world, I and my brothers against my cousins, I against my brothers." Translated into sociologese, this proverb verbalizes the existence of a clearly marked hierarchy of loyalties in which the closer kin group takes precedence over wider kin groups.

The principle of familism has been so strongly embedded in the Middle Eastern consciousness that social aggregates larger than the family have traditionally been conceived of as mere extensions of families. The actually functioning family has for uncounted generations consisted of the descendants in the male line of one common grandfather who occupied the position of family head. The tribe or the village in an un-Westernized Middle Eastern district is regarded by its members to this day as consisting of several such extended families related to one another and descended from one common ancestor. Villages located in one area or tribes wandering in one another's proximity are, again, considered to be the progeny of a more remote but still common ancestor.[8] This popular tendency has received the stamp of scholarly approval when learned medieval Arab genealogists, building upon popular traditions, set up a highly speculative but everywhere readily accepted genealogic scheme, tracing back all the Arabs to a single pair of forefathers and, through them, ultimately to one original ancestral progenitor.[9] We have only to think of the stories of the Book of Genesis to realize that this tendency has not been one peculiar to the Arabs, but had its prototype in the ancient Near East as well.[10]

Another important feature shared by the ancient Hebrews and the more recent peoples of the Middle East and having a direct bearing on the centrality of familism in the formation of *any* ingroup-outgroup dichotomy is the attribution of a kin-group character to groups of patently nonrelated individuals who happened to engage in one and the same occupation. In Biblical times all the harp and pipe players were regarded as the descendants of one single common ancestor, and so were the forgers of brass and iron and the tent-dwelling cattle owners (Gen. 4 : 20–22). Josephus Flavius, in the first century A.D., using undoubtedly expressions based on popular views still current in his days, speaks of "the tribe of prophets." And Evliya Chelebi, the famous Turkish traveler, writing less than three centuries ago, reports of several of the numerous guilds into which the artisans, tradesmen, and professional people of Constantinople were organized in his day that they venerate certain historical or mythical individuals as the original progenitors of all the members of their particular guilds.[11]

The effects of this concept complex were significant and far-reaching with regard to Muslim state organization, to prenationalistic attitudes to the non-Muslim world, and, most recently, to the specific forms assumed by nationalism in the Arab and other Middle Eastern states.

The effect of familism on Muslim state organization was, as could be expected, that the state was from the very outset of its development considered a mere extension of the family, enlarged this time not tenfold to a hundredfold as in the case of a tribe or the village, but a thousandfold to ten thousandfold. The entire Muslim realm was, from its very inception, regarded as a familial grouping, gigantically enlarged but in its essence nevertheless a social body similar to the family. Therefore, the same loyalty scale that was the guiding principle in the familial and social organization and demanded diminishing loyalty with increase of group size was applied also to the state. Loyalty to the state could thus never approximate the level of intensity characterizing close in-group loyalties. The tenuous ties that thus existed between the subject tribes, villages, and urban aggregates on the one hand and the Caliph, the remote "father" enthroned in his faraway capital on the other, could never supersede the more immediate pull that direct loyalties to locally present "fathers" such as the actual family head, the tribal chieftain, the village headman, the landlord, etc., continued to exert. In fact, the limited imagination of the simple peasant, for instance, could not even conceive of a greater or higher power position than that of the highest local official with whom he had direct personal contact, such as the *mudir*, the district officer, in Egypt. The story is told of such a peasant that when for the first time in his life he had an opportunity to prostrate himself in front of the Khedive (viceroy), he pronounced a blessing over him, saying, "May Allah make you as powerful as our *Mudir*!"

The same family-patterned relationship between sovereign and subjects made it necessary for the Caliph and other rulers in the Muslim realm to rely in the first place on that group among their subjects on whose loyalty they could count in their capacity of immediate chieftain rather than as the Caliph, king, or overlord. Similar situations are known to have existed in other empires, outside the Middle Eastern culture continent, but they reached a comparable extent only when based on a similar intensity of familism. Be this as it may, the fact remains that the Caliph ruled through his kinsmen: his immediate and more remote relatives, his tribesmen, and last but not least, his slaves, who were indoctrinated to see in him their *pater familias*, and who, in turn, were regarded as family members. This was the method by which the Ottoman Turks were able for centuries to hold sway over a far-flung empire peopled by Arabs, Kurds, Greeks, Armenians, Copts, Berbers, Druzes, and dozens of other minority groups. The entire population of the Ottoman Empire was thus divided into two sectors: there were the ruled groups who constituted the vast majority, and then there was the ruling minority of the Ottoman Turks, organized and considered, by the ruled peoples as well as by themselves, as one family with the Caliph at its head.

Tyranny and despotism too appear in a different light when viewed against the background of a familistic society. What son dare question the commands and exactions of his father? It is not for him to weigh and consider but to obey and be judged. The duty of the son is to serve the father. The father in return protects the son. Without the father's protection the son is lost; he could never hold his own against inimical outsiders. Similarly, the duty of the subjects was to serve the Caliph by paying taxes, by indented labor, by conscription. In exchange, they received protection against enemies who otherwise could have destroyed them.

Bribery, the pattern of both giving and accepting gratuities either for services rendered by a superior to an inferior or simply for receiving from a superior what is one's due by tradition-sanctioned custom, can also be explained as an extension of the familial relationship between the mighty father and the dependent sons. You want something from your father? The way to getting it is to perform a special service for him, to become a favorite, for the occasion at least. This is how Isaac's two sons competed for the blessing of their blind old father, and this is how the simple subject of a ruler attempts to gain his ear. In the family situation, after all, there is rarely a clear-cut right or wrong, independently of the will of the father. Whatever the competing sons feel and opine, the father's decision is the final factor that makes the point of view of one right while rendering the argument of the other wrong. And both sons, the one toward whose present the father did not turn as well as his more fortunate brother, know that soon a conflict may arise between them and an out-sider, and in that case they will have the unquestioning support of the father.

This is the family situation in which are rooted all types of inter-action between subject and ruler in the traditional House of Islam.

Group Attitudes and Nationalism

Some general features of the prenationalistic attitudes toward the non-Muslim world can also be considered as extensions of traditional attitudes that developed in and around Middle Eastern familism. In a familistic situation the attitude of a given group, whether an actual extended family or a larger aggregate molded after its pattern, to an equivalent out-group can be twofold. As long as the out-group is independent of the in-group, the two are rivals, competitors, actual or at least potential enemies. In the interests of self-preservation, the in-group feels impelled to attack the out-group, to reduce its strength, and to make it subservient to itself. Once this is achieved, a new attitude tends to replace the first: that of benevolent toleration, mixed with condescension or even contempt.

The best example of the working of this interaction on a level broader than that of the extended family can be found among the tribes of the Syrian Desert. The more powerful among these tribes were able to reduce the weaker tribes to a status of vassaldom and to exact the payment of *khuwwa* or protection money from them.[12] A free or noble tribe will not intermarry with a vassal tribe, this would be beneath its dignity. Nor will it attack or engage in fighting with a vassal tribe, whether its own or that of another free tribe; this again would be beneath its dignity. If the vassal tribe is attacked by an outsider, its protector tribe will rise up and defend or avenge it.

It would be an interesting task to work out in detail the analogies between this intertribal situation and the conditions in which interfamilial rivalries were utilized by energetic and fortunate family heads to advance themselves, to strengthen their own family by extending their protection to poor and weak relatives, by inviting nonrelated families to become their clients, and by acquiring many slaves and interbreeding with them, and in this manner to assure their own ascendancy over other families. While such a procedure lies beyond the scope of the present subject, it is well within it to point out certain parallels between the attitudes, arrangements, and institutions developed around the intertribal situations on the one hand and those characterizing traditional Muslim conduct in international situations on the other.[13]

An international situation—and the following remarks will largely be confined to international situations and interactions between the Muslim and the Christian worlds—used to be encountered by the Muslims with attitudes and reactions predetermined by the intertribal experience. That is to say, the outside world, the Christian world, was approached by the Muslim world as a whole as one tribe would be by another: it was an encounter with a potential or actual enemy. From the earliest days of the foundation of the new faith, when Muslim Arab conquerors swept with astounding rapidity over the entire Middle East, they viewed the world as being divided into two parts: the *Dār al-Islām*, the House of Islam, containing that part of the world pacified by the sword of Mohammed's religion on the one hand and, on the other, the *Dār al-Ḥarb*, or House of War that lay outside the former realm and against which to engage in Holy War was regarded as a sacred religious duty, invoked as late as the years of World War I. Mohammed himself enjoined upon his followers to fight both idolaters and monotheistic peoples "who believe not in Allah" (Koran 9 : 29). However, while the former had either to be exterminated or converted to Islam, the latter, "those who have been given the Scripture," had to be fought only "until they pay the tribute readily, being brought low" (*ibid.*). These "people of the Book" came very soon to be known as people under protection, or *dhimmi*-s, in Arabic. In a very ancient Muslim document, said to be the testament of the Caliph Omar II (who died in 720, that is, merely 88 years after the death of Mohammed), the duties of the Muslims toward the *dhimmis* are spelled out: ". . . and I commend to your favor the people under 'protection.' Do battle to guard them and put no burden on them greater than they can bear, provided they pay what is due from them to the Muslims, willingly, or under subjection, being humbled.' . . ."

This of course is the application of the same principle that governed in pre-Islamic days, and has continued to govern down to the present the relationship between a strong, free noble tribe and its subjected, protection-money-paying, vassal tribe.

When the idea of nationalism became the ruling doctrine in a modern Middle Eastern country, the people of that country were required or at least expected to expand the familistic attitude so as to include the entire population of their country. A good Egyptian Muslim, for instance, was now supposed to regard not only the Egyptian Muslims but also the Copts and the other religioethnic minorities as members of his national family. As a result of this changed situation the nearby close-at-hand traditional objects of the out-group hostility suddenly disappeared. There were now no more *dhimmis* to look down upon and thereby to strengthen one's own feeling of superiority. The attitude of contempt and suspicion of outsiders that was an age-old complement of familism had to look for new objects. The foreigner, the intruder, in all his variegated appearances, was the new peg on which the old hostilities could most conveniently be hung.

While these processes took place inside several Middle Eastern countries, the latter simultaneously found themselves confronted with the irresistible ascendancy of a Christian Europe. In the earlier encounters, during the Crusades, and in the centuries of Ottoman expansion in Europe, the feeling of Muslim cultural superiority was repeatedly reaffirmed and strengthened. In the nineteenth century for the first time Christian Europe appeared to the Muslim world not only as a superior opponent in armed clashes but also as a possessor of cultural attainments superior to those had by the House of Islam.

It was an unfortunate coincidence as far as the Arab countries were concerned that, before they had time truly to integrate Western culture into their traditional cultural configuration, they were brought under the control of the same Western powers which up to that period were the chief profferors of Western cultural imports.[14] A result of this coincidence was the emergence of a tense ambivalent attitude: on the one hand, Western culture continued to exert its magic pull, and even increased it; on the other, the carriers of these cultural enticements came to be regarded as hated oppressors. Thus the two main facets in Western culture that were unquestioningly accepted by the Arab countries—technology in the realm of reality culture and nationalism in that of value culture—were both utilized for the end of ridding themselves of the bearers of these gifts. The nationalistic aim of independence became paramount and it was subserved by everything that could be learned from the West. In fact, the feeling of many was that the more Westernized they became the greater the likelihood of their liberation from Western dominance.

However, in order to understand the roots of Middle Eastern and particularly Arab anti-Westernism, it is not enough to refer to the coincidence of Westernization and Western domination. One has only to mention the case of India to realize that the simultaneous occurrence of these two phenomena in itself does not automatically result in a violent anti-Western attitude. The outcropping of the anti-Western xenophobia in the Arab countries had to draw on a third root as well. This can be found in the Arab cultural complexes of religionism and familism discussed above. For a people whose national personality was conditioned

by this type of value syndrome it was much more intolerable to
be dominated by a Christian government than for a people such
as the Indians whose religions are nontheistic and tolerant, and
whose family dynamics are suffused by the *laisser faire* engendered
by a general other-worldly orientation.[15] In contrast, the Arab
ethos with its imperative emphasis on in-group cohesion, on out-
group enmity, and on the exclusive values and undoubted superiority of Islam was a fertile soil for the luxuriant growth of a
nationalistic xenophobia once the seeds of Western dominance
were sown in it.

Foreign domination, for the same reasons, was resented by the
Arabs even when it was exercised by the Ottoman Turks. Yet,
while the Turkish yoke weighed heavily on Arab necks and the
desire to throw it off was always present, to carry it was not felt
an indignity. It was, after all, merely the domination of one
Muslim group by another. On the other hand, to be subjected
and ruled by Christians was regarded as shameful in particular
because it made them into bad Muslims who did not fulfil one
of the basic commandments of their religion: to fight the People
of the Book and turn them into submissive *dhimmis*. When the new
ideas of nationalism are added to over and above all this, there
stands before us the full complement of the main factors making
exnophobia one of the pivotal facets in Arab nationalism.

THE *FÜHRER* IMAGE AND NATIONALISM

Another feature of Middle Eastern nationalism is its tendency
to embody itself symbolically in an autocratic father image.
Middle Eastern autocracy appears in two typical forms, of which
the older is clearly a heritage of the past, of the local Middle
Eastern millennial sociopolitical development, while the younger
is a focusing on a father-image reshaped after modern Western
Führer-type leaders.

The old Middle Eastern father image is, of course, that of the
paternalistic absolute monarch, the theocratic ruler, who still
functions in more or less the same sociocultural context as he used
to for many centuries in the past. From the head of the extended
family to the shaykh of the tribe, to the Caliph of all the Muslims,

to the Sultan or Emir of a given population aggregate, and finally to the king of a twentieth-century Muslim theocratic state, there leads an unbroken line of inner historical sequence. The last representatives of this old type of father-ruler image can be found in Yemen and Saudi Arabia and in the smaller Sultanates and shaykhdoms ringing the Arabian Peninsula.

There is little reliable information on nationalism in the Arabian Peninsula in general. However, it so happens that there, more than in any other Middle Eastern country, the inhabitants of each political entity largely share the same religion, the same language, the same descent traditions, the same racial characteristics, the same attitudes and values, thus forming homogeneous population aggregates which, even in their prenationalistic phase, had come very close to resembling the typical nation-states in the Western world such as, say, Italy or Sweden. What the rulers of these states try to achieve is the consolidation of their power over areas within their political boundaries that lie outside the traditional domain of the tribes proper, which used to be headed by them or their fathers. In those territories they have to overcome the traditional in-group loyalty and out-group enmity that for centuries kept Arabia in a state of utter political fragmentation. They are trying to attain this aim by the use of both old Middle Eastern and modern Western methods. The former include the handing out of "purses" to the chiefs of the tribes whose loyalty must be secured, of marrying their daughters for longer or shorter periods, and of inviting them to sit in council. The latter consist mainly of acquiring superior Western arms such as airplanes and tanks, which prevent uprisings by making them utterly hopeless; of utilizing Western means of mass communication, especially the radio (the press only to a negligible extent since most of the people in the peninsula are still illiterate), for the inculcation of a feeling of solidarity with the ruler and his house. The moment the delicate balance of loyalties is tipped definitely in favor of the ruler rather than of the local chieftain, the kingdom or principality has crossed the boundary from traditional Middle Eastern tribal organization to modern nationalism.

As far as the new *Führer*-type father image is concerned, it is interesting to note that in no Middle Eastern country has he

directly taken the place of or evolved from the old type of paternalistic monarch. Everywhere a longer or shorter period of
experimentation with parliamentary government intervened. At
first, the power of the paternalistic ruler was curtailed, and the
leaders of political parties gained predominance. (This is the stage
that Afghanistan has only just entered, while Iran and Jordan
are well advanced in it.) Then the king was altogether eliminated,
and a period of republican parliamentarianism began in which,
however, the old upper class, the same that used to support the
king and was in turn favored by him, continued to occupy a
powerful position. The next phase was the emergence of the new
leader, who was not a member of the upper ruling class but an
army officer of middle-class background. Egypt, Syria, and Iraq
have all reached this stage after having passed through the
previous one, while Turkey has left it behind and introduced a
democratic parliamentary two-party system.

In the dictatorship stage, the *Führer*-figure, of course, symbolizes
the nationalistic aspirations of the people. All these aspirations
and ideas are purposely fostered, disseminated, and by unceasing
reiteration made part of the people's consciousness. Up to this
point Middle Eastern totalitarian nationalism closely follows
German Nazism, Italian fascism, and the Communist nationalisms. Where the original Middle Eastern elements enter this
picture is at the level of contact with religious tradition. Just as
the nationalist idea cannot come in conflict with religion, so its
leader must remain a religious figure. The modern Egyptian or
Iraqi leader, although a Westernized man by education and
inclination, bent on the speedy introduction of reforms in the
social and economic life of his people, bends his knee and touches
his forehead to the prayer rug in the mosque together with all the
true believers, in strict accordance with old religious tradition
just as the early Arab and Turkish kings and sultans did for thirteen hundred years. Europen nationalist leaders may have been
regarded as anti-Christs in the secret hearts of a fearful but faithful
minority in the totalitarian countries in the 1920's, 30's, and
40's. No Middle Eastern nationalist leader in the 1950's gave
cause to be regarded as an anti-Mohammed, be his teachings and
acts as modern and as nontraditional as they may.

PAN-ARAB NATIONALISM

A third factor that distinguishes Arab nationalism from Western nationalism is its superstate character. There are, to be sure, inter-Arab rivalries and hostilities, and there are particularistic trends in Arab nationalism, and these can be strong under certain conditions.[16] The baiting Jordanian King Hussein and his country suffered at the hands of President Nasser of Egypt resulted in a strengthening of Jordanian particularistic nationalism in not insignificant sectors of the Jordanian population. But apart from such special reactions, the general trend of Arab nationalism runs in the direction of Pan-Arabism, that is to say, its ultimate aim is to achieve the unification of all the Arabic-speaking peoples in one Arab superstate. This trend is clearly noticeable not only in those Arab countries that have achieved a predominant position in the Arab world and strive to establish their hegemony by uniting all the other Arab countries under them. This in itself would be consonant with the more extreme forms nationalism has occasionally taken in the Western world, of which the Nazi German nationalistic drive to rule Europe can be cited as the most blatant example.

What is not readily understandable without reference to the specific Arab sociocultural background, is the endeavor of true Arab nationalists in the smaller and weaker Arab countries to unite their countries with a larger and stronger Arab state which, as they only too well know, means in practice the submergence of their own countries in the larger Arab body politic in question. In view of the world-wide trend of nationalism to seek its fulfillment in the breaking up of large political entities into smaller ones peopled by ethnically, linguistically, and culturally homogeneous populations, one must look for very specific factors powerful enough to counter this trend. The only explanation that suggests itself is the still forceful cultural and genealogic tradition that managed to survive and become incorporated into the modern ideologies of Arab nationalism. The Arabs or, to put it more cautiously, many Arabs in every Arab country, small or large, still hold that all the Arabs are the descendants of one or two common ancestors and therefore form but a widely furcated family of tribes. The application of nationalistic ideas to such a situation must inevitably result in the conviction that the *summum bonum* of any Arab state, shaykhdom, territory, or unit of whatsoever description lies in the unification of all Arabs in one Pan-Arab state.[17]

Considering that as recently as until the end of World War I, that is, well within the memory of many persons still alive, all the Arab states were merely administrative provinces within the Ottoman Empire, it is not at all difficult to understand the attraction of the Pan-Arab idea. Those who have deeper historical knowledge look back beyond the inception of the Ottoman rule when there were Arab empires administered from a centrally located seat of government such as Damascus, or Baghdad, or Cairo. The aim of Pan-Arabism is thus regarded as a mere reunification of territories cut up into separate political entities by European power machinations. The old cultural ties have continued to reach across the newly established international boundaries and have, in fact, been intensified by the use of Western methods of mass communication such as the newspapers, the radio, and the motion pictures.

NONRACIAL NATIONALISM

We can touch only briefly upon one additional specific characteristic of Middle Eastern nationalism. This is the remarkable *absence of racism* even in the midst of the most excessive culminations of nationalistic fervor. With the Nazi example close at hand, and with the tendency to imitate nationalistic European dictatorships in many other respects, it is truly significant that racial intolerance has been added by no Arab dictatorship to its methods of whipping up popular enthusiasm. The explanation lies in the absence of racial intolerance, of even racial consciousness, in Arab and Muslim history. In the traditional Middle East, religion was the thing in judging an individual or a group, not racial antecedents, and thus the application of race as a criterion of distinction between man and man has remained foreign to the Middle East to this very day.

The sum total of these observations concerning the social and cultural determinants in Middle Eastern nationalism seems to add up to the following:

The Middle Eastern peoples have received nationalism from the Western world, because they saw in this idea a tool they were able to put to good use in the cause of their own advancement as they understood it. But in shaping the precise forms of nationalism for home consumption they were directed by ideas and values anchored in their own sociocultural past and still constituting powerful motivating forces at the present time.

XII. The Dynamics of Westernization

THE NATURE OF WESTERNIZATION

A DISCUSSION OF the dynamics of Westernization in the Middle East can best be opened by stating that Westernization is a specific variety of culture change. Since culture change is the process by which the material equipment, the techniques, the organization, the attitudes, the concepts, the points of view, and the values of a culture are transformed as a result of contact between its carriers and those of a different culture, Westernization is the culture change that takes place in any non-Western society under the impact of contact with Western groups or individuals. It is, therefore, a cultural process in the course of which a society or part of it adopts Western culture either totally or partially. It involves the discarding of elements and complexes of the traditional culture in order to replace them with Western cultural elements and complexes.

In theory, when two groups of individuals with different cultures come in contact, changes can result in the cultural patterns of either or both groups.[1] In practice, however, when carriers of Western culture establish contact with non-Western societies the chances are heavily weighted in favor of the acculturation of the non-Western group to Western culture. Of the large number of factors that bring this about, the following seem to be among the most important:

Western people often arrive on the non-Western scene as conquerors or occupy positions of power and leadership, and form a ruling class. This is what happened in the Middle East in the former and present colonial areas (Pakistan, Southern Arabia, Cyprus, North Africa) and in the former mandated territories

(Iraq, Syria, Lebanon, Palestine, Transjordan). Elsewhere (Afghanistan, Iran, Turkey, Saudi Arabia) Western penetration has been mainly economic, but even this was sufficient to secure for the Westerners high positions as employers and as possessors of superior techniques and technical equipment. In addition, their financial situation was incomparably better than that of the average native, and they formed a closed society from which the natives were excluded. The prestige that these foreigners thus acquired among the natives was transferred to the culture they represented, and especially to the overt manifestations of their civilization, that is, their technology, their material equipment, and all the other external trappings with which they surrounded themselves. Especially among members of the urban upper class who had official business, and more rarely, social contact with the Westerners, and also had the requisite financial means, the desire was thus engendered to emulate the Westerners by acquiring their paraphernalia and learning how to use it. Incidentally, the traits adopted in this manner were in many cases of practical usefulness in addition to their prestige value, a circumstance which, of course, added to their attractiveness.

For the last two or three decades the manifestations of Westernization in the Middle East have literally forced themselves upon the attention of students of the area. At least scattered references to them can be found in nearly every book or article dealing with any aspect of Middle Eastern life. As a result, the phenomenology of Westernization is sufficiently well attested, and it would be a simple task to draw up a long list showing what traditional features in Middle Eastern culture have been replaced in the course of the past 100 or 150 years by what new features introduced from the West.

The situation is different with regard to the dynamics of Westernization. What is the nature of the forces which, in many contact situations, caused Western culture to prevail and traditional Middle Eastern culture to succumb? Why and how did the Westerners attempt to make Middle Easterners accept their culture, and what were the motivations of the Middle Easterners in welcoming and often seeking out these changes? Why were certain facets of Western culture more readily accepted than

11§

others, while some were rejected altogether? What were the effects of the acceptance of certain specific Western cultural elements on the total context of Middle Eastern culture? To these and many other related questions no satisfactory answers can be found in the available literature.

In the present chapter an attempt is made to outline very briefly some of the main features, forces, and processes the interplay of which resulted in the Westernization observable today, especially in urban aggregates in many Middle Eastern countries. A discussion of the resistance and opposition that are also incident to Westernization in the Middle East will be left to the subsequent chapter.

CULTURAL AFFINITY

When attention is focused on a comparison of traditional Middle Eastern with modern Western culture as typified by their most characteristic representatives (for example, the United States and England with their urbanized majority as prototypes of modern Western culture, and Iraq, Iran, or the Arabian Peninsula with their agricultural and seminomadic majority as those of traditional Middle Eastern culture), they appear as significantly different and even contrasting in many respects.[2] In such a purview basic affinities can receive little notice. But as soon as the horizon is widened so as to include, for instance, the Far East as well, certain similarities become apparent against the more markedly different textures of those remoter culture areas.[3] The culture of the West then appears as more closely related to that of the Middle East than to the cultures of either central and southern Asia or Negro Africa.

The cultural affinity between the West and the Middle East has historical roots. Disregarding the prehistoric and earliest historical connections between the two world areas, the Middle East was in ancient times for several centuries under Greek and Roman domination and thus absorbed much of those cultural influences that so decisively molded the culture of Europe. Soon after, the West was subjected to powerful religious influences emanating from the Middle East in the form of the young faith of Christianity. At a later age, Islamic culture penetrated deeply into the West through the Iberian Peninsula and the Danube Basin, resulting in cultural exchange, another phase of which was a concomitant of the Crusades. As a result of these interchanges, at about the end of the Middle Ages the cultures of the two adjoining areas evinced considerable similarities of a general nature.

It was only with the advent of the Industrial Revolution and the subsequent technologic, economic, and social development in Europe that these similarities began rapidly to diminish. In the eighteenth and nineteenth centuries, the distance between the two cultures increased as a result of the relative cultural stability of the Middle East throughout this period and the cumulative and accelerating changes that were taking place in the culture of the West. Thus, when toward the middle of the nineteenth century the two cultures entered a new phase of their more than two-thousand-year-old intermittent contact, the situation was somewhat as follows:

The Europeans, as they became familiar with the culture of the Middle East, recognized in it similarities with certain aspects of the medieval phase of European culture, and noticed the absence of practically all those developments to which they were wont to point proudly in their own culture as significant accretions. From this discernment it was but one step to the formulation of the reproach of backwardness, and only one more step to the endeavor to fill in with their own Western achievements those facets of Middle Eastern culture which, they felt, were lacking or lagging.

The Middle Easterners, on the other hand, were in the possession of a culture still sufficiently similar in several basic aspects to the one brought to them by the Westerners to be able to recognize without too much difficulty that in certain fields the West was definitely ahead of them. Having for centuries used water for irrigation, clay for vessels, iron for utensils, wool and cotton for clothing, stone and bricks for building, ships for water transport, etc., it was much easier for them to appreciate the Western improvements in these and other such activities than for the carriers of a culture completely lacking these elements.

CHANNELS OF WESTERN INFLUENCE

Broadly speaking, the channels of Western influences on Middle Eastern culture fall into two main categories: impersonal or mechanical influences and personal contacts. In the case of impersonal influences, the group or the individual exposed to Westernization has no direct contact with personal exponents of any aspect of Western culture. Such persons, to be sure, are present somewhere in the background, but they are unseen and unfelt. These impersonal or mechanical influences are: (1) equipment, supplies, and consumers' goods; (2) newspapers, magazines, and books; (3) the radio; (4) motion pictures; and (5) phonograph records.

As to personal contacts, these can be subdivided into three groups that can be called respectively primary, secondary, and tertiary sources of Westernization. Primary sources of Westernization in personal contacts are represented by those individuals who come to the Middle East from the Western world and are, therefore, fully saturated with their specific brand of Western culture. Such persons either purposely or involuntarily impart something of their culture to the people with whom they come in contact. To this category belong the members of diplomatic corps stationed in the Middle Eastern countries; members of religious, medical, educational, technical, economic, and other missions; members of Western philanthropic institutions; also, Westerners who have settled in the Middle East for business purposes or who are sent there temporarily to represent or to work for Western firms; and finally, tourists. Secondary sources of Westernization by personal contact are provided by natives of Middle Eastern countries who have spent some time in the Western world and who, after their return to their native land, become (again either intentionally or unintentionally) Westernizing agents. To this group belong emigrants returning from overseas countries; returning students; returning diplomatic personnel and, to some extent at least, religious pilgrims who make for a certain amount of cultural interchange between various Middle Eastern and neighboring countries. As tertiary sources of personal Westernization must be regarded all those Middle Eastern individuals or groups who, having themselves absorbed a certain amount of Western cultural traits in the course of their contact with primary and/or secondary sources, become disseminators of Western influences in their social environment.

Apart from the returning emigrants and the members of various missions and philanthropic institutions, whose personal contacts include the native peasant and working classes, all the other primary and secondary personal Westernizing agents affect directly only the members of the urban upper class. The great majority of the Middle Eastern populations, the nomads, the cultivators, and the workers (unless they happen to be employed by a Western concern such as Aramco or the defunct Anglo-Iranian Oil Company) are exposed to the Westernizing influences of tertiary personal sources and of impersonal or mechanical sources only.

It is almost impossible to make any statement as to the differential degrees of Westernization in the various countries of the Middle East and within each country in the various social classes or occupational or other social groupings without courting the danger of undue generalization and schematization. Illustrative rather than generalizing statements will therefore have to serve the purpose. The differences in the extent of Westernization between country and country can best be illustrated by referring to Turkey on the one hand and Yemen on the other, the former having gone a relatively long way, while the latter is still poised hesitantly on the crossroads. Again, the differences within a single country can be made comprehensible by stating that the ruling class in a country like Egypt is well advanced in Westernization, while her peasant majority has barely budged from the traditional mode of life followed by their grandfathers. These two observations, by the way, also indicate how difficult it is to speak of Westernization in the Middle East *in general*.

THE IMPACT OF THE WEST

A complete analysis of the diverse ways in which the Western impact has made itself felt on the Middle Eastern scene would have to include a discussion of the roles of several Western institutions in the contact situations between the two cultures. Western institutions, for instance, played an important part in shaping the reforms introduced in the Tanzimat period in the Ottoman Empire and by Muḥammad 'Ali in Egypt. Also, certain Western political concepts, notably that of nationalism, as well as several principles characteristic of Western democracy (for example, the right of self-determination, sovereignty of the people, social obligations of the state) found their way to the Middle East through educational and philanthropic channels, and were echoed in Middle Eastern ideologic developments. It is proposed, however, to limit the present discussion to two other major but hitherto largely neglected aspects of Western influence on the Middle East, namely the aspects of technology and prestige, and to an analysis of the widening range of changes resulting from these primary points of impact.

Westerners, having once set themselves up in the midst of the Middle East, began to display their technology and to spread, both purposely and incidentally, certain elements of it among the natives of the area. The technologic aspect of culture is the one that can most easily be loaned and borrowed. This generalization, of course, holds good only with regard to the *use* of technologic equipment, not its production. It may not be easy to learn how to make a motor-driven pump, but in a few minutes one can learn how to use it and recognize its advantages over the old method of lifting water with the *shaduf*.

In addition to its high degree of transmissibility and its function as an apparent index of advancement, the acceptance of the products of Western technology by the natives of the Middle East was facilitated by the fact that in their own culture technology did not occupy a focal position. Therefore, the Middle Easterners, like the carriers of many other cultures, initially regarded the switch to the use of Western equipment as a change of minor importance only, which would not affect their focal values. Only later, in fact when it was too late, did it dawn upon them that the admittance of even a single Western culture element inevitably brought in its wake more and more new elements with more and more changes, resulting in serious disturbances in the vital texture of their traditional culture.

While the technological beginnings of Westernization explain much of the success of this worldwide cultural process, other factors significantly supported and bolstered it. Among these must be mentioned in the first place the new prestige order that developed after the appearance of the Westerners on the native Middle Eastern scene. Having in many cases achieved ruling and controlling or at least leading and dominant positions in the Middle Eastern countries they penetrated, the Westerners superimposed themselves upon the native social order and became something like a topmost or upper-upper class.

It is not easy to analyze the various components that go into the making of Western prestige. The power element must have been the most important in the earlier, "imperialistic" days, to be replaced, as time went by, by varying combinations of such components as wealth, the possession of strange gadgets and awe-inspiring equipment, specialized knowledge in new fields of increasing importance (such as medicine and agriculture), positions of trust and influence given to Westerners by the local government, and entrance to and free association as equals with the highest elite of native leadership. The aura of prestige surrounding the Westerner soon enveloped his culture as well, with the result that the acquisition of Western culture became a matter of social desirability over and above its recognized utility.

Whatever the specific context of the social stratification in an area, the rich native upper class had the most opportunity for firsthand and close contact with Westerners, had the amplest financial means necessary to acquire the trappings of Western civilization, and was the first to succumb to the lure of the West. Once this movement was on the way, the other native social classes that were ranked beneath the native upper class had an additional incentive for the adoption of a Western style of life so far as this was possible within their limited means: the desire to climb up the native social ladder by acquiring at least some of the same characteristics that the upper class itself had only recently acquired from the Westerners. For instance, in the native garb there were well-defined class differences: the urban effendi, the member of the urban lower class, the fellah, or the Bedouin each had his own distinctive garb that "placed" him as soon as his figure was discerned at a distance. Now, however, the effendi had adopted the Western suit; if the urban worker was able to follow his example, he achieved two aims at once; he demonstrated his advanced social status vis-à-vis his more backward countrymen by dressing like a European, and he also assimilated to the new-style effendi, thus achieving an approximation, in outward appearance at least, of the coveted upper class status. In this manner the acquisition of Western cultural trappings became a symbol of identification with the foreign ruling group for the native upper class and of social advancement for all other classes.

SOCIAL CLEAVAGE

Generally speaking, however, Westernization in its impact upon the traditional Middle Eastern social structure resulted in a widening of the distance between the top and the bottom layers of society. Prior to its inception, the style of life of the native upper class represented the highest culmination of which the local culture was capable. Having concentrated in its hands most of the wealth of the area, the upper class was able to make use of the best cultural forces available in Islamic lands. The best Muslim architects built their palaces, mosques, and madrasahs; the best tailors sewed their clothes; the best sandalmakers made their shoes; the best swordsmiths forged their blades; the best artists and craftsmen provided them with decoration of body, lodging, and furnishing, and with exquisite *objets d'art*; the best poets, storytellers, musicians, dancers, and mimes entertained them; in brief, while greatly surpassing in quality and refinement anything that was within the reach of the lower classes, the culture of the upper class was identical with the culture of the masses. Thus, there existed what can be termed a lower-class–upper-class cultural continuum.

This continuum was disrupted with the impact of Westernization, which hit first and foremost the upper class. Members of this class, to the extent to which they were attracted to Western culture, ceased to be creators, inspirers, and consumers of native cultural products. The local culture became to all practical purposes nonexistent for them, and they became avid consumers in all fields of importations from the countries of the West.

A general decline in native arts and crafts was one of the consequences of this situation. Since the number of customers who insisted on and could pay for high quality rapidly diminished, quality itself declined. There was a vulgarization and deterioration of the traditional arts and crafts, soon to be followed by an adaptation of the native skills to patterns and styles imported from the West in an effort to compete with the imported products themselves, which constantly gained in popularity. This competition in turn resulted in an increased spread of the cheaper kind of Western-style consumers' goods now offered in both an imported and a locally made variety.

However, what the lower classes were able to afford by way of Western-style goods was extremely meager in comparison with the all but wholesale switch to a Western style of life effected or at least attempted by members of the upper class. Especially in the rural areas, where something like four fifths of the total population of the Middle East still lives, the generally low standard of living enabled the people to acquire only a fraction of even those limited offerings of Western-style products that reached them via the weekly markets, the itinerant pedlars, or the local stores.

Thus, while under traditional circumstances the upper class, sitting on the narrow top of the social pyramid, was connected with the lower classes forming the pyramid's broad and massive base by a cultural continuum, Westernization successively severed the vital cultural arteries running between the top and the bottom and created a cultural discrepancy between the two. The elite was now no longer the top exponent of the traditional culture of the same masses, upon the continued existence of which its upper-class status depended. It was Western-oriented, and having like its European preceptors identified Westernization with progress, it regarded the members of the lower classes who still represented the poor version of the traditional culture as backward and primitive.

In the reaction of the lower classes to the widening cultural gulf between them and the native controlling group, certain ambivalences were demonstrated. On the one hand, the traditional resentment felt by the needy at the display of wealth and waste by the idle rich increased when this display included a growing number of newfangled Western traits objectionable to the more tradition-bound outlook of the poor. On the other hand, there was the irresistible attraction exerted by the glitter of

Western cultural trappings, which, however, remained mostly unattainable for the poverty-stricken masses. The frustration thus engendered was not infrequently channeled into one of the special Middle Eastern varieties of nativistic movements of which the Muslim Brotherhood is the best known example.

CREATION OF AN URBAN PROLETARIAT

One of the earliest outcomes of Westernization was thus to throw into disequilibrium the traditional social balance and to disturb the age-old, well settled social strata of the Middle East by culturally alienating the native upper class from the rest of the population. Two additional changes effected by the impact of Westernization on the native society were both urban developments. They were the creation of a rudimentary urban proletariat and an urban middle class.

The social class or the occupational group in traditional Middle Eastern society that came closest to what is generally understood by an urban proletariat was that of the artisans. Yet an artisan or a craftsman, even though he may have been employed for many years, first as an apprentice, then as a journeyman, counted as a person on the way to becoming a master craftsman, and this potential position, as well as membership in the corporation or guild, defined his status as something very different from that of the urban proletarian laborer. Furthermore, in many cases the apprentice who embarked on a career of artisanship was a son, nephew, cousin, or other close relative of the master craftsman under whose guidance and control he acquired the skills of his trade. This hereditary or familial character of the crafts and guilds placed the urban artisan in a definitely higher position than that of the rural agriculturist, whether the latter was a day laborer, a tenant sharecropper, or even a smallholder. The fact of the matter was that under traditional circumstances there was no urban element which in status and social position corresponded to the rural proletariat, which constituted the majority of each country's population.

Such an urban proletariat has begun to come into being as a result of Westernization. The onset of industrialization created a demand for a labor force that was recruited partly from the towns themselves and partly from the surrounding countryside. The new industrial laborers received low wages, had to put up with hard working conditions, and were crowded into suburban slums of which the North African "bidonvilles" (or "tin-can" towns) are today the worst examples. All the conditions for the emergence of a depressed and underprivileged urban proletariat are present, and the labor aspect of industrialization has been characterized by all those evils which to overcome took the modern West several decades.

Compared with the growth of Western industrialization, Middle Eastern industrialization, though limited in extent, was sudden and spurtlike. Moreover, it did not grow organically out of local conditions, but was imposed or introduced from the outside. It was therefore likely to be accompanied by grave tensions and disturbances concomitant upon an all too rapid transition from the traditional forms of social interaction characterized by familism, personal relationships, and the prevalence of a kin-oriented ascribed status, to the modern Western forms of social interaction with its impersonal relationships and preponderance of individually achieved status.

These difficulties were further aggravated by the equally sudden disappearance from the life of this new proletariat of many of those emotional, aesthetic, and spiritual satisfactions that gave it color, content, and interest as long as it ran in its old traditional channels. In the old setting there were the friendships formed in childhood, the colorful feasts of family life accompanying birth, circumcision, marriage, and death, the annual festivals of the Muslim or the agricultural calendar, the birthdays of saints, the enjoyment of story, song, dance, and other traditional forms of aesthetic entertainment, and the trust, the peace of mind, and the equanimity that were the spiritual rewards of unquestioning compliance with the simple and few rites of Islamic worship. In a culture in which the extended family was the traditional protective frame of life and the prime locale of practically all activities, these satisfactions were severely strained by the severance of the family ties and the submergence of the uprooted individual in the disillusioned crowd of slum inhabitants.

These negative features were, however, outweighed by several compulsive factors that contributed to the steady growth of the urban proletariat. One of these was the pronounced status difference between town and country. In the town (with the possible exception of Lebanon), a goodly amount of contempt was felt toward the village and the villager, as manifested in the derogatory connotation of the term "fellah" and in the invariably comic and foolish figure the fellah cut in the shadow theater and other forms of popular entertainment. In the villages, a high status was ascribed to the town and to everything and everybody connected with it. This resulted in a constant though not very sizable village-to-town migration throughout the past centuries. With the spread of Westernization this movement increased, for the town now meant greater opportunities for industrial employment, to which was added the glamor and attraction of the Western style of life.

Another change owing to Westernization that resulted in an increased migration of villagers to the cities was the slowly but perceptibly improving sanitary and hygienic conditions, especially in villages not too distant from urban centers. These improvements enabled a larger percentage of children born to survive and reach maturity, without, for the time being at least, affecting the traditionally high birthrate of the area. This resulted in a rural population pressure not experienced by previous generations. Some of the surplus population, unable to find a livelihood in the villages, had to migrate to the towns, and for lack of skills or other opportunities, swelled the numbers of the urban proletariat.

Thus a social class came into being that was characterized by a greater dissatisfaction with its own status than any population element under traditional circumstances. One of the causes of this proletarian resentment has been discerned by Toynbee: the consciousness of being disinherited from one's ancestral place in society.[4] Another is the spatial proximity to higher social classes and the familiarity with their style of life. The tension created in rootless underprivileged groups as a result of this proximity, known from many other parts of the world, is aggravated in the Middle East by the cultural gulf that separates the two elements. Moreover, luxuries and wealth in the traditional Middle East were kept indoors, to be enjoyed in the privacy of walled-in palaces and gardens, unsuspected by those who happened to pass by the simple and drab frontage facing the street. In contrast, luxurious living in the Western style means public display to be seen and envied by all. As Carleton Coon has put it, "The West has tended to widen the social gulf between rich and poor in the Middle East by dangling in the faces of the poor conveniences and luxuries of which they had never before heard and which they now cannot have, while giving the rich new and expensive tastes, and the need for more and more income."[5]

MIDDLE-CLASS DEVELOPMENT

The second urban development resulting from Westernization was the creation of a new and increasingly numerous middle class. It is true, of course, that in the traditional Middle Eastern town there was an established and highly specialized array of craftsmen, merchants, and professional people, whose position roughly corresponded to that occupied by the middle class in the modern West. What Westernization effected, therefore, was not so much the creation of a new class as a transformation of this traditional sector of the population into a middle class more and more similar to its Western equivalent.

Since the traditional Middle Eastern craft, commercial, and professional guilds comprised literally hundreds of highly specialized occupations, their transformation, or "modernization," was a complicated and ramified process characterized by great differences in speed and extent. These differences depended, first of all, on the effective causes that brought about the transformation itself. With reference to the craft guilds, it appears that their decline and partial or total disappearance was caused mainly by the impact of Western technology and/or Western fashions of consumption. The adoption of Western clothing, for instance, contributed in every part of the Middle East to the decline of local clothing industries. Occasionally it has happened that local crafts declined and disappeared not as a result of the shrinking of their markets but in consequence of the competition of goods produced in Europe in cheap imitation of the local styles.

Articles imported from the West were the products of a superior technology with which local artisanship was unable to compete. Of later origin, but today of increasing importance, is the competition of industrial undertakings established in the Middle Eastern towns themselves, first by foreigners, then by members of the indigenous minorities, and most recently by the state and rather hesitatingly also by members of the Muslim upper class. In some cases these so-called "new industries" in the Middle East were new also in the sense that they engaged in types of production not previously practiced in the area (for example, the extraction of minerals, chemicals), in which case they did not directly contribute to the decline of the traditional crafts. In other cases, however, they were new only in the sense that they introduced Western methods of production, while the products themselves or their equivalents had been both manufactured locally and consumed in the area for many generations (for example, certain foods and textiles, especially in Turkey, Iran, and Egypt), in which case they powerfully competed with and caused the decline of the old native industries.

If in the case of the craft guilds the changing fashion, which is a matter of taste and preference, was a contributing cause of their decline, in the case of commercial guilds the same fashion changes resulted not in a decline, but in a transformation of the character of many business establishments. For the craftsman it was a matter of grave importance if he had to cease producing a certain type of merchandise, and only in rare cases could he switch to the production of the same basic goods but in a modern, that is, Western style. For the merchant, on the other hand, it was a matter of relative indifference what type of wares he carried in his store as long as he knew how to handle them and was able to make his profit. For this reason, while the external appearance of stores and shops has in many cases become modernized, with the plate glass shop window replacing the old wooden shutters, and while the contents of the stores also reflect the changing times, the merchant has suffered less from Westernization and Western competition than the craftsman.

On the other hand, deep inroads were made by changes of fashion, taste, and preference in the traditional professions of the

Middle East. Gone from the urban scene are most if not all of the bloodletters, leeches, surgeons, barbers, bonesetters, healers, readers, exorcists, diviners, soothsayers, fortune tellers, astrologists, dream interpreters, and many other professionals who ministered in traditionally accepted and specialized ways to man's desire to better his physical or mental condition. Not so long ago the confidants, advisers, and companions of kings and princes, they are gone, not in the sense of having completely disappeared, but gone, as it were, underground, withdrawn to the slums, to the quarters inhabited by the villagers recently attracted to the towns, or gone altogether from the larger cities where they could no longer find clients to the more remote small towns relatively untouched by the new ideas brought in from the West.

This development surely reflects a radical change in mental attitudes dominant for centuries. But in probing for its causes, one cannot help doubting that this change was actually accomplished by a sudden conversion to more rational thinking. The clearly demonstrated "miracles" of Western medicine had of course much to do with the abandonment of the traditional methods of improving the physical condition of the body. But even this had to be preceded by some inclination to weigh rationally and unemotionally the evidence for and against both competing systems. Whence did this inclination come? And as to those specialists who administered to the mental comfort of rich and poor alike, of both educated and ignorant, their efforts were summarily dismissed by the Westerners as "sheer superstition" without, however, having anything positive to offer in their stead. Whence, therefore, the inclination to adopt this Western attitude as well, without the backing of any new empirical evidence as to the futility of occult practices, and without anything Western to take their place?

The answer seems again to lie in the prestige of the Westerners and their culture, to which reference was made earlier. The prestige enjoyed by everything Western in the eyes of the natives created in the latter a propensity to emulate all the ways of the West. In fact, it often led to a subservient desire to acquire not only Western equipment, but also Western behavior, mannerisms, and attitudes. Consequently, Western medicine was accepted not only because it was demonstrably superior to traditional Middle

Eastern medical practices, but also because it was Western; and the Western contemptuous attitude toward traditional Middle Eastern mantic and magical practices was adopted on its face value only, merely because it was vouched for by Western prestige.

The complementary aspect of the decline of the traditional Middle Eastern guilds and corporations is the emergence of new professional elements whose totality forms the new middle class. An increasing section of the urban population aspires or is compelled to join the ranks of this new and vigorous social class, the importance of which for the cultural development of the Middle East as a whole is still growing.

Among the members of the old craft guilds who were forced out of their professions by the impact of Westernization, some had no choice but to join the ranks of the urban industrial proletariat; others managed to survive the changing conditions, retain their independent positions, and take their places in the new order by adapting their products to the new consumers' demands. An even greater percentage of the members of the old commercial guilds succeeded in retaining or even improving their positions as independent owners of stores of varying sizes with varying numbers of employees. These merchants, too, are today solid members of the middle class in the larger cities of the Middle East. The professional sector of the middle class is its newest element. Only rarely were members of the old professions able to fit into the life of the Westernized city or to adapt themselves to the changed conditions. As a rule, the new professional class is recruited from among the sons of members of the other classes or sectors of the urban population, or of the better-to-do rural population.

It has been observed in many Middle Eastern countries, as well as in other parts of Asia (for example, in India and Pakistan), that the aim of the great majority of young people who can afford a college or at least a high school education is to go into law, politics, journalism, administration, or at least into clerical, religious, and teaching positions, and to practice these professions in the towns only. Education in their eyes is the open sesame to city life and to a livelihood earned *not* with one's hands. This aversion to rural life and any type of labor that they consider to be manual is a heritage of the traditional Middle Eastern urban mentality that saw in the ability to escape working with one's hands the clinching proof of social advancement. It is interesting to note that this prejudice against village life and "manual" work is retained even in circles that otherwise pride themselves with their thorough Westernization.

As a result of this attitude the new Middle Eastern middle class is lop-sided when judged by Western standards: it has a profusion of white-collar workers and intellectuals, many of whom are chronically unemployed, or underemployed and underpaid, while on the other hand it lacks a sufficient number of doctors, engineers, architects, chemists, technicians. Another consequence is the marked concentration of professional people in the cities, which greatly contributes to the growth of the cultural distance between town and country.

Dislocation of Value Judgments

In a traditional and well-settled culture such as that of the Middle East, reality (that is, tangible) ingredients and value ingredients, to use Kroeber's terminology,[6] are usually well adjusted. The two categories reinforce each other, and the extent of their mutual support lends the culture coherence, balance, and inner consistency. Take, for example, the matter of wealth and poverty. The typical situation in the Middle East was for centuries the concentration of great riches in the hands of a very few, with great poverty the share of the many. This was and in many places still is a factual reality. The ideologic counterpart of this situation was that the division of worldly goods is willed by God, that the possession of wealth is not one of those really important things for which man should strive, that there is a certain religious virtue in poverty, and that it is a religious duty of the rich to dole out alms to the poor.[7] In this manner extreme economic inequality was organically incorporated into the culture, not only by being accepted realistically but also by being underpinned ideologically.

In a contact situation such as Westernization presents, this old balance between reality culture and value culture is disturbed. As Kroeber has emphasized, the reality ingredients of a culture can be loaned and borrowed much more readily than its value ingredients. Therefore, very often there is a lag in the acceptance of value culture, while reality culture is accepted readily. One of the causes of this lag is the emotional attachment of society to its own value culture and its resistance to the introduction of new, foreign value ingredients. Since, however, reality culture and value culture are interdependent, the reality ingredients of one culture cannot be expected to fulfill the same function in another culture if the latter retains its own value ingredients.

This thesis can be illustrated by examples from almost any field in which Western influences are felt in the Middle East. Take, for instance, the factory system introduced from the West. The adoption of all the technical equipment, the learning of all the skills and tricks of the trade, will not ensure the operation of a factory with the precision, reliability, and efficiency attained in the West as long as the basically negative attitude toward manual labor persists and the value of the work and the worker is not recognized. In other words, reality ingredients alone cannot guarantee the satisfactory functioning of an institution that in its home environment comprises value ingredients as well.

All this, of course, does not mean that reality ingredients of a culture can be transplanted into another culture without causing changes in the values of the latter, or that values from one culture can be superimposed on another culture without causing changes in its reality ingredients. Quite the contrary. The close coordination and interdependence between reality culture and value culture make it impossible to introduce changes in the one without creating changes, with some delay perhaps, in the other. Thus, once the establishment of factories introduced new reality ingredients into the life of Middle Eastern towns, it became only a question of time until changes in values would follow. As a matter of fact, some signs of these changes already are visible here and there. In eastern Saudi Arabia, for instance, where the Arabian American Oil Company offers excellent working conditions to the still largely nomadic population of the peninsula, the tribesmen, until recently utterly contemptuous of all manual labor with the exception of the only noble task of breeding camels, flock in increasing numbers to the company's recruiting stations without suffering loss of prestige.

In general, the approach of the West to the Middle East, especially in recent years, has been characterized by a careful avoidance of ideologic issues and a concentration instead on a number of practical problems. Technical, economic, and related missions sent in recent years to the Middle East by the United Nations or the United States, as well as by private business enterprises working in the area, have adopted the principle of noninterference with traditional ideologies and values as a fundamental directive.

In the case of Western religious missions, the abstention from ideologic influencing was not as much a matter of free choice as a matter of prudence in view of the hostility with which Islamic society would have reacted to open attempts at conversion.[8] The result was that while religious missions healed and treated tens of thousands of Muslim sick, gave education to other tens of thousands of Muslim children, and may have influenced by precept and example the ethical outlook of many others, they converted very few natives. Religion being a focal concern in the culture of the Middle East,[9] conversion was regarded as apostasy and resulted in an open breach with family, society, and value culture. The convert to Christianity was ostracized by his peers and, what is equally important, since Islam was held with unshakable conviction to be the only true religion, to leave it was regarded as an evidence of utter folly.

More recently, to the 150-year-old impact of the Western world on the Middle East has been added a new attack coming from the Russian totalitarian subvariety of Western culture. In contrast to its West European predecessor, the Soviet impact is directed mainly at the ideologic facet of the traditional Middle East culture. Part of the Communist effort is to convince the people whom it seeks to win that the doctrines of Communism and Islam are not only compatible, but that actually Communism is the true interpretation of the original and pure form of Islam. And, as Bernard Lewis has shown, certain external resemblances can, in fact, be discerned between the traditional Islamic forms of autocratic-theocratic social structure and the Soviet totalitarian-dictatorial state form.[10] While there is no need to exaggerate the danger of a Communist revolution in any Middle Eastern country, the Communist attack on the native culture at its ideologic roots is a serious threat that can create grave disturbances in the traditional cultural and social equilibrium even short of a political overthrow.

While the direct impact of Christian missions on the religious life of the Middle East has been negligible, Westernization has indirectly resulted in an increasing coolness toward religion as a whole. It has been emphasized repeatedly that religion in the Middle East under traditional circumstances was a total way of life.[11] The craft guilds, for instance, were religious organizations; the wearing of the locally customary garb was religiously sanctioned; medicine was a religious vocation, as was teaching. Sovereignty itself was a religious office. While there was no hierarchy or priesthood in any sense comparable to those of the Catholic and Episcopalian churches, a considerable percentage of the urban population was engaged in directly religious professions. Many additional families, both in town and country, were supported by religious foundations that concentrated in their hands a considerable proportion of each country's landed property.

The most important instrument through which religion exercised its hold on the individual was the traditional Middle Eastern patrilineal, patrilocal, patriarchal, endogamous extended family. The dependence of the individual on his family and his integration into it were so intense that Middle Eastern culture was rightly termed a kinship culture.[12] And since this family system itself was a religious institution, sanctioned and supported by religion, family and religion mutually strengthened each other. As we have seen, Westernization brought about a decline of paternal authority; a break-up of the extended family; a movement from village to town; a change-over in the towns themselves from the family economy of the old-fashioned crafts to the impersonal economic system of the factory with its employment of individuals as such, irrespective of family ties, and with its considerable labor turnover; and a conscious imitation, especially in the middle and upper classes, of Western family and social forms. All this resulted not only in a crucial change in the character of family life itself, but also in a trend away from religion and toward secularism. When the individual, and as a rule the young male individual, extricated himself from the hold of his family, he left behind an intrinsically religious atmosphere, the rejection of which thence-forward became a part of his negation of the old, tightly knit family system itself.

Another point to make is that under traditional circumstances leadership, wealth, position, power, and control belonged, with very few exceptions, to members of the ruling religion, Islam, who all vied with one another in the public demonstration of their orthodoxy and piety. Religiosity was thus one of the hallmarks of the traditional upper crust, and consequently no question could arise in the minds of the other classes as to the importance, value, and obligatory nature of religious observance.

On this scene appeared the prestige-laden Westerner, occupy-ing superior positions, carrying a culture that evoked the desire to emulate it. These foreigners were not only adherents of a differ-ent faith, but their attitude toward their own Christian religion was, on the whole, lukewarm. Among those Middle Easterners whose general attitude toward Westernization was positive, the emulation of Western ways therefore meant, among other things, to display unconcern about their own religion. On the other hand, among those whose ties to their own religion-centered traditional culture proved stronger than the Westerly pull, Western irreligi-osity became an additional cause to reject whatever the West had to offer and to seek refuge in "return to Islam" movements.

THE ISSUE OF WESTERN DOMINATION

As many Middle Easterners understand it, the basic motivation of the Western world in establishing contact with the Middle East was the endeavor to dominate it politically and exploit it economically. The Middle Eastern view is that for several decades the Western powers controlled the Middle East with the help of the Middle Eastern ruling classes who were either coerced or bribed into serving the Western interests. As a result, the peoples of the Middle East have remained poor and oppressed; in fact, their poverty and oppression have even increased. By the end of World War II however, the patience of the people became at long last exhausted; they burst forth in movements against foreign domination, against misery and poverty, and against those of their own rulers who, under the auspices and with the blessing of the foreign governments, had oppressed and exploited them. They produced strong and fearless leaders, nationalized their natural resources and the large foreign-owned industrial and commercial establishments, and declared many of the foreign residents as unwelcome. They sincerely felt, and never tired reiterating, that "We would rather die than accept British or Russian or any other domination over our fatherland."

As against this, the Western argument is as follows: Without Western initiative the natural resources of the Middle East would have remained unutilized. The Western powers were invited by the rulers of the Middle Eastern countries themselves to find and exploit their natural resources and to introduce Western technology. The Western companies that thereupon were set up shared their profits with the legal owners of the natural resources, the kings and governments of the Middle Eastern countries. These rulers, however, instead of passing on at least part of the benefits to the people themselves, pocketed all the income. They are, therefore, responsible for the poverty and degradation in which nine tenths of the Middle Eastern peoples live. They direct and foment the hatred of the West, of the "foreigners," in the hope of thus making the foreigners responsible in the eyes of the masses for the "animal-like standard of living forced on their people . . . by their own corrupt, greedy selves."[1]

In the leadlong clash of these two opposite views, the minimum measure of agreement that exists between them is apt to pass unnoticed. The fact of the matter, however, is that a major share of the direct responsibility for the poverty and misery of the people is laid by both sides at the door (or rather the luxurious portals) of the local ruling classes, whether their actions and attitudes are held to be instigated by foreigners or by their own selfish attitude.

Resentment against effendis, pashas, agas, shaykhs, beys, deys, notables, landowners, and other traditional overlords is increasingly felt by the people, is more and more overtly expressed by their educated and articulate spokesmen, and is becoming a stronger and stronger impetus for social and land reforms. Although protestations against landlord exploitation still go hand in hand with a display of antiforeign sentiments, from the view of ideologic development it has to be pointed out that the very concepts of land reform and of a more equitable sharing of material benefits were born in the West whence they have penetrated the Middle East in recent years. The traditional Middle Eastern idea, which, by the way, made poverty and misery much more easily bearable, is that the landlord or the chieftain is a sort of family head, that all his tenants or vassals are subordinate members of his quasi-family, and that therefore it is not only actually inevitable, but also right in principle for the peasants to live on the barest subsistence level while sustaining their lords in luxury. To wish for a change in this situation, to revolt against a landlord, to threaten to kill him (as actually has happened several times lately in Iran), would have been as inconceivable in the past as it would be for a son in a traditional Middle Eastern patriarchal family to take a stand against his father. A great measure of Western mentality had to be acquired before the people became receptive to reform ideas with reference to these important areas of entrenched traditionalism.

TECHNOLOGY, SCIENCE, AND MEDICINE

Of all the different aspects of Western culture that are being introduced in the life of the Middle East, the acquisition and use of technical equipment and methods encounters the least resistance. There is, of course, an innate disinclination to change old techniques that were inherited from one's ancestors and knowledge of which was acquired in early youth. A peasant father whose son returns home after three years in an agricultural school will not readily discard the old methods of cultivation that enabled him to make a living (and, incidentally, to send his son to school) for the new ones fervently advocated by the youngster. His resistance to change will be based on a preference for the familiar and a distrust of everything new, unknown and untried. Experience, shows, however, that if the son succeeds in demonstrating to the father the superiority of the method or the implement he recommends, the father soon changes his mind. Readiness to give up initial distrust and to accept demonstrated improvement was observed repeatedly in various Middle Eastern countries by social workers among the rural population.[2] Demonstrated advantages in technical improvements tipped the scale in favor of acceptance of superior Western machinery and the discarding of the old traditional implements in Palestine among the Arab weavers of Majdal.[3] Once the initial resistance is overcome, the readiness to accept demonstrated improvements soon turns into eagerness to benefit by them. This explains the numerous petitions sent by peasants from remote villages in Turkey or in Syria to the central authorities clamoring for a road, a hospital, a motorized pump, and many other technical improvements.[4]

In addition to demonstrating in practice the good results of the suggested change rather than explaining them in theory, there is a second prerequisite for successful culture change in the technologic field: innovations must be introduced gradually. A change that if sprung upon the people precipitately would meet with determined resistance can become acceptable without any noticeable repercussion if protracted over a number of years. The law that forbade the Turkish people to wear the red fez, with immediate effect, resulted in much unnecessary resentment and bitterness. In several other Middle Eastern countries the old-fashioned headgear, together with the veil, is disappearing gradually; in the absence of sudden compulsion, the discarding of these traditional items of clothing spreads by the spontaneous process of voluntary imitation.

The sum of these observations is that of all aspects of Western culture it is the material equipment that meets with the least resistance in the Middle East, and that further changes in this field can best be effected by demonstrating their advantages and by introducing them gradually.

The situation with regard to the introduction of the exact sciences and the scientific method is similar. These facets of culture *ipso facto* touch directly upon the lives of the small urban upper and middle classes only, whose contacts with Western culture are close and manifold. The great Western advances in all branches of science are fully acknowledged by these groups, and with the increasing recognition of the role and function of science in the life of a modern state there is a growing readiness on the part of the young educated group to take up the study of sciences in place of the traditional academic concentration on theology and law. As a matter of fact, the endeavor to get rid of Western interference and domination is an additional factor directing many young people into those scientific and technical occupations which until recently were the exclusive domain of Westerners.

It goes without saying that the attitude toward medicine and sanitation is the same as that toward Western technology and science. The demonstrated advantages of modern medicine and sanitation meet little resistance, and in many cases, even in the most remote villages, there is a demand for more of these modern miracles of the west than the local government can supply.

EDUCATION

The changeover from traditional Middle Eastern to modern Western educational methods and aims can serve as an additional illustration of the practicability of introducing any change, even the most far-reaching one, if it is preceded by careful demonstration and is made gradually. Both these conditions were fulfilled in the course of the modest beginnings and the slow growth of modern educational institutions in the Middle East. Thus there was little organized resistance on the part of traditional forces who would have preferred to retain the outmoded *kuttābs* (Koran schools) as the only educational institutions. The first modern schools were founded by Western educators or patterned after a Western (French, British, American) model. In a short time modern Muslim schools were founded, until eventually they outnumbered the traditional Koran schools.[5]

Another effect of the introduction of modern education was the increase in the percentage of children attending school. The Koran schools could never boast an enrollment of more than a small percentage of the male school-age population. Since the establishment of modern schools this percentage has been steadily on the increase in every Middle Eastern country. Since no corresponding increase has taken place in the Koran schools, the result is that an ever-growing majority of the children attend modern schools while a decreasing percentage of them is still sent by their parents to Koran schools.[6] Although the modern educational effort of the Middle East is still far from having reached its goal, several countries have passed laws of general compulsory elementary education, and thus have officially adopted the principle that every child is duty bound to acquire a system of knowledge much of which has been adopted from the West only recently.

At the same time, however, in the curriculum of the modern Middle Eastern elementary schools (outside Turkey) great emphasis is put on the Koran, on Islam, on Islamic history, and the history of the country in which the school is situated (including its pre-Islamic phase). Expanding modern education thus creates in ever-increasing numbers of children and youths a much greater appreciation of their own culture than was ever the case under the old *kuttāb* education. The rudiments of Western learning are absorbed together with an increased religionational consciousness that potentially contains the seeds of anti-Western feelings.

ARTS AND LITERATURE

In the realm of technology, it is relatively easy to demonstrate the superiority of a modern Western achievement over the traditional Middle Eastern one. It is not too hard to convince an Arab weaver that the wide fly-shuttle loom is superior to the old narrow-width hand loom, or to show a village population that if it cleans up a polluted source of water its health improves. Because of this, the introduction of Western technical improvements meets with least resistance.

In other aspects of culture, such as the arts, music, and literature, it is not possible to demonstrate the superiority of one culture over another. What an individual or a group prefers in these fields is largely a matter of taste and education, and the end result of cumulative previous experience. When therefore Middle Easterners rave about the greatness of Beethoven and Tchaikovsky while deprecating the primitivity of their own music, they clearly have allowed their judgment to be influenced by factors extraneous to the musical enjoyment itself. There can be little doubt that the ostensible enjoyment of jazz music by the urban Turkish youth[7] originates in the wish to be regarded as modern and fashionable. Eventually, of course, a few years of listening to a new musical variety may result in a genuine preference for it. The great majority of the Middle Easterners, however, still enjoy their own traditional music only, still sing their old folksongs and popular songs, and still prefer to hear familiar tunes in radio broadcasts.[8] They show interest, although without too much appreciation, when "modern-Oriental" songs sung by such famous performers (that is, famous in the cities) as Abdul Wahhab or Umm Kulthum are broadcast, but have neither interest in nor understanding for the Western music to which the Westernized musical directors of the Middle Eastern broadcasting stations devote a considerable proportion of the program time.

As with music, so with the visual arts, and especially their rich decorative varieties. On the one hand, traditional tastes still predominate among the "simple people"; and on the other, some of the more enlightened Middle Eastern governments have initiated measures to insure the survival of the fine crafts in which decorative art has traditionally found its expression. Only in the cities are foreign art forms, introduced from the West, becoming fashionable among the sophisticated groups.

It may be argued that the resistance to the penetration of Western musical and visual art forms is a rather unimportant aspect of the resistance to Westernization in the Middle East. It must, however, be remembered that it is precisely in the arts that the regional and local character of any culture most overtly and specifically manifests itself. A loss of the traditional character of the Middle Eastern arts would not only make the life of the area's peoples poorer and drabber, it would also detract from the sum total of mankind's artistic creativity.

Literature in Middle Eastern popular culture is of much smaller significance than the visual arts and music. The enjoyment of written literature is confined to a still very small educated urban class, and the active participation in it is the privilege of a very few individuals. Poetry, both in its artistic and popular forms, is still very much alive, and the old traditions of the great medieval Arab and Persian poets are still followed, although the resultant products are recognizedly inferior. But the Western literary forms of the novel and the short story are used almost exclusively by modern Middle Eastern writers of prose, and it is the consensus among Middle Eastern literati themselves that the original works of these local authors are less enjoyable than the translations of European and American prose prepared by the same writers.

The only persons in a position to put up a considered resistance to this form of Western cultural penetration are the religious functionaries and the traditionally educated and tradition-bound elements whose number is dwindling rapidly. They do not object to the perusal per se of Western literary products in the original or in translation; neither do they oppose in principle the fashionable trend among the young generation of authors to write in a style and in prose forms imitative of Western literatures. They protest these modern developments because Western literary forms are usually filled with a Western spirit; because the heroes of the novel and short story, as a rule, either are Westerners or behave, think, and feel like Westerners; and because thereby *belles lettres* as a whole serve as a propaganda instrument for Western attitudes, mores, and values. More has to be said on this very sensitive issue; but first it seems necessary to discuss the contrast between Middle Eastern and Western social control and intercourse that constitutes the background against which the clash over mores and values takes place.

SOCIAL CONTROL

The next aspect of Western culture that encounters a more definite resistance is social control including organization, administration, and governmental forms. In traditional Middle Eastern society, social control and political organization are based on family ties, or at least are modeled after the structural pattern characterizing the family. The tribal or village headman, and even the landowner who owns entire villages, occupies a position vis-à-vis his people not unlike that of the patriarch of the family. Even King Ibn Saud kept to this tradition as long as it was physically possible for him. Western observers have often remarked at the ease with which the simplest tribesman could gain entrance to the King, and the familiarity with which he conversed with the powerful monarch of the Arabian Peninsula. In this "kinship culture"[9] the parallelism between familial and social structure goes even further. In the family, the son has no clearly defined rights of his own, for all his rights are vested in and defended by his father. In the social order, the individual lacks legally circumscribed rights apart from those which are represented by the headman of the larger social group to which he belongs. However, just as the son can always count on the love and protection of his father, the individual is in accordance with the prevailing ethos sure of the benevolence and help of his chieftain, headman, landlord, or other leading personality. This situation became somewhat complicated with the appearance on the Arab scene of Turkish, that is, foreign governors and other officials, but even the relationship between these and their Arab subjects was never as impersonal as is the case in a Western-type governmental and administrative set-up. It would therefore be shortsighted to attribute the resistance to the changeover from the traditional to modern Western organizational, administrative, and governmental forms to vested interests of the ruling classes alone. These undoubtedly constitute a powerful contributing factor; but it will take a great educational effort to accustom the governed classes to the impersonal Western organization with its insistence on equal rights and duties for everybody, instead of the personal Middle Eastern approach[10] with its emphasis on kinship, friendship, benevolence, and conveniently purchasable good will.

The great emphasis put by traditional-minded Middle Easterners on the accustomed forms of social control and intercourse is a motivation, among those of them with sufficient insight to recognize indirect causal connections, for resistance to even the most innocuous aspects of Westernization. They observe that the acceptance of such unobjectionable elements of Western culture as technology, sanitation, industrialization, and the like inevitably brings about the penetration of Western social forms and behavior patterns as well. A young man who is sent by his father to a modern school, acquires a trade or profession, and subsequently finds employment in a factory or office, earns probably more than his father and gets accustomed to moving around in a world in which his father is a complete stranger. Such a young man will rarely exhibit to the full those traits of filial obedience, of self-subordination to the joint interests of his family, as expressed and represented by his father or possibly his grandfather, which are highly prized values in the traditional mores of the Middle East. To engage in a new occupation invariably means that the individual doing so removes himself from the closed circle of joint family endeavor. Occupational change thus brings about economic separation, and this in turn results in the creation of a social distance that would have been unthinkable in the traditional set-up. The next step usually is the assertion of a certain independence by the young man in the choice of a wife, contrary to the traditional custom according to which the parents of the young people take the initiative and make the decision with regard to the marriage of their children. This is followed by the setting up of a separate household by the young people, again contrary to the custom which demands that the young couple become integrated into the household of the bridegroom's father. In this manner, educational and occupational changes, in themselves features of Western culture desirable from the Middle Eastern point of view, result in the breakdown or at least in a considerable weakening of the traditional extended family system that is one of the mainstays of Middle Eastern society. The substitution of the Western family pattern is regarded by most people (at least by those of the older generation) as highly undesirable, and is therefore resisted.

Nor is the effect of education and occupational change confined to the breakdown of the traditional extended family. In the Middle East, as we have seen, all the larger social units, whether one of the two famous moieties, an urban trade guild, or a new political party, are firmly founded upon the extended family which, as a rule, has been committed for many generations to supporting them. In the past, since the individual was a member of an extended family, and the extended family as a whole derived its strength from its membership in such a larger unit, he was, as a rule, not able to break ranks, to change affiliation or allegiance. The result was a certain stability in the entire social structuring of the population.

Up to a certain point, the changes brought about by modern times could be accommodated within this pre-existing social system owing to its inherent flexibility. When, for instance, voting and "modern" political parties were introduced, which in itself was done in emulation of Western political forms, the groups economically dependent on the great landlords and residing in their villages were transformed without much difficulty into political constituencies: instruction had only to be handed down to all those who had newly acquired the right to vote that they cast their ballot either for the landlord or for the man to whom he in turn owed allegiance.

With the increase of literacy and of the occupational, economic, and social independence of the individual from his own extended family, the political system that had retained its traditional Middle Eastern content under the newly introduced Western forms began to crumble. Once the primary bond to one's extended family was weakened, the loyalties that the family as a whole owed to a larger group and its leaders also lost much of their hold. For this reason, if for no other, the family heads and all those who under the traditional system hold positions of importance and wield influence must be opposed to the changeover from the traditional Middle Eastern social forms to newfangled ones introduced from the West.

MORES, MORALS, AND VALUES

Before entering the very sensitive area of mores, morals, and values, a general remark seems to be in place about an all too often encountered preconception that makes difficult if not impossible the understanding of any resistance to Westernization. This preconception is the conviction that Western ways of life, Western mentality and behavior are superior to their Middle Eastern counterparts. To the average Westerner who visits the Middle East or who has any dealings with the area from a distance, the situation is a clear-cut one: "native" peoples are given an opportunity to benefit by the vast storehouses of Western experience; they are presented with the end results of a long and laborious civilizatory development; they can therefore learn within a short time what it took the West several centuries to achieve, and thus are enabled to step out of the Middle Ages right into the twentieth century. If they do not want to learn, if they do not wish to be helped, if they are "choosy," rejecting this and accepting only part of that, this is but an additional manifestation of their backwardness and stubbornness.

As against this rule-of-the-thumb explanation of any opposition to Westernization, it is well to consider that Middle Eastern cultures, as the other great cultures of the Orient, "are thousands of years older than the West . . . with aesthetic, religious, and social values in many respects superior."[11] Middle Eastern opposition to Westernization can, therefore, stem from the apprehension, even if not often clearly articulated, that a wholesale adoption of Western civilization would entail the displacement and loss of many greatly cherished traditional Middle Eastern cultural values.

The issue of modern *versus* traditional mores and morals often result in conflict even within the context of one single culture between the old and the young generation. When the old generation is in addition the exponent of the traditions of one culture and the young one that of the dominant moral tenor of another very different culture, the conflict between them can become much more pronounced and embittered.

Although from Chapters 2 and 5 it became apparent that considerable variations exist between one culture area in the Middle East and another in several important facets of the traditional mores and morals, precisely those areas that have hitherto become exposed to Western influences share a certain fundamental value syndrome negated in its entirety by modern Western culture. In many cases the contrast between the two systems of mores and values is explicit and blatant; in others, it is implicit and latent, but its existence is nevertheless felt by those whom their own full awareness and appreciation of traditional Middle Eastern values sensitize even to differences in emphasis. A few areas can be indicated, albeit with sketchy brevity.

Traditional Middle Eastern mores insist on segregation between the sexes to varying degrees; the modern West has built its entire social life on the mingling of the sexes, allowing and even prescribing intimate bodily contact between members of the opposite sex barely acquainted with each other as, for example, at dances. The Middle East has developed a garb that reveals neither the feminine nor the masculine body form; in fact, the long robes traditionally worn reveal the sex of the wearer only by their color and decorative pattern, and not by outlining the shape of the physical frame. In the modern West, clothes emphasize rather than hide the difference between the physical shapes of the two sexes, and, on certain occasions, reveal almost the entire body.

In the traditional Middle East age is a value; the older a person becomes the more he is honored and the more prestige he has. In the West, age is considered a drawback and, with few exceptions, the older a person is the less his importance for society and even for his own family.

Education and socialization in the Middle East aim at making the young ones into obedient members of their families. Both during maturation and after having reached adulthood, the younger generation must follow the instructions of the elders, and subordinate its own interests to those of the family. In the West, the purpose of education is to make the youngsters independent as early as possible; it is anticipated that they will soon "fly the coop," make their own decisions, find their own way, and fight their own battles. Family cohesion is minimal and neither expected in actuality nor upheld in theory.

In the traditional Middle East, the drive for material success is mitigated and balanced by a religious outlook that stresses the need to be prepared for afterlife. In the Modern West, work for success here and now, measured primarily in income and property, completely absorbs most people.

The above items are merely examples of a long list of contrasting values whose sum total is the ethos in each of the two cultures. That people steeped in traditional Middle Eastern culture object to the abandonment of their own value system for that of the modern West should not be difficult to appreciate. Most people, and especially those who are carriers of traditional cultures, tend to regard their own values as "right," and different values as "wrong." This tendency becomes even more pronounced in a culture permeated by religion to the extent to which the Middle Eastern is. For Middle Eastern religiocentricity the adoption of Western value culture appears not merely as the exchange of a proved set of values for an inferior one, but as a fatal deviation from the "straight path" (Koran 1 : 5).

In traditional Middle Eastern society, whether rural or urban, nomadic or settled, the daughter's place is at home until such time as she is safely married off by her parents to a man as closely related to the family as possible. Formal schooling for girls is a Western innovation the acceptance of which still lags behind that of the schooling of boys.[12] But those girls who are sent to school are by this single act placed in a position largely similar to that of the educated young man in relation to their families.

Outside the family circle itself, the educational facilities granted to varying percentages of the women in Middle Eastern countries bore results that were alarming to those who clung to traditional social forms and mores. In one country only, namely in Turkey, complete political equality of women with men was made law in 1934. In other countries women are still demanding such rights with varying intensity. In Egypt, for instance, there is a strong feminist movement, but there is also strong opposition to it on the part of the 'ulamā of el-Azhar and other orthodox Muslims who maintain that woman's place is in the home and that according to Islamic law public authority is confined to men. In Syria only literate women won the franchise (in 1949) while both literate and illiterate men are permitted to vote.

Any change in the traditional position of women in the Middle East is a step in the direction of Westernization and is advocated by feminists in their desire to secure for women a position similar to that held by them in the Western world. On the other hand, opposition to these feminist aspirations stems from the socio-religious attitude of the conservative elements who see in the feminist movement an infringement of traditional religious law and custom.

THE REALM OF LAW

Religious conservatism is the ideological and emotional founda-tion also of the opposition to the introduction of new systems of laws. Law in the Middle East has been the domain proper of religion for the past five thousand years. The Islamic versions of religious law, although the youngest of indigenous legal systems in the area, are by now about a thousand years old and therefore do not cover all the contingencies of later developments. They are especially out of touch with the legal needs arising as a result of Westernization. In the more Westernized states Islamic Canon Law (*sharī'a*) has been supplemented by a modern civil law taken over from the West, while in the more tradition-bound countries the older tribal or local (*'urf, 'āda, izref, ittifāqāt*) law is still ad-hered to by the nonurban population. These three legal systems function independently and without coordination, and the observance of one of them occasionally entails a breach of the other.

The survival of the *'urf* after thirteen hundred years of Islamic legal domination is an eloquent testimony to the religiolegal conservatism of the Middle East. In relation to the problem of further modernization of the realm of law this conservatism is expressed by the opposition to any additional expansion of the domain of modern civil law at the expense of traditional Islamic law. In most countries the present stage of legal development is considered satisfactory, whether modern civil law has made

considerable headway as in Egypt, or is still completely excluded
as in Yemen. Secularization of the law is opposed in many countries not only by individuals and public bodies with vested
religious interests, but also by thoughtful people who are otherwise not particularly conservatively minded.

As to the conservative element, they feel keenly that Westernization, as von Grunebaum put it, "develops what secularizing
tendencies there are in the Islamic heritage, it relegates the Canon
Law, in a sense the greatest achievement of traditional Islam, to
the background and it assails the social basis of traditional society
by changing the status of women, introducing democratic pro-
cedures, and a new kind of education."[13]

ISLAM AND THE "INFIDEL"

Islam, the ruling Middle Eastern religion, is thoroughly
Oriental insofar as it exercises as strong a hold over the thoughts
and emotions of the great majority of the population as do the
great religions of southeast Asia, in sharp contrast to the modest
place of religion in the modern Western world. In one fundamental aspect, however, Middle Eastern religion is basically
different from the other major Oriental religions, and falls into one
category with Western religion (Christianity), in keeping with the
common origin of the two. The major South Asian and Southeast
Asian religions (with the exception of Shinto) are nontheistic and
tolerant of other faiths. Islam, like Christianity and like the parent
religion of both, Judaism, is theistic, proselytizing,[14] aggressive,
and often intolerant. Common to all theistic religions is the tendency to regard "religious views other than their own as heathen,
erroneous, or inferior."[15] Thus while in South Asia and Southeast
Asia the presence of Europeans who were of a different religious
persuasion did not arouse resentment on religious grounds, the
appearance of Christians in the Muslim world evoked the typical
impatient reaction of a theistic religion to an encounter with
members of another faith. The appellative "Christian" (like that
of "Jew") has remained to this day an expression of contempt in
the more isolated parts of the Middle East. The traditional attitude
of Muslims to "infidels" has almost the same quality that characterized the missionary and inquisitorial zeal of the Spaniards after

their arrival in the New World: the "infidel" (in the Middle East) or the "idolatrous pagan" (in New Spain) must be saved by conversion to the only true faith (Islam in the Middle East, Catholicism in New Spain) in his own interest and even against his will. This attitude explains the periodic outbreaks of violence, subsiding only when formal conversion was accomplished, perpetrated by Muslim mobs against Christians and Jews living in their midst who, in normal times, were merely treated with varying degrees of contempt as *dhimmi*, tolerated subject people. Violence against foreigners has been rare even in those countries of the Middle East that have preserved much of their isolation, but the feeling of contempt against those who are not "believers" is still present. The self-assurance of these foreigners in the superior positions they occupy, their impolite manners,[16] and even their eagerness to teach and instruct are in striking contrast to the accustomed submissive behavior pattern of the *dhimmi*, the native Christians and Jews. And not only does the foreigner do all the things from which a *dhimmi* (if he ever dreamt of presuming) would be immediately and most effectively discouraged, he cannot even be reproached for it. Here is an unbeliever who is an adherent of the same churches (regarded by the Muslim as places of semi-idolatrous worship since they are decorated with pictures and statues) as the native Christian. Yet instead of following the customary pattern of *dhimmi* submissiveness, his bearing betrays his pride; he expects all and sundry to comply with his wishes, and to follow his instructions; instead of asking for favors, he has the power to grant them. In this emotion-guided chain of reactions there is little place for such practical considerations as the actual usefulness of the foreigner or the economic advantages and material benefits his presence means for the country at large. An emotional tension is thus built up that can find no outlet (apart from rare outbreaks of violence usually discouraged by the authorities) and therefore leads to what to the Westerner appear as completely unreasonable demands aiming not at the benefit of the Middle Eastern people concerned but at the elimination of the "stone of offense," the foreigner.

Like all other phenomena connected with Westernization, the variations of this religiously grounded antiforeigner feeling constitute a scale of fine gradation from the "most intense" on the one end to the "minimal" on the other. Nor must it be forgotten that the population of no Muslim country is homogeneous, and that considerable differences can be found in the attitude to foreigners among the various classes and groups of the urban population, as well as among the urban people in general on the one hand and the inhabitants of the villages, especially the more remote ones, on the other.

WESTERNIZATION AND SECULARIZATION

This antiforeign feeling is a heritage of past centuries when the whole world was in Muslim eyes divided into the *Dār al-Islām* and *Dār al-Ḥarb*, the House of Islam or Peace, and the House of War. In this view, every country and individual not belonging to the *Dār al-Islām* was *eo ipso* an enemy. In modern times, increasing familiarity with people who were characterized above as primary personal sources of Westernization, and many other kinds of contact with the Western world, have rendered this view obsolete. In the meantime, however, a new motivation started to serve as fuel for the old fire.

It has been observed by Middle Eastern people in the last two generations that wherever Westerners and with them Western civilizatory attainments penetrate, traditional religiosity suffers a setback. This has proved to be the case even if nothing but the most external and mechanical phases of Western civilization were introduced. Not as if these were accompanied by a danger of conversion to Christianity (in no other culture has Christian missionary activity been crowned with less success than in the Middle East) but because the adoption of Western civilizatory trappings tended to loosen the hold religion traditionally has had over all aspects of life, and to make people negligent in the fulfillment of religious ritual. Westernized Middle Easterners will assert that they are good Muslims in their feeling and thinking even though they do not observe the Fast and the Prayers, the prohibition of drinking wine and eating pork, and other ritual injunctions of Islam. Tradition-bound Muslims, however, attach to these assertions even less value than similar statements by nonpracticing Catholics have in the eyes of practicing Catholics. To the average Middle Easterner, in whose life religion is still the fundamental motivating force[17]—religion not expressed in formal observance is unthinkable. There is therefore an opposition even to the culturally "harmless" or "neutral" components of Western civilization such as technical and organizational improvement, not because these in themselves are deemed undesirable, but because it is understood that they are almost inevitably followed by a decline of religious observance. It is felt that a breakdown or even a mere cracking of the religious-spiritual-emotional edifice, a total or partial loss of the traditional mental climate, and a narrowing down of the wide outlook would be too high a price to pay for mere material betterment.

SUPERFICIAL WESTERNIZATION

It has been noticed by both Western and Middle Eastern observers that the first effect of Westernization is to focus the interest of those caught in it on the overt manifestations of Western culture, such as technology and organizational know-how; that a true absorption of Western cultural patterns with their implicit ideational mainsprings takes place very rarely; and that in many cases the individual nevertheless tends to abandon his own traditional cultural values, and becomes rootless and superficial.[18] Especially younger people often suffer serious personality damage because, having acquired the external trappings and mastered the overt mannerisms of the Westerners, they feel free to throw off the traditional restraints of their old culture without having first grasped and often without even suspecting the existence of the different set of restraints invisibly controlling Western behavior patterns and directing them into morally sanctioned channels. In contacts between males and females, parents and children, teachers and pupils, elders and youths, employers and employees, the rejection of the old social forms, a seemingly unavoidable concomitant of Westernization, often means the complete disappearance of any check or constraint.

It is not hard to see why thoughtful Middle Easterners should be disquieted by these developments, and why some of them should advocate a policy of cultural isolationism. It simply amounts to rejection of the honey for fear of the bee's sting.

AMBIVALENCE

Complete rejection, however, of everything offered by Western culture is rare. It is an extreme, polar position. More frequent is an attitude that can best be described as ambivalent, as composed of both negative and positive factors. On the positive side there is the irresistible glitter of many features dangled by the West before the eyes of the Middle East. The reaction to these is a strong desire to acquire them, to imitate them, to master them, to enjoy them, and to profit by them. Hand in hand with attraction, however, goes repulsion; there is the feeling that the people who seem so ready to teach and to impart these good things are themselves not virtuous, that any or all of the following objections apply to them: they are unbelievers; they are foreigners; they wish to gain (or retain, or strengthen, or renew, as the case might be) domination over the country; their ultimate aim is exploitation; their mores and morals are undesirable. There is, in brief, the fear that if the peoples of the Middle East swallow the bait of the attractive offerings of the West, they will soon be unwittingly influenced by Western thinking, outlook, points of view, behavior, and will in the process lose their own values, individuality, ideals, concepts, which make them the true sons of their fathers and bring them honor, status, and respectability. Thus the desire to learn from the West in the material and other fields in which Western supremacy is unquestioningly acknowledged is powerfully counteracted, or at least inhibited, by the fear of being contaminated by those Western traits against whose acceptance traditional, moral, ethical, religious, emotional, and ideational scruples militate.

Few are the people in the Middle East who are consciously aware of this ambivalence in their attitude to Western values. Fewer still are those who are able to resolve the conflict created by it. In many cases one of the two contrasting attitudes gains dominance in consciousness while the other is forced back, repressed, and relegated into the subconscious where it becomes an irritating factor and a source of frustration.

Outlook

In conclusion it should be pointed out that the development of the traditional Middle East appears to have lingered for several centuries close to the beginning of that road which, according to Redfield, led precivilized human society toward its bifurcation into urban civilization and folk society.[19] Furthermore, in accordance with Redfield's generalized statement to the effect that the technical order is the destroyer of the moral order,[20] the increasing new ramifications of the technical order in the cities have made the ancient walls of the Middle Eastern moral order begin to crack and crumble. The literati of the Middle Eastern urban society have viewed this breakdown of their highly prized moral order under the impact of Westernization with understandable alarm, and have issued impassioned pleas for resistance. It is difficult to foretell what the results of these efforts will be, especially in view of the fact that the growing "intelligentsia," as Toynbee calls those members of the native community who "have learned the tricks of the intrusive civilization,"[21] exerts a powerful pull in the direction of Westernization. But certain signs indicate that the Middle Eastern developments will bear out the correctness of Redfield's observation that "the effects of the technical order (also) include the creation of new moral orders."[22] This constructive and recreative effect of the introduction of a new technical order lags behind its immediate effect, which is destructive, but its manifestations are becoming more and more evident each day, and in them lies the justification for looking with confidence towards the cultural future of the Middle East.

As to the future relationship between the Middle East and the Western world, the experience of the last two decades has shown that economical aid and technical assistance, though important and even imperative, are in themselves not sufficient to make for understanding and cooperation between peoples belonging to two different cultures. Aid offered on the basis of what is important and desirable in Western culture can meet with conditional or grudging acceptance or even forthright refusal by people sharing a different culture and having therefore a different scale of values. The air lift organized by the U.S. Air Force a few years ago to

help thousands of pilgrims reach Mecca in time and thus fulfill a
lifelong dream undoubtedly did more to create among the peoples
of the Middle East an appreciation of the sincerity of America's
attitude towards them than millions of dollars of economic aid
could have done.

In order properly to evaluate what Middle Eastern culture will
willingly accept from the embarrassingly rich storehouses of
Western civilization, a better and sounder understanding of
Middle Eastern culture must first be acquired. The same prerequisite is necessary in order to gauge the probable effects of
newly introduced traits on the cultural context of tradition-
directed peoples. Also, the ways and means in which new cultural
offerings can be made palatable must be studied much more
thoroughly than was hitherto the case. In brief the only way in
which the Gordian knot of resistance to Westernization in the
Middle East can be unraveled is that of studying the Middle East,
of obtaining a fuller picture of its traditional culture, a better
understanding of the processes of change taking place in it at
present, and a deeper insight into the psychology of human groups
brought up in Middle Eastern culture. The task is taxing, but the
prize, harmony between the West and a neighboring world area
of crucial importance, is well worth it.

Notes

CHAPTER 1—

1. The latest and best cartographic representation of this basic trichotomy of the Old World can be found in the *Atlas International Larousse*, 1950, p. 23A.

2. M. J. Herskovits, "The Culture Areas of Africa," *Africa*, Vol. III, London, 1931; *idem.*, *Backgrounds of African Art*, Denver, 1945; *idem.*, *Man and His Works*, New York, 1948, pp. 190–93; G. P. Murdock, *Africa: Its Peoples and Their Culture History*, New York, 1959; E. Bacon and A. E. Hudson, "Asia (Ethnology)," *Encyclopaedia Britannica*, 1945, Vol. II, pp. 523–25; E. Bacon, "A Preliminary Attempt to Determine the Culture Areas of Asia," *Southwestern Journal of Anthropology*, 1946, II: 117–32; W. Schmidt and W. Koppers, *Voelker und Kulturen*, Regensburg, 1924.

3. This delimitation is at variance with the presently accepted one. Generally, only the Asiatic part of this area plus Egypt is regarded as the Middle East or the Near East. Cf., for example, R. Linton (ed.), *Most of the World*, New York, 1949, where a separate article deals with the Near East and another with North Africa. W. B. Fisher, in his recent geography of the Middle East (*The Middle East: A Physical, Social and Regional Geography*, London and New York, 1950), includes also Cyrenaica in addition to the above in the Middle East.

4. Clark Wissler, *The American Indian*, New York, 1922, pp. 217–57.

5. The expression is taken from the title of Gertrude Bell's well-known book, *Syria: the Desert and the Sown*, London, 1907.

6. R. Patai, "Nomadism: Middle Eastern and Central Asian," *Southwestern Journal of Anthropology*, 1951, Winter.

7. Feilberg, *La Tente Noire*, Copenhagen, 1944; Patai, "Nomadism."

8. A similar comparison between each significant culture trait discerned as characteristic of the Middle Eastern culture continent and the equivalent elements in the contiguous culture continents of Europe, Africa, Central Asia, and India, would be highly desirable.

9. R. Patai, "Musha'a Tenure and Cooperation in Palestine," *American Anthropologist*, 1949, Vol. 51, No. 3; Fisher, *The Middle East*, pp. 180–81.

10. R. Maunier, *The Sociology of Colonies*, London, 1949, Vol. II, 613–35.

11. This brief description could make no allowance for local variations, of which there are many.

12. Edith Gerson-Kiwi, "The Musicians of the Orient," *Edoth: A Quarterly for Folklore and Ethnology*, Jerusalem, 1946, Vol. I, pp. 227–33.

13. Jacob, M. Landau, "Shadow Plays in the Near East," *Edoth*, 1947, Vol. III, pp. xxiii–cliv; *idem.*, *Studies in the Arab Theater and Cinema*, Philadelphia, 1958, pp. 9–47.

14. In Arabic: *arkān ad-dīn*. The five pillars of the faith are: confession of the faith (*shahāda*), pilgrimage to Mecca (*ḥajj*), legal alms (*zakāt*), daily prayers (*ṣalāt*), and fasting in the month of Ramadhan (*ṣawm*).

CHAPTER 2—

1. Cf. Ruth Benedict, *Patterns of Culture*, Boston and New York, 1934, p. 230.

2. M. J. Herskovits, *Man and His Works*, New York, 1948, p. 199.

3. Franz Boas, *General Anthropology*, New York, 1938, p. 671.

4. A. L. Kroeber, in *Encyclopaedia of Social Sciences*, Vol. IV, pp. 646–47.

5. Cf. Clark Wissler, *The American Indian*, New York, 1922, pp. 217–57.

6. Clark Wissler, *The Relation of Nature to Man in Aboriginal America*, New York, 1926, p. xv.

7. Kroeber, *loc. cit.*

8. These differences are treated in greater detail in R. Patai's "Nomadism: Middle Eastern and Central Asian," *Southwestern Journal of Anthropology*, Vol. 7, No. 4, Winter 1951, pp. 401–14.

9. Cf. Tor Irstam, *The King of Ganda: Studies in the Institutions of Sacral Kingship in Africa*, The Ethnographical Museum of Sweden, Stockholm, New Series, Publ. No. 8, 1944; Raphael Patai, "Hebrew Installation Rites," *Hebrew Union College Annual*, Cincinnati, 1947 (Vol. xx), pp. 143–225; *idem.*, *Man and Temple in Ancient Jewish Myth and Ritual*, Edinburgh, 1947, p. 207.

10. Cf. K. G. Lindblom, "Spears with Two or More Heads Particularly in Africa," *Essays Presented to C. G. Seligman*, London, 1934, pp. 149–81, 175–77.

11. Cf. Robert Hartman, *Les Peuples de l'Afrique*, Paris, 1886 (?), p. 165, with two figures on p. 164; C. G. Seligman, *Egypt and Negro Africa*, London, 1934, pp. 12, 63–65, with pictures; C. K. Meek, *A Sudanese Kingdom*, London, 1931, p. 458.

12. Cf. Sir James George Frazer, *Folk Lore in the Old Testament*, London, 1919, Vol. I, pp. 52–65.

13. Cf. Hans Abrahamsson, *The Origin of Death, Studies in African Mythology*, Uppsala, 1951.

14. G. P. Murdock, *Africa: Its Peoples and Their Culture History*, New York, 1959, pp. 71, 223, 272, 315.

15. Cf. R. Patai, "Nomadism: Middle Eastern and Central Asian," *Southwestern Journal of Anthropology*, Vol. 7, pp. 401–11.

16. Cf. A. de Préville, *Les sociétés africaines: leur origine, leur évolution—leur avenir*, Paris, 1894.

17. Cf. Jerome Dowd, *The Negro Races*, Vol. I, New York, 1907.

18. *American Anthropologist*, Vol. xxvi, pp. 50–63.

19. New York, 1948, p. 191, and subsequent editions.

20. Cf. M. J. Herskovits, *Backgrounds of African Art*, Denver, 1945, pp. 15 ff.

21. Herskovits, *Man and His Works, op. cit.*, p. 192.

22. Cf. *Africa: Journal of the International Institute of African Languages and Cultures*, London, Vol. 2, 1929, pp. 221–43, 352–78.

23. Field Museum of Natural History, Anthropological Series, Vol. 26, Chicago, 1937, pp. 325 ff.

24. New York, 1959.

25. See Chapter 3 "The Desert and the Sown."

26. Wissler, *The American Indian, op. cit.*, pp. 217–57; A. L. Kroeber, *Anthropology*, New York, 1923, pp. 335–39.

27. Cf. Henry Ayrout, *Fellahs d'Egypte*, Cairo, 1952, p. 171.

28. Max v. Oppenheim, *Die Beduinen*, 3 volumes, Leipzig, 1939—Wiesbaden, 1952.

29. Cf. R. Maunier, *The Sociology of Colonies*, London, 1949, II: 634.

30. E. F. Gautier, *Le Sahara*, Paris, 1928, pp. 209 ff.; C. G. Seligman, *Races of Africa*, London, 1930, pp. 142, 146–52; C. G. Feilberg, *La Tente Noire*, Copenhagen, 1944, p. 144; J. Greenberg, *The Influence of Islam on a Sudanese Religion*, New York, 1946, pp. 1–2; R. Patai, "Nomadism."

31. Murdock, *Africa, op. cit.*, pp. 14, 129; Joseph H. Greenberg, *Studies in African Linguistic Classification*, New Haven, 1955.

32. A. Vámbéry, *Skizzen aus Mittelasien*, Leipzig, 1868; *idem., Encyclopaedia of Religion and Ethics*, VIII: 888.

CHAPTER 3—

1. Cf. W. F. Albright, *From the Stone Age to Christianity*, Baltimore, 1940, pp. 120–21.

2. Genesis 13: 6. Cf. v. 2.

3. Albright, *op. cit.*, p. 121.

4. See below, Chapter 7, "Dual Organization."

5. E. Chiera, *Sumarian Religious Texts*, 1924, pp. 20 f.

6. Alec Kirkbride, "Changes in Tribal Life in Trans-Jordan," *MAN* March–April, 1945, No. 23, London.

7. K. S. Twitchell, *Saudi Arabia*, Princeton, 1953, pp. 47 ff., 171 ff. Ameen Rihani, *Ibn Saud of Arabia, His People and His Land*, London, 1928. Cf. also Dwight Sanderson, *The Rural Community*, 1932, Chapters 2 and 3, on transition from the nomadic tribe to the subagricultural state.

8. Jeremiah 35: 1–10.

9. Jeremiah 2: 2.

10. Joseph Braslawski, "The Composition of the Bedouin Tribes of the Negev," *Edoth, A Quarterly for Folklore and Ethnology*, ed. Raphael Patai and Joseph Rivlin, Jerusalem, 1946, Vol. 1, No. 2, in Hebrew with English summary.

11. *Op. cit.*, p. 95.

12. Cf. C. S. Jarvis, "Southern Palestine and Its Possibilities for Settlement," *Journal of the Royal Central Asian Society*, Vol. xxv, Jan. 1938, p. 205.

CHAPTER 4—

1. Charles W. Churchill, *The City of Beirut: A Socio-economic Survey*, Beirut, 1954, p. 4.

2. Hashemite Kingdom of Jordan, *1952 Census of Housing*.

3. Lebanese Ministry of National Economy, *Kasmie Rural Improvement Project*, Beirut, 1953, p. 8.

4. Government of Palestine, "Survey of Social and Economic Conditions in Arab Villages," *General Monthly Bulletin of Current Statistics*, 1945, p. 432.

5. Bryan Clarke, *Berber Village*, London, 1959, pp. 75–76.

6. Francis R. Rodd, *The People of the Veil*, London, 1926, pp. 148, 150; cf. 136.

7. Rom Landau, *Moroccan Journal*, London [1952], p. 55.

8. Gerald de Gaury, *Arabian Journey and Other Desert Travels*, London, 1950, p. 92.

9. Survey 1945: 435.

10. Ilse Lichtenstaedter, "An Arab-Egyptian Family," *The Middle East Journal*, Vol. 6, No. 4, Autumn 1952, p. 382.

11. Survey 1945: 436

12. Ian D. Suttie, *The Origins of Love and Hate*, New York, 1952, p. 105.

13. Lichtenstaedter, *op. cit.*, p. 385.

14. Koran 60: 10; Cf. Reuben Levy, *The Social Structure of Islam*, Cambridge, 1957, p. 103.

15. Cf. Fulanain, *The Marsh Arab*, Philadelphia, 1928, pp. 251–73.

16. Bräunlich, "Zur Gesellschaftsordnung der heutigen Beduinen," *Islamica*, Vol. vi, 1934, pp. 186–87.

17. Alois Musil, *Manners and Customs of the Rwala Bedouins*, New York, 1928, pp. 136–37, 139.

18. H. R. P. Dickson, *The Arab of the Desert*, London, 1949, pp. 140–41, 602–3.

19. Bertram Thomas, *Arabia Felix*, New York, 1932, p. 67; cf. G. Wyman Bury, *The Land of Uz*, London, 1911, p. 278.

20. A. C. Jewett, *An American Engineer in Afghanistan*, Minneapolis, 1948, p. 262.

21. Horace Miner, *The Primitive City of Timbuctoo*, Princeton, 1953, p. 180.

22. G. Wyman Bury, *op. cit.*, p. 278.

23. Hilma Granqvist, *Marriage Conditions in a Palestinian Village*, Helsingfors, 1931–35.

24. W. E. Lane, *Manners and Customs of the Modern Egyptians*, Everyman's Library, London–New York, Chap. xiii, p. 301.

25. Lichtenstaedter, *op. cit.*, p. 387.

26. Weulersse, *Paysans de Syrie et du Proche-Orient*, Paris, 1946, p. 221.

27. Kazem Daghestani, *Etude sociologique sur la famille Musulmane contemporaine en Syrie*, Paris, 1932, pp. 21–22; cf. below, Chapter 6, Cousin Marriage.

28. Burckhardt, *Arabic Proverbs*, London, 1830, p. 118.

29. *Encyclopaedia of Islam* (old edition), s.v. Arabia.

30. Bertram Thomas, *Arabia Felix*, New York, 1932, p. 97.

31. William S. Haas, *Iran*, New York, 1946, p. 58.

32. *Encyclopaedia of Islam* (old edition), s.v. Berbers.

32a. Lloyd Cabot Briggs, *Tribes of the Sahara*, Cambridge: Harvard University Press, 1960, p. 174.

33. Survey 1945: 443.

34. Cf. Survey of the Khiss-Finn Camp. U.N. Doc. No. ME/3S/20.

35. Cf. Abbas M. Ammar, *A Demographic Study of an Egyptian Province (Sharqiya)*, London, 1942, p. 36.

36. Churchill, *op. cit.*, p. 5.

37. Alois Musil, *Arabia Petraea*, Wien, 1908, Vol. III, p. 207; *idem.*, *Manners and Customs of the Rwala Bedouins*, p. 230. Cf. the story of Rachel, Leah, and the mandrakes, Genesis 30:14; cf. R. Patai, *Sex and Family in the Bible and the Middle East*, New York, 1959, pp. 43 ff.

38. Michel Feghali, "La famille Catholique au Liban," *Revue d'Ethnographie*, Paris, 1925, pp. 291 f.

39. Kingsley Davis, *Human Society*, New York, 1949, p. 51.

40. Sania Hamady, *Temperament and Character of the Arabs*, New York, 1960, pp. 28, 94.

41. Gertrude Joly, "The Woman of the Lebanon," *Journal of the Royal Central Asian Society*, Vol. 38, 1951, pp. 17 ff.

42. Kasmie 1953: 25.

43. Feghali, *op. cit.*, 292 f.

44. Survey 1945: 441.

45. *United Nations Demographic Yearbook*, 1958, pp. 321 ff. The marriage rates, that is, the number of marriages registered annually per 1,000 population, cannot serve as a basis of comparison. In the United States the marriage rate in 1957 was 8.9; in Jordan, 1957, 11.5; in Aden Colony, 1950, 16.1. In other Middle Eastern countries they are lower than in the United States: in Iraq, for example, as low as 3.8 in 1955, which only shows how incomplete is the registration of marriages, just as that of births and deaths. Cf. *loc. cit.*

46. U.N. Economic and Social Council Document No. E/CN.9/82, 24 April 1951.

47. *U.N. Demographic Yearbook* 1949–50.

48. Ammar, *op. cit.*, I:257.

49. Churchill, *op. cit.*

50. Survey 1945:440.

51. H. R. P. Dickson, *Kuwait and Her Neighbors*, London, 1956, pp. 84–86.

52. Survey 1945:442–43.

53. *U.N. Demographic Yearbook*, 1958, pp. 472 ff.

54. *Arab Women's Congress in Cairo 1944*:320.

55. Antonin Jaussen, *Coutumes Arab au Pays de Moab*, Paris, 1908, p. 20; Victor Muller, *En Syrie avec les Bedouins: Les Tribus du Désert*, Paris, 1931, p. 270.

56. A. H. Hourani, *Syria and Lebanon: A Political Essay*, London, 1946, p. 92.

57. Sources: *United Nations Demographic Yearbook* 1949–50, 1958; *Statistical Abstract of Palestine*, 1942, 1944–45.

58. U.N. Social Welfare Seminar, Cairo 1950:298.

59. Nadel, *The Nuba*, Oxford University Press, 1949.

60. United Nations General Assembly. Information from Non-Self-Governing Territories, Doc. No. A/1269, 20 July, 1950.

61. Cf. R. P. Davies, "Syrian Arabic Kinship Terms," *Southwestern Journal of Anthropology*, Vol. 5, 1949, pp. 244–52.

CHAPTER 5—

1. M. E. Hume-Griffith, *Behind the Veil in Persia and Turkish Arabia*, London, 1909, pp. 96–97.

2. Eleanor Bisbee, *The New Turks*, Philadelphia, 1951, pp. 23–24, 31.

3. Jewett, *Afghanistan*, p. 48.

4. For example, among the Copts in Egypt, Cf. Lane, *The Manners and Customs of the Modern Egyptians*, Everyman's Library, 537; C. B. Klunzinger, *Upper Egypt: Its People and Its Products*, London, 1878, p. 90; S. H. Leeder, *Modern Sons of the Pharaohs*, London (ca. 1918), p. 21. Among the Christian Arabs of Palestine and Syria, cf. F. J. Bliss, *The Religions of Modern Syria and Palestine*, New York, 1912, p. 284, note 1. Among the Jews in Egypt, cf. Lane, *op. cit.*, p. 559.

5. Bisbee, *op. cit.*, p. 37.

6. E.g. In Dhahran in Saudi Arabia, Cf. H. St. J. Philby, *Arabian Highlands*, New York, 1952, p. 389; Egypt: Lane, *op. cit.*, p. 561.

7. Cf. Sources adduced by Josef Henninger, "Die Familie bei den heutigen Beduinen," *Internationales Archiv für Ethnographie*, Leyden, 1943, Vol. 42, pp. 94–95.

8. *Ibid.*, p. 94.

9. *Ibid.*, p. 95.

10. The writer's observations in Palestine.

11. Henninger, *op. cit.*, p. 95; *Encyclopaedia of Islam* (old ed.), s.v. litham.

12. Klunzinger, *op. cit.*, pp. 41, 122; Winifred Blackman, *The Fellahin of Upper Egypt*, London, 1927, pp. 59–60; Ayrout, *Fellahs d'Egypte, op. cit.*, p. 99.

13. Rodd, *The People of the Veil, op. cit.*, p. 67.

14. Alois Musil, *Manners and Customs of the Rwala Bedouins*, New York, 1928, pp. 122–124.

15. H. R. P. Dickson, *The Arab of the Desert*, London, 1949, p. 155.

16. Dickson, *op. cit.*, pp. 154–55.

17. Charles M. Doughty, *Travels in Arabia Deserta*, Cambridge, 1888, I: 336.

18. G. Wyman Bury, *The Land of Uz*, London, 1911, pp. 198–99.

19. Freya Stark, *The Southern Gates of Arabia*, New York, 1936, p. 136.

20. H. St.-J. B. Philby, *Sheba's Daughters*, London, 1939, p. 211.

21. Bury, *op. cit.*, pp. 189–90; Stark, *op. cit.*, picture opp. p. 226.

22. Philby, *op. cit.*, p. 410.

23. Bertram Thomas, *Alarms and Excursions in Arabia*, p. 151.

24. Bertram Thomas, *Arabia Felix*, New York, 1932, p. 227.

25. George Haddad, *Fifty Years of Modern Syria and Lebanon*, Beirut, 1950, p. 198.

26. Leeder, *op. cit.*, pp. 21–22.

27. Donald N. Wilber, *Iran, Past and Present*, Princeton, 1955, p. 218.

28. Bisbee, *op. cit.*, pp. 23–24.

29. Doughty, *Arabia Deserta*, I: 350, 367.

30. E.g., Teyma, cf. Doughty, *op. cit.*, I: 336.

31. Philby, *op. cit.*, pp. 79, 211.

32. Musil, *Rwala*, p. 232.

33. Cf. Doughty, *op. cit.*, I: 365.

34. *Voyages d'Ibn Batouta*, ed. Defremery, Vol. iv, pp. 388 ff.

35. Musil, *Rwala*, p. 240; Philby, *Sheba's Daughters*, p. 356.

36. Lane, *Modern Egyptians*, Chap. iv, p. 184.

37. *Ibid.*, Chap. xxiv, p. 435–37.

38. Cf. A. M. Hasanein, *The Lost Oases*, London, 1925, p. 101, as quoted by Levy, *The Social Structure of Islam*, p. 109.

39. Cf. Walter Cline, *Notes on the People of Siwah and El Garah in the Libyan Desert*, General Series in Anthropology, No. 4, Menasha, Wis., 1936, pp. 42–43.

40. Cf. Patai, *Sex and Family*, *op. cit.*, pp. 138 ff.

41. Rodd, *People of the Veil*, *op. cit.*, pp. 173–75.

42. Cf. Henri Lhote, *Les Touaregs du Hoggar (Ahaggar)*, Paris, 1944, pp. 288–94; cf. Count Byron Khun de Prorok, *In Quest of Lost Worlds*, New York, 1935, pp. 45–46.

42a. Lloyd Cabot Briggs, *Tribes of the Sahara*, Cambridge: Harvard University Press, 1960, pp. 220–21.

43. Horace Miner, *The Primitive City of Timbuctoo*, pp. 176–77, 192.

44. William S. Haas, *Iran*, New York, 1946, p. 58.

45. Gertrude Joly, "The Woman of the Lebanon," *Journal of the Royal Central Asian Society*, Vol. 38, 1951, pp. 179 ff.

46. "Arab Women's Congress in Cairo 1944," *Moslem World*, 1945, p. 322.

47. Feghali, "La famille Catholique au Liban," *op. cit.*, pp. 292 ff.

48. B. Yebamot 37*b*; B. Yoma 18*b*.

49. *Kitāb al-Aghāni*, VII, 18; as quoted by Reuben Levy, *The Social Structure of Islam*, Cambridge, 1957, p. 116.

50. *Muslim's Collection of Traditions with Nawawi's Commentary*, III, 309–14; as quoted by G. A. Wilken, *Das Matriarchat (Das Mutterrecht) bei den alten Araben*, Leipzig, 1884, pp. 11–14.

51. Cf. Count Carlo Landberg, *Etudes sur les dialectes de l'Arabie méridionale*, Leiden, 1909, II/2, p. 935.

52. Cf. Ignaz Goldziher, *Die Richtungen der Islamischen Koranauslegung*, Leyden, 1920, p. 13.

53. Cf. Wilken, *op. cit.*, pp. 23, 25.

54. Hamilton, *New Account of the East Indies*, I: 52–53 (about Ṣanʿa, capital of Yemen); Guarmani, *Neged*, 113–16; Alois Musil, *The Northern Nejd*, New York, 1928, pp. 85, 253; Snouck Hurgronje, *Mekka*, 11: 109 f.; Heffening, *Encyclopedia of Islam* (old ed.), III: 838*a*; Henninger, "Familie," p. 47; G.-H. Bousquet, *La morale de l'Islam et son ethique sexuelle*, Paris, 1953, p. 104.

55. Lane, *Modern Egyptians*, p. 384.

56. Harold Ingrams, *Geographical Journal*, Vol. 88 (1936), p. 537.

57. Arminius Vámbéry, *Meine Wanderungen . . . in Persien*, Pesth, 1867, p. 71; Dr. A. M. Djamdudi Djahausouzi, *Les Pelerinages de l'Islam Schiite*, Paris, 1930, p. 85; G.-H. Bousquet, *op. cit.*, pp. 103–4; S. G. W. Benjamin, *Persia and the Persians*, London, 1887, pp. 451–53; Marie Anastase, "La Femme du désert autrefois et aujourd'hui," *Anthropos*, Vol. 3 (1908), p. 186.

58. Reuben Levey, *The Social Structure of Islam*, Cambridge, 1957, p. 117, and sources there, in Notes 1 and 2.

59. *U.N. Demographic Yearbook* 1949–50, p. 254; *Census of Palestine* 1931.

60. *U.N. Demographic Yearbook* 1949–50.

61. Cf. "Conditions of Work in Syria and Lebanon," *International Labour Review*, April, 1939, p. 513, as quoted in ILO Regional Meeting for the Near and Middle East, Cairo, Nov. 1947, *Report on Protection of Industrial and Commercial Workers*, p. 21.

62. Cf. ILO Report of Regional Meeting for the Near and Middle East, Cairo, 1947, p. 32.

63. Widad Sakakini, "The Evolution of Syrian Women," *United Asia*, Bombay, May–June, 1949, Vol. I, pp. 531 ff.

64. "Arab Women's Congress in Cairo 1944," 316 ff.

65. "Arab Women's Congress in Cairo 1944," 320.

66. Joly, *op. cit.*, p. 178.

CHAPTER 6—

1. Cf. Gait, *Census of India, 1911*, Vol. I (India) Report, pp. 252, 256; Matin uz-Zaman Khan, *Census of India, 1911*, Vol. XX (Kashmir), Report, p. 139; quoted after E. Westermarck, *History of Human Marriage*, Vol. II, p. 71.

2. Cf. Sibree, *The Great African Island*, p. 248; Grandidier, *Ethnographie de Madagascar*, Vol. II, p. 167.

3. Cf. Sibree, *Journal of the Royal Anthropological Institute* IX (1880), p. 50; quoted after Brenda Z. Seligman, "Studies in Semitic Kinship," *Bulletin of the School of Oriental Studies* III (1923–25), pp. 277–78.

4. G. McCall Theal, *The Yellow and Dark-Skinned People of Africa South of the Zambesi*, London, 1910, p. 219; idem., *History of the Boers in South Africa*, pp. 16 ff., quoted after Westermarck, *op. cit.*, Vol. II, p. 71.

5. Cf. Westermarck, *op. cit.*, Vol. II, pp. 71–81.

6. Ayrton, Curelly, and Weigall, *Abydos*, III: 44; Pausanias, *Descriptio Graeciae*, I, 7, 1; Johannes Nietzold, *Die Ehe in Ägypten zur Ptolemaisch-Römischen Zeit*, Leipzig, 1903, pp. 12 ff.; Hastings, *Encyclopaedia of Religion and Ethics*, VIII: 444; Erman, *Life in Ancient Egypt*, p. 153; Westermarck, *op. cit.*, Vol. II, p. 91.

7. Nietzold, *op. cit.*, pp. 12 ff.; Erman, *op. cit.*, p. 153; Griffith, in Hastings, *Encyclopaedia of Religion and Ethics*, VIII: 444.

8. Cf. Nietzold, *op. cit.*, p. 14, and Song of Solomon 4:9.

9. In the royal family after the time of Cambyses, cf. Herodotus III: 31; Spiegel, *Eranische Altertumskunde* III: 678 f.; otherwise: Rapp, *Zeitschrift der deutschen morgenländischen Gesellschaft* XX: 112 f.; Hubschmann, *ibid.*, XLIII: 308 ff.; Gray, in Hastings, *Enclyclopaedia of Religion and Ethics* VIII: 457; Westermarck, *op. cit.*, Vol. II, p. 86.

10. Darab Dastur Peshotan Sunjana, *Next-of-kin Marriages in Old Iran*, p. 16 ff. and *passim*; Westermarck, *op. cit.*, Vol. II, p. 87.

11. West, *Sacred Books of the East*, XVIII: 427 f.; Moulton, *Early Zoroastrianism*, p. 207; Westermarck, *op. cit.*, Vol. II, p. 87.

12. Darab Dastur, *op. cit.*, p. 45; Westermarck, *op. cit.*, Vol. II, p. 89.

13. William Robertson Smith, *Kinship and Marriage in Early Arabia*, p. 163.

14. Cf. R. Patai, *Sex and Family*, *op. cit.*, pp. 23 ff.

15. Robertson Smith, *op. cit.*, p. 192, and also pp. 82, 138, 164, 285; Wellhausen, *Nachrichten der königlichen Gesellschaft der Wissenschaften*, Göttingen, 1893, No. 11, pp. 436 f.; Wilken, *Das Matriarchat bei den alten Arabern*, p. 59.

16. Krauss, *Sitte und Brauch der Südslaven*, pp. 221 f., quoted after Westermarck, *op. cit.*, Vol. II, p. 97.

17. Reuben Levy, *The Social Structure of Islam*, Cambridge, 1957, pp. 102 f.

18. Cf. Bruno Meissner, "Neuarabische Geschichten aus dem Iraq," *Beiträge zur Assyriologie*, Vol. v (1906), pp. 48–51; idem., "Neuarabische

Gedichte aus dem Iraq." *Mitteilungen des Seminars für Orientalische Sprachen zu Berlin*, Vol. V, 2 (1902), p. 101; Enno Littman, "Märchen und Legenden aus der Syrisch-Arabischen Wüste," *Nachrichten von der königl. Gesellschaft der Wissenschaften und der Georg-August Universität zu Göttingen*, 1915, pp. 4–17; Schmidt und Kahle, *Volkserzählungen aus Palästina*, Vol. I, Göttingen, 1918, pp. 126–35, 158–61, 200, 203, 204 f.; Vol. II, Göttingen, 1930, pp. 72, 77, 95, 195; E. S. Stevens, *Folk Tales of Iraq*, Oxford–London, 1931, pp. 194, 233; T. Ashkenazi, *Tribus Semi-Nomades de la Palestine du Nord*, Paris, 1938, pp. 57 ff.; Leo Haefeli, *Die Beduinen von Beerseba*, Luzern, 1938, p. 106.

19. Eleanor Bisbee, *The New Turks*, Philadelphia, 1951, p. 41.

20. Among the Mandaeans of Iraq and Iran, cf. E. S. Drover, *The Mandaeans of Iraq and Iran*, Oxford, 1937, p. 59: "Marriages between cousins are usual, and the paternal cousin is preferred to the maternal cousin." In southern Arabia, cf. Landberg, *Etudes, op. cit.*, II/2 : 841 f.; Bent, *Southern Arabia*, London, 1900, p. 144. Among the Kababish, Beni Amer, and Hadendowa of Upper Egypt and the Sudan, cf. Brenda Z. Seligman, "Studies in Semitic Kinship," *op. cit.*, pp. 268, 279.

21. Ella C. Sykes, *Persia and Its Peoples*, New York, 1910, p. 201; cf. also idem., "Persian Family Life," *Journal of the Royal Central Asian Society*, 1914, Pt. I, p. 7.

22. *'Aqd dukhtar 'amu wapesar 'amu ra dar behesht basta and;* communicated by a Persian student in Philadelphia to Mr. William Stockton, Jr., to whom the author is indebted for it.

23. C. Colliver Rice, *Persian Women and Their Ways*, London, 1923, p. 68; cf. Bess Allen Donaldson, *The Wild Rue*, London, 1938, p. 48: "Marriage between cousins is common." Cf. also Henri Massé, *Persian Beliefs and Customs*, New Haven, 1954, pp. 40–41: "Unions between cousins are quite frequent in the upper classes."

24. H. N. Hutchinson, *Marriage Customs in Many Lands*, New York, 1897, p. 67.

25. Ernest F. Fox, *Travels in Afghanistan, 1937–1938*, New York, 1943, p. 195.

26. Lane, *Modern Egyptians*, pp. 161–62.

27. Ilse Lichtenstadter, "An Arab-Egyptian Family," *The Middle East Journal*, Vol. 6, No. 4, Autumn 1952, p. 387.

28. Winifred Blackman, *The Fellahin of Upper Egypt*, London, 1927, p. 37.

29. C. G. and Brenda Z. Seligman, *The Kababish, A Sudan Arab Tribe*, Harvard African Studies, II, Cambridge, Mass., 1918, p. 131.

30. Oral information supplied by my Coptic student Mr. Fawzi Fahim Gadallah. Cf. also C. B. Klunzinger, *Upper Egypt*, London, 1878, p. 90; Brenda Z. Seligman, *op. cit.*, p. 276.

31. Cf. Walter Cline, *Notes on the People of Siwah and el Garah in the Libyan Desert*, General Series in Anthropology (ed. Leslie Spier), No. 4, Menasha, Wis., 1936, p. 46.

32. Adolf Erman und Hermann Ranke, *Aegypten und aegyptisches Leben im Altertum*, Tübingen, 1923, p. 180.

33. Cf. Gertrude H. Stern, *Marriage in Early Islam*, James G. Forlong Fund Vol. xviii, The Royal Asiatic Society, London, 1939, pp. 60, 65–66, 172, 177–78.

34. Henry Ayrout, *Fellahs d'Egypte, op. cit.*, p. 143.

35. Klunzinger, *Upper Egypt, op. cit.,* p. 196.

36. Georges Legrain, *Une Famille Copte de Haute Egypte,* Brussels, 1945, pp. 33–39.

37. Fredrik Barth, *Principles of Social Organization in Southern Kurdistan,* Oslo, 1954, p. 68.

38. Fredrik Barth, "Father's Brother's Daughter Marriage in Kurdistan," *Southwestern Journal of Anthropology,* Vol. 10, 1954, p. 167.

39. Hilma Granqvist, *Marriage Conditions in a Palestinian Village,* Helsingfors, 1931, Vol. I, pp. 82–83, 192–95.

39a. Horace M. Miner and George de Vos, *Oasis and Casbah: African Culture and Personality in Change,* Ann Arbor: University of Michigan, 1960, pp. 37, 43, 57, 61; Lloyd Cabot Briggs, *Tribes of the Sahara,* Cambridge, Harvard Univ. Press, 1960, pp. 86, 91, 198, 220.

40. Horace Miner, *The Primitive City of Timbuctoo,* Princeton, 1953, pp. 143–44.

41. *Ibid.,* p. 154.

42. Cf. for example Lane, *Modern Egyptians, op. cit.,* p. 166.

43. Ilse Lichtenstadter, *op. cit.,* p. 388.

44. Ayrout, *op. cit.,* p. 144.

45. Cf. John Lewis Burckhardt, *Notes on the Bedouins and Wahabys,* London, 1830, p. 154; Kazem Daghestani, *Etude sociologique sur la famille Musulmane contemporaine en Syrie,* Paris, 1932, p. 22.

46. Alois Musil, *Manners and Customs of the Rwala Bedouins,* New York, 1928, pp. 444–45; Cf. also Charles M. Doughty, *Travels in Arabia Deserta,* Cambridge, 1888, I : 491 (the Muwahib in northern Hijaz); P. Antonin Jaussen, *Coutumes Arabes au Pays de Moab,* Paris, 1908, pp. 46 f. (Moab in Transjordan).

47. Granqvist, *op. cit.,* I : 23–32, 69–71, 75 note 3, 122 f.; Daghestani, *op. cit.,* 22, 27; Khaled Chatila, *Le Mariage chez les Musulmans en Syrie,* Paris, 1933, pp. 184, 192.

48. Fredrik Barth, "Father's Brother's Daughter Marriage," *op. cit.,* pp. 167–71.

49. Cf. Josef Henninger, "Die Familie bei den heutigen Beduinen," *Internationales Archiv für Ethnographie,* Leiden, 1943 (Vol. 42), pp. 73 f.

50. Bertram Thomas, *Alarms and Excursions in Arabia,* London, 1931, p. 275.

51. Burckhardt, *Notes on the Bedouins and Wahabys,* London, 1830, pp. 64–65, 154. In a footnote Burckhardt refers to the Biblical parallel of Ruth 4 : 7–8.

52. Richard F. Burton, *Personal Narrative of a Pilgrimage to Al-Madinah and Meccah,* London, 1913, II : 84.

53. Doughty, *op. cit.,* I : 231, 236.

54. Lady Anne, Blunt, *A Pilgrimage to Nejd,* London, 1881, I : 42.

55. William Robertson Smith, *Lectures and Essays,* London, 1912, p. 563.

56. L. W. C. van den Berg, *Le Hadhramaut et les colonies Arabes dans l'Archipel Indien,* Batavia, 1886, p. 45; Theodore and Mrs. Bent, *Southern Arabia,* London, 1900, p. 144; Bertram Thomas, *Alarms and Excursions, op. cit.,* p. 275.

57. Bertram Thomas, *Arabia Felix, op. cit.,* p. 99.

58. Ailon Shiloh, private communication from Beit Mazmil, Israel, based on field observations among Yemenite Jewish immigrants.

59. S. D. Goitein, "Portrait of a Yemenite Weavers' Village," *Jewish Social Studies,* January 1955, p. 20.

60. Musil, *Rwala Bedouins, op. cit.*, pp. 137–140.

61. Lady Anne Blunt, *Bedouin Tribes of the Euphrates*, New York, 1879, p. 308 ; le Comte de Perthuis, *Le Désert de Syrie, l'Euphrate et la Mesopotamie*, Paris, 1896, pp. 98–102; L. Bouvat, "Le droit coutumier des tribus Bedouines de Syrie," *Revue de Monde Musulman*, Vol. 43, 1921, p. 39; Musil, *Rwala Bedouins, op. cit.*, 137.

62. Cf. J. G. Wetzstein, "Sprachliches aus den Zeltlagern der syrischen Wüste," *Zeitschrift der deutschen morgenländischen Gesellschaft*, xxii (1868), pp. 102–12; F. H. Weissbach, *Beiträge zur Kunde des Iraq-Arabischen*, Leipzig, 1908–30, pp. 41 f.; 25; Musil, *Rwala Bedouins, op. cit.*, 137 f.; *idem., Northern Negd*, New York, 1928, pp. 112 f.; Burckhardt, *Notes, op. cit.*, 64 f.; G. A. Wallin, "Probe aus einer Anthologie neuarabischer Gesänge in der Wüste gesammelt," *Zeitschrift der deutschen morgenländischen Gesellschaft*, iv, 1852, p. 125; Victor Müller, *En Syrie avec les bedouins*, Paris, 1931, p. 227.

63. Perthuis, *op. cit.*, pp. 98–102.

64. Blunt, *Bedouin Tribes of the Euphrates*, pp. 308, 322–24.

65. Alois Musil, *Arabia Deserta*, New York, 1927, p. 175.

66. *Ibid.*, p. 285.

67. *Ibid.*, p. 240.

68. Alois Musil, *Arabia Petraea*, Wien, 1908, III : 174.

69. Antonin Jaussen, *Moab, op. cit.*, pp. 45–47; Jaussen and Savignac, *Coutumes des Fuqara*, Paris, 1914, p. 24.

70. Jaussen, *Moab, op. cit.*, p. 46.

71. *Ibid.*, pp. 46–47. The case happened in the Hajāya tribe.

72. P. Marie Anastase de St. Elie, "La femme du désert autrefois et aujourd'hui," *Anthropos*, Vol. 3, pp. 186, 189.

73. Jaussen, *Moab, op. cit.*, p. 47.

74. G. Robinson Lees, *The Witness of the Wilderness*, London, 1909, p. 121.

75. Omar el-Barghuthi, "Judicial Courts among the Bedouin of Palestine," *Journal of the Palestine Oriental Society*, Vol. 2, 1922, p. 28; Antonin Jaussen, *Coutumes Palestiniennes. I. Naplouse et son district*, Paris, 1927, p. 62; T. Canaan, "Unwritten Laws Affecting the Arab Woman of Palestine," *Journal of the Palestine Oriental Society*, Vol. 11, 1931, p. 178; Granqvist, *Marriage Conditions, op. cit.*, p. 72.

76. Canaan, *op. cit.*, p. 178; Musil, *Rwala Bedouins*, p. 137.

77. Barghuthi, *op. cit.*, p. 28.

78. Jaussen, *Coutumes Palestiniennes, op. cit.*, p. 62.

79. Philip J. Baldensperger, "Women in the East," *Palestine Exploration Fund Quarterly Statement*, London, 1900, p. 181; T. Ashkenazi, *Tribus semi-nomades de la Palestine du Nord*, Paris, 1938, p. 63.

80. F. A. Klein, "Mitteilungen uber Leben, Sitten und Gebräuche der Fellachen in Palästina," *Zeitschrift des deutschen Palästina Vereins*, 1883, p. 84; Philip J. Baldensperger, *The Immovable East*, London, 1913, p. 121; Jaussen, *Coutumes Palestiniennes, op. cit.*, p. 62; Granqvist, *op. cit.*, p. 72.

81. Granqvist, *op. cit.*, pp. 67–72.

82. Enno Littmann, *Neuarabische Volkspoesie*, Berlin, 1902, pp. 32–33 (Arabic text) and 119—120 (German translation).

83. Granqvist, *op. cit.*, pp. 72–75.

84. Daghestani, *Etude, op. cit.*, pp. 21-22; Jacques Weulersse, *Paysans de Syrie et du Proche-Orient*, Paris, 1946, p. 221.

85. Daghestani, *Etude, op. cit.*, p. 22; Musil, *Arabia Petraea*, p. 174.

86. Daghestani, *op. cit.*, pp. 21-23; cf. above, p. 152.

87. Chatila, *op. cit.*, p. 93.

88. *Ibid.*, pp. 91-94; Daghestani, *op. cit.*, pp. 21-22.

89. Leonard Bauer, *Volksleben im Lande der Bibel*, Leipzig, 1903, p. 98 ; Jaussen, *Coutumes Palestiniennes, op. cit.*, p. 66; Daghestani, *op. cit.*, pp. 18, 19, 173.

90. Daghestani, *op. cit.*, pp. 20, 23, 24, 32, 173; J. Castagné, "Le mouvement d'émancipation de la femme musulmane en Orient," *Revue de Monde Musulman*, Vol. 43, 1921, p. 261.

91. H. R. P. Dickson, *The Arab of the Desert, op. cit.*, p. 140; cf. also George L. Harris (ed.), *Iraq: Its People, Its Society, Its Culture*, New Haven, 1958, pp. 272 f.

92. Bruno Meissner, "Neuarabische Geschichten aus dem Iraq," *Beiträge zur Assyriologie*, Vol. 5, 1906, pp. 48-49, 74-75.

93. Jacob M. Landau, Private written communication from Jerusalem, based on field work.

94. John B. Glubb, "The Bedouins of Northern Iraq," *Journal of the Royal Central Asian Society*, London, Vol. 22, 1935, p. 24.

95. H. R. P. Dickson, *Kuwait and Her Neighbours*, London, 1956, pp. 228-235.

96. W. R. Hay, *Two Years in Kurdistan*, London, 1921, p. 45.

97. Barth, "Father's Brother's Daughter Marriage," pp. 167, 169; *idem., Principles of Social Organization in Southern Kurdistan*, p. 26.

98. Hay, *op. cit.*, pp. 71-72.

99. Hellmut Ritter, "Aserbeidschanische Texte zur nordpersischen Volkskunde," *Der Islam*, Vol. 11, 1921, p. 185 (Turcic text) and 198 (German translation).

100. C. G. Feilberg, *Les Papis*, Copenhagen, 1952, p. 136.

101. Burckhardt, *op. cit.*, pp. 154-55.

102. G. W. Murray, *Sons of Ishmael: A Study of the Egyptian Bedouin*, London, 1935, pp. 179-80.

103. Charles G. and Brenda Z. Seligman, *The Kababish*, p. 81.

104. *Ibid.*, p. 131; Brenda Z. Seligman, *op. cit.*, pp. 269-70.

105. Edward Westermarck, *Marriage Ceremonies in Morocco*, London, 1914, p. 53.

106. Cf. Major A. J. Tremearne, *The Ban of the Bori*, London, n.d. [1914], p. 121.

107. Dozy (ed.), *Commentaire historique sur le poème d'Ibn 'Abdan*, pp. 27, 29, as quoted by I. Goldziher, "Endogamy and Polygamy among the Arabs," *The Academy*, London, July 10, 1880, p. 26.

108. Cf. Julius Wellhausen, *Nachrichten der königl. Gesellschaft der Wissenschaften zu Göttingen*, 1893, No. 11, pp. 437 f.

109. *Kitāb al-'Aghāni*, ed. Bulaq, viii : 113, as quoted by I. Goldziher, *op. cit.*

110. E. W. Lane, *Arabian Society in the Middle Ages*, London, 1883, p. 227.

111. Lane, *Modern Egyptians, op. cit.*, pp. 161-62.

112. Chatila, *op. cit.*, p. 92.

113. J. R. Jewett, "Arabic Proverbs and Proverbial Phrases," *Journal of the American Oriental Society*, 15 (1893), p. 86.

114. Barghuthi, *op. cit.*, p. 28.

115. Snouck Hurgronje, *Mekkanische Sprichwörter*, Haag, 1886, p. 17.

116. Gertrude H. Stern, *Marriage in Early Israel*, *op. cit.*, pp. 60, 158 ff.

117. Chatila, *op. cit.*, p. 91; Westermarck, *op. cit.*, pp. 53–54; Ella C. Sykes, *Persia and Its Peoples*, *op. cit.*, p. 201; etc.

118. Barth, "Father's Brother's Daughter Marriage," *op. cit.*, pp. 167, 169, 171; *idem.*, *Principles*, *op. cit.*, pp. 69 f.

119. Goldziher, *op. cit.*, p. 26.

120. Wilken, *Matriarchat*, *op. cit.*, pp. 59, 61.

121. Ghazālī, *Iḥyā 'ulūm al-dīn*, Book xii, Chapter, ii; cf. the German translation by Hans Bauer, *Von der Ehe. Das 12. Buch von al-Gazali's "Neubelebung der Religionswissenschaften,"* Halle a.S., 1917, p. 66.

122. Westermarck, *op. cit.*, pp. 54–55.

123. Goldziher, *op. cit.*, p. 26.

124. Westermarck, *op. cit.*, pp. 54–55; *idem.*, *Ritual and Belief in Morocco*, London, 1926, I : 164.

125. Chatila, *op. cit.*, p. 93.

CHAPTER 7—

1. The following is a partial and incomplete list of the most important studies in which dual organization is treated and defined: W. H. R. Rivers, *Social Organization*, London, 1932, pp. 29–30; A. M. Hocart, *The Progress of Man*, London, 1933, pp. 238–44; R. Linton, *The Study of Man*, New York, 1936, p. 207; B. Malinowski, *Crime and Custom in Savage Society*, London, 1940, pp. 24–26; I. Schapera, in *Encyclopaedia Britannica*, 14th ed., Vol. 8, p. 70; M. D. W. Jeffreys, "Dual Organization in Africa," in *African Studies*, Vol. 5 (1946), p. 84; G. P. Murdock, *Social Structure*, New York, 1949, pp. 47, 90, 124–25.

2. Josef Haekel, "Die Dualsysteme in Afrika," *Anthropos*, 1950, pp. 13–24.

3. Again only a selective list can be given: India: W. Koppers, "India and Dual Organization," *Acta Tropica*, Basel, 1944, Vol. i, Heft 1–2; Ugric people: J. Haekel, "Idolkult und Dualsysten bei den Ugriern," *Archiv für Völkerkunde*, Wien, 1947, Bd. I; Indonesia, Oceania and North America: W. J. Perry, *The Children of the Sun*, London, 1923, *passim*; Negro Africa: Jeffreys, *op. cit.*; Haekel, *op. cit.*

4. Dominik Josef Woelfel, "Die Hauptprobleme Weissafrikas," *Archiv für Anthropologie*, Braunschweig, 1942, p. 118; Jeffreys, *op. cit.*, pp. 159–62; Haekel, *op. cit.*, p. 18.

5. Bräunlich, E., "Beiträge zur Gesellschaftsordnung der Arabischen Beduinenstämme," *Islamica*, Vol. 6, p. 185.

6. *Handbook of Arabia* (Naval Intelligence Division), Oxford–London, 1920, I : 43.

7. One is tempted to compare with this popular tendency the Biblical account of the ten generations from Adam to Noah, and the ten generations from Noah to Abraham, telescoping the entire history of the world from Genesis to the first ancestor of the Hebrews into a mere 20 generations.

8. Bräunlich, *op. cit.*, pp. 77–78.

9. *Ibid.*, p. 69.

10. Cf. Procopius, *History of the Wars*, I, xix. Loeb Classical Library, London, 1944, I : 181.

11. Wm. Robertson Smith, *Kinship and Marriage in Early Arabia*, Cambridge, 1885, pp. 7, 247.

12. *Ibid.*, p. 7.

13. E.g., Ḥaṣarmaweth, Hadhramaut; Sheba, Saba; Yeraḥ, Mahra, etc. Cf. Gunkel, *Genesis*, 4th ed., Göttingen, 1917, pp. 91–92.

14. Cf. *Encyclopaedia of Islam* (old edition), s.v. Ḳaḥṭān.

15. Cf. Wüstenfeld, *Genealogische Tabellen*, Göttingen, 1852, table A.

16. Cf. *Encyclopaedia of Islam* (old ed.), s.v. Ḳais-ʿAilān; (new ed.), s.v. al-ʿArab, Djazīrat, p. 544; Wüstenfeld, *Gen. Tab.*, D.

17. Cf. R. Dozy, *Spanish Islam*, London, 1913, p. 65; Philip K. Hitti, *History of the Arabs*, London, 1937, p. 32. It is remarkable that this important and patent fact escaped the authors of the otherwise thorough *Handbook of Arabia*; on p. 44 (Vol. I) both the Qaḥṭān and the Ishmaelite tribes are stated to be the descendants of Abraham. Prof. Majid Khadduri repeats the same statement in his *Area Handbook on Iraq*, xerographed preliminary edition, New Haven: Human Relations Area Files, 1956, p. 122.

18. *Encyclopaedia of Islam* (old ed.), s.v. Ḳaḥṭān: cf. also new ed. s.v. al-ʿArab, Djazīrat, p. 545.

19. Cf. Philip K. Hitti, *Origins of the Druze People and Religion*, New York, 1928, p. 21.

20. Cf. Julius Wellhausen, *Das arabische Reich*, Berlin, 1902, pp. 44 f. I. Goldziher, *Muhammedanische Studien*, Halle, 1890, I : 94 ff.

21. Wellhausen, *op. cit.*, pp. 44 f.; *Encyclopaedia of Islam* (old ed.), s.v. Ḳais-ʿAilān; Dozy, *Spanish Islam*, *op. cit.*, p. 68; Hitti, *History of the Arabs*, p. 280.

22. Charles M. Doughty, *Travels in Arabia Deserta*, New York, 1937, I : 282; cf. p. 418.

23. Hitti, *History of the Arabs*, *op. cit.*, p. 281.

24. *Encyclopaedia of Islam*, *loc. cit.*

25. Dozy, *Spanish Islam*, *op. cit.*, p. 126.

26. *Ibid.*, p. 66, quoting Abu al-Fidāʿ II : 64 and Ibn ʿIdhārī's *Bayān*, II : 84; 265.

27. Hitti, *History of the Arabs*, *op. cit.*, p. 281.

28. S. B. Miles, *The Countries and Tribes of the Persian Gulf*, London, 1919, II : 419. The above account of Omani dual organization is based on data contained in this book. Cf. *Encyclopaedia of Islam* (new ed.), s.v. al-ʿArab, Djazīrat, p. 545.

29. British Admiralty, *Handbook of Arabia*, London, 1916–17, p. 273.

30. *Handbook of Arabia*, *op. cit.*, pp. 240–41, 334–35; Bertram Thomas, *Arabia Felix*, New York, 1932, pp. 111–12, 273.

31. Thomas, *op. cit.*, p. 273.

32. *Ibid.*, p. 26.

33. Wüstenfeld, *Gen. Tab.* 1.

34. Thomas, *Arabia Felix*, *op. cit.*, p. 26; Harold Ingrams, *Arabia and the Isles*, London, 1942, pp. 179, 223, 312; *Handbook of Arabia*, *op. cit.*, I, 213.

35. S. B. Miles and M. W. Muenzinger, "Account of an Excursion into the Interior of Southern Arabia," *Journal of the Royal Geographical Society*, London, 1871, Vol. 41, pp. 234–36.

36. Landberg, *Arabica*, Leyden, 1897, IV : 12–16.

37. Landberg, *Arabica*, Leyden, 1898, V : 3, 5, 12; *Encyclopaedia of Islam* (new ed.), s.v. Bayḥān al-Ḳaṣāb.

38. Miles and Muenzinger, *op. cit.*, p. 234; Landberg, *Arabica*, Leyden, 1897, IV : 52; *Handbook of Arabia, op. cit.*, I : 214. But according to G. Wyman Bury (Abdullah Mansur), *The Land of Uz*, London, 1911, p. 164, "the Ba-Kazim with its numerous sub-divisions composes the entire tribal population of Lower Aulaki."

39. Bury, *Land of Uz, op. cit.*, p. 216.

40. Miles and Muenzinger, *op. cit.*, pp. 229, 234; Landberg, *Arabica*, V, Leyden, 1898, p. 230.

41. Sir Bernard Reilly, "The Aden Protectorate," *Journal of the Royal Central Asian Society*, London, April, 1941, p. 139; *Handbook of Arabia*, I, 229, 232.

42. Thus according to an early authority, S. B. Heines, "Memoir of the South and East Coasts of Arabia," *Journal of the Royal Geographical Society*, London, 1841, Vol. 15, p. 112; cf. Thomas, *Arabia Felix, op. cit.*, pp. 47–48, 142–43. Wüstenfeld, *Register*, 1853, 280.

43. Wüstenfeld, *Register*, p. 280. Although none of the three names appearing in the popular tribal genealogy of the Mahra is found in Wüstenfeld's list, the claim to be a Noahide tribe makes this genealogy more plausible than the alternative of 'Adnānī descent.

44. Ingrams, *op. cit.*, p. 223.

45. Wüstenfeld, *Gen. Tab.* 1 and 9, *op. cit.*

46. Thomas, *Arabia Felix, op. cit.*, p. 269, note.

47. Leo Hirsch, *Reisen in Südarabien, Mahra-Land und Hadramaut*, Leiden, 1897, p. 11.

48. *Handbook of Arabia, op. cit.*, I, p. 229; H. St. John Philby, *Sheba's Daughters*, London, 1939, p. 154.

49. Thomas, *Arabia Felix, op. cit.*, p. 36; Sir Bernard Reilly, *op. cit.*, p. 139.

50. Ingrams, *op cit.*, p. 204.

51. Miles II, *op. cit.*, p. 515; Ingrams, *op. cit.*, pp. 189–90; Philby, *Sheba's Daughters, op. cit.*, p. 167.

52. Miles II, *op. cit.*, p. 515; Thomas, *Arabia Felix, op. cit.*, pp. 4, 13, 112, 181, 269.

53. *Encyclopaedia of Islam* (new ed.), s.v. 'Awāmir.

54. Thomas, *Arabia Felix, op. cit.*, pp. 112, 142–43, 269, 273.

55. Philby, *Sheba's Daughters, op. cit.*, pp. 35, 60, 65, 66; Ingrams, *op. cit.*, pp. 288, 319, 320–22.

56. Philby, *op. cit.*, p. 218.

57. *Encyclopaedia of Islam* (old ed.), s.v. Hashid and Bakil; cf. Amin Rihani, *Arabian Peak and Desert*, Boston and New York, 1930, p. 235; Carl Niebuhr, *Beschreibung von Arabien*, Copenhagen, 1772, p. 260.

58. *Encyclopaedia of Islam, loc. cit.*

59. *Handbook of Arabia, op. cit.*, pp. 479 ff.

60. H. St. John Philby, *Arabian Highlands*, Ithaca: Cornell University Press, 1952, p. 161.

61. *Handbook of Arabia, op. cit.*, pp. 430, 441.

62. Wüstenfeld, *Genealogische Tabellen*, 4; *idem., Register*, p. 132; Philby, *Arabian Highlands, op. cit.*, pp. 405, 494, 502, 503, 537–38, 561.

63. Philby, *Arabian Highlands, op. cit.*, pp. 36, 111, 116, 119, 121, 123, 124, 129, 130, 133, 139, 144, 177, 449, 454, 456, 458.

64. Wüstenfeld, *Gen. Tab.*, 4; Philby, *Arabian Highlands, op. cit.*, p. 225.

65. Philby, *Arabian Highlands, op. cit.*, pp. 225, 384, 388, 405.

66. *Ibid.*, pp. 150, 217, 225, 242, 245.

67. Oppenheim, *Die Beduinen*, Leipzig, 1952, Vol. III, pp. 142–43.

68. H. R. P. Dickson, *The Arab of the Desert*, London, 1949, pp. 264, 284, 363.

69. Philby, *Arabian Highlands, op. cit.*, p. 245.

70. Oppenheim, *op. cit.*, III : 149–50.

71. Harry W. Hazard, *Saudi Arabia*, Subcontractor's Monograph (xerographed), Human Relations Area Files, Inc., New Haven, Conn., 1956, pp. 58, 60, 61, 64.

72, H. St. John Philby, *Sheba's Daughters, op. cit.*, p. 19; *idem., Arabian Highlands, op. cit.*, p. 405.

73. Cf. for example Bertram Thomas, *Arabia Felix*, 208 ff.; Philby, *Sheba's Daughters, op. cit.*, pp. 19, 26–27, 333.

74. Cf. *Encyclopaedia of Islam* (old ed.), s.v. Hilal.

75. Cf. *Handbook of Arabia, op. cit.*, p. 44.

76. Wüstenfeld, *Genealogische Tabellen*, F; and *Encyclopaedia of Islam*, s.v. Hilal.

77. Cf. H. St. John Philby, *The Heart of Arabia*, New York–London, 1923, II : 23, 217; *idem., The Empty Quarter*, New York, 1933, Index, s.v. Murra; Thomas, *Arabia Felix, op. cit.*

78. Fu'ad Hamza, *Qalb Jezīret al-'Arab*, Cairo, 1352/1933, pp. 195 f., as quoted by Oppenheim, *Die Beduinen*, III : 159.

79. Oppenheim, *Die Beduinen, op. cit.*, III : 160–61.

80. *Ibid.*, III : 159.

81. Philby, *The Empty Quarter, op. cit.*, pp. 409 ff. (Table). A somewhat different account of the Murra divisions is given by H. R. P. Dickson, *Kuwait and Her Neighbours*, London, 1956, p. 96.

82. Cf. Oppenheim, *Die Beduinen, op. cit.*, III : 106; *Encyclopaedia of Islam* (old ed.), s.v. Kahtan.

83. Doughty, *Arabia Deserta, op. cit.*, I : 418; Philby, *Arabian Highlands, op. cit.*, 109.

84. Oppenheim, *Die Beduinen, op. cit.*, III : 112–15.

85. Philby, *Arabian Highlands, op. cit.*, pp. 18, 30, 34, 110, 128, 136, 144, 161, 181, 193, 196, 352, 366, 374, 442, 444, 445.

86. An older enumeration of the Qaḥṭān tribes of 'Asīr (Rufaydat el-Yemen, Benī Bishr, Senhān el-Hibab, 'Abidah, Wada'ah and Shereyf, six separate tribes), found in the *Handbook of Arabia*, I : 430, is also unsatisfactory.

87. Philby, *The Heart of Arabia, op. cit.*, II : 228–29. The inconsistencies between the structure of the Yām as appearing above and the one appearing in the 'Asīr district can be explained by the different tribal traditions prevalent in 'Asīr on the one hand and in inner Southern Arabia on the other.

88. Burckhardt, *Notes on the Bedouins*, London, 1831, I : 1, 10, 27; II : 6.

89. *Encyclopaedia of Islam* (old ed.), s.v. Harb.

90. Philby, *Arabia of the Wahhabis*, pp. 393–94; Oppenheim, *Die Beduinen, op. cit.*, III : 65–66, 362 f., 379.

91. Oppenheim, *op. cit.*, II : 362 ff., 379.

92. Harry W. Hazard, *op. cit.*, pp. 61–62, 64, 67.

93. Cf. Dozy, *Spanish Islam*, *op. cit.*, p. 68.

94. Cf. Robert Montagne, *Le Civilisation du Désert*, Paris, 1947, p. 51.

95. *Encyclopaedia of Islam* (new ed.), 1957, s.v. 'Anaza.

96. Cf. Oppenheim, *Die Beduinen*, *op. cit.*, I : 113, 114–23.

97. Cf. R. Patai (ed.), *The Republic of Syria*, HRAF Subcontractor's Monograph, New Haven, 1956, I : 160 ff., 170 ff., 181 ff.

98. Oppenheim, *Die Beduinen*, *op. cit.*, I : 159–63; Henry Field, *The Anthropology of Iraq* (Papers of the Peabody Museum of American Archaeology and Ethnology), Harvard University, Vol. 46, No. 1, Cambridge, Mass., 1951, pp. 19–21; Vol. 46, No. 2, 1952, pp. 89 f.

99. Oppenheim, *op. cit.*, I : 169, 176–77

100. Alois Musil, *Palmyrena*, New York, 1928, p. 151.

101. Oppenheim, *op. cit.*, I : 245 ff., 264–65, 335–36; II : 203 ff., 244 ff.; Frederick G. Peake, *History and Tribes of Jordan*, University of Miami Press, 1958, pp. 143–221; R. Patai (ed.), *Jordan*, Country Survey Series, Human Relations Area Files, New Haven, 1957, pp. 181–88.

102. Harry W. Hazard, *op. cit.*, p. 67.

103. H. R. P. Dickson, *Kuwait and Her Neighbours*, *op. cit.*, pp. 97–101.

104. Oppenheim, *op. cit.*, I : 196 ff., 211 ff.

105. Cf. Macalister and Masterman, *Palestine Exploration Fund Quarterly Statement*, 1905, p. 343; 1906, pp. 33–34.

106. Michael Assaf, *History of the Arabs in Palestine* (in Hebrew), Tel Aviv, 1941, II : 279.

107. Hitti, *History of the Arabs*, *op. cit.*, p. 281.

108. A. N. Haddad, *Journal of the Palestine Oriental Society*, I : 210–13; E. Robinson, *Biblical Researches in Palestine*, London 1841–1856, III : 283.

109. C. F. Volney, *Travels Through Syria and Egypt in the Years 1783, 1784, and 1785*, London, 1788, II : 325; Robinson, *op. cit.*, II : 17.

110. Cf. Robinson, *op. cit.*, II : 344.

111. Cf. Assaf, *op. cit.*, II : 279.

112. *Ibid.*, II : 278.

113. Volney, II : 177, as quoted by Gibb and Bowen, *Islamic Society and the West*, Oxford, 1950, I : 268, English translation, II : 302.

114. Volney, II : 203; English translation I : 325–26, 333–34; Gibb and Bowen, *op. cit.*, I : 268.

115. Cf. Elihu Grant, *The Peasantry of Palestine*, New York, 1907, pp. 159, 225.

116. Cf. Ya'qov Shim'oni, *'Arvē Ereṣ Yisrael*, Tel Aviv, 1947, p. 175; Omar el-Barghuthi, *Judicial Courts among the Bedouins of Palestine*, reprint from the *Journal of the Palestine Oriental Society*, Jerusalem, 1922, p. 9.

117. Mariam Zarour, 'Ramallah: My Home Town," *The Middle East Journal*, Autumn 1953, Vol. 7, No. 4, pp. 431–32.

118. Gibb and Bowen, *op. cit.*, I : 222.

119. Cf. Hitti, *The Origins of the Druze People and Religion*, *op. cit.*, p. 8; cf. also Niebuhr, *Reisebeschreibung nach Arabien und andern umliegenden Ländern*, Kopenhagen, 1778, II : 447.

120. Cf. Niebuhr, *loc. cit.*

121. Cf. R. Montagne, *La Civilisation du Désert*, *op. cit.*, p. 62.

122. Cf. Shim'oni, *op. cit.*, pp. 172–73; Granqvist, *Marriage Conditions in a Palestinian Village*, Helsingfors, 1935.

123. Mahmud, Bavār, *Kūh-Gīlūyē wa Ilāte ān* (Kūh-Gīlūyē and Its Tribes), Gachsārān, 1324 (1945), 158 pp.

124. *Ibid.*, 86 ff., 116 f., 130 ff.

125. C. S. Coon, *Caravan*, New York, 1951, pp. 217–18; Herbert H. Vreeland (ed.), *Iran*. Country Survey Series, Human Relations Area Files, New Haven, 1957, p. 42; *Encyclopaedia of Islam* (new ed.), s.v. Bakhtiyārī.

126. Cf. Henry Field, *The Anthropology of Iran*, p. 123, quoting Sykes.

127. *Encyclopaedia of Islam* (new ed.), s.v. Afghān, Afghānistān, and Abdālī; Donald N. Wilber, *Afghanistan*, Human Relations Area Files Subcontractors Monograph, New Haven, 1956, I : 73, 81–85; S. G. W. Benjamin, *Persia and the Persians*, London, 1887, pp. 142–43.

128. *Encyclopaedia of Islam* (new ed.), s.v. Balūčistān.

129. Cheikh Abd-el-Rahman el-Djabarti, *Merveilles Biographiques et Historiques ou Chroniques du* ... Traduites de l'Arabe. ... Le Caire, 1888, Tome I, pp. 50–54, 209; II : 157.

130. Gibb and Bowen, *op. cit.*, pp. 268–69, citing Girard, Chabrol, and Volney.

131. M. de Chabrol, *Essai sur les moeurs des habitants modernes de l'Egypte, Description de l'Egypte*, Paris, 1822, Tome Seconde, IIe partie, p. 372–73.

132. M. P. S. Girard, *Mémoire sur l'Agriculture, l'Industrie et le Commerce de l'Egypte, Description de l'Egypte*, Paris, 1823, Tome Seconde, p. 514.

133. Lane, *Modern Egyptians*, *op. cit.*, p. 202.

134. Oppenheim, *Die Beduinen*, *op. cit.*, I : 295.

135. G. W. Murray, *Sons of Ishmael: A Study of the Egyptian Bedouin*, London, 1935, pp. 253, 264–65.

136. Ibn Battuta, *Travels in Asia and Africa*, ed. Gibb, London, 1929, pp. 53–54.

137. *Encyclopaedia of Islam* (new ed.), s.v. Bedja.

138. Winifred Blackman, *The Fellahin of Upper Egypt*, London, 1927, pp. 129–31.

139. Cf. C. G. and Brenda Seligman, *The Kababish: A Sudan Arab Tribe*, Harvard African Studies, 1918, II : 113.

140. Hamed Ammar, *Growing Up in an Egyptian Village*, London, 1954, pp. vii, 44, 45, 47, 61.

141. *Encyclopaedia of Islam* (new ed.), s.v. Bishārīn.

142. Cf. G. Marçais, *Les Arabes en Berberie du xie au xive siecle*, Constantine & Paris, 1913, p. 59; E. E. Evans-Pritchard, *The Sanusi of Cyrenaica*, London, 1949, pp. 48, 49, 56.

143. Ibn Khaldun, *Histoire de Berberes*, Paris, 1934, Vol. iii, p. 181.

144. Ibn Khaldun, *op. cit.*, I : 168–69; III : 181.

145. Cf. Leo Africanus, *Description d'Afrique*, Paris, 1896–1898, I : 327; English edition: *History and Description of Africa*, London, 1896, 3 vols.

146. Cf. Henri Lhote, *Les Touaregs du Hoggar*, Paris, 1944, p. 115, referring to a note sent by a Marabout of the Tuareg tribe Kel es-Suq in 1907 to Captain Cortier and reprinted in the latter's volume *D'une rive a l'autre du Sahara*, p. 394.

147. Ibn Khaldun, *op. cit.*, I : 169, 170, 172; II : 11 ff.; III : 180, 181, 190, 300.

148. C. S. Coon, *Tribes of the Rif*, Harvard African Studies, Cambridge, Mass, Vol. ix, p. 17.

149. Cf. Eugène Guernier, *La Berberie, l'Islam et la France*, Paris, 1950, I : 338; Marçais, *op. cit.*, pp. 643–44, 709; Bryan Clarke, *Berber Village*, London, 1959, p. 96. The term *ṣoff*, in the form *ṣuff*, was met above as designating the factional alliances in Oman. The same term, pronounced *ṣaff*, is used by the Terābīn Bedouins of the Negev (today in Israel), for warlike alliances. Cf. Aaref el-Aaref, *The History of Beersheba and Her Tribes* (Hebrew translation), Tel Aviv, 1937, p. 65.

150. Robert Montagne, *Les Berberes et le Makhzen dans le sud au Maroc*, Paris, 1930, p. 197.

151. Coon, *Tribes of the Rif, op. cit.*, pp. 18, 169, 172–73.

152. Josef Haekel, "Die Dualsysteme in Afrika," *Anthropos*, 1950, p. 18, quoting Montagne, *Les Berberes*.

153. Coon, *Tribes of the Rif, op. cit.*, p. 19.

154. Montagne, *Les Berberes*, p. 197, 212; *idem., La Civilisation du Desert*, 261.

155. Jean Despois, *L'Afrique du Nord*, Paris, 1949, p. 145; Haekel, *op. cit.*, p. 18.

156. Cf. Despois, *op. cit.*, p. 145; Haekel, *op. cit.*, p. 18; Montagne, *Les Berberes, op. cit.*, p. 197; Clarke, *loc. cit.*

157. Montagne, *Les Berberes*, p. 212; *idem., La Civilisation du Desert*, p. 261.

158. R. Turnbull, *Sahara Unveiled*, London, 1940, p. 25, as quoted by Jeffreys, *African Studies*, Vol. 5 (1946), p. 159.

159. Dr. H. Barth, *Travels and Discoveries in North and Central Africa*, London, 1867, I : 99, 100, 148; as quoted by Jeffreys, *op. cit.*, p. 162.

160. Walter Cline, *Notes on the People of Siwah and El Garah in the Libyan Desert*, General Series in Anthropology, Menasha, Wis., 1936, No. 4, pp. 12, 46.

160a. Lloyd Cabot Briggs, *Tribes of the Sahara*. Cambridge: Harvard University Press, 1960, pp. 78–80.

161. E. E. Evans-Pritchard, *The Sanusi of Cyrenaica, op. cit.*, p. 58.

162. Edward Westermarck, *Ritual and Belief in Morocco*, London, 1926, I : 178.

162a. Lloyd Cabot Briggs, *Tribes of the Sahara, op. cit.*, pp. 195–96.

163. Doutté, *Magie et religion dans l'Afrique du Nord*, Alger, 1909, p. 509.

164. Westermarck, *op. cit.*, II : 72. On other ceremonial fights between children in Morocco, cf. *op. cit.*, I : 601; II : 65; between men and women, II : 72.

165. *Ibid.*, II : 73, 115, 131–33, 171, 188, 197–98, 272.

166. Ibn Khaldun, *op. cit.*, I : 273.

167. Francis R. Rodd, *The People of the Veil*, London, 1926, pp. 349–53; Lhote, *op. cit.*, p. 127.

168. Henri Duveyrier, *Les Touareg du Nord*, Paris, 1864, p. 329.

169. Lhote, *op. cit.*, p. 156.

170. Cf. H. Barth, *Travels in Central Africa*, London, 1859, IV : 552 f.

171. Rodd, *op. cit.*, p. 387.

172. Cf. Henri Lhote, *Les Touaregs du Hoggar (Ahaggar)*, 2d ed., Paris, 1955, pp. 216–18, 239, 248.

173. Hocart, *The Progress of Man*, London, 1933, p. 241.

174. G. P. Murdock, *Social Structure*, New York, 1949, p. 80.

175. Perry, in Appendix III to Rivers, *Social Organization*, London, 1932, pp. 208 ff., maintains that the superiority of one moiety over the other was one of the original traits of ancient Egyptian dual organization which became diffused from there as an integral part of the "Archaic civilization."

CHAPTER 8—

1. Cf. H. R. P. Dickson, *The Arab of the Desert*, London, 1949, p. 515; Charles M. Doughty, *Travels in Arabia Deserta*, New York, 1937, I : 324 ff.; John B. Glubb, *The Sulubba and Other Ignoble Tribes of Southwestern Asia*, General Series in Anthropology (ed. Leslie Spier), Menasha, Wis., 1943, No. 9, p. 14.
2. Cf. Dickson, *op. cit.*, p. 516.
3. H. R. P. Dickson, *Kuwait and Her Neighbours*, London, 1956, p. 102.
4. John Lewis Burckhardt, *Notes on the Bedouins and Wahabys*, London, 1831, II : 19–20.
5. Alois Musil, *Manners and Customs of the Rwala Bedouins*, New York, 1928, p. 136.
6. Glubb, *op. cit.*, pp. 15–16.
7. Cf. G. W. Murray, *Sons of Ishmael*, London, 1935, pp. 269, 285.
8. Burckhardt, *op. cit.*, II : 15.
9. Cf. Carleton S. Coon, *Caravan, The Story of the Middle East*, New York, 1951, p. 200.
10. Bertram Thomas, *Arabia Felix*, New York, 1932, pp. 46 f.; Richard F. Burton, *The Land of Midian (Revisited)*, London, 1879, I : 161.
11. Cf. E. E. Evans-Pritchard, *The Senusi of Cyrenaica*, Oxford, 1949, p. 51; G. W. Murray, *Sons of Ishmael*, *op. cit.*, pp. 273 ff.
12. Cf. Henri Lhote, *Les Touaregs du Hoggar*, Paris, 1944, p. 150; *Encyclopaedia of Islam* (new ed.), s.v. Ahaggar.
13. Cf. Max Freiherr von Oppenheim, *Die Beduinen*, Leipzig, 1939, I : 23.
14. Cf. Musil, *op. cit.*, p. 60.
15. *Ibid.*, p. 136.
16. Glubb, *op. cit.*, p. 16.
17. Burton, *op. cit.*, I : 170–71.
18. Musil, *op. cit.*, p. 137.
19. Murray, *op. cit.*, p. 245.
20. Doughty, *op. cit.*, I : 325.
21. W. B. Seabrook, *Adventures in Arabia*, New York, 1927, p. 53.
22. Glubb, *op. cit.*, p. 14.
23. Seabrook, *op. cit.*, p. 53.
24. Musil, *op. cit.*, p. 453.
25. Doughty, *op. cit.*, I : 324; also Musil, *op. cit.*, pp. 452–53.
26. Cf. Seabrook, *op. cit.*, p. 52.
27. Murray, *op. cit.*, p. 268.
28. Doughty, *op. cit.*, I : 325.
29. Glubb, *op. cit.*, p. 15.
30. Murray, *op. cit.*, p. 269.
31. Glubb, *op. cit.*, p. 15.
32. Murray, *op. cit.*, p. 268.
33. Dickson, *The Arab of the Desert*, *op. cit.*, p. 515.
34. Glubb, *op. cit.*, p. 14.

35. Burton, *op. cit.*, II : 118.

36. Dickson, *op. cit.*, pp. 571–72.

37. Glubb, *op. cit.*, p. 15.

38. Dickson, *op. cit.*, pp. 516–17.

39. Musil, *op. cit.*, pp. 136–37; Glubb, *op. cit.*, p. 16.

40. Cf. Ernest Main, *Iraq From Mandate to Independence*, London, 1935, pp. 253 ff.; John Van Ess, *Meet the Arab*, New York, 1943, pp. 69–70.

41. Cf. Musil, *op. cit.*, p. 282; Coon, *op. cit.*, p. 201.

42. Dickson, *op. cit.*, p. 516; Glubb, *op. cit.*, p. 14.

43. Burton, *Personal Narrative of a Pilgrimage to al-Madinah and Meccah*, London, 1893, II : 121.

44. Glubb, *op. cit.*, pp. 15, 16.

45. Pierre Ponafidine, *Life in the Moslem East*, New York, 1911, p. 133; Dickson, *op. cit.*, p. 517; Musil, *op. cit.*, pp. 118, 134, 325, 406–7; Coon, *op. cit.*, p. 200; Glubb, *op. cit.*, p. 15.

46. Glubb, *op. cit.*, pp. 15–16; Musil, *loc. cit.*

47. Musil, *op. cit.*, pp. 281–82; Coon, *op. cit.*, p. 200.

48. Bertram Thomas, *Alarms and Excursions in Arabia*, London, 1931, p. 152; idem., *Arabia Felix*, p. 47.

49. Musil, *op. cit.*, pp. 278—81; Coon, *op. cit.*, p. 203; Murray, *op. cit.*, p. 285.

50. Murray, *op. cit.*, pp. 265–66.

51. Dickson, *op. cit.*, p. 518.

52. Burton, *op. cit.*, II : 121.

53. Cf. Dickson, *op. cit.*, pp. 516–17; Coon, *op. cit.*, p. 200; Jarvis, *Desert and Delta*, London, 1938, pp. 154–55; Seabrook, *op. cit.*, pp. 52–53; Ponafidine, *op. cit.*, p. 132; Gerald de Gaury, *Arabian Journey*, London, 1950, p. 140.

54. Jarvis, *op. cit.*, p. 153, Seabrook, *op. cit.*, p. 53.

55. Glubb, *op. cit.*, p. 14.

56. Coon, *op. cit.*, p. 200.

57. Cf. for example Murray, *op. cit.*, pp. 268–69: " . . . these Hiteim represent ancient broken clans, who have lost their independence. . . . Some may contain non-Arab elements, but these must be rare." Glubb, *op. cit.*, p. 16, says, " . . . they are known to be of base descent."

58. Coon, *op. cit.*, p. 200.

59. Musil, *op. cit.*, pp. 136–37, 282.

60. Glubb, *op. cit.*, pp. 15–16; Gerald de Gaury, *Arabia Phoenix*, London, 1946, p. 143.

61. Cf. Murray, *op. cit.*, p. 265; Jarvis, *op. cit.*, p. 119.

62. Thomas, *Arabia Felix*, *op. cit.*, pp. 46–47.

63. Fulanain, *The Marsh Arab*, Philadelphia, 1928, p. 254.

64. Dickson, *op. cit.*, pp. 550–51.

65. Cf. E. E. Evans-Pritchard, *op. cit.*, pp. 48 f.; Murray, *op. cit.*, pp. 272 ff.

66. Henri Lhote, *Les Touaregs du Hoggar (Ahaggar)*, 2nd ed., Paris, 1955, pp. 145, 166, 188, 213–14, 239, 247.

67. Lloyd Cabot Briggs, *Tribes of the Sahara*, Cambridge: Harvard University Press, 1960, pp. 126–27, 136–38.

68. *Ibid.*, pp. 168–71.

69. *Ibid.*, pp. 194–95.

70. *Ibid.*, pp. 216–17, 219.

CHAPTER 9—

1. Gustave E. von Grunebaum, "The Structure of the Muslim Town," *Islam: Essays in the Nature and Growth of a Cultural Tradition.* Comparative Studies of Cultures and Civilizations, No. 4. The American Anthropological Association, Memoir No. 81, April, 1955, p. 142.

2. H. A. R. Gibb, and Harold Bowen, *Islamic Society and the West*, London, Royal Institute of International Affairs, 1950, Vol. I, p. 276.

3. W. E. Lane, *Modern Egyptians*, Everyman's Library, p. 4.

4. Cf. R. Patai (ed.), *The Republic of Lebanon.* Subcontractor's Monograph, Human Relations Area Files, New Haven, 1956, Vol. I, pp. 223 ff.

5. Cf. R. Patai (ed.), *The Republic of Syria.* Subcontractor's Monograph, Human Relations Area Files, New Haven, 1956, Vol. I, p. 341.

6. Lane, *op. cit.*

7. Freya Stark, *Winter in Arabia*, London, 1945, p. 44.

CHAPTER 10—

1. The author is indebted to Professors H. H. Rowley, F. S. C. Northrop, Edward J. Jurji, David Bidney, and Dr. Everett R. Clinchy for their comments on this chapter.

2. Cf. above, pp. 13 f.

3. Cf. above, Chapter 1, pp. 33 ff.

4. John Clark Archer, "Hinduism," in E. J. Jurji (ed.), *The Great Religions of the Modern World*, Princeton, 1947, p. 49.

5. Daniel and Alice Thorner, "India and Pakistan," in Ralph Linton (ed.), *Most of the World*, New York, 1949, pp. 571, 574, 577, 646.

6. A. K. Reischauer, "Buddhism," in *The Great Religions of the Modern World*, pp. 138, 105–06.

7. Lewis Hodous, "Taoism," in *The Great Religions*, pp. 41–42.

8. Hodous, *op. cit.*, pp. 24–43.

9. Hodous, "Confucianism," *op. cit.*, pp. 6–7.

10. *Ibid.*, pp. 7–18.

11. *Ibid.*, p. 20.

12. Joachim Wach, *Sociology of Religion*, Chicago, 1944, pp. 274 ff.

13. Cf. above, p. 36.

14. Rebecca West, *Black Lamb and Grey Falcon*, New York, 1943, p. 298; as quoted by F. S. C. Northrop, *The Meeting of East and West: An Inquiry Concerning World Understanding*, New York, 1946, p. 431.

15. B. L. Atreya, "Indian Culture; Its Spiritual, Moral and Social Aspects," in *Interrelations of Cultures*, UNESCO publication, Paris, 1953, p. 144.

16. Younghill Kang, *The Grass Roof*, New York, 1931, pp. 7, 12; *idem, East Goes West*, New York, 1937, p. 233; as quoted by Northrop, *op. cit.*, p. 314.

17. Kurt Singer, *The Idea of Conflict*, Melbourne, 1949, pp. 50–52.

18. Northrop, *op. cit.*, p. 388; cf. also p. 496, where in the closing sentence of the book the same statement is repeated with slight variations.

19. Arnold J. Toynbee, *A Study of History*, abr. ed., Oxford, 1947, p. 487.

20. Edward W. Lane, *The Manners and Customs of the Modern Egyptians*, Everyman's Library, p. 241.

21. Northrop, *op. cit.*, p. 401.
22. Archer, *op. cit.*, p. 51.
23. E. S. Geden, "God (Hindu)," in James Hastings (ed.), *Encyclopaedia of Religion and Ethics*, Vol. 6, p. 285; Archer, *op. cit.*, p. 76.
24. Passages followed by this reference number are based on written communications from Professor F. S. C. Northrop.
25. Reischauer, *op. cit.*, p. 139.
26. M. Anesaki, "Prayer (Buddhist)," in *Encyclopaedia of Religion and Ethics*, Vol. 10, p. 166.
27. One must carefully distinguish between this Western term and the Eastern concept of "transcendence." In the Eastern sense the Tao transcends sense objects. Cf. Northrop, "The Complementary Emphases of Eastern Intuitive and Western Scientific Philosophy," in *Philosophy—East and West*, ed. Charles Moore, Princeton, 1944, p. 219.
28. Hodous, *op. cit.*, pp. 24–25.
29. *Ibid.*, p. 40.
30. Edward Sell, "God (Muslim)," in *Encyclopaedia of Religion and Ethics*, Vol. 6, p. 300.
31. W. T. Davison, "God (Biblical and Christian)," *op. cit.*, Vol. 6, pp. 265 ff.
32. F. S. C. Northrop, *The Meeting of East and West*, *op. cit.*, p. 409.
33. Atreya, *op. cit.*, p. 126.
34. Max Weber, *Gesammelte Aufsätze zur Religionssoziologie*, 2d ed., Tübingen, 1923, Vol. 2, pp. 22, 24.
35. Raymond Kennedy, "Southeast Asia and Indonesia," in *Most of the World*, pp. 675, 677.
36. Francis L. Hsu, "China," in *Most of the World*, p. 766.
37. Northrop, *op. cit.*, pp. 409–10.
38. Hodous, *op. cit.*, p. 41.
39. Douglas G. Haring, "Japan and the Japanese," *Most of the World*, p. 856.
40. Reischauer, *op. cit.*, p. 90.
41. Northrop, *op. cit.*, p. 412.
42. Krishnalal Shridharani, *My India, My America*, New York, p. 298.
43. Toynbee, *op. cit.*, pp. 299–300.
44. *Ibid.*, p. 485.
45. Northrop, *op. cit.*, p. 411.
46. Toynbee, *op. cit.*, pp. 300–301.
47. *Op. cit.*, p. 553.
48. F. S. C. Northrop, *The Taming of the Nations: A Study of the Cultural Bases of International Policy*, New York, 1952, p. 77.
49. Hodous, *op. cit.*, pp. 1–23.
50. Northrop, *The Meeting of East and West*, p. 339.
51. Oral information supplied by my student, Mr. Timothy Lin.
52. Archer, *op. cit.*, pp. 62, 75, 88.
53. Reischauer, *op. cit.*, p. 97.
54. *Ibid.*, pp. 98–100, 103, 105.
55. Hodous, *op. cit.*, pp. 27, 32, 37, 39.
56. Singer, *op. cit.*, p. 52.

138

CHAPTER 11—

1. Prof. John B. Whitton of Princeton University, in the *Encyclopedia Americana*, article "Nationalism and Internationalism."

2. *Ibid.*

3. Hazem Zaki Nuseibeh, *The Ideas of Arab Nationalism*, Cornell University Press, Ithaca, N.Y., 1956, p. 203.

4. Cf. Hans Kohn, *A History of Nationalism in the East*, London, Routledge, 1929, pp. 231–32.

5. Philip K. Hitti, *History of Syria*, New York, Macmillan, 1951, p. 667.

6. After the above was written, my attention was directed to a statement by Shaykh Muṣṭafā al-Sibāʿī that expresses basically the same idea. Advocating "The Establishment of Islam as the State Religion of Syria," the shaykh says in an article published in the Syrian newspaper *al-Manār* (in February, 1950): "Although it is understood that the nationalism of Europe decrees as a fundamental tenet the expulsion of religion, that step is not incumbent on us, the Arabs. Nazi Germany may have found in Christianity a religion which was foreign to it. Turanian Turkey may find in Islam a religion foreign to it. But the Arabs will never find in Islam a religion foreign to them. In fact they believe that Arab nationalism was born only when they embraced Islam. . . ." Trans. R. B. Winder, *The Muslim World*, XLIV (1954), p. 223. Quoted also by G. E. von Grunebaum, "Problems of Muslim Nationalism," in Richard N. Frye (ed.), *Islam and the West*, The Hague, 1957, p. 22.

7. Cf. R. Patai, *The Kingdom of Jordan*, Princeton University Press, 1958, pp. 136 ff.; *Idem.*, *Sex and Family in the Bible and the Middle East*, New York, Doubleday, 1959, pp. 19 ff.

8. Cf. R. Patai, *The Kingdom of Jordan*, pp. 275, 287 f.

9. Cf. above, Chapter 7, "Dual Organization."

10. R. Patai, *Sex and Family, op. cit.*, p. 17.

11. Cf. for example Alexander Pallis, *In the Days of the Janissaries: Old Turkish Life as Depicted in the "Travel Book" of Evliya Chelebi*, London, 1951, p. 120.

12. Cf. R. Patai (ed.), *The Republic of Syria*, I : 154 ff.

13. Cf. Reuben Levy, *The Social Structure of Islam*, Cambridge University Press, 1957, p. 66.

14. Cf. below, p. 350.

15. Cf. above, p. 307.

16. Cf. Nabih A. Faris and Mohammed T. Husayn, *The Crescent in Crisis*, Lawrence, The University of Kansas, 1955, pp. 130 ff.

17. The creed of Pan-Arab nationalism has been summarized by G. E. von Grunebaum, *op. cit.*, pp. 15–16.

CHAPTER 12—

1. Cf. Melville J. Herskovits, *Man and His Works*, New York: Alfred A. Knopf, 1948, p. 523.

2. Cf. Raphael Patai, *Israel Between East and West*, Philadelphia; Jewish Publication Society 1953, pp. 27 ff.

3. Cf. above, Chapter 10, pp. 286 ff.

4. Arnold J. Toynbee, *A Study of History* (abr. ed.), New York and London, 1947, p. 377.

5. Carleton S. Coon, "The Impact of the West on Middle Eastern Institutions." An address before the Academy of Political Science, Columbia University, New York, 1952.

6. A. L. Kroeber, *The Nature of Culture*, Chicago, 1952, pp. 152 ff.

7. Cf. p. 36.

8. Cf. pp. 364–65.

9. Cf. p. 34.

10. Bernard Lewis, "Communism and Islam," *International Affairs*, Vol. 30 (January, 1954), pp. 1–12.

11. Cf. p. 34.

12. Ali Othman and Robert Redfield, "An Arab's View of Point IV." University of Chicago Round Table, No. 749, Aug. 5, 1952.

CHAPTER 13—

1. Typical and forceful expressions of these two opposing points of view were given in a meeting of the American Academy of Political and Social Science, held in Philadelphia in the spring of 1952. Cf. N. Saifpour Fatemi, "Tensions in the Middle East," and Ray Brock, "Report from the Middle East," in the *Annals of the American Academy of Political and Social Science*, July, 1952, pp. 53–59 and 64–68. The two quotations are found on pp. 57 and 65.

2. This was the experience, for example, of Mr. Abdel-Aziz Allouni working in Syria under the auspices of the Near East Foundation in the Village Welfare Service, and of Mr. Mohammed Shalabi working in Egyptian villages under the sponsorship of the Egyptian Association for Social Studies. (Oral communication from both.) These examples could easily be multiplied.

3. Raphael Patai, *On Culture Contact and Its Working in Modern Palestine*, Memoir No. 67, American Anthropological Association, October, 1947, p. 42.

4. Oral communication from Mr. Nuri Eren, Director of the Turkish Information Office in New York, and Mr. Farid Zeineddine, Permanent Representative of Syria to the United Nations.

5. Roderic D. Matthews and Matta Akrawi, *Education in the Arab Countries of the Near East*, Washington, 1948, pp. 540–41, and *passim*.

6. In Iran, for example, 28,991 children attended *Maktabs* (Koran-schools) in 1942–43, while no less than 152,168 attended modern schools. The total number of school-age population (children aged six to fourteen) in Iran was estimated at more than 3 millions. Cf. Abdullah Faryar, "Rural Education in Iran." *The Iran Review*, Jan.–Feb., 1950, p. 22; UNESCO Publication No. 133, p. 27.

7. Eleanor Bisbee, *The New Turks*, Philadelphia, 1951, p. 154; E. W. F. Tomlin, *Life in Modern Turkey*, London and New York, 1946, p. 63.

8. The entire issue of preference for the old and the new (Western) in music has received much attention in *The Passing of Traditional Society: Modernizing the Middle East*, by Daniel Lerner, Glenco, Ill., 1958.

9. Cf. *An Arab's View on Point IV:* an NBC Radio Discussion by Ali Othman and Robert Redfield, The University of Chicago Round Table, No. 749, August 3, 1952, p. 10, where the dispositions that developed in Arab kinship culture are discussed.

10. Cf. Sania Hamady, *Temperament and Character of the Arabs*, New York, 1960, p. 229.

11. F. S. C. Northrop, *The Meeting of East and West: An Inquiry Concerning World Understanding*, New York, 1947, p. 4.

12. This is shown statistically by the much higher numbers of boys enrolled in schools in all Middle Eastern countries as compared with those of girls.

13. G. E. von Grunebaum, "Problems of Muslim Nationalism," in Richard N. Frye (ed.), *Islam and the West*, The Hague, 1957, p. 23.

14. In many places, as for instance in Africa south of the Sahara, in Central Asia, in India, and in the East Indies, Muslim missions or missionaries have been more successful than Christian.

15. Northrop, *op. cit.*, p. 411.

16. Since the Middle East and the Western world have two different sets of etiquette, the Westerner may be behaving impeccably according to his own pattern, and still be regarded as offensively impolite by Middle Eastern standards which, of course, are the only ones a Middle Easterner can apply, unless he has had sufficient experience to become acquainted with what the Westerners regard as polite manners.

17. Cf. above, p. 34; Carleton S. Coon, "The Impact of the West on Middle Eastern Social Institutions," *The Academy of Political Science*, Columbia University, New York, 1952, p. 7: " ... religion provides the dominant tone to Muslim civilization. ..."

18. As an example of how conservative Middle Easterners view what we called above "superficial Westernization," let us quote a passage from an editorial in the conservative Pakistani paper, *Al-Islam: An Independent Exponent of Orthodox Islam* (Karachi, Pakistan, Jan. 1, 1955, Vol. 3, No. 1, p. 1; as quoted by G. E. von Grunebaum, *op. cit.*, pp. 23–24): "Our intelligentsia, utterly ignorant of the scientific implications of the progress made by the West, sing the praises of Western culture only because it gives them opportunities of indulging in frivolous and vulgar pursuits. ..."

These phenomena are not confined to the Middle East. Very similar processes have been observed in Indonesia where the new factor making its impact on the old traditional native cultures of the islands is Islam. Cf. Justus van der Kroef, "Patterns of Western Influence in Indonesia," *American Sociological Review*, Vol. 17, No. 4 (August, 1952), pp. 421–30.

19. Robert Redfield, *The Primitive World and Its Transformations*, Ithaca, N.Y., 1953, p. 23.

20. *Ibid.*, p. 77.

21. Arnold J. Toynbee, *A Study of History*, abr. ed., New York and London, 1947, p. 394.

22. Redfield, *op. cit.*, p. 77.

Index